MEDITATION
THE CURE

Published by

NV·life

Author

NAVEEN VARSHNEYA

Meditation The Cure

© NVLife

Price : ₹ 1551

Published by

NVLIFE

www.nvlife.net

Illustrations by

Rajat Bose

Cover design by

P. Raghuveeran (DAT, MFA)

Printed by
COMPUPRINT
9, Second Street,
Gopalapuram, Chennai 600 086.
Phone : +91 44 2811 6768
www.compuprint.in

GRATITUDE & ACKNOWLEDGEMENT

My father once said that his father went to his uncle to borrow INR 2 to start some small trade. I do not recall whether he got that money or not but I grew up watching my grandfather running a successful clothes shop and together with my grandmother, they educated their seven children. I saw them leading a very content life in a small village, Chattari, India.

When my father and his other siblings moved to different cities within the state of Uttar Pradesh, India, with their respectful jobs within the government, it was only natural for my father to invest in educating his children and bringing us up with strong values. So when my mother once said to my father that she wants to live in her own house, my father moved all his resources to give the best which none of his colleagues or peers could have imagined in those days.

As I look back after writing this book, It seems logical for me to scale the same values and take them to a much bigger level by doing things with joy. For that one moment, when my mother lost faith which turned fatal, I have spent all these years trying to find this faith for her. This is how it feels today after writing this book. I felt guided and inspired by wisdom and courage of my father who raised six of us teaching us the value of health and virtues.

I feel contented passing on the values and wisdom of my family to all of you. If just one person reads this book and discovers the faith and inner wisdom, my contentment will become my joy.

In a chance meeting, in my young days, I married a gorgeous woman and together we saw a vision of home. Over the years she has turned out to be an anchor, a guide and a solid pillar of support without whom there is no way I would have arrived here.

My daughter brought the finest expression, of fatherhood, out in me and my son has made me celebrate it each moment.

I still do not know how to acknowledge the contribution of my siblings for their love, the support of my friends and immense love and respect I receive from the family of my wife.

This is still in the family, love and support is understandable but how do you explain cosmic relationships which are created by the universe to make the journey beautiful and effortless.

A hand on my back which blessed me, set me on this path. This is the hand of my Guru Pt. Rishiraj Maharaj ji.

Around the same time, seven years back, I was connected to Kirti Narang who has been an integral part of my journey. I sleep because she remains awake the whole night working on me. She is an amazing healer and a generous soul who has been like a shadow to me during the writing of this book from the very beginning. She has worked untiringly to heal my subconscious so that deeper insights could flow through me into the book.

When I closed my healing centre to write the book last year, Anjana walked in after curing her terminal blood cancer. Like a mirror, she has worked selflessly with deep love and devotion to allow me to write the book and made sure nothing deviates me from this path.

Kirti, Anjana anchored the space for me round the clock from the start. Towards the second half, the team expanded and I was again showered with love and support from Simren Sawhney and her ability to see visions for the book, reminding all of us to stay with our silence. But the book was still incomplete and it needed a western perspective and editing by someone with deep wisdom about this subject. Charan Surdhar came in with her infinite love, wisdom, and sharp editing skills.

Each one of you, who have come to NV Life in the last seven years have helped me arrive here today, for that I am deeply grateful.

PAUSE

***E**xistence exists in the moment of pause. To experience it, observe your breath.*

It was very easy for me to have a distinguished personality to write the foreword for this book. I decided not to have a "Foreword" for this version" and rather have a "Pause". There is a reason why I chose not to.

The core value of NV LIFE has been to let the work speak for itself. Let transformation be visible to the person within and around. The energy of this transformation will attract others on its own. If there is any effort or salesmanship done by me in these years, then it is about educating them, helping them experience and then allowing them to make the choices. There were conscious efforts made not to convince people to believe us.

The lady who cured her blood cancer of 10 years is now being instrumental in the transformational journey of many people. This corporate executive who was shown the door by her husband, has now a happy family with the same partner and has a top management position. The mother whose child was declared autistic has her child going to normal school. The schizophrenic woman who never had a day without medicine for 27 years slept several nights peacefully without medicines. Such stories and more are endless and have been a routine for us. They are all celebrities. They all are heroes in their ecosystem and as they continue to make a positive impact in and around, their aura is growing their influence and their sphere of influence is also growing. With this book, I live with a vision that there will be a celebrity in each home. In this connected world, I do not think it is too much to ask for the remaining years of my life.

You must have tried many things so far and must have failed. This book is with you because you believe there is some hope and this exactly, is what this book offers you. A hope - within you. It is as simple as breathing and this is going to be the hardest thing for you to believe that it can be a cure. There is no way you will believe it unless you experience the cure. The testimonials, case studies and various examples used in the book, are only to ignite hope within you to experience the transformation. They shall not be viewed as validation of your cure. Your cure is in your hands and only you can create that in you. Leave your past learnings aside, drop the baggage of your failures for the moment. Keep your skepticism alive and continue to live your daily routine the way you live it. With absolutely no changes in your sufferings or in your schedules and value systems, experience the cure every day for 30 minutes with the first technique and almost zero effort required to trigger healing in you through processes as mentioned in Section three.

Can you do that everyday for three to six weeks to see the transformation in you? Regardless, whatever your issue is or if you feel there is no issue. If so, you will be the celebrity of your life and this celebratory ecosystem will only grow with time.

This book is not just for people with sufferings. It is meant for everyone. You can start your journey from any point and this book will only help you go higher. If you are healthy and happy, it will make you reach much bigger heights in your life in all spheres.

Rather than moving forward to try this book out, It is important that you "Pause" for few minutes. I like to share some insights into my work and my vision. It shall help you understand the subject much better.

1. If you have urgent need for a cure, I suggest you to go to section three directly and start to experience the cure before reading through the book.

2. Feel free to read through the book as you like. The whole book is written as integrated and linked with each previous chapter but each chapter is complete in itself. The best way could be to read the case studies of some of the celebrities to warm up.

3. This book is not written by me. It is written through me. It has been a blissful one year that I have been writing it full time. I teach this program in workshop in two days for last four years and it was simple to have a shadow writer in the workshop. Each chapter and page and word is structured with an intent to offer you healing. I am confident you will experience it as you read through the pages. Be aware of the shifts in your energies as you read through.

4. My key challenge in writing the book was what not to write and keep it simple to first let everyone accept the concept and start to practice. I see each chapter holding a potential to be a book in itself. I have also attempted to use a language which even non-English speaking natives can relate to. Conscious efforts were made to ensure that glorification and intellectualization of the concept shall not be promoted, unless needed for healing purposes.

5. This book has been written with the intent that it shall be one book for one household. It is your scripture and it is meant to heal only one postal address. It is an energy game. Do not let anyone borrow the book from you.

6. There will be training programs for you to gain deeper insights on the subject and an online support forum on Facebook where you can raise your queries and we will attempt to resolve them to help you practice better.

7. I like to encourage all of you to consider in becoming a well-being expert and take this as a profession to lead a holistic life. Though I have given all the secrets in this book, you may need some grooming and guidance to become an expert to be able to help others in their transformations.

8. To become a well-being expert with us, there is nothing which you need to learn from me. You only need to go deeper within, using the science and techniques of this book and my job is to only help you reach it deeper and faster, and not let you get trapped by the Maya(illusion) and obstacles.

9. To become an expert, we do not make you a healer. We help you arrive at a stage where *healing chooses you*. Whether you become a healer or not, you will be aligned to the purpose of your life. If healing is the purpose, then let that be.

10. I would like to encourage institutions and research organizations to collaborate for further work in this field of integrative medicine.

11. Do not look for specific points related to your suffering in the book. As you read through the book, this will be revealed to you on its own. When you practice Section three, then each day, you will find you are getting better and becoming aware of the root cause of your suffering. By the time, you are healed, you will know what was ailing you. So, walk towards the cure, that shall reveal the cause of the suffering.

12. As you read through the pages, please do not try to make any decisions or judgements about yourself. Do not try to bring any changes as you become aware of yourself reading through the book. Just become aware and live that awareness.

13. As you start practicing the techniques, you may feel feverish, have loose stomach, vomiting, pain in body parts, emotional outbursts etc. This is very normal as the energy starts move in you, healing you and eliminating the toxins which have been in you.

TESTIMONIALS

I am 51, from Delhi. I got an opportunity of getting connected with Naveen at the time of critical illness of my husband. Unfortunately he is not with us but somehow he made that connection with Naveen. After my husband left us for heavenly aboard, I was in a state I can't either express or had experienced ever earlier. The first October workshop I attended helped me to overcome up to some extent but I was not consistent in NV practices and I continued with deep grief within. When I attended this recent February workshop I felt Naveen poured his heart into it and it reached to the core of my being. It has made a difference within me I'm on the way back to normal life and hopeful to develop my hidden potential to lead blissful life. Thoroughly grateful to NV life, Naveen and the team, all the way.

Anu Sachdeva, New Delhi

NV life..... the thread of breath binds me to myself.... liberating my core and giving power to strive & thrive in vast infinite spaces, yet cuddles me like a weaned child with my mother unconditionally along life's sharp edges and smooth curves.'

Sarika Aggarwal, Shillong

I'm really very much indebted to the NV Life Science Techniques for changing my life in such a small period. I got my Frozen Shoulder Healed on the 2nd day of the Workshop itself. It resolved my age-old issues with Mother miraculously by transforming my Hatred for my Mother into Unconditional LOVE. Now I enjoy all Her Love and Blessings unconditionally. My life has changed remarkably. My reactive relationship with my wife has been healed. It has transformed me to such an extent that I no more feel any anger at all when my Soul Mate scolds me at regular intervals.

Something inside me has changed within me without least personal effort. Now I'm able understand any event or problem at the core level miraculously. I can guarantee that this will be a wish fulfilling Tool, the Best so far. I just can't explain how it works. But it's working miracles every moment. For example I wanted to go for morning walks but could not as I used to get up at 10/11.00 AM regularly. But now I'm going on morning walk regularly like a automated robot. How neither I can Understand nor explain. NV LIFE has melted all my worries and anxieties and has made my life so beautiful I can't imagine.

NV Lifestyle grants you unimaginable wisdom so spontaneously. Now I've made it a Mission of my life to take this Life - Transforming Tool to every doorstep to help change Life from inside out, so that the very Hell will be Transformed into Heaven.

NV Life Science is a Miracle Tool, no less than a wish fulfilling tree.

Mihir Mohanty, Bangalore

I came into belief seeing and hearing miraculous happenings.... My childhood pal introduced me to NV techniques... Initially I found myself gaining insight on a daily basis but now I am struggling and that is due my non adherence to daily practice... But I am on.....

Maushmi, New Delhi

Quest for Calmness Of Mind has its answer in NV TECHNIQUES. The most wonderful part of all these is that these techniques keep guiding you naturally to further experiences; and each one holds amazement ! My faith in NV TECHNIQUES works great.

They have made me lighter, less worrisome and more focused.

The most important thing is that they attract one to pursue them in a routine. Everytime you look forward to new experiences while doing them. These 'No-effort techniques' are like gliding, you enjoy the journey, the wind makes it smooth for you.

Aditi Sirothia, New Delhi

I know a little girl

She hid in her self

Wanted to be strong and fight the world and never take any help

She never could be vulnerable as it was not good to be so

She always had to be strong

To show the world that she was ready for the worldly blows

Till one fine day

Came a fresh breeze

It made her shed her shadows and made her breathe

The little girl got up from her deep slumber

A feeling so beautiful she could always remember

She became vulnerable and wanted to live

Life as it comes and not on how rules of one should live

The only fear she has now that the breeze may flow along ahead

And she may be left alone again in the casket that she dreaded

Till the breeze whispered that it's all so easy

Just keep breathing and feel me inside u forever

Let the casket go and let the dawn be

I will be there forever only if you allow me to be

So the little girl decided that I will live my life through

Breathe and feel each breath as if it is meant to be only for you.

Puja Khatri, New Delhi

Might be a baby step towards a transformation, I am a person who does feel and wants to help and do stuff for family and friends. I am known as the fill in the blank for all family matters. After being a part of NV I realised that I am the person who needed most help and every one can be fine without me too. So next step to work on myself i.e the toughest part as had never given myself any importance!! I admit that I am not a regular practitioner of techniques. But surely the essence of all this has initiated a positive change in my personality and that is the beginning, not blaming others, not being critical, not being overly concerned about others. I have a better view of situations. I am after 52 years of existence acknowledging myself. Feel wasted my earlier years !!! This the beginning.

Mrs Puneet Kaur, New Delhi.

Nvlife is a path which often confused me and at times brought me to my wits end. But after spending almost 16 months in Nvlife now I feel my life totally changed and my being full of peace within, in spite of huge upheaval in my life recently.

Meeta Thapa, Jaipur

After recovering from encephalitis and coming back home, I had a lot of fear inside me. That fear has reduced a lot.

Confidence on myself has increased. I had no sincerity and consistency for myself. But now I feel like doing things for myself.

Feel so connected with my breath. Have never felt this before in my life. Have never seen my breath from this perspective.

I would definitely like to recommend it to others as this can solve a lot of mind related problems, change the insight towards life, hence keep you fit and fine both mentally and physically.

Punam Gupta, New Delhi

Looking back at my journey from the time I joined NVLife..Life has been a roller coaster ride. Things took a turn for the good under the guidance of Naveen. I am now better equipped to handle the things and situations which otherwise would have adversely affected me. Kabhi upar kabhi neeche (sometimes up, sometimes down). But how to equip oneself to handle the churning of this roller coaster is what NV life is all about. My gratitude to Naveen for guiding us through thick and thin, to Anjana and Col Ajay for guiding us to NV life, to all the NV Lifes for being there providing constant support and guidance during hours of need.

Love to all.

Regards
Ritu Kaushik, Gurgaon

It is rare for human beings to think beyond 'what about me' all their lives and here is Naveen Varshneya, an extremely intelligent, human, evolved, sensitive man with a clear mission to reduce the sufferings of us mortals based on pure intellect, strong data base of pure scientific knowledge and a clear and soft heart. I was routed to him at a stage in my life wherein he came as a ray of hope and a promise that things will be alright. I wish loads of good luck to him and for his book and wish and pray that he may continue to heal and guide many lives to eternity.

May life never ever throw any kind of pain hardships on anyone, but the truth is that to grow and evolve we are sometimes bound to experience it.

NV Life promises a hope against all hopes, a bounty full of energies that has the ability to bring you out of deepest of gutters only if you can breathe, well it's that simple.

Everybody who is anybody must experience it because then breathe you will, but now it will be with a twist!!

Shweta Bedi, Udhampur

Life Transforming!! Enriching!! Helped me understand my Soul's Journey!! Pulled me out of Chronic Mental Disorder.

Rajat Bose, Kolkata

I was hiccupping non-stop for eight days when I was advised to go on medication. It was the 12th day and I could not see the end of my agony. I called Naveen at NV life. I have known Naveen for the last 31 years and his interests in helping others. I also knew that he continues in this quest to help others. It was a long shot (as I was in Melbourne and he was in Bangalore) to see if he could suggest any yoga or meditation technique. He did and told me that in one hour the hiccups would stop. Exactly one hour later my hiccups had subsided to 10-15% and the next day it stopped. It was interesting, intriguing and unbelievable that my hiccups had to subside exactly one hour later.... I do have a very scientific bend of mind and can say medicine that I started taking on eight day acted exactly one hour after the technique on 12th day and after the remote healing Naveen sent. What was equally unbelievable that the reasons he eluded to (which I don't need discussed here).

My summary of everything. There are things that are hard to believe in but they seem to work too. Keep up the good work Naveen. God Bless!!!!

Sameer Babbar, Australia

Reflections don't need testimonials because we are aware of their existence. We need light to see our own reflection, whether external or internal. Living in the darkness of my own emotions and karmic baggage I couldn't see any ray of hope, I was fortunate to meet

Ms. Renuka who told me about this source of light. The magnanimity of the curator and his workshop is only experienced; words can't describe how easily everything flows here, including energy and divine grace. The transition is so fluid and huge that I recommend every human who suffers at this moment should be in vibrations and frequency of NV so that they personally experience transfer of energies and healing. NV Life and its techniques helped me rise from the physical form of distress, disease and disorder and aided me towards my soul journey of inner reflections. NV helps you consciously to expand your subconscious and brings to your awareness of who you are. When we see the light within we wish to see none other, when we embrace our love for ourselves we have immense compassion and empathise with the one who intended no harm. I came to NV with obesity, thyroid, skin rashes and a huge sack of emotional baggage within six months I was physically free of disease and within the year I have bliss joy and wealth and good health. This is my truth and I got the confidence to accept it through my guidance and effortless coaching at NV LIFE. My true source of confidence, stability, strength,joy and ultimate bliss is NVLIFE and Naveen Varshneya.

Simren Sawhney, Chennai

I participated in remote healing though mid-way. What altered was my perceptions and interpretation of emotionally triggering events. For all those who wish to practise the impossible task of being peaceful in an extremely triggering and hostile situation. This is for you. I have a different perspective of an event that was bothering me since 2010. I can now experience love & affinity that was blocked. I found wisdom and inner peace.

Nami June, Ahemdabad

In 2006, I, Anjana, mother of a three-year-old boy, was diagnosed with a serious health condition, Multiple Myeloma. Everything I had tried using conventional and alternative medicine had failed, until I tried simple breathing techniques that I learnt being in NVlife. Nine years into this blood cancer, I had given up on life and took NVlife as a last resort to give life a chance to treat me with empathy. I took up NVlife seriously and with every passing day I just got better. Amazed that I had cured myself almost of all small issues instantaneously, I started to use these techniques under the guidance of Mr. Naveen Varshneya, founder of NVlife and saw myself miraculously heal.

Having had just begun my journey into the discovery of breathing, NV Life's techniques provided an extensive, practical and tangible introduction to the physical release of the stored trauma I held in my body. This is an introduction to the powerful healing available to all of us through the power of our breath, and the surrender to the intuitive knowledge of our own physical bodies that for so long we have often ignored, blocked or shut down.

NVLife was different from what I had imagined, and it was better than I had imagined. I personally experienced it as a way to speak to myself more freely, on a deeper level, and much more sincerely than I had been trying to do on my own (and I had been trying long and hard for some time). There was no blacking out, no loss of control like I was nervously expecting. There was just this calm opportunity to concentrate and open up somewhere within yourself. What really helped me a lot, was Mr. Varshneya's personality: he was very thoughtful, sincere, easy going, and just extremely comfortable to be around, both outside of the session and during the healing session. He explained everything very distinctly, made sure that I followed everything and overall treated me both very politely and with all his anger. And to this day I believe, I would never have realized some important things about myself if not for him and his ways.

I will be forever grateful and indebted for your existence in this lifetime Mr Naveen Varshneya. You are my Pole Star. I wish you keep scattering your kindness all around like confetti for everyone to get a taste of what I had. I wish you all the love and serenity there is in this world.

Anjana Sharma, Jaipur

For the two days in which I attended the workshop, I gathered so much of peace, tranquility, new insights that I wished those moments never ended. During those two days, a thought occurred to me. Usually, to get a break from our mundane lives, we gather our baggage, and travel to far off places thinking that we will enjoy the vacations, will become refreshed and be happy. But once we return back, again the same routine and life starts. NV Life is like a tours and travel company which take you to exotic holidays within yourself.

Pragati Bhatnagar, Bangalore

I learnt breathing from Isha. It begins with a prayer, Aum chanting, pranayam, *kapalabhatti*, neck lock n meditation. Everything focus on breathing, when reached final stage, we are in that meditative state. Have experienced Theta too. Tried shoonya, which is kinda of yoga nidra. After that NV LIFE happened, now I'm practicing NV LIFE alone, which gives me much more clarity and understanding. Happy to share this.

Renuka shah, Chennai

I am amazed by the power of NV TECHNIQUES, and Naveen's research that he has so very sincerely and widely undertaken. I have a special liking for NV Swimming which I have been almost regularly doing since attending his workshop. The logic behind all TECHNIQUES holds water and when followed sincerely, they DO work perfectly well for all individuals even though they might be in different situations. My sincere thanks to Naveen, I look forward to learning more from him.

Thanks and kind regards.
Anaadi Sirothia, New Delhi

Before NV life I used to cringe away from thinking about the events which were negative in my life. The techniques learnt made me braver to face them head on.

And the effect is that now when I think or the mention of those people and events come I'm better equipped to handle the emotions associated with it.

Though I miss doing NV Swimming regularly, NV Hunting is something I need to work on more.

I'm thankful to Naveen as he in his own way has touched my life and made it actually better to live with all the emotions. No hiding away, suppressing, shying away, now from all the emotions after NVLife. So thanks Naveenji for nudging us both to go through the workshop.

Ishita, Shillong

NV Life... 'khud se khud ki pehchaan' (recognizing oneself)

The most beautiful gift that NV life has given me is ME... a stronger, calmer, powerful, happier, confident and complete ME who is falling in love with herself.

The NV life techniques are the most powerful tools I possess now and they enable me to heal myself physically and emotionally. I feel sheltered and protected in the cocoon of NV life and this empowers me to take on the world. There is a sense of peace in my heart, a sense of purpose too. Thanks to our great teacher, our Guru, for putting me on a flight to self discovery and I am getting there and will reach my destination soon. Thank You Naveen for being the MIRACLE of our lives. Heartfelt gratitude, best wishes, regards and tons of love to our Messiah!!

Rekha Singh, Shillong

It was a turning point in my life having met Naveen, I feel totally blessed I think everyone should do NV life workshop at least once!! It does change your life...

Sukhwinder, Shillong

Naveen has a wonderful and warm healing ability, clearing away negative and heavy pressures, whilst shedding light upon the boundless potential of our own healing energies. The best thing which happened to me in his two days workshop was that I was able to let go all my grudges against my parents all my life. I had just love and gratitude for my parents after I completed my first NV Hunting. Thank you Naveen for your profound and powerful healing sessions, for sharing the effective tools and techniques that you have designed and developed over the years, and your knowledge, compassion, and understanding. I appreciate the generous gifts of your time, your ongoing research, and your meaningful book. Thank you for helping me in the specific ways in which I have needed help and healing. I am going steady with my practice of the techniques and each day is a new day. My sincere and most profound wish is that your techniques and book reaches every corner of the world, to the rich and the poor. My recommendation is that your book should be available in Hindi and other regional languages as well. I feel a great sense of appreciation and gratitude for you. Blessings and love forever.

Brig KRS Panwar (retd.)

I came to this workshop because Charan asked me to, and my intuition led me to go to the workshop. Because I was looking for something like this before, something that was easier than struggling with your mind, and focusing on something. Breath is so important, natural, and observing the breath, and relaxing into it, learning to do this, and experiencing how the body and mind comes into harmony, helps throughout the whole day and life. I am very curious now looking towards my future and how I can apply these techniques. I recommend it.

Jennifer R, Medical Doctor, Germany

I have attended this wonderful, and extraordinary workshop in Birmingham, UK, April 29th and 30th with an off the charts, amazing man, Naveen Varshneya. It has been one of the most transformative experiences I have ever had. It was beautifully organised, and well run workshop. We came away with so much information about how to continue to do the work we did in the workshop and how to transform our lives from this day forward. I can't recommend it more highly for anybody in the world, so please, please think about it and get to a workshop if you can. I have done many, many modalities, and this is by far been the most extraordinary one I have ever been involved with. I have been involved with healing modalities for years and they have been helpful but I have a gut feeling that this will be transformative for me. I appreciate it so much thank you. My transformation from this weekend, has been from going from being a very anxious person to a much calmer one, and one who can now use her breath whenever the anxiety comes up or there is some issue, I can use the breath to calm down and to refocus my life. Highly recommend it to everyone.

MLD, USA

I had a really good experience and learnt a lot. The spirituality side of things I was very much in tune with but Naveen has done is bring the scientific, so I now I have a much better understanding along with the techniques he has taught us. Also the work I have been doing on healing myself and other people, his techniques are the next level I feel. And I can feel the improvement in myself already. I have released some deep emotions that I had previously worked on and knew they weren't completely finished with but I didn't know how to go about it, and two of them have been released in this workshop. After this workshop, I am going to start a new ritual for myself, which will include NV swimming, which I really love as it is going to get me back into meditation practice. So I am very grateful.

Emma Thomas, UK

My experience of the workshop with Naveen and NV-Life began to show me is how to shift my awareness from my distress from the past or the future to the present. We examined all the different sources of the layers of distress that had built up in my life from my early life onward. There are many things he teaches and explains, but the key for me was experiencing what it felt like to separate the pain of the past or the anxiety of the future from the need to do anything to compensate or cope in the present. All the healing and unburdening happens here. Here and now is where the space in the mind is recovered to be used for living rather than remembering the past or fearing the future. What I particularly appreciated about the set of thoughts, techniques and experiences NV-Life taught me is how a small shift in the space of the present, can have a lasting and freeing impact on my idea of the future. Out of the seeds of contentment grows the optimism and a glad anticipation of the future. I would recommend the workshop for anyone who feels overburdened with grief or immobilised by the presence of distressing or hurtful events in their day-to-day life. It's not an easy journey by any means, but definitely a worthwhile one.

Ben O, London

I attended the UK NVLife workshop, because having listened to Naveen speak on Facebook, it was clear to me that using the breath in very specific ways was something I hadn't fully explored.

Through a mixture of teachings and practice, I started to see how my breath was the invisible bridge between my physical body, mind and emotions. Meditation, which I have experienced before, quietens the mind. Then, using the breath in a particular way enables shifts in our blocked emotions. It made me feel different. Better. And through recent advances in scientific research I know this can positively impact our biology.

As a medical Dr, who has explored different healing modalities, I felt excited. This made sense. I lay on the mat, remembered my biology textbooks and thought how if a breathing technique could calm down my thoughts, my brain and my autonomic nervous system, this would in turn help the body achieve homeostasis. I thought of hormone feedback mechanisms and neurotransmitter balance. I even thought of quantum physics and fields of healing energy.

Then I was out of the zone. Into my thoughts. Out of the healing field. This was the main lesson I learned.

All of 'this', our innate healing ability, is beyond thought, and that is the key. To help ourselves we must stop purely thinking, reacting and doing to survive. Instead we need to be in that empty space between thoughts.

I didn't find this easy, but with the group all experiencing this together for 2 days, I did find it possible. I experienced many old unhappy memories. I tried to stop thinking about it and feel it instead. It hurt. But only in doing that could I clear them with my breath as we were taught. I felt lighter and more relaxed. It was lovely to see the sun through my closed eyelids, and feel it's warmth as I lay on my mat. I opened my eyes thinking the sun had come out. But it hadn't. Outside was still cloudy. The curtains were half drawn. I realised this was something else. The light was inside and so I shut my eyes and went inside again.

These techniques are easily taught, anyone can do them, and they are healing. You are not dependent on another person or system. Your breath is free. You are only dependant on yourself, and your discipline to practice, and that that is the key.

Just as there are side-effects to meditation, there are side-effects here too. Dealing with negative emotions which surface when we calm our thoughts isn't easy. But these past hurt feelings, or at worst traumas, are there, driving our mental state, whether we consciously acknowledge it or not.

But once they resurface you are not just reliving them, or trying to block them for your own sanity. You can finally clear them. Yourself. Using your breath. Under your control.

I walked away from this workshop thinking of hundreds of patients I know whose traumatic experiences replay over and over, causing severe anxiety, depression and PTSD, despite medication and cognitive or analytic psychotherapy. This type of approach is deeper. Like meditation, the method is based on an understanding of the healing properties of the deep mind. Like energy work and bodywork, it can be understood using an expanded model based on esoteric philosophies of who we really are. But you don't need to care or believe in that.

For anyone seeking more health and balance in their lives, I would recommend learning how to use your breath in this way.

I can't help thinking of the potential of using the breath to hit this sweet spot in consciousness, which calms the mind, the brain, and the whole body, allowing our innate biological healing design to repair and optimise itself. So I'm going to carry on with these techniques, seeing if I can BE in that sweet spot, instead of just thinking about it.

Dr. N Crowley, Medical Dr, UK.

As a scientist, and now an epigeneticist, I was very curious to learn more about NVLife. So keen that I coordinated, organised and attended Naveen's first workshop outside India, in the UK. I was always curious about how he was integrating the concepts of quantum physics with spirit and breath. This workshop, was well attended by people from the UK as well as other countries. In the whole two day workshop, Naveen was amazing to watch and learn from. His skills included being able to read into the energies of each participant, and teaching at the level that was required, allowing each participant to gain such depth and insight into their lives, allowing the transformation within to begin to unfold. Also the ability to teach such concepts as the science of healing in a way that was accessible to all. What amazed me is the simplicity of the techniques taught. This simplicity is the golden key, to the cure that resides within each of us. This to me was so profound, as this simplicity had hidden in it such ancient wisdom, all tied in with the science, to bring about an approach to helping each person awaken to the healing power within. I personally, have received a treasure trove from this workshop, that I know I will continue to integrate allowing my own innate wisdom to unravel. I can't recommend this workshop enough to anyone who may have health issues, or to anyone that is looking to open up to the huge potential that exists within them. This workshop does that.

Charan Surdhar, Epigeneticist, UK

Having been operated upon, for Carcinoma of left Kidney in May last year I found myself vulnerable. A recurrence of the problem in some other organ of the body is a possibility. During review it was seen that my Gallbladder has some Polyps.

It is around that time that I went through a workshop and treatment with NV Life, towards end of Oct 2016. My major concern was also, my wife Manju's condition as a Diabetic for over 20 years. She too underwent the treatment with me. The 6 week follow up turned out very beneficial for us both.

An Ultrasound indicated that the Polyps had diminished. My wife's condition too has improved reasonably.

We got busy with a lot of travelling December onwards and are presently not being able to devote desired time to the techniques of NV Life as much as we would like to. Though we follow the discussions on WhatsApp.

I do believe that NV Life is making a great positive impact on our lives.

Thanks Naveen, for you guidance and indulgence.

Lt. Gen V S Tonk, PVSM, AVSM (Retd.)

SUPPORT AND FEEDBACK

This book is an intense subject. It is the most intimate layers of each one of us. There is no way, I could have covered every aspect in detail. Please provide us feedback about the book, contents or errors, if you find some. You are also supported in your journey. We will be personally supervising each one of you who is facing any issues in implementing the cure.

You can reach us at www.nvlife.net and best is to join us on our FB page https://www.facebook.com/nvlifescienceofhealth/ to interact with us. You will even find our numbers to have WhatsApp support. There are several of us here that can guide you and this tribe will only be growing with time.

Disclaimer:

This is The Cure. This happens on its own as you begin to practice as described in the book. It works on the principle that you do not make any changes in you. Allow changes to change you. We have never asked anyone to leave any of the medications or stop engagement with their healthcare provider. In fact you will need them more now because as you begin to reverse your suffering, they will validate this through their tests and diagnostics. Continue with your lifestyle and as you experience the transformation, you will know yourself what changes need to happen in your lifestyle and you will find it easy to do it.

CONTENTS

PREFACE

"God does not play dice" – Albert Einstein

My birth took place in the village in Uttar Pradesh, India, and it was a celebration for my family. I was born after two girls, therefore I was considered special. Soon, my younger brother was born, he was often sick, and needed more attention and care.

For the next thirteen years, life wasn't any different from that of any other boy in a middle-class, rising family moving from a village to the city. My father taught in a university and enjoyed the status of a teacher, which was a respected profession then. I was a simple, ordinary, and obedient child – just like every child of that generation. All I wanted was to play, and that is why I hated going to school. Once inside the school, I would look forward to the two-minute break between classes or the free period or even during the classes to get up to some mischief. It was a routine to finish lunch before the lunch break in order to have plenty of playtime. I was wise enough to be a backbencher in the classroom and intelligent enough to rank among the top four students of the class. This was despite the mischief and extra-curricular activities I was involved in. My only pain-point was that winters were shorter, and it was tough to fly kites or play cricket in the dark. I am sure this is the story of every boy, and was not anything unusual.

Being born in a Hindu family was a real celebration back then and more so if you had a large family. Every month, there would be some celebration or the other – a wedding, the birth of a child and festivals. The preparation of such events, several weeks ahead held the joy and excitement of life. I remember becoming very sad on the eve of every such celebration, as I realized it would be over the next day. If there was anything exceptional about my childhood, it was my ability to stick to a promise even when it was not really required, which I believe I hold even today. I do not know how, but reading became a habit and I would read anything and everything I could lay my hands on, and it did not matter if I understood it or not. My father would often laugh and call me *bhondu* (dumb/mentally slow) and an emotional fool. It would be a surprise in the family if I was sent to buy potatoes and I actually came back with potatoes. Apparently, I was always lost in my own world, which I have no clue of even now. My father would read out chapters of *Ramayan* to us and my school would narrate stories of freedom fighters and sages of India which fascinated me. My aspiration was to become a spy and join RAW (Research and Analysis Wing) when I grew up; still remains to be a secret aspiration to this day. I was admired for my endurance regarding my ability to fast for 9 days during Navratri and chant fifty *slokas* (a couplet of Sanskrit verses) at a stretch without knowing the meaning of any one of them. I was an ardent follower of rituals and very religious in worshiping every morning and evening as advised by my mother. I was in *bliss* round-the-clock for my first 13 years as I recall.

Then one day, God played the dice. It happened on a festival. Four of my siblings were inside the room, and I was sitting in the veranda with my mom, dad and my aunt (dad's sister), who was visiting us for that festival. Rituals were yet to start, and I was starving because on festival days, mom would not give us anything to eat till the (prayers) puja was done. I was hungry, waiting for their conversations to get over and their rituals to start, so that we could devour the delicacies, which for several days, we were all waiting for. I was sitting next to my mom on the floor, with my head buried in my knees. They were talking in a normal tone, but I was sensing that it was not pleasant for my mom. Something happened and in that split second, when I lifted my head up sensing some commotion, I saw my mother engulfed in flames in the adjacent kitchen. It was an accident, and took place within a split second. That very instant everything changed. I was numb and helpless as I watched her for several minutes while my father tried to douse the fire and in the process burned his hands severely. Life changed in the next 24 hours when the news from the hospital came. Suddenly, my numbness transformed and I had more questions than all the stars in the sky. My *bliss* changed into pain and faith into anger. My nights knew no sleep and nightmares were a routine till I learned Reiki when I was 24. I spent my days feeling dejected, humiliated, lonely, frustrated and infinitely angry for several years with one pertinent question; why me?

There is *bliss* in the innocence that every child is gifted with, and this is one of the highest frequencies of emotion a human life can experience. Given the choice, no one would want to grow up and lose this *bliss*; but life is a journey to attain the same *bliss* through consciousness and not remain stuck in ignorance for a false sense of *bliss*. The protection we feel in the presence of our father and the love which we experience in the warmth of our mother do not have any parallel in any realm. To be loved, to be appreciated and to be accepted are the only three states we strive to attain through our choices in our formative years. As normal human beings, we strive for the same in one form or another and as *Mystics* we search for the same in mysticism through religion and/or its derivative in spirituality. After losing the *bliss* at age 7 when the left brain joins the right brain, our entire lifespan goes into a futile search for a purpose and for the *bliss*, and very few are fortunate to find it.

I forgot about my dream to join RAW but the detective in me became active as my curiosity grew to decode the meaning of life. I began to question everything and anything internally. One day, my father came into my room and saw 2 fiction books which in his opinion were not good for children to read. He took them out (I still do not know where he threw those books) and replaced them with a book of over five hundred pages on naturopathy consisting of home remedies for various ailments, I look back at this event and believe it was the turning point of my life. I am sure and certain that angels and fathers are synonymous. I read all of it, though I forgot about it, it left me with hope as I read so many diseases being claimed to be cured in the book and that opened the door for me to explore the world in a whole new way. Soon, my father became in charge of the library at his college where he was a professor and I had two friends while preparing for their engineering degrees, who also had wall to wall shelves of books. Now I had a huge access to books on anything and everything from all over the world. Preparing for admissions to engineering college — studying, reading, debating became a total obsession. Choice and compulsion both merged into it. Each book gave me some solace but fired my curiosity for more. Internally, I felt like I had found something but was clueless on how to comprehend it. Each answer gave rise to many more questions, and I spent my youth and married life chasing the answers.

By the time I was a father of two, I found out that all this while I had just two questions: *Who am I?* and *Why do things happen to certain people and not to others?* This brought me some peace though I had no idea on how to find answers to them.

I wanted to know why things had happened the way they happened to me and why I felt the way I did? What was so unique about me that things happened to me and not to any of my friends? It was an accident but by now I knew it could not be an accident in the eyes of the universe.

Human behavior became my biggest fascination. I would review each sentence and conversation spoken for deeper underlying meanings, debating the choice of words spoken and mentally imitating the body language or gestures to decode the emotion which I felt must have caused it. This remained a tacit obsession, which I applied while reading books as well. I would begin to track patterns in their life and would be able to sketch a trajectory of their life with the probability of potential outcomes on few variables as choices. In other words, I was making an algorithm of every case I would come across. Fiction or nonfiction. All my friends, family and relationships were my research lab, who I believe, I have disappointed many a time.

When I was told smoking causes cancer, I was intrigued to see smokers healthy at eighty years old and yet on other hand, it was common to hear of many religious vegetarians living a disciplined life, who never smoked, drank or looked at another woman outside of their own relationships, succumbing to cancer and other fatal illnesses. When a friend's parents divorced, I was keen to know the background and the history of their life and would silently listen to their story to figure out how love turned into divorce for them and not for others. Bangalore is known for its high pollen count, known for its high cases of asthma and yet a vast majority of the population is living without asthma.

It is possible that smokers may get cancer. It is possible that if you are in Bangalore, you may get asthma due to pollen. But all of these are external triggers and not the root cause and that is why it happens to a few vulnerable people and not to all. There must be an algorithm which creates a unique path, unique situations and a unique destiny for each one of us and it cannot be that someone sits at the top and controls these algorithms because if it is being controlled, he would have offered enough wisdom to every person not to suffer or live with ailments or constraints. The code or the path to reach the code shall exist in each one of us. Throughout history, there have been many people who found that code and lived their life blissfully. If some people could find it, then why couldn't I find it and if I could find it why not each one of you?

These arguments kept growing, and I could not keep them concealed. Soon it began to form my personality and lifestyle. My eccentricity began to interfere with my pretence to be normal and reached a stage where I had no option but to accept them. To accept them meant accepting being different, lonely and someone with whom no one wants to relate with except being polite and social.

Seven years ago, in the year 2009, the universe conspired and I had clairaudience in the middle of the night. Since then, driven by insights and synchronicities, I have been led to find the answers to both my questions. Over the years, I discovered how to help people find their two questions and help them with their answers. This book will allow you to first arrive at those two questions in Section 1 and 2 and then help you find the answers through Section 3.

With this book, I am finally home, within. It seems to me that my search for my mother ends here. For many years, I had the illusion that I had found her in things, people and my aspirations. The funny thing about illusions is that they always feel real till broken, and God kept breaking my illusions. All these years each festival or celebration meant a lot of pressure to be happy at a frequency that I would find very hard to imagine. It caused me a lot of stress. It was always a relief to wake up in the morning after the festival was over.

It took me 33 years to reach where I am today, and I feel content knowing that I have arrived at my answers. I invite you, and promise you that if you read this book, there is no way it will fail you in finding your questions, and if you practice the three techniques, you will find your answers. So that when God plays the dice in your life, you do not spend decades in emotional turmoil.

SECTION I
SCIENCE OF LIFE

INTRODUCTION

"*A*s a Child, we were in *bliss*, and healthy. As we grew up, we eroded our well-being and lost *bliss*. This affected our health. If we can bring back well-being, *bliss* will come and health will be restored on its own."

For about twenty years of my career, till 2009, I largely remained a serial technology entrepreneur. This was when being an entrepreneur was a bad word and no one would get their daughter married to such a man. My ventures were disruptive, innovative and almost always much ahead of time. I stood for reforms and empowerment of the masses through technology and my two TEDx talks have details of all such misadventures. I gained and lost wealth quite a few times and landed up broke in 2009 with my ten-year-old start-up, which had begun to bleed profusely. Everyone my start-up touched, began to be prosperous. By then, I had realized, through various such start-up successes and failures that my personality was very fragile compared to my courage and capabilities of causing such mass level disruptions. I was unable to sustain the success of my own creation.

By then, though I was married for almost fifteen years with two kids, it occurred to me for the first time that I should first focus on feeding my family. So, I left my start-up in a bleeding state with my wife to nurse it because I did not have the courage to kill it. A close friend helped me find a small assignment to turn around a software start-up, which I did successfully within four months and moved on to take another job in digital space for money and stability. Life was good as it fulfilled my promise to myself to be stable and be a normal guy, who goes to office, comes back, plays with kids and pays the bills.

Within a few days of joining this company, it was becoming evident to me that it was a bad decision to join it. It felt like they were making the same mistakes that I had made several times in my start-ups. It was a no-brainer for me to see the trajectory of the company and predict that it would close down in eighteen months. I forecasted each step to my colleague in HR for the next eighteen months – the steps that the management would eventually take, leading to the company's closure. I also predicted how it would all start with me being fired. Not wanting to make the same mistakes, I wanted to resign, but didn't for the sake of my promise to myself to be a normal guy, I continued for four months, feeling suffocated.

Then God played the dice again. My prediction came true. The same colleague invited me to my boss's room, and I was given five minutes to pack up and leave. Involuntarily, it brought joy to my face, which I could not hide, and it stunned the gentlemen in the room including me. Feeling insulted, he insisted to know the reason of my happiness and I got up, holding his hand and bowing down to him in gratitude for liberating me from the *suffering* for which I had no courage to liberate myself from, this time. Within three minutes, I came out of the office and my colleague from HR joined me for a smoke with an absolute sense of joy and freedom. I was guilt-free and I had clear justification to myself that I did not break my promise.

Reality hit me as I drove back home with this mixed feeling of inner joy and shame in facing my wife. I had promised stability to her and she had been seeing such upheavals very frequently living with me.

As I came home, seeing papers, few other belongings in my hands and a face beaming with happiness, my wife said what she always said in such moments. I did not have to say anything as I had the advantage of being married to a wise woman who would always read me much before I knew what I was feeling. She said, "Nice to see you happy for the first time in the four months since you joined this company. Did you resign or did they do the honors?" So, she touched my arm gently which healed me from my shame and left me with joy.

The next morning, I woke up with an insight. I am an honest, hardworking, intelligent, compassionate, and have a track record of helping and reforming the lives of several thousands of people with my initiatives. I mean well for everyone, so why is it that my family and I are the only ones who struggle when I make a decision. I thought that there was definitely something wrong with me because people need such initiatives. It cannot be that I suffer while trying to eradicate the *sufferings* of others. This led me to a very strong insight, which evolved into a resolution I had no control over. I decided that I would do nothing for now. I would continue to perish, if needed till I was shown a clear path.

When I announced this to my wife, in a rather toned down manner so as to not create drama yet get her consensus, she did what she always did in such situations – smiled, agreed and touched me with the same kind of love. Her touch in such situations always had a very deep healing effect on me. All such life-changing moments in our home have been short-lived, and then we start to work on such decisions without any further conversation about them. I had a simple task. Chill out during the day, drink chilled beer at night and live life for three months for which we had enough money or till the universe showed me the path, whichever came first.

One day I was browsing through a book I had picked from the bookstore some time ago but had never opened which mentions that breathing should be deep and slow to reach a state of meditation. I checked my breath and found that it only went till the chest. I was so amused with myself. For over two decades, I rarely missed my ritual of meditating daily after a bath and was very proud of myself for being spiritual only to discover that I did not even know the basics of meditation. Would you still want to know how I felt that day?

In the next few days, I spent all my time observing my breath. Nothing happened for the first three days, and I was not looking for any results. Someone said that breathing should be deep and slow. My obedience helped me to do just that. One afternoon, while sitting on the dining table having tea with my wife, I suddenly remembered the day my mother died tragically, which I had buried deep down. For the next two days, I was in tears and my wife who watched while doing her chores, encouraged me to continue to cry. I felt lighter each time I cried, as if a huge stone was lifted off my chest. My breathing got better with each such episode.

I was beginning to sense that each time I observed my breath, it led to the surfacing of some old memory or trauma. If I did nothing and continued to observe my breathing, it would leave me feeling lighter; that memory would not disturb me anymore. This had a unique impact of feeling very intimate and comfortable with myself and my past, without causing me any disturbance. This set the ball rolling and got me curious to learn more about myself. I started to understand what it meant to be in meditation. I found that I was getting quieter and I was unable to have chaos in my mind. I would sit in silence, through the day and evening, just observing my breath.

During these oblivious periods, one day, my father visited to stay with us for a few days. He had been the biggest and most persistent critic for all my misadventures. He was an exceptional orator and possessed rare skills to diagnose any problem and get to the root cause of it. To top it all, he was very passionate about solving problems and had an extraordinary energy to stay with the issue till it was resolved. It was a fatal combination, and we could never escape his sharp scan. He would see my face or hear my voice over the phone, and in that moment, he would know everything I was going through or would tell me an aspect of my personality which in that moment, I needed to know the most. Being in conversation with him meant that all your hidden files were downloaded and visible to him, and at times it felt like being hacked by him.

He had enormous energy, patience and versatility to be able to pick a topic and ponder over it for several days or weeks till he explained it using various techniques and perspectives. He would bring that insight to a logical end by either learning through our discussions or ensuring that his point of view was incorporated. He would never force a decision. He had a lot of patience and conviction in his insights. If he failed with us directly, he would find a different way to pursue the same topic again after a few weeks or months. In short, his intervention would always change something in you. In my case, he persisted relentlessly for almost fifteen years that I accept a normal stable life by going back to a job. Since I was a child, he always came across as a friend and yet I would fear doing anything that hurt him or break the values he taught us. Hence, emotional outbursts, loud conversations, arguments were normal, which to others seemed like fighting and shouting scenarios. We could spend several hours and days laughing, discussing and debating. I regret the times when we could not be friends. He would listen to my lame excuses patiently, often smiling within, and then rip me apart with logic, sarcasm, humor and wisdom.

He saw a very happy family each time he visited us but this time, he probably sensed something more in the family and in my energy. I was unusually silent and did not have much to share or talk. Being very observant, he did not attempt his usual session with my wife or me to convince me to take up a job again.

On one of these days, late in the evening, he got up abruptly and looked straight in my eyes and uttered something so prophetic. His voice had the conviction of a *Mystic* and his face was filled with pride. I had seen this face a few times before on several occasions when it felt like some divine power was speaking through him. I vividly remember that face and his words reverberate in my mind all the time. He said, "I do not know what you are searching for but whatever it is, it is something very big and it is beyond my imagination. My son, let me assure you today, you will get it one day and no one can stop you. From now onwards, I will not come in your way. You have all my blessings."

A few weeks later, his blessings manifested and I witnessed clairaudience. I heard a voice and I saw a design with colors. I discarded it as a bizarre episode and went back to sleep but till today, I have not been able to forget the sound I heard, and the design I saw.

Soon after, one day, my sister-in-law asked me to visit a relative of hers in the hospital, who was in the ICU for over a month due to multi-organ failure and the doctors were giving up. She said, "Everyone has paid a visit and you shall also pay a visit. Since you know Reiki, maybe you can do something." I had long forgotten Reiki which I learned in the mid-nineties and felt very weird at her suggestion to heal someone. I went the next day and as I entered the ICU and stood in front of the unconscious patient, something happened. He partially opened his eyes and closed them. Involuntarily, I saw my hand rising up to bless him and a very strong voice came from inside saying, "He will not die."

Something took over me in that moment. I spent the next one hour coaching the elder brother and the pregnant wife of the patient to do certain things in the form of a chant while observing their breath and promised them that I would perform remote healing. The patient's elder brother had not left the hospital even for a day the entire month. I sold them hope.

As I drove out of the hospital, reality took over and I had to pull my car over and catch my breath as it hit me that what I had said to them had no basis. I was feeling quite embarrassed about my actions and felt anger towards myself for fooling people and giving them false hope. I felt that I was trying to become important and fabricating a new career and it scared me if it was true. I knew myself as a hard core, rational, technology entrepreneur and had always looked down upon such irrational things as jargon that uneducated people use to exploit the society and poor people.

I came home and confessed to my wife. She said, "Why don't you go to your room, meditate and see." I did as she suggested – closed my eyes and did the only thing I knew to do; observed my breath. I was amazed at how visions started to come to me about the patient. Some of these visions were clues for the future and some were mystical. Since then, it was all a guided process for five days during which the patient was declared out of danger. During these five days, I started to take inputs from his brother on what changes in the patient's parameters would help the doctors become hopeful. I also started to tell them what would happen in the next twelve hours. It surprised me that all the predictions kept coming true. Fifteen days later, this patient visited me on his way back home after getting discharged and I recently heard that he is the proud father of a six-year-old boy. I did not make much out of it and to be honest, I was reluctant to attribute it to myself. My rational mind was way too strong to believe that I could cause such a turn around. I kept it a secret for several months.

I was a man with an embarrassing level of ignorance regarding medical terms or the human anatomy. My only encounter with doctors was for a fever once or twice or taking my wife to her doctor. I would not know the names of the simplest of diseases and potential reasons or even the internal functioning of the human body. During the time, I was doing this work on the patient; I used to interact with my elder sister who was a gynecologist in Bangalore. I would ask her various questions on the function of various parts of the body and what it meant to have low blood pressure or multi-organ failure and how it came in the body and why? She was aware that I had a tendency to relate emotions and events of life with illness and would know how to reply in layman's terms. One day I received a call from my brother-in-law (her husband) telling me that his colleague's nephew was in the ICU in Nagpur for the last four weeks or so due to multi-organ failure and the doctors were not hopeful any more. My first patient was still in hospital but out of danger by this time. In a way, within a week, I had a second case.

When the mother of the patient called from Nagpur and briefed me, again the same inner voice came to me so strongly that I could not resist it. It said he will not die. Much before she could put the phone down and send me more details, I started connecting with the patient (God knows how I was doing it). Again, the same type of rituals started for almost ten days. I would observe my breath, see a vision, and know what was going to happen next. I remember waking up in the middle of night once and starting to meditate because it felt like this patient was beginning to slip away. Who woke me up? I had no clue. Within a week, this patient was declared out of danger and is now a successful advertising executive.

This time, by now, I knew two things about healing, using cotton wool to balance the electromagnetic field (read Section 3, Treatment) and observing breath leads to the state of meditation. In addition, it was evident to me that two significant factors which were common in both the cases, contributed to the success. In the first case, it was the elder brother and in the second, the mother who did not step out of the hospital till they took their patient out of the hospital in a healthy condition. The second common factor was that both the patients were young (first one in his thirties and second one an engineering student).

Reading the book on *Kriya Yoga*, I stumbled upon a statement, "No disease can set in the body if the electromagnetic field of the body is in a balanced state." In a different culture and time, the electromagnetic field actually meant yin and yang, left and right brain, male and female energy in the body, respectively. This is regulated by breathing through both nostrils which alternate every forty-five minutes to restore the balance in every healthy human being, hence keeping us in health and harmony.

The electromagnetic field is dynamic in nature and it fluctuates with the breathing. Breathing is a function of our emotions. We breathe differently in different emotional states hence disturbing our electromagnetic balance. In an ideal scenario, such as with a child, emotions move through the body all the time and leave the child in his default state of *bliss*. Breathing is then not affected. But due to our *belief*, we begin to store emotions in our body which affects our breathing through both the nostrils and this causes imbalances. If an emotional state stays for too long in our body, it results in consistent, faulty breathing which gradually becomes a pattern and the electromagnetic field seeks to stabilize at that imbalanced state following the law of nature that everything in the universe can exist only if it is stable. The very first sign of such an imbalance can be seen in body structure, postures, language and voice modulation. It changes to contain the emotion inside the body. Try walking while feeling extreme self-pity, or anger and then walk after deep meditation to feel the difference. As emotions alter breathing, altered breathing alters emotions to seek the new-found stability. For instance, if you are angry and keep that anger within, it alters your breathing. This altered breathing rate will now attract emotions of similar nature, which is anger, following the law of attraction, through various events or thoughts so that you remain stable in that quantum level at which anger vibrates.

Though I began to realize that there was something I was gifted with and had found vital information about health and life, I did not know what to make of it. I had begun to enjoy practicing the power of observing breath and its impact on my consciousness with so many insights coming into my awareness.

A few days later, I felt like I could heal people. This felt as strong as a woman in labor being sure that she was delivering and I could not deny or ignore it. I was burning with an unknown power to cure, and I knew it was possible. One day, I received an email from a healer friend that there was a schizophrenic patient in the mental hospital.

The next day, the patient's family was at my house and they decided to work with me. I met the patient, a MBBS, MD doctor who had written a book a big book on medicine, was now in the mental hospital in Delhi. I asked him to be on cotton (Section 3, Chapter Treatment). I asked his family to meet me three days later. They came back jumping with joy.

They informed me that 80% of his hallucinations and delusions had stopped. Wow! Till then, I was still struggling to pronounce and spell schizophrenia; I did not even know the symptoms or cause entirely. Over the next ten days, this became my first paid assignment and I was certain by now that I had something which could help people. After partially recovering, (though he left the treatment in between) he became the Head of Department at a medical college. If he hadn't been a medical doctor, I would probably not have believed in myself.

Human body and its internal functioning is the subject matter of the engineering inside the body. It has been the same engineering work since the origin of life on the planet. Health is regulated by well-being. There is a correlation between health, well-being and *bliss*. Well-being in its definition covers emotional, spiritual, mental and physical harmony. Well-being is dynamic in nature and is affected by our everyday experiences that influence health. If our experiences are more negative than positive, our well-being begins to deteriorate. If our experiences give us more positive feelings, we have a sense of well-being. Hence, well-being shall be considered an instrument which would help attain health through *bliss*. This creates a need for human beings to have certain guidelines in their lifestyle as routine which takes care of their well-being. A holistic life means choosing the aspirations and decisions which will contribute to well-being.

The *bliss* experienced by a child in innocence is the same *bliss* experienced by mystics, consciously in the meditation. These mystics who had revelations while meditating shared them with common people. Through these guidelines, they had the intent to help people stay connected to the divine energy, which would continue to give hope for the future. They created these guidelines in the form of religion and rituals. The set of *belief* were created to help them evolve in a structured manner as individuals. As they followed these guidelines, they experienced well-being and that kept them healthy. These guidelines were designed in such a way that common people could pursue the *bliss* in their routine experiences and did not have the need to become a *Mystics*.

When I looked at the history of the schizophrenia patient, I knew there was a strong link between his life experiences and his mental illness. I sensed that his symptoms had the seeds for his cure. His life was traumatic throughout his adolescence.

I posted my success regarding the schizophrenia case on Facebook. One after the other, I started getting mental disorder cases and I started to learn common things in their life experiences. Within months, I was tempted to write the book on the cause and cure of mental disorders to reach out to the masses. I wrote to Dr. Deepak Chopra hoping he would share this wisdom, so it got the attention it deserved. I was so sure that I had found logical explanations for the cause of mental disorders. As I began to gain confidence in my healing power, my conviction to believe in myself started to magnify, though I continued to remain cynical about myself. It is the science which was unfolding, that supported my mystical powers, which did the trick. I was very repulsive to the idea of becoming one big healer and control everything. I used to contemplate coming out of it so I kept it low profile. One day, In meditation, I saw a vision and that is where I began to make sense of all the experiences of my professional life.

1. How do I help people discover the same healing powers within themselves? If I can discover that, then this is scalable. Otherwise, it will die with only a few hundred people benefiting, I being the bottleneck.

2. If it is scalable, then it has to be so logical that everyone can feel and experience it. If so, then it will be a science and not an *art*.

3. It must be so robust that no one shall be able to challenge it. Yes, I needed more than perfection in the science and its ability to be practiced by common people. It had to be something which worked for everyone and it had to explain why for some cases it could not be done, if so. The most important was the medium through which it is passed on to people so that it does not get diluted or misused.

Since then, for seven years, every day, I have lived with the vision of birthing this book that you are holding in your hands.

Our emotions are functions of our life events. Every moment is an experience that generates specific emotions in us. Emotions are an expression of our spirit; hence our experiences always try to bring us in touch with our spirit. Each experience, offers to form a *belief* and this is how we create a conscious mind. Experience formulates *belief* and *belief* creates reality. This is a 'chicken and egg' situation and as we unravel it further, it takes us into the theory of karma. *Belief* is formed by the environment we see around us, at home and outside. The environment is chosen by our soul based on our karma. Our birth is an endeavor to choose the environment and experiences which will liberate our spirit from the clutches of karma by breaking the limiting *belief*. This leads to the selection of parents, thus the selection of environment becomes its playground for a particular lifetime.

This, for example, explains why two brothers can have different emotions having experienced the same event due to different *belief*. This causes different patterns of infinite choices through the same event and affects the breathing of the two brothers differently. This shall explain why the same environment produces different destinies for two people, which is due to their different *belief*.

Analyzing the simple science of breathing, I arrived at the karma and reincarnation theory. The task was to discover why a specific disease happens due to permutations and combinations of various emotions and *belief*. By the time this theory unfolded in front of me over the next year or so, I had already successfully started to reverse all complex mental disorders, lifestyle diseases and distressed relationships with conviction. A large part was still my healing powers and less of a science. At that time, people came to me as the last option when they were not even hopeful about hoping.

Experiences, emotions, choices, karma and its role in well-being were visible, however, these were still loose pieces of information. I did not know how to link them to breathing and then to a specific problem and then to trigger healing. Since I was working largely on mental disorders, this question led me to look at the role of the mind. The mind is a regulator of emotions. We use it to direct our attention, provided it is in our control. A strong mind is able to suppress any emotion and a weak mind is driven by emotions causing a situation of distress. Extended exposure to distress disturbs the mental functioning, eventually turning it into a disorder. A strong mind keeps emotions suppressed and over a long period this suppressed emotion seeks to express itself by causing a disease in the body. This also made me realize that symptoms of a disease comprise the cause of the disease and the seed of the solution. So how do we re-work our mind so that it is governed by us and not the other way around?

Breathing is inversely proportional to thoughts. So, as we observe our inhalation and exhalation, it will begin to reduce our thoughts and finally, we shall reach a stage of no thoughts. This is the state of meditation or *Yog Nidra*. Self-healing can be achieved if the state of meditation or *bliss* can be attained, and practiced over a period of time. This is the sole reason why the cure, which exists in Pranayama and Ayurveda principles, does not deliver healing anymore. There is a phenomenal difference in the way the mind worked in those days compared to the present. Cure is attained when the mind is in a zero thought state. Any existing holistic treatments such as Pranayama, Homeopathy or Ayurveda or Yoga do not have the universal results in healing that they once had. This is because we are now dealing with an active and entangled mind that consumes most of our life force energy, which in turn leaves very little energy for the body.

Realization of the role of the mind and meditation being cure raised the question of how we make a patient attain the state of meditation (*Yog Nidra*). It is easy for a *Mystic* in the Himalayas to attain this state. How do we make patients with mental disorders reach the zero thought state when it's known that their mind is not in their control?

My discovery of healing principles was far from being very basic because it was too complicated and intuitive. I was so far able to bring people relief within a week, and it was important for me to learn a process that could quickly give relief but more important than cure was to trigger hope in the patient and the family so that they pursue the cure. One week was not good enough to trigger hope and hope will not trigger unless they see relief. I needed a simple process to teach common people so that they could validate their experiences against the set outcomes and quickly gain faith in the treatment which would raise their hope.

I discovered there were three factors common to all the cases – sleep, breath and sexuality. If breathing was observed, deep sleep was restored, and sexuality was restored. I saw vague link between thoughts and sexuality being inversely proposal. It appeared that health means restoring sleep, breath and sexuality. This became the validation point for me. To know if you are healthy, you shall have these three points in a balanced state. Sleep keeps the partition between the subconscious and conscious mind intact. If there is loss of sleep, interference of the subconscious with conscious makes the mind malfunction causing distress or disorder. Insufficient sleep wipes out the life force energy (sexuality) from the body and powers up the mind for a negative spectrum of thoughts. This gives rise to the state of mental disorder and if the mind is very strong and able to keep emotions under wraps, it manifests as some other disease later on. Hence, I perceived that disease is a disorder of the body, disorder is distress of the mind, distress is disease of the spirit (emotions) and all three can be healed by restoring the breathing, which will reinstate sleep and that in turn will regulate the flow of sexuality (life force energy). So, the secret of health is in the ability to breathe deeper with awareness in such a way that it breaks down the compulsion of the mind to remain active with thoughts. By sheer coincidence, I happened to come upon a book about Tantra again. It took my intuitive knowledge about breathing into the science of breathing.

Swarn Yog is the branch of Tantra which is the complete science of breathing. It states that every human life is designed to have 946,080,000 breaths. The electromagnetic field is in a balanced state if we take fifteen breaths per minute, which means human life is designed for one hundred and twenty years. This made a lot of sense to me as to why people die at different ages, have different paths and choices and hence differing destinies which are driven by how fast they consume their breath. It conforms to the theory of quantum physics and the law of spirituality that each moment is uncertain and we have choices to make in that moment which determines our destiny. It also validated my quote that "everything in the universe is vibrating and nothing is fixed, nor is death and destiny". Each moment which is an experience, affects your breath. So if insufficient love was discovered as one of the primary drivers of cancer, then among all the people who experienced lack of love, it depends on how their *belief* system was which potentially led one to have cancer but others probably had other issues or none at all. Breathing rate goes up due to emotions which keeps the mind active all the time to regulate them or suppress them, causing hyperactivity of the mind. It was, in any case, my observation, from the beginning that each of the patients had a much higher breathing rate, obsessed mind, loss of empathy, were unable to feel emotions and experience sexuality. *Swarn Yog* further says that eight breaths per minute is the state of *Yog Nidra* (meditation). This means a state in which emotions, mind and body are in harmony. When they are in harmony, disease cannot exist. This is what the cure is. To arrive at eight breaths per minute daily, is the state of meditation (*Yog Nidra*) and this will restore the normal breathing rate of fifteen breaths per minute!

This was now making sense. I could understand why the ICU patient did not die and how disease and disorder could be cured through breathing. By now, I had extensive experience with infertility cases while working with the Fertility (IVF) center and that turned out to be a path breaking experience to understand the human body – mind and spirit. It now went deeper into understanding the role of life force energy, ego, male and female imbalances and importance of sexuality in well-being. There was a lot of wisdom unfolding about how we humans translate various *belief* into emotions which continue to play a pattern of failure in our lives. This gave me confidence to mobilize the energy in the body within hours to restore the balance. You learn about that in the treatment section. I discovered that infertility is a very fragile disorder and a small intervention is enough to let women conceive naturally in three to nine months.

I discovered that the human body carries all the wisdom and that wisdom can be tapped through breathing by paying attention to a specific part of the body. This led me to start creating a structure of treatment and logical explanations for the patients. I started reducing healing people and increased my coaching to bring the root cause to the awareness of the patients. It surprised me that such coaching session brought shift in the people more deeply and long lasting than doing healing on people. I understood that if we raise the consciousness of people and help them discover their truth, healing triggers on its own.

By now, my exposure to diseases were still very limited but I discovered that people who had some issues with thyroid, sugar, spine related issues were getting cured though they probably came for some mental disorder or relationship distress. Things turned around when I was asked to work on a terminal liver cancer case from Delhi. The family of the patient in any case was not expecting me to cure the patient but provide relief as doctors had given him only 6 to 8 weeks. By this time, remote healing was at its peak and I was handling cases remotely without meeting patients and healing them over six to twelve weeks through a daily healing program. Hence, I took up the cancer case by doing remote healing for this sixty-eight-year-old man. I taught his wife to handle what you shall discover in the 'Treatment' section and the rest was handled remotely twice a day.

To my surprise, after five weeks, the family of the patient informed me that there was a 33% reduction in cancer and a leading cancer hospital in Delhi, which took the scan, spent several hours examining the new reports vis-a-vis old reports. This broke my fear and my theory of the cause of cancer was proven right. Most importantly, it was the fact that rather than being bed-ridden when I started the work, the patient had no sign of cancer in his daily life. He could walk five kilometres every morning, with a healthy, good diet and sleep. A sign of well-being.

This opened up my confidence to take up any complex and rare case. In April 2013, I started conducting a workshop to teach the science and techniques to help people learn and cure themselves. Since then, more than thirty workshops and more than a thousand people have been taught the program. This book has wisdom acquired through each of them and difficulties faced by them in implementing the program learned in the workshop.

This book consists of three sections as a part of your complete cure. Section 1 and 2 are the theory where you discover the structure or engineering of life on the planet and can relate it with your own life. Section 3 consists of the treatment section, which is meant for a caregiver to administer on their patient in the family or for you to heal yourself. This section is the reality so that everyone can prepare the person for self-healing. If you are in dire need of healing, I suggest that you skip the theory and directly start with the treatment section and follow the process of reversal of symptoms. Same section has the three techniques, which are based on breathing and are, in essence, the cure for you.

You shall be able to find all your answers. Each of the patients were able to reverse their *sufferings* and get cured. Limitation of this program is only your decision to go slow to reverse your *suffering*. People like to work on their recovery in phases, and this is perfectly fine. The cure is now in your hands and you can always choose to go back to your *sufferings*. This is the reason cure does not exist and will never exist outside human beings. Healing is innate to us and our freewill is the fundamental driver of our choices. There are no exceptions when it comes to this cure. You are free to keep your skepticism and devote yourself to practice it with commitment and sincerity. You do not need to have faith in these techniques to practice it and you can continue to believe in your God and Guru while still practicing these techniques and as you begin to experience a difference in your life, you will find correction in your thoughts happening on its own making you believe in this treatment program.

This treatment program has been applied to people, aged 7 to 85, with diverse profiles, across various faiths, cultures and *belief* systems. You need no alteration in anything you do or believe, including your eating, drinking, praying or socializing habits, except that you start to include this in your schedule. The rest of the work is done by the energies as it begins to open up. This is an experience-based science; hence, all you need to do is to trust your experience.

You do not need to change your schedule. You can continue to take your medication or allopathic treatment. In the last seven years, none of our patients have had to leave their allopathic treatment to be with us. Once their *sufferings* started to diminish, their doctors themselves happily reduced or eliminated their medication. This works best because allopathy is best at diagnosing, and we have worked with allopathic doctors hand in hand as an integrated medicine.

For someone who could just blindly go on implementing the treatment and learn to practice three techniques, their truth will surface on its own. This is how I started. The essence of the cure is in the ability to observe your breath and as you do that, various emotions, *belief*, thoughts and patterns come into awareness and dissolve making you vibrate at a higher quantum plane where no low frequency emotion can come. Hence, it is a cure as long as you are vibrating at that frequency zone. If some event happens in your life, you may lose that higher state again and fall to a lower frequency zone and attract suffering. The good news is that the cure is now in your hands, and you can come back to a higher frequency zone using the same techniques. Having said that, you will find it hard to fall back if you practice the techniques and each day, you will be able to create a barrier for a downward fall.

All these years, I have used phone calls, video and audio calls to handle cases globally. I have attempted to explain the techniques and processes and people have been successful in following the steps. Therefore, any argument that you can only learn in a workshop or face-to-face in a meeting, does not hold much merit.

After the book is published, I will in any case be creating various support formats for you. We will start to train people who can be certified as they begin to help you. Anyone can become an NV Life well-being expert by first working on self and then either through formal training with us or just from this book, you can start to help others in your family and friends and then grow from there.

I have not gone into the specifics of any specific type of *suffering*. It does not mean that your rare case is not covered. Any form of *suffering*, you can think of, is imbalance in an electromagnetic field and that can be restored by following the treatment written. It is safe to assume that each one of you can reverse the *sufferings* by 80% and rest 20% heals with time or you can take the support of our online forums, Facebook page to interact with us or engage with our trained experts or attend our workshops to learn at a deeper level.

As I discovered the science, I understood why a degree in engineering was essential for this work. It was to decode the secrets, break down the components of each aspect and find the algorithm that governs our lives. This is potentially the first book of its kind in the history of humanity, which is not a self-help book or theoretical, but based on actual work and results proven over seven years with diverse and complex cases. I am confident that there is no way this book will fail you, and I dream that this community will grow and contribute further to the research carried out so far. This book is for each one of you to discover the light within.

ORIGIN, HISTORY AND INTRODUCTION OF BELIEF

I want you to travel in time imagining how life on this planet must have evolved from the first few people. In the beginning, there were two types of human beings:

1. The one who accepted the existence of self and went on to survive by discovering food is called a *Survivor*. It is assumed that if we have life, we must do something about it. Either we attempt to live or make an effort to not die. There exists a very tiny micro-moment between living and dying, in which we exist with realization of existence, in which we receive all the insight to carry out what we need to do with the life including discovering the need to survive.

2. The second, is the one who questioned his or her existence and went deeper into the forest to discover the meaning and purpose but more importantly attempted to discover the answers to questions like "What is life?" and "Who am I?"; he is called the *Mystic*. The *Mystic* is a person, who refuses to attempt to live if he or she does not understand the deeper meaning behind the purpose of their existence and rather than staying with the existence, attempts to know the answers.

Origin of *belief* lies in the journey of *I exist* to *I survive*. *I exist* is a realization of self in the body and surroundings but that still is not enough motivation for a human to explore the world or try to retain existence. It is a passive state and there is no action in it any way.

I survive is a state in which acceptance of self comes in with a desire or need to retain or to survive. Journey from *I exist* to *I survive* has the origin of a *belief* that since I have a life, I must *survive*. If not this, there was no reason for humanity to care for its own existence and try to survive by discovering food and protecting against the dangers of nature.

Hence, *belief* is originated from the realization of *need* i.e., *need to survive*. This *need to survive* became the origin of *belief,* which in turn became the mother of all *belief* for humanity to evolve. *Need* to *survive* has a sense of indifference toward existence of cosmic power or God due to ignorance. If *Survivor* was to believe in God, then movement from *I exist* to *I survive* would not take place because then a paradigm like *being taken care of* or *being provided for* would become the *belief*, which will not let existence work toward their survival. Hence, being a *Survivor* in essence evolved into taking charge of existence.

On the other hand, the *Mystic* looked at existence and began to seek answers as his own existence and surroundings appeared to be full of wonder, mystery, and he was curious. He formed no *belief*. It was fine if he perished in the process of finding more about nature.

The *Survivor* discovered hunger and then food as a means to survive. As he began to feel certain about surviving through food, it created an insecurity and uncertainty about the availability of food. Gradually, regime of three meals a day was created not as a need for the body but to ensure the certainty of survival. Body was beginning to get trained and a *belief* of three meals a day was created. Discovery of sex as pleasure created a sense of joy in living. Through this process, as humanity discovered birth of a child, it brought pressure on resources like providing three meals a day. Women demanded food when they could not make it available for themselves due to pregnancy and later for the child.

This led man and woman to work together. Hence, concept of monogamy was invented. This was done to ensure that they survive together due to mutual need, which by now included food and pleasure through sex. Pleasure through sex was felt by man and woman internally and that began to give them joy and *bliss*. Hence, food ensured certainty of survival and sex became the motivation to live. Monogamy was essentially the first contract ever signed between a man and a woman to ensure that a woman stayed back home and did not search for food, which was to be provided by man. Similarly, the woman provided him with sex to ensure that he could go and get food. It worked well for both of them to ensure the fulfillment of mutual and collective needs, which offered them a sense of certainty. After the birth of the child, food became a bigger issue as man had to take larger responsibilities of being the provider of food which, by now, included himself, his woman and the children. Clearly, he did not want to hunt for food for months to come back home and discover that he must provide for one more child who was not his own. Hence, sex and food were interwoven and traded.

Seeking loyalty from the woman was a natural outcome of this trade contract as that gave men certainty, purpose and survival. Same were the reasons for a woman to ensure that her man remained loyal to her and continued to provide food, certainty and does not divert food by building another home. If not for food and non-availability of contraceptives, humanity would not have agreed for something as unnatural as monogamy and loyalty. Since that time, there have been people and communities in every era, which when felt abundance of food, and sense of security began to break away from the clutches of monogamy.

Hence, loyalty and commitment were invented through marriage to ensure a higher degree of certainty by growing interdependency. Gradually, to further grow security and certainty, same interdependency was enhanced by living in the community to defend themselves from natural calamities and attacks by the neighbor's tribes. Survival through food was not a challenge for men and women as they both were capable of finding food for themselves. If not for sex, birth of child and emotions, institutions such as interdependency, monogamy and marriage wouldn't have developed. The need to survive, by now, had created many *belief*, which were passed on from one generation to another generation and gradually became an automatic response system by being coded in the genes.

Life was still quite mechanical, though enjoyable. Until this point, humanity did not have enough curiosity beyond the need to survive. Having discovered food, sex and interdependency, life was turning out to be more joyful. They had some sense of emotion but the *Survivor* did not know how to react to it till procreation, which gave birth to emotions. Birth of a child gave birth to one distinct emotion. Wonderment. This sowed the seed of a *Mystic* into a *Survivor*.

In wonderment, he discovered himself merging in the flow of nature. There was now a sense of celebration and that made humanity explore themselves more inward than outward. He began to integrate nature and its cycle of sunrise and sunset as much as the laughter or cry of a baby. It triggered hope, optimism and the desire to experience life and searched for creating his own identity which is unique. But this was still not enough for him to dig deeper into life as it generated no such need to know more about, "Why this life?" Wonderment does not create curiosity as much as it creates the feeling to dissolve all questions. On the contrary, new-found emotions filled with hope, joy and wonderment were giving rise to a degree of uncertainty triggered by the search for identity to start to store more food for the future and this is how the thinking was developed. The birth of the mind took place with the objective to survive longer to continue to enjoy life.

Then one day, God played the dice. Death, which humanity had seen up till now had not been such a big problem and had not allowed people to become curious about the nature of life. Post the birth of emotions and discovery of joy in living together rather than living alone, when death of the loved one caused pain and, it disrupted interdependency, threatened survival, and changed the confidence humanity had about certainty and future, it became a problem. It forced them to take more responsibility. It hit them hard that their joy was not permanent, certainty was an illusion and life was unpredictable and could be full of pain and burden. Fear was now born.

Death was never an issue for the *Survivor*. For him, it was just like a friend leaving a bit early from the late night party. So the party was still on unless, that death caused disruption to his joy. *Survivor* grew curious and asked the same question, "Who am I?" and "What is Life?" The seed of the *Mystic* in him began to grow and become active. The nature of pain is such that it raises questions and connects us to the mystery of life. It is through the mystery that we connect with deeper layers to decode the meaning of life and pain is its driver. Applying the mind to their curiosity, their quest to know the deeper meaning of life began.

At the outset, it appeared that the *Survivor* had begun to ask the same question asked by the *Mystic*. His questions about life kept growing to seek the purpose of his living and to discover the reason for the pain he felt within. He resembled his quest with that of the *Mystic*, but there was one clear difference in asking the same question. The *Survivor* wanted to know the answers to resolve the pain, to be able to come back to life, enjoy it and if possible, avoid pain so that the enjoyment could continue. The idea was to gain victory over pain and create a higher degree of certainty.

And then one day *Survivor* met the *Mystic*.

The *Mystic* by now, knew a lot about life. He knew that *bliss* was infinite, and could be experienced through meditation. The deeper the state of silence, the higher the *bliss*, and the bigger the wonderment. In this state, where a *Mystic* was going deeper by the day, he began to have a revelation and the mystery began to unfold about life and nature. He discovered the cycle of life and death, and *bliss* and pain are but a state of being one with nature. He found out that basic survival on the planet centered around food, sex, pleasure and certainty was a primitive view. He realized such a primitive life experience would limit the spirit of humanity and create many emotions which would result in humanity remaining stuck, without realizing the higher dimensions of life and would gradually perish.

The *Mystic* understood that life was a continuous process beyond birth and death and the same spirit till one realizes the highest potential needed to be born again. He found there was no accident but instead a design. Acceptance of self, taking life as a journey into the unknown and surrender to the mystery is the only way to dissolve temporary pain into *bliss* of living life by realizing the deeper wisdom of nature and by helping humanity evolve to a higher dimension of living.

Having realized the truth, the *Mystic* faced two key challenges in communicating the same wisdom to a *Survivor*. On one side, he knew that the only way a *Survivor* would believe him was if the *Survivor* also began to realize the same truth as seen by him. The objective was not to teach the truth as realized in the state of *bliss* through silence and attaining state of wonderment, but to teach how to attain *bliss* through silence which would reveal to them their own truth. On the other hand, the *Mystic* did not know the ultimate answer to the question "Who Am I?", and to be able to teach and explain it to the *Survivor*. This was because the ultimate question after attaining all the *bliss* and decoding all the mystery would be "What is the next step?" and "What is it for?". Hence, mystery is the basic nature of living on the planet and exploration of it seems to be the natural path to live.

Realizing that the *Survivor* was stuck to pleasure and seeking the permanence of it; seeing the *Survivor suffering* the loss of near and dear ones and unwilling to accept life and its cycle; seeing the *Survivor* being ignorant about the mystery of the universe and his or her inability to see beyond their own needs, the *Mystic* came up with a solution. To teach the *Survivor* two things:

a) A process through which the *Survivor* could gain insights the way the *Mystic* experienced *bliss*.

b) Teachings about the existence of the universe as a mystery to make mystery acceptable so that the more a *Survivor* finds an answer and still remains clueless in decoding all questions, he or she shall be able to accept that perennial state of quest in themselves. This called for a two-fold approach. On one side, faith was invented to help the *Survivor* go beyond questions and connect with the mystery to experience *bliss* and find answers within and on other hand, rituals and *belief* were created to generate energy in the human body to attain this state of faith.

This is how religion and rituals to perform religious acts as a way to seek deeper meaning of life were created by the mystics and God was invented as a symbol of mystery with supernatural powers. To tap into God, faith was the way, rituals and processes were there to reach the state of faith in which *bliss* could be experienced. The intent of the religion was never, to turn a *Survivor* into a *Mystic* but to make him or her better at surviving and exploring life in a higher dimension. The objective was to help the *Survivor* self-realize wisdom, a deeper sense of existence and to grow compassion and raise the consciousness which was stuck in needs. Realization of *bliss* within was the realization of God within. Hence, every process given to him or her was to help them see the purpose of life which was always meant to contribute towards the evolution of the planet.

This brought a paradigm shift in human evolution. As the *Survivor* began to practice rituals by following religion with the objective to understand the deeper learning of life. This facilitated the acceptance of destiny, compassion and pain at one end and on other end, fear of God and insecurity, when they failed to find the inner connection or made mistakes in rituals and *belief*. They began to create a culture which was nurturing the rituals and offering a holistic living to the entire community. Hence, religion gave birth to rituals and rituals created culture. There was a need to pass on this knowledge to the next generation and that needed a value system to be created so that knowledge is preserved. Morality was born out of the need to preserve the value system, through which a culture could be passed on to have a ritual, which the next generation could continue to use to gain insight and explore a new dimension.

But wisdom alone could not be the driver in passing knowledge to the next generation. On one hand, the constant insecurity and temptation for indulgence was very enticing and on another hand, fear of failing to connect with God was raising morality. On the top of it, the *Mystic* was not around on a daily basis to pass on the culture and values. When *Survivor* did that, they passed on a higher morality than wisdom due to their fears and failures.

Hence, they inflicted fear and created a form and identity of nature and called it God. This made it easy for them to make a new generation adhere to culture and rituals with higher levels of morality. Heaven was an incentive to stick to values and culture and hell was the punishment in failing to do so. Coupling 'Wisdom-Fear', they continued retaining their culture by growing fear over wisdom. That is how faith became the driver of the human *belief* system, to explore inner powers and realize a fulfilling life beyond mere survival. Development of mental faculties enabled humanity to believe that they do have choices and can design their own destiny. *Mystics* offered a case study of what humans can possibly achieve by demonstrating superhuman capabilities and inspired them to shed their fears and break their *belief*, which was tying them down. Mythological stories depicting heroic acts were the way wisdom and courage was passed on.

Over a period of time, since no one questioned them, it became a way of life. It moved from the consciousness of humanity into the subconsciousness as it began to get passed on to the next generation. Gradually, it got coded into the DNA of the next generation and so on. This meant that when the child was born and began to grow, he began to respond to some unknown program, which was actually nothing but the values, *belief*, wisdom and fear passed on from previous generations. This was then dubbed as a more intelligent race. The wisdom coded in our DNA which we may not be consciously aware of, is actually the tendency and patterns (*sanskar*) of the soul, which showed up in specific situations or unknowingly feels as a tendency to break free from programmed *belief* for survival. Each time, humanity tried breaking a ritual or tradition; they were faced by an unknown fear as if their ancestors were watching them or God would punish them. In reality, each new generation was only trying to break free from old *beliefs*, which were passed with higher morality through the fear to arrive at the same question, "Who Am I?".

The need to survive, thus, is the origin of all *belief* and lack of faith creates the need to survive. Hence, faith is inversely proportional to *belief*. The more you surrender and experience faith in mystery, the more you feel oneness. That is how you feel guided with the insight to pursue a purposeful life. Faith gave rise to feeling contentment, which is the base emotion for experiencing *bliss*.

So it went very well for humanity. They had clear roles, responsibility and accidents and the calamities were called destiny, which further grew their faith in mystery. Choices were rather limited and the family along with the community was a grounding mechanism to various emotions in which people felt needed, acceptable and secure. Faith offered them the possibility that they were being watched and guided. For thousands of years, this continued very well and the linear gradual evolution was normal and accepted pace of life till the Industrial Revolution took place and disrupted the process.

Part of humanity, which was experiencing faith through fear instead of wisdom felt helpless and controlled. It resulted in feeling a lower degree of control and dissatisfaction, and feeling manipulated. With decreased value, benefits of faith and restlessness among the society grew. That began to give birth to a new kind of conversation and search for a solution outside, instead of above (in God), which led to the Industrial Revolution.

The Industrial Revolution thus started on a premise that religion was obsolete and taking control of life was worth trying. They began to search for a new way of life and felt purposeful in their creation and achievement. Evolution now meant doing more than what you can rather than being more content and compassionate. This gave birth to a sense of inadequacy within which humanity sought out to heal by achieving more. Having broken the trust in 'Faith', they began to experiment with all old beliefs around relationships, community, family and a classic definition of men and women. Insights were replaced by thoughts and thinking was considered to be supreme, hence came the slogan "I think, therefore I am". On the other hand, the custodian of holistic living began to reform their faith and replaced religion with spirituality. It grew on the premise that one can experience *bliss* within self without placing faith in a specific religion or form. Polarization began. Instead of looking above for guidance, one side of humanity looked outward to explore the potential, and another side of humanity turned inward to seek guidance. Regardless of the path, once again, humanity was ailing with a sense of inadequacy and the belief of survival still existed.

Having gone full circle in attaining more than basic survival, the seeker of the world typically driven by the Industrial Revolution, arrived on the same question once asked by the *Mystic*; *"Who am I?"* and *"What is the purpose of my life?"*. They arrived because they broke all the *belief* by breaking institutions, rituals and culture. On the other hand, seeker of the inward journey was also not better off. They could not find a credible solution which could replace religion.

Since then, humanity has been living with a growing void within, while the question still remains the same. This inner void has caused a lower degree of contentment and *bliss* has become elusive. It is driven by a higher degree of inadequacy, which gave rise to ego. Since *bliss* is the natural frequency humanity has sought out to be, it is now being looked for in sex, drugs, alcohol, violence and inadequacy dispelled by hoarding money, power and relationships.

Rise in ego means staying more in our mind and consuming more resources to stay in the mind than letting it be used by the body for nourishment. This has disturbed the balance of spirit, body and mind which has severely affected the well-being of humanity in the last 100 years. Now, again, in distress, disease and disorder, we are asking the same questions; *"Why am I suffering?"*, *"Why me?"*, *"What is the purpose of my life?"*.

After polarization a few decades ago, we are now in the convergence stage, out of desperation trying all possible ways to find an answer to the same question but now the nature of the question has changed. It is now about how to find my well-being. If I have it, I am content and if I am content, I will find *bliss* and then I am guided.

There is a need to have a credible, measurable, quantifiable spiritual process which allows the *Survivor* of today to attain *bliss* within and continue to get the guidance to lead a purposeful life. This actually means integrating a *Mystic* within the *Survivor* through such a process. This would mean that as he breaks each *belief* layer by layer, and unlocks his infinite potential, there shall be a process to make him feel grounded and guided without any external help. Breaking of *belief* has gained momentum and is an irreversible process for the coming generations. Hence, the spiritual process (or spirituality) which can support this momentum of self-discovery is not an option but the compulsion of our time. This book attempts to offer you the same credible, measurable, quantifiable processes to find your *bliss* and guidance within and pursue your aspiration effortlessly feeling guided and protected.

Belief: A Brief Note

Every moment is an experience and each experience creates a feeling. By nature, each of these feelings tend to take us into the state of either wonderment, *bliss*, mystery or pain. But if we bring our mind in between, we create thoughts and combining thoughts with feelings becomes a *belief*. I grew up with a fondness for the rose and my *belief* was that the rose was the only good flower. Later on, I discovered living around the world that whenever I saw any other flower, I would search for a rose and would not appreciate the flower I was seeing. Instead, if I had just experienced roses for their color, smell and beauty and not created a *belief*, it would have made me curious to look for other varieties of flowers and would have led me to wonderment seeing so many colors and smells created by nature.

Belief limits the consciousness and expansion of consciousness is possible by breaking *belief*. The first step to break *belief* is to bring it into awareness, for e.g., when I became aware of my *belief* about roses, I began to experience beauty in all flowers. Hence, the path to integrate the *Mystic* is to become aware of our *belief*.

Nature of *belief* is to search for certainty, and we have accumulated infinite *belief* over various lifetimes coded as the tendencies in our soul. Hence, if I wish to see flowers, my subconscious would ignore all other flowers and would always bring me in touch with a rose. This is how we create patterns as that gives us a feeling of security. In life, this is what we do with relationships and self. We create patterns of failures and misery because that gives us a feeling of certainty and a sense of security.

A *belief* has two components to it: an emotion (Yin) and a thought (Yang). Together they become an electromagnetic field as per quantum physics which states: "Everything is vibrating and nothing is fixed in the universe." So, when we form a *belief*, we begin to limit the variety of frequencies in which we vibrate. For example, consider that you have various options to choose from for your career and you decide on engineering. This choice begins to cut off various frequencies and limits you to think only within a spectrum of frequencies which supports your choice. Years later if you decide to be a painter, this would be hard from the energy point of view as now your various frequencies will begin to open up and make you feel unstable for some time. If you believe that you are born in a Muslim family, you have a set of *belief*, which comes with it but if you believe that you are a human being first who happens to be born in a Muslim family, you will pursue your religion but would remain curious and open to other religions and potentially adopt good things which support your being a human.

Parents pass on *belief* to their children, which ensures that they are safe and can survive. Hence, parenting is done not in a manner where the child is allowed to explore life and be on his or her own path, but to ensure that the child survives, on the best knowledge available to the parents. For instance, if you are an engineer, the safest bet for you is to see that your son also becomes an engineer and that way, you have fulfilled your responsibility toward your child and provided best of the certainty. However, it has to be realized that such type of parenting operates at a bare minimum fulfillment of their responsibility than realizing the true, infinite potential of the child and opens him up for new experiences to form his own frequency range to operate upon.

Belief is for human life like an operating system is for computers and mobiles. *Belief* sits in the subconscious. *Belief* defines the range and type of experiences one shall have. It is similar to how an application designed for Windows will not run on Apple. If your operating system says that "money is the root of all evil or the more you laugh", "the more you will cry" or "all men are the same", you will find your experiences will support this *belief* through life.

IN, ABOVE AND OUT – INSIGHTS INTO M.A.S.T

> *"Everything is determined, the beginning as well as the end, by forces over which we have no control. It is determined for the insect, as well as for the star. Human beings, vegetables, or cosmic dust, we all dance to a mysterious tune, intoned in the distance by an invisible piper."* – Einstein

My father would tell me stories during my childhood. This was his way of passing on his wisdom to me. Here is the story which always inspired me to be holistic in my approach and took away temptation of greed very early on in my life.

There was this man in India who wanted to hoard a lot of land. So he worshiped round-the-clock for several months in the forest to receive a boon from God. God appeared in front of him and granted him a boon that from sunrise to sunset, as much distance he could cover, that much land would be granted to him. The man started at dawn the next morning and walked in a straight line till sunset to acquire as much land as possible. Upon arriving at a place, at sunset, he called out to God to grant him the land he had traveled. God appeared, smiling at his stupidity, told him, "You have the whole line of land you walked on for yourself. You should have created a space to reach back where you started off to have a large area for yourself. Now enjoy this single thread of land which has no value."

What was once a quest driven by curiosity to add more meaning to life is now driven by irrational ambition to accomplish a way to fill the void in our lives. This is the tragedy of the humanity of our age. It is rooted in the *belief* that we are inadequate where we are. The greed, to hoard and own, to hide our void, is what defines us being adequate about our existence. Hence, extreme cases of hoarding wealth, relationships and power, seeking freedom for no cause, treating stability and harmony as status quo or lack of life are common trend of our life. Being disappointed or failing to hoard, again feeling inadequate, we begin to hoard divinity or indulge into spirituality. Like a pendulum, we keep swinging between materialism and spirituality to hoard to fill the void. Our needs have now turned our greed. Failing to hoard, we yet again swing into drugs, sex and multiple relationships again to hide our void.

We are yet to learn to respect ourselves the way we are. We do not feel we are adequate enough and we do not believe we are guided. We are in constant search but clueless about the direction.

Life is always driven by insight, and guidance comes on its own if we have acceptance of our solitude. In such cases, wherever life takes us, it automatically becomes a journey which is fulfilling and purposeful.

At the time in our history, when Newton was working on optics and calculus, he observed in wonderment how an apple falls from a tree. There was nothing in his education to suggest he was qualified to think that way. There was no logic why Kekule saw the formula of Benzene after having a reverie or day dream, after years of studying carbon bonding. There was no justification that all the Vedic scriptures, which unfolded layers of mystery, were revelations during meditation to our Rishis and seers. There is no logic in so many others stars and leaders who were not qualified yet created large discoveries, inventions or caused transformation. All those legendary songs and their tunes are conceived from some mystery which some artists were capable of tapping into. They were all driven by some insight which came to them when they were lost in some mystical state celebrating their existence and being one with their solitude. They stayed with these insights and used their creativity or intellect to nurture themselves. They did not think the way they were trained or were expected to.

All insights live in mystery and one needs to be connected to the mystery to receive them. It is like you need to have an internet connection before being able to surf the net. Insights are like embryos in the womb, nurtured on their own for nine months. Like each embryo has its own unique possibilities, inner wisdom and vision, insights if nurtured long enough, unfold its purpose and wisdom on its own. After the Industrial Revolution, we began to look outwards, discarding the idea of looking above. We did so, on a premise of hopelessness with the *belief* that faith above to drive our inward journey is not a solution for humanity and we can take control of our lives by creating our destiny. All the inventions, new records achieved in sports, arts, humanities and academics were symbols of human capabilities through which we exhibited our own spirit and infinite potential which once religion promised that we could tap into by surrendering to God. Inner peace and sense of contentment were then replaced with ambition and striving for excellence and we began to demonstrate our capabilities of what is possible for humans to achieve. We did this because we felt we were not being loved and we were a lonely planet. Exactly this was the essence of every religion and culture to help people see their own potential within and evolve collectively celebrating the human race with compassion. Our achievements in less than three centuries have been exemplary. We have evolved much faster during this period than the thousands of years prior to this.

Our basic premise for excellence, rooted in hopelessness which made us lonely and insecure was fundamentally flawed. The more we felt disappointed, the more we turned outward to acquire stability and a sense of belonging. In place of that, had we started by summarizing that mystery is something which unfolds on its own as it did for Newton and many others, we would have remained in awe of nature and pursued our insights. We would have attained the same or more excellence but would have created a more compassionate and peaceful world. Due to our insecurity, vision was replaced by greed, compassion by selfishness and holistic view towards life got lost during this process. This resulted into more chaos, despair, violence, distress and competition for excellence instead of cooperation to evolve. We have arrived at a stage now where our basic stability in the form of well-being is in question. We live in a world now where half of the world is fighting for the basic definition of survival and the other half, the better off, is fighting for the well-being and health.

Each time we experienced excellence and disruption; it gave us more choices but left us with a larger inner void. Like any other teenager in India, I worked very hard to get into engineering college and when I got the result, the only solace was that I could now survive. It was an achievement to survive because otherwise, it was rooted in my *belief* that I would not be worth surviving if I did not get into engineering. I looked at the result to seek happiness in it, which I had imposed on myself all along that I would be but I failed to see. I had a far bigger insecurity and instability now thinking about the next steps of my journey in which I felt drawn to without knowing why?

Our search for purpose and contentment within still remained unanswered. We moved up in our lifestyle and choices to the next quantum level but carried this void all along.

Hopelessness, with which we started our journey outward three centuries ago, began to show up as a pattern in front of every generation as a challenge to deal with. The more we hoarded or accomplished, the bigger the inner void grew. We developed all the capabilities and advancements in our mental powers based on emotions of helplessness and feeling being rejected by God when we looked above and did not find our answers to. All along, we suppressed the emotional body and made it taboo for someone to exhibit it. Being emotional meant being foolish and weak. When we sought a solution from above, even then, we felt that we were not adequate and when we got the solution through our capabilities by expanding mental powers, we carried the same sense of inadequacy. So, where has humanity evolved in all these centuries? We seem to be in a maze searching our way out instead of being in a garden enjoying the nature.

In reality, all our achievements in these years were carried out by running an internal process where we received an insight much like Newton. There is no way, we could achieve what we did purely based on mental faculties. Since we were disappointed and lost touch with our own self, we could not see that we are being guided all the time. Once we had insights, we processed them through our inspiration and worked towards manifesting them using our minds. Being obsessed in defining adequacy in ourselves, we wrongly perceived these insights as a thought and ambition and attributed to our own unique capabilities gifted to us. Again, we created this ego to feel adequate by being loved by some God. We have been trying to place our faith in something one way or another and that has not changed as much as inner void.

Once again, we are making the same mistake by placing the same blind faith, now in our logic and capabilities, called science and technology, which we once helplessly placed in God. The brokers of power, who once lived in temples and churches, now live in laboratories of large corporate houses. Instead of meeting our hope in temples and feeling loved, we now visit them in hospitals hoping that they would at least manage our misery quickly if not reverse them. Have we really evolved?

Till now, inner-self, inner wisdom, self-realization of the divine within, holistic view about life and being one with nature remained elusive for humanity and only a select few people continued to carry the torch of it from one generation to another. Typically, there are four types of people who actually understood life. These are *The Mystic, The Artist, The Scientist, and The Technologist.* (read more about them in Part 3, Science of Healing)

They all nurtured an insight, stayed in the *bliss* and were concerned about survival only as long as it supported their quest. Life for them meant pursuing the connection with the inner-self, receiving and nurturing the insight that gave them the *bliss*. They did not have a plan B, and had no backup or respect for life if they failed. Take the example of a *Mystic*. In his company, when we meditate or pray, due to his being in *bliss*, and his aura (electromagnetic field) being big, it automatically lifted our vibratory level. A higher level of vibration leads us to connect with the mystery and as that happens, our lower level frequency such as stress, worry, anxiety or *suffering* like disease begin to fade away. We are raised in our vibratory level and as we connect with the mystery, it leads us to an insight or cleanses our aura. We feel connected with our inner-self which makes us feel adequate. We feel healed and conclude that it is the blessing of the *Mystic*. Once again we make this same mistake by considering ourselves inadequate or capable and placing our faith in the *Mystic*. We began to feel that the *Mystic* was the person who had access to God and his blessings made us feel calm. Desperate to place our faith outside ourself, we begin to devote ourself to the *Mystic*. Of course, that *Mystic* or that temple or church or that mosque did the trick of raising your vibration but the same could have been done by you while working in your kitchen, had you known the same formula that the *Mystic* knew. It is a function of creating an environment which we see in a garden, mountain or with a *Mystic,* which raises the vibration and cleanses the energy field and we feel guided.

Contentment is the seed of *bliss*. It comes with acceptance of life the way it is and this means acceptance of the environment in which we were born. This leads us to accept our parents, our gender and everything connected with our past. You will learn in the next Section how insecurity is the virus that erodes into contentment, resulting in boredom if we do not do anything about removing it. This is where need turns to greed and more greed gives more insecurity leading to a higher state of boredom. Since *bliss* is a natural state every human experience seeks, we begin to seek out by indulging into alternate sources of *bliss* like sex, drugs and hoarding money, material and relationships.

Insecurity is driven by fear and that keeps us stuck with the issues of survival, and this is where the gap between contentment continued to widen while our excellence continued to grow but it produced material abundance only to very few selected people. Vast majority of people living in urban and rural areas are still working for survival except that their acceptance of life and contentment is now replaced by fear and insecurity. As they disturbed their inner balance, they lost their well-being and are now *suffering* with health issues. This is the reason prayers do not work nowadays and worshiping does not bring contentment because we have moved out from the spot within us from where effortless connect with mystery to gain insight and feel guided could take place. We are no more qualified to talk about inner peace. We have downgraded ourselves and the glaring issue is well-being and health. Now, we no more dream of joy and peace but are desperate for restoring well-being and health. If in the process of restoring well-being and health, we gain wisdom, peace and joy, this will be end of our search.

The other set of people, traditionally, who stayed with faith continued to reform their *belief* to keep the hope alive for humanity. Instead of turning outward, they turned inward while others turned outward or above. This gave birth to spirituality which worked on the premise of *I am the universe and the universe is in me*. Unlike religion, which sought out to patronize masses, spirituality began to brew in every culture inventing its own local mechanism and its interpretations of inner journey to restore their well-being. It treated mystery as mystery and did not attempt to decode or seek but to connect and receive guidance. This went very well with people as they were finally going by what they experienced, believing it to be their truth.

Since, it was irrational, but empowering because it gave adequacy, the logical and rational mind began to see it as a threat. Rightly so, because now they were seeking to patronize masses, which once religion did in the name of science and technology and spirituality and feeling of empowerment came as obstacle in their path.

Gradually, in the last few decades, tribes of spirituality grew and come together through technology and the seed of spirituality or quest for the inner journey grew and started to reach every household, largely with women holding the forte of inner quest and men still continuing to seek outward. It made perfect balance of In and Out between Yin and Yang except that it still did not have credible solutions for inner peace and *well-being*.

A new breed of priests in the form of healers mushroomed, armed with various modalities of healing to handle well-being. They had easy access to perform experiments with healing powers. Disappointed by modern medicine and science, people came to them as a last resort. In the beginning, people came for peace and healing from distress but much before these healers could advance to a level where they could have a cure for terminal or fatal diseases, the epidemic grew and they were flooded with inquiry to heal disease and disorder. Those who could mystically heal themselves from fatal cases, turned into healers but more often than not, they failed to translate the same success to others. Hence, their healing or cure became incidental and not a science. They could not teach the same to others but became local anchor in their own community to be a messenger of hope. It was a trial and error. Worked with some people, for some time, for some of the issues giving some relief. This was enough to draw larger audiences to have hope and faith in the inner journey.

At the bottom of it, every form of spirituality still asked for faith in mystery which did feel like religion at the outset, but since it was all experience-based, the argument dropped and people began to leave it by individual choice. This created more space for spirituality and healing to grow, but it still lacked a mechanism. If any, it was an art or gift of a healer who could somehow translate success from one case to another becoming an expert in one type of case.

Regardless, the concept of spirituality continued growing like the content grew on Wikipedia with independent contributors.

The rational mind that feared losing the battle, first laughed it off, then started ridiculing it as irrational, demanding proof. The debate between science and spirituality continued growing in the last few decades regarding health. However, well-being and health began to go down at a much faster pace than the debate. At this point of time, the science is unable to sustain its own failures in providing health care. Instead of fighting it, they are now integrating spirituality and science. Medical practitioners are beginning to join to offer solutions to their customers to retain their own survival. The pharmaceutical industry is the next in line of fire to accept it. In reality, science and spirituality are nothing but the Yin and Yang of nature, and there will be a day when they both will work together by contributing to each other and benefiting humanity. Humanity will not win the day modern medicine or science adopts spirituality, but the day spirituality integrates science. That will be the real empowerment of humanity and will accelerate evolution on the planet at a faster pace to reach out to the world population living below the poverty line. This is where institutions and corporate of next generation find their business model and individual will find their purpose. It will happen in search of compassion and not the earlier model of search for excellence.

Exploring the inner journey was probably not enough a reason for modern human beings to look at spirituality in all seriousness. There is a growing void which has been created between inability of spirituality to offer credible and tangible results and the fall of modern medicine in treating diseases and its epidemic. We are forced to question today, if we are headed in the right direction. Not knowing which way to go i.e., In, out, above, we are now confused and attempt anything which has easy access and whatever is available through whichever means holding a promise of hope, no matter how fragile.

We need a solution which does not ask us to bend our ways because we are very tired now. But we are very curious to try anything which if we practice, can automatically bend our ways to bring us to a state of harmony within. It shall take away our temptation for indulgence on its own as a result of practicing the techniques and reverse our greed. Of course, all these are optional; first it shall offer health and eliminate our *sufferings* and we shall be able to feel ourselves. If something like this works effortlessly, then even the most serious skeptics will not be able to oppose it when they experience a gradual shift in their well-being as they practice. Till then spirituality has a huge task to adopt a science and come out with an effortless, credible and quick solution which can work in all cases with each one of us all the time.

There is a story about Buddha. After renouncing the world when he decided to meditate to find his answers, he apparently took a vow that he would not eat anything till he found answers. He sat in the forest, meditating for days without eating and fell unconscious one day due to the fasting. A lady who was passing by nursed him and fed him juice and herbs. He gained back his consciousness. When he realized he had been fed, he felt cheated because his vows were now broken. This was when this woman explained to him, what will you do with truth if you do not have a healthy body? All the wisdom or search for truth exists in the physical realm and needs to be experienced in this body and before anything, this body is your temple. Respect this first as a visible truth.

We all need the same pretty woman today to tell us that our health is far more important than our search for any purpose or truth. This is where our quest to discover our inner-self has reached, if we do not turn inward, we lose our well-being. This is the biggest truth, bigger than the search for any truth.

In search of solutions for health and well-being through spirituality, various eastern and western techniques came into being - Yoga, Pranayam, Reiki and Pranic healing, Ayurveda, Homeopathy, Chinese medicine, various breathing techniques and mind based techniques such as past life regression. While Ayurveda, Yoga, Pranayama, chinese medicine and Homeopathy and various other ancient systems have a credible history to provide tools for health, others are all new-age experimentations for well-being.

In the absence of a scientific mechanism, which could be comprehended by the mind, each of them began to fail as they were effective only for some people some of the time and in some of the situations. This remained mystical for most of us. As that happened, hard core believers found some relief through healers and Gurus who were *Mystic* enough to open up their emotional body and trigger healing. But this again is not very different from religion where common people are still dependent on some middle men. On the other hand, early adopters of such well-being tools were the ones who traditionally believed in looking above and were searching for a new way to look for what works. Even when healers asked them to turn inward to tap into their own healing powers through their tools, they continued worshiping those healers as Gurus and magicians of their life being elusive about how to turn inward. This placed lot of power in the hands of those otherwise normal human beings with some extraordinary gifts which they could seldom sustain in the face of growing expectation of the people to deliver. These Gurus were also not aware of any science which they could explain to the rational mind convincing enough for them to turn into practitioners of an inner journey. Their language was an old wine in a new bottle when they spoke of universe in place of God, and defining themselves as just a channel to transfer divine light and asking people to have faith. How to have faith? no one knew but everyone said to everyone else. To a rational mind, their language sounded the same as of a priest speaking.

Yoga practice of various postures is a way to release held up emotions in the specific part of the body by regulating the breath in that posture. This is a very subtle, swift and holistic process to bring Emotion-Body and Mind in union by releasing the toxins and making mind thoughtless to arrive at the state of *Yog Nidra (Meditation)*. It is a way to regulate breathing to rejuvenate each cell. The postures are designed in such a way that each type of emotion, held in the that specific organ of the body is released. It was assumed that as you perform Yoga, it shall bring your attention to your body by dropping the mind. As that happens, *Yog Nidra* (meditation) state arrives and this is union of matter and spirit or gross and subtle and that was used as prevention and part of lifestyle. The way this is taught in the West and now in the East as well – power Yoga with rapid dance styles on loud music – is not Yoga but a circus. This is akin to people going for a drink and then hitting the dance floor till the body cannot take any more. They bring such rigourous movement to the body that to sustain this movement, more breath is needed. This forces the attention on body and thoughts are suspected (not dropped). As body gets tired and can not handle anymore, they feel better for some time as thoughts and emotions can not be addressed in that fatigued body state.

The body needs to come back to normal first. This is your wellness program which gives you break from your misery for few hours and then comes back to haunt you again. The best it does is that it attempts to normalize your breathing. The more we numb ourselves emotionally and turn insensitive to it, the more we stay in our minds and lose touch with our bodies. Mechanically shaking the body does not bring you in touch with your emotions and does not rejuvenate your cells.

Internal system works in very subtle ways. A soft touch, a kind gesture or a compassionate view is able to bring us toward *bliss* and our thoughts drop on its own in this state and we feel connected with our core self. It does not need such an indulgence in rigorous acts. It is like your inner system is working at 3 to 15 V and you are directly plugging it into 230 V sockets hoping that at least 15 V will go in. You are using lot of mechanical energy to generate tiny amounts of power. This power, is what we have in abundance inside which we can tap through our breath. We are actually angry with ourselves and desperate due to our ignorance about our infinite power within.

In modern times, in the name of spirituality, no one had a larger consciousness than Osho. He, through his work, had built the operating system of spirituality and each one of us for many generations further would have no option but to operate upon principles laid out by Osho. But he made the same mistake by introducing dynamic meditation and making people imagine they were in the *bliss* when they were not. They danced so long that when the body began to get exhausted, their minds could not support any thought, hence they attained sleep. Some could do some healing but it was a lot of hard work to dance for hours to impose the *bliss* into their lives.

Two drunk men reached their homes in the morning when sun was rising. Since they came out of a dark pub, they found sunlight very disturbing. They decided to shift their house toward the West so that they never had to see the sun again every time they come home from pub in dawn time. The whole day, they kept pushing the house. When the sun set, they started celebrating their achievements of being able to relocate the house to the West. This is how the modern, urban generation is doing wellness program.

Yoga came from India as a tool for well-being, Reiki from Japan as a path for inner peace and past life regression (PLR) from the West. Each of these offered instant results. The work was legendary as a foundation stone for growth in the consciousness of humanity and to bring acceptance to people for their inward journey. Reiki through its founder Mikao Usui alone set the tone that the cosmic energy can be accessed by anybody for healing. Dr Brian

Weiss through PLR broke the artificial barrier created by most of the West to deny the reincarnation principle, and Yoga from India was so ancient and proven over centuries that people did not have any issues in adopting it.

Each of these techniques and many more by now, do have some solution and exceptional success stories but they were still missing links in terms of scalability and quantification of results. Hence, rather than the main course meals, they remained as the side dish so far and did not become the preferred choice of altered lifestyle for *well-being*.

In the meantime, during the last few decades, as well-being and health both deteriorated and existing solutions were not helping, we were now forced to connect with the mystery again albeit through misery. As small as a case of thyroid or migraine or high BP is, it is able to confine our free expression and bring our attention to our lifestyle and seek a deeper meaning in life for our *suffering*. Women, *suffering* from PCOD, infertility, breast cancer are the ones who have discarded their basic essence of femininity and tried aligning more with male energy. In last seven years, in every case of disorder/disease and distress I have met, were good people and kind souls, yet they suffered severely. The distortion in our lifestyle has reached a stage where we have now passed on the seeds of illness and distress to our next generation. This is forcing us to turn inward and arrest our lifestyle because in this *suffering*, we are now finally realizing that the solution does not exist outside ourselves.

So we are back to the same question, though now through misery, which we have been asking since eons of time, but now with the advantage that we have a higher degree of consciousness and ability to take the responsibilities of our life.

In the last three centuries, if anything good has happened, it is the fact that now we know we are not helpless beings and if we want, we can make a difference to ourselves. Our ability to believe that we have choices is by far the best gain. The next step, which humanity is facing and will have to address in the next few decades is what choices to make, how to make those choices and then how to walk those choices. We are untiring fighters in our quest to seek solutions and do not spare any effort in trying the various options available. We do not resign to destiny and in the utmost of hopeless situations, we hope. If not for this, we would have perished long ago as a race.

Pranayama is the process of balancing male and female energy (electromagnetic field) within the body which leaves us in the state of meditation and that alone is the cure for everything. Yoga also does the same; brings us into the state of meditation. Pranayam like

Yoga has been distorted and in addition, our mental faculties have grown so much that the purpose of Pranayam which in essence is to bring our minds to a zero thought state, seldom brings results. Besides, we are so ignorant about its process and its effect that we use it more as an aid than a process to turn inward.

None of these are working on its own unless done under the guidance of a Guru in some health resort. You come back home and do not find enough inspiration to continue what you learned unless forced by some situation. It is not like a mobile phone which we once bought and got hooked on to. Any solution for our well-being, if to be adopted by masses, must be just like mobile phone usage like mobile phone usage when used up, continues to inspire one to top up more, to continues to inspire to do it more and keep bringing benefits into our daily lives on its own effortlessly without having to change anything.

The missing element has been our emotional body. The missing element has been a virtue of faith in all these practices. So people who could practice all these techniques with faith, could restore their Spirit-Body-Mind and could even cure their cancer with Reiki, and paralysis with Pranayama, which rational people called the placebo effect. The placebo effect is the essence of life and is the base at which any cure works.

We have had a huge problem with the emotional body since the Industrial Revolution. We are conditioned not to feel emotions the way they are. We are taught either to suppress them or to convert them into something else to escape them. A *Mystic* would convert all his emotions into pain or *bliss* and that would connect him or her to mystery and the Survivor will deny it and seek *bliss* outside by converting an emotion into a thought and the thought into some action seeking its manifestation. Either way, acceptance is missing.

Emotions are beyond time and space. They have no expiry date. That is why we can always visit our childhood and recall our trauma or happy moments as fresh as if they are happening to us right now. It is all about inter play of the emotions and the mind. The mind is used to regulate or suppress emotions thereby distorting access to being wholesome.

Buddhists discovered this secret by advocating *living* in the *now* by witnessing their existence. *Living* in the *now* is an ability to keep your consciousness at the fusion point of emotional, mental and physical body and not let it interfere with any *belief*. If you are in pain, witness it. If you are angry because you are disappointed by your partner, then witness that anger or your ego. Accept it. It is a simple concept and is easy to practice under guidance but if practiced by us in our daily life, it creates the risk of losing balance with our survival related issues.

This is the reason why Eckhart Tolle's book *"The power of NOW"* became a bestseller and yet none of the people who read it, were able to 'Live in the Now'. Each word written by him is a word of deep wisdom and people understood him well at the mind level but having a poor connection with their emotional body and in the absence of proper techniques given by him, they were unable to experience what the author was trying to convey.

On the other hand, *You Can Heal Your Life* by Louise Hay created a huge success which essentially promised to come across as diagnosis, cause, and cure for various emotional trauma and disease. For the first time, people read what they always suspected or intuitively knew – that emotions are stored in various body organs and they are the cause of *suffering* or ailment. Between Eckhart Tolle and Louise Hay, they spoke great wisdom and found space with the mind and emotional body but still it could not become the path for people to imbibe as a well-being solution. Her visualization techniques to heal specific *suffering* or ailment with corresponding emotions had three major limitations to be successful as a cure apart from missing out on the rationality and science behind it.

1. Visualization requires a stable mind. Often people in distress do not have a stable mind to access their trauma and through the auto suggestion witness it being healed. To be able to heal through this approach, mind must hold itself in that space long enough for trauma to diminish.

2. Visualization is an egocentric approach; hence, any cure through it is just incidental. It does not change a *Belief* but hides the trauma inside and new belief shifts the conscious away from it.

3. Any cure must lead to expansion of consciousness by breaking the *belief,* which caused that trauma or *suffering*. Healing trauma and not becoming aware of the *belief,* which caused it, is like wiping the water from the floor while the leaking tap is still on. Hence, it is a relief for some time but it comes back again.

Sri Aurobindo and Ma, from Pondicherry, knew the science of well-being from quantum physics and energy perspective but spoke in a mystical language and chose philosophy over mechanism. His book "Integral Healing" has the essence of well-being and causes of *suffering* but coded in a language you will find hard to understand. He advocated the inner journey as a way to heal based on his diagnosis but it meant having faith to begin with, which became a roadblock in the absence of mechanism and a guided process which people could follow. In my view, he was a modern quantum health and well-being scientist which people mistook as a spiritual Guru.Probably he wanted to come across that way.

Around the same time as Sri Aurobindo, Carl Jung began to work on the subconscious, and he discovered the root cause of mental disorder. His only point of departure from his teacher Freud was that Jung respected spirit and spirituality as a driving force in the development of the subconscious which Freud took as repressed sexuality. In 2010, when I had helped my first ever patient with schizophrenia and working with a few more cases of a similar disorder, I had developed a theory as to the root cause for mental disorders and more specifically schizophrenia. When I researched and came across the work of Carl Jung, I was ecstatic to learn that he knew the exact cause of schizophrenia one hundred years ago which I had also concluded now. His attempt to interpret dreams and the subconscious was more like counting the drops in the ocean rather than converting it to drinking water. Integration of Carl Jung and Freud, has complete process of cause and science of cure of mental disorder. i.e. integration of sexuality and spirituality.

All of this legendary work to address issues at all deeper layers. Someone solved the issues through the mind, others through emotions or through faith. The role of all these components and its interrelationship with each other affecting the well-being and health at a physical level was missing and this is where the remarkable work of Dr. Deepak Chopra holds the merit. He was the first one to start with physical body, went to the mind and linked them up. He avoided any connotation to faith

Dr. Deepak Chopra with his degree in modern medicine and his research in Ayurveda and spirituality approached the same subject combining spirituality and ancient medicine and attempted to find the link between body and mind. He successfully cured people in the early days using Ayurveda as concluded in his book, *Quantum Healing*. He has clearly shown why modern medicine has a handicap in looking at the symptoms and how mind can bring the healing. His work clearly establishes that there is something called consciousness connected to well-being and health. But he was limited by his own two major strengths i.e., his qualification in medicine and his wisdom about Ayurveda and spirituality. He worked tirelessly to prove to the West, a vital link between the mind and body and attempted to heal by using the mind as a gateway to spirituality to attain the state of meditation. He missed out on the vital interconnecting layer of the spirit and emotions and drifted into consciousness and divine bypassing emotional body and its link to mind and body.

In his book, *Quantum Healing*, he concluded that he is unable to see why patient X got cured and why patient Y did not get cured through the same process. So his work to approach consciousness and spirituality through scientific perspectives is legendary and brought a new paradigm to help people explore their replies outside modern medicine. The missing link between mind and spirituality is spirit, which speaks through emotions generated through experiences forming *belief*.

When I read his book after 2010 trying to formulate the theory for cure, I was excited to read where he says something to this effect, I am sure healing is all about "awareness, attention and intention". I sensed that he had a formula for cure but lacked in making the recipe. You will discover that my entire work is linked on these three parameters one way or other.

All of these legends have brought quantum shifts and have accelerated a movement of spirituality and intent to seek within. Their work in the last hundred years was legendary and history will always revere them for their contributions.

I write about them because I see them as my Gurus through whom I learned everything. Their limitation is not spoken as a limitation but a limitation of time and space in which they operated. I, in no way mean to justify my discovery being superior to them as I seek no justification for my work. I present to you everything I have gained so that you also learn and begin to differentiate. I know someone will someday talk about the limitation of my work and that is good news for all of us to be hopeful about the future generations and evolution. The torch of light shall continue to light higher and higher passing from one hand to another.

The missing link is a mechanism through which layers of hidden wisdom come to us effortlessly, and it will come if all our seven layers are interconnected. The physical body is just a TV screen and it will display what is programmed. The important thing is to have the ability to access those programs and change them by witnessing them which enlarges our consciousness. Consciousness is directly proportional to well-being and health.

I found this missing link in the ability to observe breathing which connects all seven layers of our lives. The formula is simple. observing breathing is inversely proportional to our thoughts. Thoughts are the regulator of emotions, hence breathing is inversely proportional to emotions which we can access as thoughts drop. The universe is dynamic and flowing every moment. If you observe your breath, your thoughts will reduce and reach a stage of zero thoughts. In the process, emotions will surface.This gets you in touch with your *belief* which are not letting you access your spirit. Become aware, continue to breathe and allow the law of nature to take its course by letting those emotions leave your body. You would require three things to do so as Dr. Deepak Chopra said i.e., Intention, Attention and Awareness. The intent to heal, pay attention to breath and become aware of your emotions and *belief*.

Leonard Laskow in his book *Healing With Love* has said that "when your intention is to transfer loving energy, there is no way you can fail... because in subtle realms, intention is action."

MEDICINE AND SPIRITUALITY

> *Health is the function of well-being and well-being is the reflection of authenticity. To be authentic is to be spiritual.*

Any type of *suffering* can be put in one of the three categories – distress, disorder or disease. Distress is the disorder in the emotional body. Disorder is the distress in the mental body. Disease is the distress in the physical body creating a disorder in its functioning. Disorder happens if we cannot contain or resolve distress. If we can contain distress through our mental powers, then distress is hidden in the body till it causes disorder or surfaces as a disease. Take an event, which results in you experiencing anger. You are not willing to accept the situation and try to contain your anger. You would need mental powers to do so. Your body needs to contain the anger with stiffness in your palm and jaw muscles and gradually it gets absorbs into some organ of the body. Imagine having this anger in your subconscious and not being absorbed in the body, it remains there for long durations, and becomes your distorted body language now. Potentially one day it will surface as high blood pressure or gradually manifest into more severe kidney issues, eventually spreading into other parts due to disorder in your internal engineering. If you are able to contain the anger somewhat, then it may show up in your behavior sometimes which will label you as short-tempered or if it is periodic, hampering your normal function, it is called anger disorder.

Among the three types of *suffering*, if we talk about well-being, it needs to be addressed at the root cause level which is to handle distress at an emotional level. It originates through our experiences. This is where suffering originates starting with distress and moving on to become disorder or disease. Each moment in life is an experience. It is our *belief,* which creates distress in any event or if no *belief* creates *bliss* or pain.

Traditionally, or to say, till the Industrial Revolution, our institutions of family, and community, rituals and cultures were built in such a way that if there was any distress in the emotional body through experiences, then first the family, consequently the community would come forward to bring relief from distress by offering compassion, acceptance or vision of hope for the future or providing relief from distress by offering justice to the distressed person. If nothing worked, the concept of destiny was invented to help people accept events of life which caused distress. Rich culture meant development of art forms and creative pursuits through which people sought to express their spirit to release distress without addressing them. This became a way of life and people had faith that they are being supported. Now, such rituals and art forms are called hobbies and considered optional.

Mental disorder was sought to be solved through faith and religious practices and was considered paranormal energy influences of bad or dark. This was further developed as an energy healing mechanism by tribes realizing that some bad energy had gone to the head, hence all the work done, by such a Tantrik, was on the head (third eye and crown chakra) or by cleansing the aura.

Disease in the body was the only area directly considered to be *sin* or a karmic thing and cure meant blessings from God or nature. Every culture developed a natural way of curing themselves from diseases on their own knowledge of local plants and herbs or using energy principles or religious faith. Hence, it was called traditional medicine. The stronger and older the culture, the better were the traditional medicine practices.

Distress, disorder or disease in any case was considered an imbalance in well-being of a person and cure was attempted by regulating rituals, culture, family intervention or local herbs and plants – sometimes combining most of these. Hence, health was considered a function of well-being which if disturbed would cause health issues. With the knowledge of various diseases, cultures evolved to adopt certain rituals and *belief* to ensure prevention rather than going in for treatment. Hence, reform in lifestyle evolving rituals and *belief* as prevention was the most effective way to cure illness of any nature, which also in some way restricted further research on medicine. With time, lifestyle itself was coming under stress to be followed by every new generation and this stress reached its critical mass with the Industrial Revolution.

Hippocrates (460 BC-370 BC) regarded as the father of modern medicine was the first person to advocate that diseases are a natural phenomenon and not the punishment of our sins given to us by God. This was a very liberating truth for humanity who had begun to curse themselves if they were diseased. Hence, the acceptance of disease as natural and search for medicine as professional practice began. As ironical as it sounds, although his name was synonymous with being the father of modern medicine, his teachings were far from what we know as modern, western or allopathic medicine. He was rather more aligned to naturopathy as we call it now. He taught that if you allowed disease to continue, it would reach a point where either the patient would die or the disease would lapse. He influenced the nature of the human body to cure the disease by practicing the diet, hygiene and silence. It is now rather common sense if we say, the only foreign thing going into the body is food, but human internal engineering is the same. Hence, food regulation and variation shall act as prevention and as a catalyst to cure. If not taken properly, it can trigger disease. Hence, when he said allow "food to be your medicine and let medicine be your food" it made sense then and it is true even now.

On observing women's health, "bloodletting" was the most common form of surgery in the West for more than two thousand years till about the 19th century. It was on the fact that women release blood during menstruation. Women's health was potentially considered exemplary in nature till then because every month, they release all their held up emotions at the time of menstruation. The more they suppressed their emotions, they experienced pain during those days and the pain was the instrument for them to ground all their distress from their emotional body. The pain is not normal during menstruation period if well-being is optimal, but they were gifted to release every month rather than it getting accumulated over a period of time. Hence, bloodletting, where blood is taken out of a specific part of the body for a specific disease became the modern medicine till the eighteenth century, when a qualified German MD doctor, Samuel Hahnemann, quit his practice on moral grounds of being instrumental in causing death to patients through bloodletting or making them suffer more. Later on, he invented homeopathy and is regarded, now, as Father of homeopathy.

Post Hippocrates days, treatment began to differentiate between surgery (bloodletting) and medicine which till the discovery of homeopathy in eighteenth century was essentially restoration of well-being. Homeopathy in that sense can be regarded as a medicine system to restore internal balance of the body.

Allopathy (Greek word allo=other or different, pathos=effect) as a term was first used by the father of homeopathy, Samuel Hahnemann in the eighteenth century to define the principle of treatment which had effects, other than the symptoms the disease was displaying. This means that if you have fever and you take some medicine, then it will create symptoms other than the fever (we know it as side effects). In those days, allopathy was regarded as a derogatory word and was not respected.

While Hippocrates demystified that the cause of disease was not a curse of God, and relied on nature to heal or perish, homeopathy became the first experiment to use chemicals other than natural food and herbs to restore well-being. This is where medicine began to depart from spirituality or nature and allopathy came into being with full force without even a promise of the cure. It became very convenient to have any lifestyle and yet eat some medicine and suppress the symptoms. It had a double impact. On one side, allopathy, which was not meant as a cure and till today is not, got perceived by people as a great discovery of humanity which had the potential to make them immortals. On the other side, it made people abuse their lifestyle and inner-self, assuming that they can always take medicine and keep going.

While this was happening in the West, India had developed a most comprehensive holistic well-being and medicine system with the aim for spiritual living known as Ayurveda. It is known to be the most ancient medicine system known to the mankind.

In contrast, Ayurveda did not look at health in isolation but the integral part in pursuing holistic living. Holistic living meant integrating a *Mystic* into a *Survivor* to lead life with faith and in harmony with self and nature. Lifestyle was built around four pillars to have optimal level of well-being:

1. Dharma : Righteous duty
2. Arth : Wealth and abundance (survival)
3. Karma : Desires and aspirations
4. Moksh : Enlightenment

Lifestyle for Ayurveda meant that one should pursue wealth and abundance doing their righteous duty with the desire and aspiration to attain enlightenment.

Desires and aspirations cannot go wrong if one is rooted in the vision of enlightenment, which was served by faith. Faith ensured that desire and aspiration are in accordance with journey and that would ensure righteous duties. When everyone did that, it became harmony and peace. With the fall of faith, it had a trickledown effect, through desires and aspiration getting distorted and duties becoming the aim of acquiring wealth through any means and hoarding became the purpose of living.

The root cause of distress is the fear of dying due to *belief*. If this fear is not there and death is accepted, then no event in your life can be big enough to cause distress. Ayurveda knew the basic nature of humanity, hence they invented holistic food and its recipe using local herbs and plants in such a way that it not only provided relief from hunger or fear of dying but also took away any distress. This gave contentment and was enough to dispel fear. My childhood was full of this wisdom and food was always prepared and also served in such a way that it created this impact of giving contentment to the person eating it.

Hence, cooking at home was always a meditative process with the vision for well-being, it was an elaborate and time consuming process. It had wisdom about each individual's digestive system, weather of the season, individual tendencies. Various recipes, nurturing the ingredients and specific tastes were cooked to address specific issue of well-being to restore Spirit-Body-Mind balance. If something failed here, then home remedies itself were very well-developed medicine systems to heal any distress.

Medicine system in Ayurveda was used as a last resort when everything in well-being failed and was practiced by the *mystics* of those days, who in addition to having knowledge of the root cause of the disease, carried healing powers by virtue of being a *Mystic*.

In other words, Ayurveda had a complete lifestyle solution consisting of holistic living, prevention, diagnostics and treatment as shown in figure 1, and it was all rooted in spirituality. This became a culture which was passed on from one generation to another.

HEALTH AND WELL BEING - AYURVEDA TRADITION

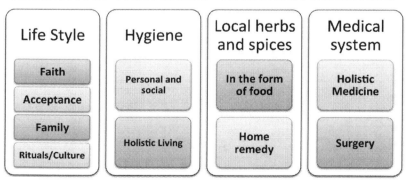

Figure 1

Ayurveda believes that we are made of the same elements as the universe. There are five elements – earth, water, fire, air and space. Permutation and combination of these 5 elements determine our own unique nature (called prakriti), and it is defined at the time of birth itself through the process of nine months. Hence, prakriti (tendency, sanskar), which is in play in our bodies through five elements is regulated through breath and is classified as the three doshas, which are Vata, Pitta, Kapha. It says – when breath mixes with space and air, it is Vata, with Fire and Water, it is Pitta, with Water and Earth, it is Kapha. When we breathe, we breathe Prana (life force energy) and every breath consists of five elements which go into the body when we breathe in. All three doshas exist in each of us but have two out of three doshas active at any time. All three active elements are rare in one person at any given point and are considered to be the rarest of the rarest case. This defines our nature and uniqueness. Hence, deviation from our prakriti (nature) is known as vikruti (symptoms). On our vikruti, Ayurvedic doctors will bring changes to your diet, lifestyle and give some medicine to align your prakriti and that is the treatment provided. It is essentially restoring your well-being. This treatment by the Ayurvedic doctor is never without suggesting changes in your lifestyle, hence Ayurvedic medicine alone was never supposed to work for full recovery. Medicines in some cases were such that they triggered restoration of lifestyle by reversing vikruti into prakriti.

Imbalance in the three doshas is caused by the change in the combination of the five elements, the change in the five elements' combination is caused by the change in our breath. Therefore, change in breath turns prakriti into vikruti. Any intervention or combination of intervention by the Ayurvedic doctor is meant to regulate the breath to reverse vikruti into prakriti.

Through these three pillars, it remained certain that breathing would continue to keep doshas in harmony and well-being will be optimal. Yoga was that tool which restored breathing to keep three doshas in balance. Hence, the entire system of Ayurveda was not just medicine but a way of life, which kept the dynamic nature of five elements, three doshas in harmony, through breathing. It was clear that if you went through extraordinary circumstances like death in the family or the loss of a job or distress in a relationship, if you did not bring acceptance to it, medicine alone would not work. Medicine, food or various techniques were all meant to regulate and restore breathing. This is in line with quantum physics, which says everything is vibrating and nothing is fixed. The combination of five elements is not fixed. Your breathing type is not fixed which changes the combination of the elements. Hence,

Ayurveda as a medicine worked wonders as long as prescribed holistic living was practiced by people. As lifestyles changed and no further advancement was ever done in Ayurveda, its success rates began to fall. It continued advocating lifestyles to be brought back, but that has been under tremendous change since the Industrial Revolution. The last piece of work on Ayurveda was written in the eighth century, and since then, there has been no institutional level innovation to enhance it with changing or evolving the prakriti of humanity. Today, Ayurvedic medicine has reached a stage where vikruti of the patient is much higher as breath is disturbed and medicine does not affect almost all those cases where no changes in the lifestyle for long periods of time were made. Quality of breath, which was supposed to be constant in Ayurvedic treatment, was by now no more a constant.

According to Tantra (science of breathing on which the cure in this book is based), when we breathe, we breathe all five elements. There are eight time zones in a twenty-four hour period. The science of breathing goes in such detail to reflect in which time zone, which element is prominent in our breath. You can experience elements by placing the finger below your nose at "breath out" for its thickness, intensity and the distance it travels, to get an idea on which element is being breathed out. I did this experiment once. One day an old lady (above eighty years old), who was weak and fragile, fell down and was bleeding profusely from her head. She was our neighbor, one floor up. Everyone thought she was not going to survive. I quickly brought my finger below her nose and found out she was breathing very intensely, which was connected to the element earth. To me, that meant that she would survive. And she did.

Breath is dependent on your emotional state and mental state. So the key question, which emerged with changing time and remained unaddressed by Ayurveda or any other stream of medicine or culture is – what is the secret of breathing? What changes our breathing? How do we address the dynamics of breathing so that our doshas are in balance?

According to Ayurveda, our dosha type is defined at the time of birth. Which of the three dosha types will be prominent and which other two types will be the supporting ones, is defined. This means that during the nine months, when the baby is in the womb, the cause of a specific tendency (prakriti) in the child depends on how mothers are breathing. The embryo is breathing the same permutation and combination of five elements as the mother is in that moment. Astrology as a science attempted to understand the same through sheer mathematics, to predict choices to be made by the child based on the same prakriti of the mother and family, to reflect in which kind of choices, it will not turn into vikruti. This would decode why two children of the same mother have different tendencies, different choices, and hence a different destiny. It is based on what tendencies the mother has breathed and passed on to the child in nine months. After passing on those tendencies, after the delivery through the pain, she has healed those tendencies in her and starts to address her other tendencies. During the next pregnancy, she passes on the tendencies she is breathing. Her tendencies are not just her own but are also acquired through the family she comes from and is married into. Her husband has already passed on the tendencies through the sperm. Therefore, a pregnant woman holds infinite possibilities, which she can architect in whichever way she wants. She has a choice to contain certain bad tendencies and not pass it on to the child. This is the reason, in every culture; pregnant woman as pampered and treated like a Goddess, so that she can make loving choices. Any bad tendency found in the child is also pointed at the mother for not doing a good job. This becomes the basis of genetics which in soft code, is prakriti, but if it reflects the symptoms of some disease from the previous generation, it's referred to as a genetically acquired disease.

Three doshas are function of the five elements and these five elements are a function of breathing. Change in breathing converts prakriti into vikruti.

After a stressful day, you come home. You either go for a massage, take a shower, have a drink or your mother gives you your favorite food. When you receive a massage, it attempts to take away hidden emotions from the body and brings your attention to your body, which by default occurs and breaks away your tendency to stay in your mind. This restores your breathing and takes your stress away. You spend some time with a glass of wine and attend to your stress and breathe your space, and it attempts to calm your mind down by releasing stress, which is being attended to with a drink. The shower changes the electromagnetic field of the body and cleanses the aura. Food directly attempts to bring contentment and certainty which takes away the stress and fears. In each of these cases, your breath is regulated and well-being is restored.

This is the reason for our *suffering* and no medicine or healing is effective in all cases. The distortion in our lifestyle and our tendency to stay in our mind has caused serious distortion to our breathing. Various methods such as faith, Yoga, Pranayama, medicine systems, various breathing and healing techniques to relieve us from distress as deployed in earlier times, are not working, due to growth in mental body which does not allow breathing to be restored. Our stress to survive and to excel is so high that we cannot change our lifestyle to restore the breathing. We need a system, which if adopted in our routine without trying to change anything shall be able to restore our prakriti by reversing any form of vikruti. We have no option but to directly address the science of breathing, which was earlier packaged in the healthy lifestyle. We were not aware of how it was working. But before we understand the science of breathing, we need to understand how breathing is affected and how that brings changes in the body which Ayurveda calls vikruti.

In order to do that, we need to depart here from Ayurveda. We now turn to Tantra and chakra system to look for solutions.

If you look at the diagram in figure 2, you can see that every experience creates a *belief* and every *belief* creates an experience. In the process, it generates some emotion and some thought. Breathing is inversely proportional to thoughts and thoughts are a means to regulate/suppress or transmute emotions. Hence, breathing is inversely proportional to emotions.

WELL BEING-BREATH-HEALTH

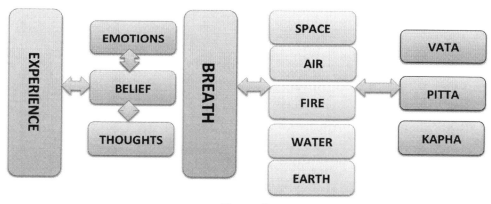

Figure 2

As your breathing changes, it changes the permutation and combination of the five elements which you are taking as lifeforce energy. This changes the prakriti by disturbing the balance of Dosha. In others words, As the combination of five elements change, this regulates the endocrine glands to readjust the hormones which are mixed in the blood with the oxygen you inhale. This is the physics which changes the chemistry of your body. Any treatment you try, if it is not regulating your breath back to normal is not the cure but a relief or disease management. Call it management of *suffering* to be more inclusive in expression.

Do you still believe we shall do research at the cell and chemical level to search for the cure and not invest in correcting the parameters which will restore the formula of physics, which changes the chemicals?

If we need to work on physics then we shall know the following,

1. What is the science of breathing? Is there one?
2. Subconsciousness is full of *belief* from various lifetimes and even in this lifetime, which will continue to affect my breathing. How do I clear the *belief* to keep my breathing optimal?
3. How do I cleanse my mind so that it does not trigger the thoughts which trigger various *belief*?
4. How do I ensure on a daily basis, that I am moving towards health and bliss?

In this book, Section 3 gives you three techniques to answer questions 2, 3 and 4, and your first question is answered by *Swarn Yog* in the next chapter.

SWARN YOG

Everything is vibrating in the universe. Nothing is fixed, nor is death and destiny.

Breathing is the link between the life and the mystery. It is an autonomous process, which means it happens on its own and does not require intervention from us. There is no way, you can stop this process. Put this book aside and hold your breath with the intent that you will not breathe and keep on holding your breath. You shall discover that you have no power to do it. The system will live through you. You will have to take a breath and no willpower will work.

Breath is like a broadband connection. Once your computer is connected to the broadband, you can go on the web and surf whatever you wish to. You can explore, learn, move from one topic to another on your curiosity. We only need to know our question and all the answers exist on the web. The same way, all answers exist in nature, and we only need to get our question right. So when we struggle with our lives seeking answers and do not get them, we tend to blame and curse ourselves or our lives or destiny or God. You should check three things before looking for answers,

A) Is your broadband connection On: Only in the state of meditation, which you attain by quieting the mind through breathing, is when you are connected with nature.

B) Do you know your question: I can assure you with my experience as a coach that you do not know the right question. It will take me quite a place to explain this and it is not possible in this space. First work on getting your question right. We only need to find the right question and once we find that, we will be get an answer on its own. For example, you will ask the question, "Why did he cheat on me or dump?", me instead of asking, "Why was this experience of being cheated important to me?". You would rather ask for a bungalow, than ask for a life full of purpose, which will automatically support that you live in a bungalow. You'd rather pray to get admission in a good university, than pray to be guided to pursue the purpose of your life.

C) And willing to accept an answer? Often, we are fixed in our mind and want a specific answer. If so, you either need a genie or a funny man, who wears red underwear over blue trousers, but certainly not God.

If you have all three points taken care of and still haven't received your answer, then the only thing you need to work on is to keep refining the question because answers are instant.

This is why *mystics* practice breathing, to stay in meditation with just one question, "Who am I?" or just to be in *bliss* without any question and that reveals all the truth it must. When in meditation, your consciousness enlarges, bringing light into subconscious. Your subconscious as it comes to light, pops the question and fires your quest. So, it is not important that you must go into meditation with a question.

There is a branch of Tantra (*Kriya Yoga*), which has the complete work on the science of breathing and is called *Swarn Yog*, and it is written in the scriptures, Shiva Swarodaya and Gyan Swarodaya, which, incidentally I have not read in whole. I have read a few books, only a tiny part of it, and on that basis, if I can write such a comprehensive book and help people reverse their *suffering* of any nature, you can fathom the wisdom written in those scriptures thousands of years back. My entire work is on the principle of *Swarn Yog*. Most of the books I have read about *Swarn Yog* had made the mistake of misinterpreting the science. They all wrote in way to lure people to adopt the science by giving them quick solutions. For example, they wrote that males should breathe through the right when signing a contract. This is enough for you to get hooked on to it and then feel frustrated that it does not work because it does not work that way. This is given as a check list and not as medicine to sign a contract.

I write this chapter, in reverence to all the mystics, seekers and practitioners of this wisdom since eons of time. I seek their forgiveness, should I make any mistake. I feel fortunate that the universe has gifted me this wisdom, which is the base principle of the cure, and I have the honor to share with you all in such a way that you can make the most of it for your well-being.

Hence, for all those readers, who will read today or many years afterwards, there is a huge scope to go deeper in this subject of breath. I have taken out only the science of *Swarn Yog* and built the science of Cure. Once you get comfortable with first technique (NV SWIMMING), there is so much you can do by playing with it. You can tap infinite wisdom hidden in your cells just by bringing your attention on breathing and feeling the flow of breath in your body. These are advanced stages of breathing, even as fatal as cancer sounds to us, is cured by this simple first technique and then the remaining two techniques make you heal the root cause. Do you see the power of breathing?

Science of breathing

I grew up hearing elders talk about how death can happen any time to anyone. I also heard them agree with one another when one of them said, without his will (often looking up to the God), we cannot even take an extra breath. I found this very mystical and contradictory at the same time.

As per *Swarn Yog*, human life is designed for 946,080,000 breaths. Rate of breath for well-being is 15 breaths/minute, and that makes the human lifespan equal to one hundred and twenty years. Of course, it is with terms and conditions, much like a car manufacturer gives out a car with average rate for fuel consumption under test environment, which are different from actual on-road average.

This is the reason we die at different ages depending upon how fast or slow we consume our breath. One breath means one breath in and out. I found it very fascinating to learn that every species has a specific breath rate and corresponding life span (figure 3). So God does not play the dice and there is actually a design and our life is the finest example of engineering. Our breath rate is designed for healthy and optimal living. This also means that we need to have a lifestyle, which supports such a rate of breathing. Yet there is a free-will given to human beings, more than to any other species to alter the breath rate and choose their lifespan. This clearly means, God is not deciding your age or destiny but you are making the choices, which alter your breath rate and then you arrive at a spot, where you cannot sustain life, and hence choose to die. If the birthing process starts becoming visible nine months in advance, there has to be the same or similar process for death. If so, there is a choice available not to choose to die. Our consciousness is limited, and hence we do not see, until very late that death is coming, but there have been people with a large consciousness, who are not necessarily *mystics*, but often found in our own families, who could predict death much in advance for themselves or for their loved ones. In my view, over the centuries, this science has been misused more than used for the purpose it was developed. For this science to become a cure for you, you need to follow the process and not get mechanical about attaining a specific breath rate. Many people in the workshop start to count their breath rate while deepening the breath. No such act will help you because now your mind is involved, and it will not allow emotions to surface, which are the reason behind *suffering*. So read this chapter carefully. Use this data for diagnostics. The cure is in the processes that are laid down in Section 3.Trees, birds, animals, aqua life do not have the five elements. Hence, they have different breath rates and different lifespans.

Breath rate and Life span

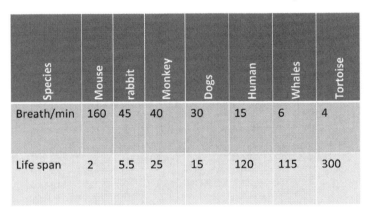

Species	Mouse	rabbit	Monkey	Dogs	Human	Whales	Tortoise
Breath/min	160	45	40	30	15	6	4
Life span	2	5.5	25	15	120	115	300

Average breath rate and average life span shown for the purpose of demonstrating relationship or breath rate with life span. Number of breath per minute is as per Swan Yog

Figure 3

The chart in figure 3, will tell you that if you breathe slowly, you will live longer. A tortoise takes 4 breaths per minute and lives longer than human beings and a rat breaths around 160 breath per minute and has very short lifespan. The whale takes fewer breaths per minute than humans, yet have a shorter lifespan than humans. This is an exception and shall be a subject of research, how aqua life though breathing slower than human beings live shorter lives. They do not have the five elements, with an exception of the tortoises who have earth, which aqua life does not have otherwise.

Coming back to human beings, here is the chart for people in various situations:

SWARN YOG: SCIENCE OF BREATHING

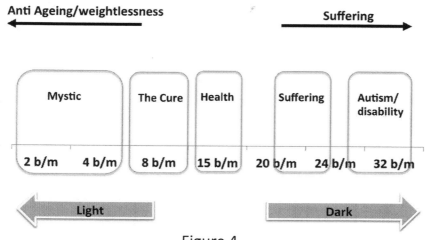

Figure 4

Normal, healthy, corporate, people with a fair degree of stress are at around 18 breaths per minute, people with lifestyle illness and depression are at around 20 breaths per minute, chronic illness and mental disorders are between 22 to 24 breaths per minute, autism and disability are at 26 or above breaths per minute. (Figure 4)

In general, as your breathing rate goes above 15 breaths per minute, emotional level of distress begins to set in and then further up, it turns into behavioral changes causing some type of mental disorder. Above 20 breaths per minute, this emotional distress has either become a mental disorder in case the ego is low. If the ego is high, then it has already set in as disease of one kind or the other. That is why, emotional outbursts, attention seeking drama, and frequent crying sessions, help you release distress and act as a barrier from getting into a mental disorder or disease but is a warning that you are unstable and suffering may stabilize sooner.

Rapid breathing (more than 15 breaths per minute) stimulates the mind or the stimulated mind causes rapid breathing and consumes more energy in the mind leaving lesser oxygen in the body for nourishment.

8 breaths per minute is the cure. This is the state of *Yog Nidra* (state of meditation). If you reach this stage daily for a few minutes (and you will learn to do that with NV Swimming technique), then gradually, you begin to reverse any disease, disorder, and distress. As you practice it, gradually, it begins to stabilize your normal breathing around 15 breaths per minute during your routine and that keeps you stable at that quantum level and arrests

any relapse. This is an automatic process. Hence, meditation is *The Cure*. All you need to do is-attain this state daily for few minutes. Additionally if you make the observation of your breath a habit while doing whatever you are doing, you can expedite your recovery.

At 4 breaths per minute, a *Mystic* attains siddhi (special powers.) This is the state in which if you fire any intent, it will always manifest. However, 8 breaths per minute itself is the *bliss* and in that state, normal humans like you and I have no desire or ambition to seek, so you will find that you are not able to have an intent at 8 breaths per minute or below. That is why those who wanted to attain extra powers go to a forest and practice meditation (tapasya) to get a boon from God. A boon from God is nothing but 4 or less breaths per minute practice. We have heard stories of people worshiping God and God appearing to grant them some boon. This is the state in which they witness the appearance of God. That is not because God appears but because they have devotion of that God. At such a low breath rate mass begins to transform into energy and then into light, and virtual manifestation of the intent happens by manifesting an image of the God. It is a virtual appearance of your *belief* system to manifest any reality. So, I often say to my participants that if you go to forest, practice NV Swimming and reach that 4 breaths stage, whether you worship Rajnikant (popular superstar of India) or anyone else, you will be gifted with a boon and their face will appear in front of you. It is about your *belief,* which can make anyone a God but the process of manifestation of that God is 4 breaths per minute or below.

At 2 breaths per minute, you do not need food. You are fed directly by light by hyper activating your pineal gland. That is where you see so many seekers demonstrating how they are able to live without food for so many days.

Figure 4 tells you that slow breathing gets you to health, slimming, anti-aging, *bliss* and how rapid breathing is in distress, disease and *suffering*. This is the reason, weight loss programs do not work and everyone who has practiced the techniques is losing weight by default along with experiencing anti-aging effects. Your breath needs to reach an area, which is typically the lower abdomen where it starts to accumulate weight. This is the area of emotions (gut), and if you are hiding your loneliness, weight gain is generally the outcome. There is more to the science of weight loss, which in this book, is hard to cover but the techniques explained, in any case, handle it.

So, how do you get back to slow breathing to discover the cure? Why is this book in so many pages if it is just about slowing down the breathing rate? After all, the same story could be told to you with the technique in three pages.

Though I have given you the path to the cure, which is as simple as observing your breath, the complex part is that your breathing is dependent on your thoughts and emotions. Hence, it is dynamic in nature as emotions are flowing in you all the time and that is due to a *belief* system, which is due to karma. That means no matter what you do, breathing will be disturbed as you will go through various experiences which will trigger various *belief* and then corresponding emotions and thoughts.

So when you begin to observe your breathing, your thoughts will begin to disappear and will leave you with the emotions and your *belief*. Further down, your subconscious begins to open up, which has patterns and tendencies affecting your breath without you being aware. So, you can attain 15 breaths per minute, but due to the tendencies in your subconscious, you will tend to disturb this breathing as some an emotion hidden inside will affect your stable state. You can fathom now that the whole process of cleansing starts with observing the breath but good news is that without going to such deep levels within 3 to 6 weeks, people have been able to reverse any *suffering* and restored health. Once stable, by and large, your curiosity is the only limitation. You have now the tool to decode the mysteries and forces hidden in your subconscious and heal their influence on creating *suffering* for you.

In summary, as you begin to practice the techniques, a lot of stuff will surface. Next sections is an attempt to make you aware of all those components which will help you remain aware when your transformation towards the cure begins.

Breathing is inversely proportional to thoughts. Thoughts are generated to regulate emotions. Emotions are created based on experience. Experience is manifested due to *belief*. *Belief* is created based on the environment we are born in. Environment is chosen by choosing parents and parents are chosen based on the karmic journey to release the dark energy from our karma and come into light. (Figure 5)

This is the reason breathing is dynamic and is never stable. A *Mystic* spends a lifetime observing his breath in caves, mountains or forests and yet does not attain enlightenment. Since eons of time, we have accumulated karma and our breath is held by our subconscious, unconscious tendencies and patterns. But wait before you leave the chapter to jump to the cure in section three of the book. Essence of all the techniques and this entire book is here and some of you can really use it and may not need further knowledge. When you observe your breathing, your thoughts start to drop. When those thoughts start to drop, you begin to get in touch with your emotional body, which your mind was regulating or suppressing.

Observe your breath for some more time and feel that emotion fully, and you will find that all emotions and thoughts have disappeared. You do that daily, and you will find so many of your memories surfacing from the past. Keep feeling them while observing your breath, and you will be surprised how without any techniques, you are getting aligned to the purpose of your life and your *sufferings* are disappearing on their own. This exactly happened with me when I knew nothing but was observing breath round the clock sitting at home, seven years ago.

Factors effecting Breath

Figure 5

Complexity of breathing lies in balancing its electromagnetic field. In a different culture and time, electromagnetic field actually means yin and yang, left and right brain, male and female energy in the body, respectively. This is regulated through the two nostrils we use while breathing.

In a healthy human being, breathing alters every forty-five minutes. This means that we breathe through one nostril for forty-five minutes and then switch to the other nostril on its own for the next forty-five minutes. Do not get stuck with the forty-five minutes. Some books talk about ninety minutes, so get the concept right. We breathe through one nostril at a time, and then through the other one for the same time, and that is how we remain in a healthy state. The science of breathing is so advanced that in ancient India, your grandparents will ask you (*kaun sa sur laga hai?*), meaning which nostril are you breathing through before you go to write an exam or go to sign a deal. Through this, they will know if you will be successful or not. For example, if you are going for a Maths exam, you shall be breathing through your right nostril, so that your logical mind is active, and if you go for an art examination, your left nostril will be active. It even goes to the extent of discovering your health status by checking which nostril you will be breathing through when you wake up. It further states a difference even for males and females. But if you go into a deep level of mathematics, you will develop OCD or will lose the essence of this science, and you will either become fearful or superstitious. The essence is slow breathing and through the technique given, you reach *Yog Nidra* (Meditation) state and the rest will be taken care of by the nature, as it restores your well-being. You shall not get stuck with monitoring the count of breathing to fifteen breaths per minute. This will change during the day, many times in any case. But as often as you can, if you observe your breath, it will slow down your breathing rate in any case. You job is to arrive at Yog Nidra as given in the process and to experience well-being. This means you have reached the required level of breaths per minute.

There are only three stages when we breathe in and out from both nostrils. One in extreme mental disorder case and second in deep meditation state (when *ida*, *pingala* and *sushumna nadi* all open up at the same time) or before dying. No one dies breathing through one nostril.

Largely on this principle, while I handled all ICU cases, I used to first ask the family members to check if the patient was breathing through both nostrils. If not, we could work on reviving him. Many non-ICU cases, in extreme distress have demonstrated breathing through both nostrils – one being prominent, and another one, a little less. That does not mean the patient will die. It means the distress level is high and no medicine will work effectively to revive the patient. Hence, the first job for a very quick recovery is to close one nostril with cotton and the patient gets relief within a very short time and whatever medicines he is taking, become effective.

In case of a stroke, this alone is able to revive the patient and substantially reduce the damage within minutes. In the moment of stroke, one nostril will get defunct in the initial hours. If as a caregiver, you can gradually start blocking the functional nostril, patient has potential to revive much before he reaches the hospital. However, it must be done very carefully. Block the functional nostril for two seconds and release and then keep doing it for very short intervals. It has the potential to dissolve a clot. I have often directed people to carry it out in a few ICU cases. Doctors have been surprised with the speed of recovery in such cases.

The electromagnetic field is dynamic in nature. We breathe differently in a different emotional state, hence disturbing our electromagnetic state. If an emotional state stays for a while in our body, thus stabilizing faulty breathing, we generate disharmony and instability through various negative emotions and thoughts. Since emotions alter our breathing, altered breathing alters our emotions to seek stability as per the law of nature. Let us understand it a bit more. You have the feelings of lonely and unworthy. This stays in you for a long period. In order to hold these emotions, your body would seek to change something to keep these emotions contained. The purpose now is that you feel stable with this *belief* inside. You cannot feel stable if the world around you does not resonate with your *belief*. This will be very hard. To be stable, you will begin to withdraw from happy people and situations and begin to attract people who resonate with you. They will share the same emotions and that will make you feel more stable. It now makes sense to you because the world around you is exactly the same as you are inside. You can do reverse engineering now. Make a list of three sets of people. Most intimate, close ones and acquaintances and see what emotions you experience through them. You will know that these are your own *belief* and emotions, which you manifest through them.

Our emotions are functions of our life events. Furthermore, they are functions of our *belief*. This, for example, explains why two brothers can have different emotions during the same events, hence different breathing patterns are experienced leading to different *belief*, further leading into different destinies through their own unique choices. But balancing the electromagnetic field is not as difficult as it sounds. As said above, we do not need to go into karma and reincarnation and identifying emotions and *belief*. This happens on its own. You only need to observe your breath and arrive at *Yog Nidra*. You do not need to count the breath rate. It happens on its own as you slow down the breathe using the technique NV Swimming. When you arrive at *Yog Nidra*, that is 8 breaths per minute, and if you start to count, then you will never arrive at *Yog Nidra* because your mind is active. The whole game is to gradually shut the thoughts, which happens on its own when you observe breath. So once again, you do not need to shut the thoughts. When you observe the breath, it happens on its own.

In seven years, we were able to help everyone attain balance of electromagnetic field. Almost everyone gets hooked to the breathing after the workshop. When I say, almost everyone, please spare those special human beings with much higher intelligence, who strongly believe that they have a problem far more complex, for a simple breathing to solve. Some even came carrying their Guru in the pocket, fully miserable through their life but their faith in their Guru is ever growing, hence wanted to see if they can make me their disciple. Barring such genius, everyone else got it.

It is all about observing your breath and this has cured everyone including cases of cancer, just by doing it. It, sure, is an effort if you are having chronic disease to restore your breathing. Same is the case with people with mental stress or disorder because they cannot observe their breath no matter how hard they try. For them and actually, for everyone, I have listed down the process in the treatment section through which you can start to get better at the ability to observe your breath or do treatment on your loved ones at home. The good news is that now, you actually have a possibility to cure yourself sitting at home. This will take away any anxiety or nervousness, and will direct your attention to start allocating your energies working toward the cure.

Based on observing your breath, I have developed three techniques. While the first technique (NV Swimming) is the cure in itself. You will realize as you practice, its effectiveness from the first time itself. For example, many cases of depression, PCOD and several other situations of *suffering*, I have only taught them the first technique to bring them into a stable state. In addition, I have used the treatment processes (Section 3, treatment) so that they can effortlessly reverse their symptoms. Many of them do not need more than that.

But as you can see, as you begin to observe your breath, your mind begins to drop, and emotions open up. You need another technique to strengthen up the divide between conscious and subconsciousness. For example, you regret that you reacted. That is because of the influence of the emotions on your mind. Through the second technique (NV FISHING) you will be able to turn non–reactive, and you will operate from deep wisdom as you go to deeper layers of your mind. It purifies your mind. Your traumas from this life and tendency to attract such a trauma and form a pattern is hidden in your subconscious, this is where you would need NV HUNTING, which purifies your spirit from the imprints of trauma and allows deeper wisdom to flow.

With these three techniques, call it courseware, each passing day, you will reduce your chances of attracting misery again in your life. It will take you to next quantum level where tendencies to attract low vibratory events do not exist.

By curing yourself, you do not cure a cancer or disorder but start to vibrate at a quantum level where such low frequencies like cancer cannot reach. Through complete courseware, you will have that barrier getting so strong, that in the future, you will not be able to slip back to that level again. But of course, you can. So neither your *suffering* nor your cure is permanent. The Cure is now in your hands and you are empowered to make your choices. Choose the *bliss* or choose misery. It is now your choice.

I have dedicated Section three only to the practical aspects of cure. It is written to replicate the same environment and processes, which I have followed at treatment on any of the individuals. No matter, how bad your situation is, if you can just start with this treatment process, it alone will start to arrest the speed at which symptoms are worsening in you. Of course, if you are healthy and reading the book for your loved one who is too sick or in distress to be able to read and follow, you are in the best situation to start to help your loved one recover. You can directly go to the Section 3 and start the process now if your need is very dire. Skip the next Section on which you can always come back once you have experienced relief. This is the reason, I said before, I do not need your faith, trust, conviction and *belief* in this process. The process is powerful enough to change your experience and any experience which makes you feel better will automatically instill your faith in it.

SECTION 2
SEVEN LAYERS OF HUMAN BODY

PARENTS

> **No understanding of evolution is adequate that does not have at its core that we are on a journey toward authentic power and that authentic empowerment is the goal of our evolutionary process and purpose of our being.**
>
> **Gary Zukav - *Seat of the Soul.***

I am writing this chapter using the reincarnation principle. It is not essential that you subscribe to the idea of reincarnation if it conflicts with your *belief*. As far as the cure is concerned, you do not need to believe in reincarnation, though it is recommended that you take an academic interest, with curiosity, to learn what is being shared here based on my realizations and learnings so far.

I hereby assume that you as a human being have always been reborn as a human being and there is no other incarnation possible. But if your *belief* tells you that you have been something else before, please feel free to integrate this chapter with your *belief*.

If Bill Gates was a dropout in India, he would have been running a traditional family business like a drop out in India and Steve Jobs could not have created Apple, which he eventually did. The Nirbhaya rape case in Delhi could not have got the global attention if it was to happen in some other country or any other city of India. Millions of people who die an unfortunate death in road accidents happen in split seconds and in that split second, a million more escape that. If one of the parameters about the birth of each one of the above examples is changed, they would not have done what they did.

A soul is born to fulfill the purpose of its life but that is the third step in the three-step selection criterion. The first one is to choose the time and space of evolution for humanity where there is a need to participate. The second is to select the region and the third is the selection of parents.

For Gates and Jobs, they were meant to participate in the digital revolution and Nirbhaya in spreading the awareness of women's safety in India. If a soul wants to participate in bringing awareness about road safety or air pollution, by sacrificing their life, then he or she would be reborn in a region where this issue is most glaring and will choose parents who will allow/ facilitate the soul to experience the same.

Therefore, we are at the right place, doing the right things and have a purpose, which is very much in harmony with the plan of the universe. If not, then nature will intervene to seek to restore itself.

This is not about Bill Gates or Steve Jobs or Nirbhaya. This is about each one of us who are born. We are all born for a specific reason. We choose our environment by choosing parents to participate in the evolution of the universe. For example, your purpose in this life could be to experience feeling financial security and raising a family. You could be born to a family where such values are respected or you could be raised in a family where you learn the hard way by seeing the family being broken and you grow up and marry a person with a financially secure government job and can nurture the children and the whole family. This is very much enough to be the purpose to celebrate the dance of life. It is not necessary, in fact, it is not the case that everyone has to do something very significant and large for humanity and only then will they feel fulfilled in their purpose.

As a soul, since billions of years, ever since we have had life on this planet, we have been born in numerous families. Numerous people from different cultures, values and *belief* have been our parents. We have acquired our own *belief* in so many lifetimes. None of this information is lost. It is all stored in your microchip just like Uber gives you details of all your rides or your browser has history of every transaction you have made. The more powerful soul is the one which has the experience of the dark and the light in several lifetimes, like a versatile actor who has played all kinds of good and bad roles, not just by being a hero or a villain. Being born is actually a very aware and conscious process, which you choose in accordance with the highest wisdom (This is equal to saying, "God sent me for this task and chose parents for me").

All this information based on our experiences become dark or light or infinite combinations of the same, which is acquired by having gone through so many wombs in which such quantum states of frequencies of our experiences are stored in the spirit as our *belief*.

For example, at the soul level, you wish to experience the importance of love in life and its significance. Let us say, it requires ten lifetimes to learn this lesson. You will then choose parents where the mothers pass on those frequencies during the nine months, which either enhances your resolve to look for love or creates so much hate that you look for love. Your father may create situations in such a way that either through will or through choice, you begin to seek love. This is how your specific frequencies are either kept dormant or active, which in the nine months of pregnancy begin to create your blueprint. It depends on what your driver is. Wisdom or fear? If you are learning through fear, then in some lifetime, you will have to learn the same lesson through wisdom and this exactly is the purpose behind faith, worshiping, seeking blessings from our elders and now through meditation, to expedite your process of learning through wisdom. Faith heals our soul from the cloud of dark karma and moves us towards the light.

The most remarkable thing about the journey of human life is that there is no way the universe will judge you or guide you to remain focused on your path if you do not wish to. It seems your free will is far bigger than anything else in life. You choose to deviate from your plan where you were either supposed to take the pain of rejection and reform as a painter, writer or singer or just live an anonymous life through pain or choose to become a Hitler and take revenge by attempting to force the world to accept you. This is a choice of free will. Free will if exercised out of fear would require power of dark karma to be able to manifest. If free will is exercised through wisdom, then it has to be backed by a lot of good karma of the past several lives to enable manifestation.

Coming back to your need to experience love. You have made experiences about love in a few lifetimes and you know what love is. You now need to learn a lesson of trust in love because there is a tendency in you to get fearful in love due to previous experiences. You choose parents where your mother brings you up with love, and your father trusts you and this reduces your negative tendency but of course you are not aware of it. Since you grew up in a loving environment, you feel loved. You grow up and meet someone and love and trust is flowing now. Loving environment is now created and you feel loved and respected. Now it is time for the subconscious to clear up dark tendencies and *sanskars* (patterns) your dark karma of fear of losing love coming in. You either try to control your partner or get addicted to love ignoring your tendencies of fear of losing love. You suffocate the life of your partner, who now wants to leave to exercise the free will. Your partner could be on a journey to experience free will rather than being desperate to feel your love. In this process, by leaving you alone, your partner offers to be your teacher to teach you the meaning of real love and trust in love. You realize what love is and expand your consciousness in this lifetime. Having realized and being aware, in your next life, you want to experience how to trust in love. You now choose a very wise woman as your mother, who during the nine months passes on lot of wisdom and vision for your future. Your mother is probably a woman who has gone through a lot and is on a journey to see a better future for her children and chooses to be a mother with a vision that her child shall not make the same mistake as she had made in the past. You are being healed in the womb itself from all your fears and when you grow up, all adversities on one side but your faith in love is so high that you become a light for everyone around. You learn love and trust in this life now by giving the same and seeing how it all comes back to you.

But it is equally possible that you choose a woman in distress who has been rejected in love as your mother and she passes on her sufferings and pain to you making you to feel more insecure about love and trust. This is why parents are like a regulator who fine tune your frequencies in such a way that you have the least amount of struggle in arriving at your purpose. By you holding any grudges against them actually cuts you off from their energy field in which they hold the space for you even after they die to see that you have evolved and arrived at your purpose on your own or through your next generations.

Indians decided to have arranged marriages and make it a lifelong event to provide a sense of security to the couple towards each other. This gives them enough time to help each other evolve without any insecurity. Marriage then and even now, is never about love but about evolving through a loving and safe environment.

Choosing the purpose of life, is like a maze with many possible exit points. A series of choices made after being born lead you to closed doors or an open exit. Among many such possibilities, one of them is the most optimal destiny. Let us say, you decide to rise in your career to become Prime Minister of the country. You saw that you have high possibilities to become one before being reborn and you chose this path. It is possible that in this birth, you actually die one step before being a prime minister. You were aware before being born that there is an algorithm of choices, which will lead you to become a Prime Minister, and you knew the chances are less than 1%. You still chose it because the journey of your soul gives you the courage to take more risks and evolve faster for some ultimate mission for which experience of the journey of a Prime Minister in this lifetime is very crucial.

Hence, each choice has the power to take us closer to our purpose of life or deviate us from it. The universe does not intervene except in giving you insight, but if you are not connected with your inner-self, you will fail to hear it. The journey to fulfill your purpose of life, is a journey toward authenticity. Spirituality is nothing but being authentic, or else it is just another ambition like people have for materials gains.

Before being conceived in a mother's womb, we existed in the form of light. Across all cultures and religions, this form of light is called the soul. While all of us could debate and argue about the existence of the soul, we cannot deny that there is some mystical power through which the process of giving birth takes place, and the sexual act is just a process to facilitate the conversion of that light (called the soul) into a physical mass in the nine month period in the womb.

Coming back to the design of choosing parents we choose the best parents among the most probable who are ready to start a family. You will think, how would it make a difference if a soul decided to be born on the twenty-third of a month or on the twenty-fifth of a month, but then it changes the zodiac, thus the star position and astrology changes, which means that the electromagnetic field of the universe, which is most conducive to support your journey may change, and this can have an impact on the probability of you making the right algorithm of choices.

Take a family of three children – a simple, middle-class family with a stable income. The goal is to raise kids with a good education, build a home and live respectfully in the community of this small town. The father is committed but something goes wrong, as the wife begins to suspect him of having an affair. It is a breach of trust. She develops the curiosity to know the truth. This leads her towards experiencing Obsessive Compulsive Disorder (OCD). Fights and arguments become a routine in an otherwise loving and God-fearing family of five. All three kids begin to witness the change and go through misery as parents argue and fight.

The elder son of the family, watching this drama resolves to remain very loyal to his wife and creates a value system based on the *belief* that he will not let his children suffer. He cultivates a habit of commitment to build relationships of trust and resolves issues in a private, loving manner.

The second child, a girl, begins to see the misery of the mother and starts judging the father. She learns to sympathize with the mother and concludes that men cannot be trusted. As she grows up, she learns to be very cautious in love and to be on her own rather than being dependent on men. She excels in her education, qualifies to be financially stable and has a life of her own. However, she feels cheated in all her relationships because of her *belief* about men. The third child, a boy, feels very unsafe and unprotected. He grows up feeling vulnerable, starts to withdraw from people and remains lost in his world. A series of events where he is mocked by colleagues and ditched by girlfriend takes place, and he lands up with depression and OCD.

At a soul level, all three kids chose the right environment and parents who offered them the right opportunity to learn the lesson of trust.

The eldest child learned and reformed himself to become a successful negotiator and a loving family man. The girl learned a partial lesson to be independent but judged her father, hence, she could not trust men in her life. The third child, who was actually born to go deep into this subject, was born to feel the pain of loss of trust and reform as a painter or writer but lost out to be so by choosing depression and OCD of the mother which is nothing but a lesson of trust which he could not learn like his mother. This tendency still remains in the DNA of the family, including their siblings, and continues to be passed on from one generation to the next.

All possible choices were existent for all three kids. Their mother triggered a journey to dive deeper into the aspect of a relationship. This curiosity she had was supposed to trigger the youngest child to pursue art. Her lack of trust should have been a lesson for the girl to learn to trust. All of these possibilities for each of these souls were known before being born.

These choices are being breathed by your mother during the nine months of pregnancy. If she is in despair and hopelessness, negative tendencies are passed on. That is why a pregnant mother needs to be in the state of *bliss* or to be wise enough not to pass on negative tendencies to children. She is so powerful that she can hold all the negativity in her and not pass it onto the child, if she holds on to that vision.

In selecting parents, we take over their strengths and shortcomings. The purpose is to enhance the spectrum of frequencies the family operates within by healing the negative and by taking the positive to the next quantum level. The purpose of life is often misunderstood as being the need to discover if there is a rock star or a Bill Gates hidden in them. While it is true that each one of us carries such infinite potential in our soul, the fact is that this infinite potential is released to you only after you overcome the first layers of your karma. This is the reason, people who pursue their inner journey come across adversities one after the other because they are rapidly opening up various layers and clearing them up. This is a sign that they are moving toward their authenticity rapidly. If they continue to witness and accept, they will arrive at their purpose of life after which they shall be able to witness an effortless joyful journey.

There is an old saying in India – whatever good parents do, children get the fruit of it and whatever bad they do in their life, their children have to pay for it.

Your mother is your ground through her unconditional love and your father is your wings through his appreciation and protection. Together, they define the space within which you shall vibrate. In this process, they give out various pluses and minuses to you in infinite combinations as your tendencies. At a physical level, you know it when someone says, "Your nose is like your mother's and ears like your father's." Or, "You eat like your father's brother but sleep like your mom's sister."

Your resemblance is not restricted to just your looks and habits but deep down your purpose to be born in a particular family is – to heal the lower frequencies of the family. For example, your purpose might be to turn around your father's business that is running at a loss, but by following ethics and learning from the mistakes your father made due to which his business suffered. You now have choices to make the business successful by following the values of your father and not making his mistakes. You have a choice to invent new values clashing with the values of your father but make it a successful business. The other choice is to leave your father and go out and find a job. In the first case you have healed your father's karma and you are blessed and your entire family now starts to vibrate at a much higher level. In the second choice, you will survive but pain of your father in terms of his values will continue to conflict with you and will erode your contentment. In the third case, you chose a safe path and as soon as you succeed in being safe and secure in your job, values of the family and being successful will start to clash in your career for further advancement or with your spouse, you shall see the clash of values. This is now hanging in the DNA of the family. This has to be addressed by somebody some day in your family.

In seven years, I have worked on so many children by working on their mothers. It is alarming to know how casual motherhood has become as a process. Children are born with so much stress in their mother's energies that to clear it, we first need to transform their mothers by healing their pregnancy time. This subject is very exhaustive and probably requires another book, but I am including these concepts, which are essential for restoring your well-being. Autism, ADHD, Infertility, PCOD, breast and other female sexuality based cancers and various varieties of distress are rooted during the pregnancy of a mother. If you are reading this book for the purpose of healing your child, be loud and clear, do not do anything on your child. First practice all three techniques, and the third technique will help you heal your pregnancy time which will heal your child. You will be amazed to see that today you heal yourself for anger (for example) and tomorrow your child does not show hyperactivity with anger. There are few case studies in fourth section which shall help you understand better.

There are only two things we look for in our lives through our various endeavors — unconditional love and appreciation. We spend a lifetime seeking appreciation from our fathers because that is the only thing that matters to us. It is a myth that we hold on to our children and look at their future hoping to see them grow. The fact is that we always hold on to our parents, and they are the only ones who matter to us. At an energy level, we are aware that children are born through us for their own journey.

It is a norm nowadays to consider our parents obsolete and redundant to our evolution because we believe we are intelligent enough to be on our own. This is the root of all our *suffering*. At the energy level, we are not grounding into the energy of our mother and we are not tapping into the wisdom of our father. It does not mean that you have that conversation with your mother and feel that you are now sorted. Your disconnection with your parents happens between the ages of 0 to 7 and that is what requires healing. The third technique is totally dedicated to this aspect by making you travel into the past and healing the wounds. Its results will bring the biggest shift in your consciousness within minutes and will leave you intimate with self and content with your life.

Consider this — in one of the cases, a girl had been sent to live in a hostel when she was three years old and grew up emotionally numb because she felt a deep separation from her mother. She had memory about separation but had no recollection of pain, and grew up *suffering* from infertility. She could not recall any disconnection with her mother because as far as she could go in the past, she only saw her mother by her side. She was aware as to why her parents sent her to a hostel from a small village to a big city for education. When she went through healing and used the third technique (NV HUNTING), where she discovered how aloof and angry she was with her mother for sending her away and took that as rejection.

She formed a *belief* that she was not worthy of love and began to subconsciously reject her femininity. She blocked her femininity and grew up more like a male. She grew up fearful about being a mother so that she does not cause the same pain to her child. To her, it was better to not have a child. Once healed, a year later, she gave birth to twins, and there are more than fifty such cases of infertility and PCOS resolved by connecting with one's parents.

Any pattern or habit is a display of the emotional body, which reflects the darkness in the spirit. If it is unresolved, or if it remains in the subconscious, it gets passed on to the next generation. One of your children will take that pattern with a resolve to heal it. Now, this tendency, which is passed on to the following generation gets larger in the subconscious, which if suppressed through one or more generations, will get coded into the DNA. Let us take the short-tempered behavior of your grandfather. He did not think it was harmful and felt it was justified. It goes to your father or an uncle who makes it a tool to deal with a situation. You or your cousin, then have it in your DNA resulting in high blood pressure very early on, forcing you to deal with the chronic emotional outbursts in your family.

Take another case of struggling artists who give birth to a child prodigy. We see such cases on TV talent shows every day. The reason the talent of a struggling parent gets passed on to the next generation is because parents take all their *suffering* and dedicate their lives to pursue the art, but cannot make it big due to some flaw in their personality which is needed to make it happen on a large scale. But throughout their life, they do not care about anything but nurturing the art, which in essence is a movement to become a *Mystic* from a *Survivor*.

This means they are being authentic and have healed all their dark karma and hold a burning desire to make it big in art. Such a couple who has nothing else in the consciousness and everything dark is cleaned up from the subconscious, when they conceive, they nurture not a child but all that which is required by that child to be a prodigy at large canvas. The world around them can call them a fool and a sufferer, but in pursuance of authenticity, one gets a sense of contentment and they themselves never feel the *suffering*. When a child is born to such an authentic couple, it is also encouraged to pursue the art because parents are living and breathing the art with hope and vision.

It is easy to bring healing to yourself right away before you go to next chapter,

1. Make a matrix of your parents' frequency by plotting the emotions they exhibit – for example, you father stood for curiosity, humor, leadership and solving problems, but was emotionally very vulnerable and non-trusting. He wished to do something for the

community or to impart values to the youth. He could not work for the community. You took over all his good intentions and nurtured them as you grew up. You built your career around empowering youth through compassion. Now, you are being blessed by your father and for that you neither need to call him nor visit him in heaven. Blessings are granted, and you will have a huge contentment even if the whole world criticizes you. This is how you can tap into the wisdom of your parents and ancestors, which is waiting to be showered on you. They never go away. It is us, who considering them obsolete, move away from their energy field through which they have possibilities of passing the wisdom. Your challenge now is to deal with the emotional vulnerability, due to which your father suffered and now you have it glaring at you.

2. Your mother was a weak woman. She felt dependent and helpless and was not decently educated. You grow up independent but still carry her values of endurance, patience and femininity. You pick her positivity and not her negativity becoming independent. You are now blessed by your mother.

By doing so, you are not only fulfilling the purpose of the lives of your parents, but also healing all your ancestors and their karma. If you keep doing it, you can sense that the effect of that is being enjoyed by all your cousins and others in the family by them raising their vibrations in their pursuance. But that is a side effect. First you will find yourself effortlessly getting aligned to the purpose of your life.

Likewise, make a chart of your parents and their siblings, and you will be amazed with how you have applied permutations and combinations of their various tendencies in yourself.

Once, you have done this, keep it in your awareness while observing your breath, which is explained in Technique One (NV Swimming), and this exercise is part of your NV HUNTING in any case. Through this exercise, you move from *suffering*, giving you adequacy and a sense of contentment, which is the basis for *bliss*.

The process of conversion of light into mass (physical being) shall go through conversion of light into energy and energy into mass. There exist two different prisms in the universe. For the non-initiated, prism is a glass object, which converts white light into seven colors. We see a rainbow effect in the sky. The first prism converts light into infinite combinations of seven colors as spirit in the energy form and then spirit takes a combination of a certain spectrum to make a soul out of it. The spirit of various spectra is created, the same way various departments are created in a company, to experience a range of emotions for those specific functions. If you are a finance guy, it does not mean that you don't relate with the spirit of business development.

A simple way to understand the concept of a spirit is by understanding the family you are born in. Your family would have one or two religions which are being practised. Each of these religions has a specific frequency. For example Hindus are for self-actualization, so their value system is to work toward that. Christians are for compassion hence kindness and community service are key frequencies for them. Now, there are specific value systems for example, if you are an Indian, you would have a specific caste, hence, your family spirit will be aligned toward those values. You being born in that family, would always be kept confined in those frequency ranges. Each time, you are born, if your choice is not authentic, it will contaminate your spirit. You will inherit a lot from your various environments, which suffocates your soul based on how mature your evolution level is, or else you will just accept constraints of your family as your destiny and remain safe. So, if you are from a Hindu family and walking with a Christian friend and you see someone in need of help, you will do whatever you can possibly do without affecting yourself and allow him to continue the journey to make an actualization but compassion of the Christian may want to go out of the way to help the person in need. Both are right and exhibiting the spirit they are born to express. But if you do not make an authentic choice, your spirit shrinks, you begin to accumulate so much dark that in next birth, you choose a more tougher environment by choosing such parents where restrictions on expressing the true spirit is high. If you are driven by wisdom, then to break the constraints, you will need to revolt and that power will be given or activated in nine months. Yes, you may revolt against your parents using the power they have given to heal the family and express your spirit. Your purpose is not to find fault in your family or ancestors, but to liberate your soul to free up your spirit, to align with the light. For example, you are born in a family where you see women are not respected. You have a choice to accept it and continue to behave like this with your wife and other women as your ancestors did or bring about a reform. By doing this, you will liberate karma from your soul and delete such tendencies from the family spectrum. Treat yourself as a trainee in a new company which has some plus and minus. Your task is to work towards enhancing the value of the company.

The first prism converts light into energy and the second one converts energy into mass in nine months. The code of humanity is written in this form; generic and specific. Generic code represents the range of frequencies a spirit has originally been set in. A specific code is the code the soul takes by choosing a specific family or environment to liberate itself from the contamination in the spirit. This is the reason why bad appears to happen to good people. It is because they have been born to quickly release as many karmic clearings as possible. So called bad people have been born to experience the height of darkness so that in their next birth, they can quickly come back to light and start to transform.

SEVEN LAYERS OF THE HUMAN BODY

To understand breathing as a base of meditation and realize that meditation is the cure, we need an understanding of the various layers that we are made up of. If we only look at the physical body, then there is no existing cure; we have seen how allopathy has failed in providing any cure because it was never meant to be a cure. The diagram in figure 6, is the fundamental view of the book and the next chapters are dedicated to explain these layers. If you want to first experience the relief for yourself or your loved one, please skip this part and directly go to section three, the treatment section, of the book. You do not need any diagnostics and understanding to get relief from any kind of *suffering* you are seeking cure for.

Light: We are light beings. We have heard it from various religious sources, and it is by now a common assumption in the spiritual world. This is supposed to be a pure state of being. Infinite *bliss* exists here. Each of you shall be able to experience this state through the first technique very quickly. Everyone gets there within two days during our workshop. We do not need to be in some trance to experience the light. Faith is light. Faith is nothing but hope. Hope is the most undermined phenomenon. Pause for a minute, and you shall discover that unknowingly, you are hoping. Each moment we hope. When hope begins to fade, we see dark. This is the starting point of all mental disorders. They just lose hope in situations and get connected with dark, which triggers negative emotions. Through our two eyes, when light is reflected, we see the world outside. Third eye (pineal gland) is used for seeing inside. They are interconnected in "either-or" mode and that is why we close our eyes during meditation and love making to experience the light within. We close our eyes to begin to turn inward and activate the pineal gland, which is regulated by the dark and light and has photosensors. When we close our eyes, and observe the breath to be in meditation, the pineal gland is activated, which in turn connects us through the light and insight comes as guidance. If you are hopeless, you will will witness the dark within because you now are disconnected with the light. So we are light beings means we are eternal in hope. In reality, in our growing years, we first create a very perfect world and have desires, these are fueled by our hope for life. Gradually, we begin to come to reality and start turning hopeless about certain things and hopeful about other things. We are a mix of dark and light, a grey shade. This grey shade is the cause of *suffering* because it does not allow you to be authentic and stops your journey from turning inward. If at age 40, you conclude that no one loves you, it will either make you drown in the dark and lead you towards depression or if you have a strong ego, you will pull up enough power to manipulate your environment to make yourself feel you are loved. Either way, you are now connected to the dark. This is how we continue to swing between dark and light. People close to you feel you are a nice person, and people in your social and professional circle know your dark side, because you reflect the instinct to survive in front of them by trying to hide the dark. Then you justify to yourself that no one loves you and the world is a cut throat place and one must do anything to survive.

Spirit: For life to evolve on the planet, light is further divided into spirit to represent the various frequencies as representation of light. For example, when you are born in a Hindu family, you have the spirit of the Hindu ideology and ritual through which you experience this light. When you play a sport, you represent the spirit of a sportsman, through which you display light to self and to large audiences. This spirit is experienced through various emotions.

Karma: Dark exists where light is not. This is where the concept of duality kicks in. As we create karma through each of our experiences, any place where we fail to demonstrate our true spirit, we fail to see light and create a karma. That creates an entry of dark energy within and aligns with the dark in the universe. The 'Hand of God' goal scored by Maradona in the 1986 world cup against England was against the spirit of the sportsmanship and humanity as this was cheating. Had Maradona come forward and spoken the truth, Argentina would have probably lost the match but would have created history and made England their friend, which until then was a rival in football. When you steal money from your father's pocket, come back and confess, you show spirit. If you do not display this spirit, you create a dark energy inside by hiding, having fear, guilt and shame. Such dark energies are created by our karma and this obscures our spirit, thus light.

Emotion: This is the language of the spirit. At the war front, as a soldier, you die for the nation showing the spirit of a true soldier displaying emotions like courage and sacrifice. As a man, your spirit to protect the nation comes alive. What if you are caught by fear or greed? You run away and then you spend your whole life, trying to cleanse this darkness from your spirit, living with negative emotions of unworthiness, shame and guilt. Hence, emotions are the language of the spirit and each human experience is an opportunity to see our spirit and be with the light or to hide the spirit and align with dark. This is why it is said that life is made of choices, and we make a choice in every moment. We are what we choose to be. Light, dark or grey.

Mental Body: This is created in order to survive. When an experience generates an emotion, we bring the mind in between to contain, regulate or suppress the emotion in order to survive. When a curious child sees the flame of a candle and goes out to touch it, they could burn their finger. You can shout at the child to stop, which might instill fear in the child and make the child become aware that survival is important. You can also take the child into your lap, come closer to the flame and lovingly guide the child to experience how close the child can get to the flame with the curiosity and yet be safe. In the first case, you killed the curiosity ensuring the child understands survival, and the child now remembers this. Next time when the child is curious about life, he or she would be scared of you if not the flame as he or she grows up. In the second case, you have made the child wiser and the child learns to trust insights and curiosity and knows how to test for the safety. In the first case you created mind for survival and in the second case consciousness. The mind can be expanded to become consciousness by infusing wisdom and releasing fear of the *Survivor*. Typically, we are a fear-driven society, we have many such fears and remain focused on survival. The mind acts as a gatekeeper between emotions and energy, and if we remove that, we shall be able to experience our true spirit of nature and be light.

Energy Body: This is represented by the seven chakras system and can be demonstrated through Einstein's equation $E=MC$.

You stand at a noisy traffic light or live in a toxic relationship; you feel the bad vibes. You are on the beach or in a temple, you feel good vibes. Energy is a function of the five senses and additionally the sixth sense (insight). Through the insight, we either receive light or dark directly and that converts into energy based on our *belief* system.

Energy is a direct function of our experiences. We breathe the five elements as life force energy (Prana) based on our experiences, and that creates the energy in us. Our experiences are based on our belief and karma which is a function of light or dark. Energy is an interface layer between light (or dark) and Mass. Through the layers of spirit, karma, belief and mind, energy is released into the body and through experiences, it is released towards the spirit through the various layers. It is a two way connector.

In the state of *bliss*, when you are thoughtless, you are one with all the seven layers and directly experience the phenomenon of oneness. In that moment of oneness, E, M, C as separate entities cease to exist and feel as just one unified wholesome experience. If you are in deep misery, your energy as a representation of the dark, feels heavy in your body.

The energy layer is the key between light and mass and is explained through the chakra system. This energy layer is your aura around the physical body. Any positive or negative events of the future, as it unfolds in our physical realm, appear in the energy layer first. This is why it is so easy for any *Mystic* or your parents to read your energy and predict. Disease, before manifesting is already available in the energy body, and it is easy to remove it from there if caught on time. Call it prevention. Therefore, any work done in the name of healing, or toward *bliss*, works in any case by cleansing your energy and clearing up karma.

The other way round is also true. You are angry because your child or spouse misbehaved breaking your expectation. As long as you are angry, it is in your energy field, and you have a choice to keep it here, but if you conclude and make a *belief*, your anger from the energy level will move to the karma layer (subconscious). Instead if in that moment, your child apologizes, the anger disappears and is replaced with love. The reason is that it was only in the energy layer and was not yet made into a *belief*.

7 LAYERS OF HUMAN BODY

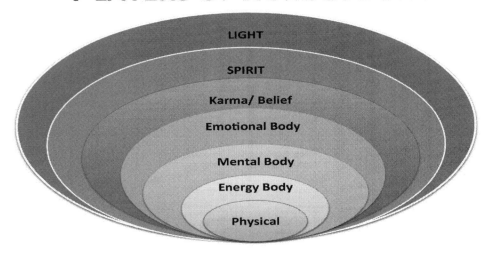

Figure 6

Physical Body: Physical body is just the screen on which light and energy are displayed and experienced. Through our experience and our choices, we generate those energies which are then formed as *belief* and either they contaminate the spirit or purify the spirit.

It is a two-way process. Light is trying to be evident in our life all the time, and it comes as coincidences, insights, dreams, miracles and giving us a chance to experience positive emotions. The other way round is in each of our experiences, we make a choice and based on that, it shifts us toward light or dark.

Every cell in the body has intelligence, and one can tap into this intelligence through breathing as oxygen goes to each cell. Every single piece of information/knowledge you need during your lifetime, is coded in these cells. You can tap into this information any time you have a question or feel stuck.

Hindu scriptures say, "I am the universe and the universe is in me." This is the reason middlemen of religion never want us to focus on our bodies because if you do, then you would not need them as it consists of all the wisdom one would ever need in a lifetime in any of the situations. Of course, original intent of such people was to bring the attention of the *Survivor* to the mystical aspects of the universe to grow the consciousness and dissuade people from getting addicted to mortal life. To be able to tap all the deep layers of wisdom which exists in your body and has existed in your family tree for thousands of years, you would need to have a very good practice of the first technique (NV Swimming). In general, you will gain wisdom from your body as you begin to practice the technique almost from day one, and that will be enough to cure you from your *suffering*. The process of curing ourselves from any type of *suffering* (distress, disorder, disease) is simple. If we remove the mind (zero thought state), the light will travel through the spirit expressed as emotions and become an energy into our physical body. Obviously, we will see a lot of unrest surfacing as this process unfolds. Negative emotions will destabilize you. This destabilization process is dissolving your ego. This is how all your held up toxicity effortlessly surfaces, and if you breathe while witnessing it, it leaves your body free from toxicity and brings you to more and more into the light. It is like opening up the water tap of a house, which has been closed for ages. You first get muddy, dirty water before clean water is seen flowing out of the tap. Of course, we are not trained to do this. This is why you are reading this book which will help you do that.

SPIRIT AND SOUL

Spirit is like a river and the soul is like a container of water taken out of the spirit for a specific task. Soul, like a microchip or SIM card is designed for a specific task in one lifetime for the purpose of cleansing the patches of dark from the spirit. When a soul is reborn and fails to exhibit the spirit, it acquires dark shades on the spirit and ends up contaminating it through karma. It then sets out again to be born to release that karma, which in essence is releasing the dark shades acquired by the soul. Its endeavor is always to seek those opportunities in a lifetime, which offers it fastest and best possible scenarios to release its karmic debt to get in touch with its pure spirit.

A child and grandparents go together very well because they have very little to worry about the future or survival. The child's survival mind has not yet cultivated, and the grandparents no longer need the survival mind. Therefore they both remain with their spirit and since a child always tends to be in the state of *bliss*, it automatically brings joy to the grandparents and raises their vibration, which is often wandering in the emotions of the past. The mind has very little role to play in these two cases to interfere with the spirit. It makes them live moment to moment together. It is common to see how they both can laugh one moment and then cry in the next moment.

We stand united to seek justice against rape or murder. We raise our voice against various issues such as global warming or pollution in our rivers. We do that to keep the spirit of humanity alive, which shall provide a more harmonious environment for the soul, enabling an enriching experience to fulfill its purpose in a more loving environment.

We listen to music and call it soulful music as our experience of listening to music moves us away from thoughts by generating various positive emotions, brings us in touch with the spirit.

When someone offers to help us unconditionally and selflessly, it breaks our negative *belief* about people and restores trust in humanity, which is an exhibition of spirit, and we feel something has touched our soul in that moment. As a community, it is easier to relate with the word spirit, and as an individual, it is easier to connect with the word soul as that's exactly what it is. Spirit is representation of the community of a frequency range and soul is a specific and individualized expression of the spirit.

So two individuals, unique in their life experiences can come together to protect the victim, conduct a candle vigil, and yet have different purposes and various unique *belief*, which is the function of their soul journey, but they are made of a common spirit. This is how we are all connected with each other cosmically.

In the same manner, as we exhibit our spirit in the external world, we do the same internally. Tendency of our soul is to always offer an opportunity to feel the pure spirit. The container of water always wants to merge in the river. Due to our karma, and the lessons to be learned, we attract scenarios where we have a choice to suppress the spirit and survive or trust and allow the spirit to purify. This process of purification is consciousness. Every experience we have, will always generate emotions and these emotions are the ones which are being the expression of our spirit. If it is negative emotions, it reflects adding to the contamination of the spirit, which it will seek to purify through some other experience, and if it is a positive emotion, it is an expression of the soul to cleanse the spirit to merge back to the spirit. Or simply said, it reflects your spirit in that emotion.

In an experience when we feel rejected, our spirit feels down, and we tend to be hopeless and non-trusting in the universe. This container of water now feels the pain of being lost in the physical realm and cannot find its source i.e. river in which it can merge. In an experience where we are in love, we feel that highest expression of our spirit in which our soul feels merged and one with the spirit. When we feel fear for our lives, it is our spirit that we feel is in the danger of existence as the soul feels it is losing the chance to exhibit its spirit by not fulfilling the task for which it is born. Hence, every experience we have in the physical world has an impact on our spirit, which either contracts it or expands it. Each expansion is an attempt to align the soul to its purpose, and each contraction of the spirit is the contamination for which now the soul would need to work at to clear up in this lifetime or another. Expansion and contraction in spirit is experienced by the emotions we feel in a specific moment.

Every *suffering* (distress, disease and disorder) exhibits contamination in the spirit which cannot be absorbed any more by the body. In any of our *sufferings*, emotions experienced by us carry the seed of healing. If we can pay attention to the source of the emotion and by consciously breathing that emotion, we can heal our *suffering* in that moment itself. Take the example of cancer, which results in pain in the body. This pain is the pain kept suppressed by the person for a long period of time and results in a continued contraction of the spirit. Since this pain, as and when it occurred, was not experienced consciously it reached a point when spirit could not be kept contracted, it revolts by surfacing as cancer and disrupts the engineering of the body. High blood pressure makes us feel very unstable, which indicates discomfort (guilt) in expression of anger. Anger is the result of loss of expectation and this loss of expectation causes a threat to survival. Not being comfortable in expressing the anger, yet not being good at suppressing it, it stays in the energy body and as we breath it, goes into blood stream causing high blood pressure, not finding an outlet for its release makes us feel unstable.

It is easier to feel our spirit than our soul. To feel the spirit is like an art form. While the soul is a mystery because it carries the purpose of life, which we often spend a lifetime to decode. This is, infact, where the trick is. By experiencing the spirit, we can begin to decode the purpose of our lives. Emotions are a science because we always need to find out which *belief* is creating that specific emotion and the mind is the technology where just by one thought (like pressing a button), we access or block the flow of spirit.

If you are passionate about decoding the purpose of life, it is simple, but could be a long drawn process. By simply starting to do what you love to do, you can begin the process of getting in touch with your spirit. As your spirit begins to expand, your emotions will begin to change from negative to positive and soon your energy field will become so large that you will not be able to do anything else but pursue the task, which exhibits your spirit. In the practical world, you may choose the pace at which you like to decode and get aligned. It does not mean that you leave your high paying job as a corporate and start to paint. You could paint very badly, and yet it gives you joy, which enriches your life while still at your job. Your purpose could be that you continue to work for a corporation and keep finding ways to express yourself through such paintings, and creative endeavors which allow you to feel soulful.

I am often asked in my workshops, what is the difference between emotions and thought?

If you stand in the sun and you feel heat, it is an emotion. It is a feeling you know, so even if God tells you it is cold, you will not believe it. When you feel you cannot survive this heat and start to look for a tree or shade – that is your thought process to survive. One step before this, it is your mind which registers that you are feeling hot, and then depending upon your *belief*, it starts working on finding survival. However, if you are with your lover, and you just have a few moments, you will sweat but not try to survive. Here love is your survival and thought is to experience emotion of love in the heat.

This example tells you that while emotions are inevitable, thoughts are optional. Emotions are the eternal truth. So heat at 45 degrees Celsius feels the same to you and me, but depending upon our conditioning, you and I may feel its impact differently and may have different responses to it. However, neither of us can deny that we feel hot. Our response to emotions, which is a display of our spirit, is unique based on our *belief*, and that creates infinite choices and our own uniqueness, and thus a unique destiny.

Each moment, no matter how micro that moment is, is an experience, and each experience creates an emotion. Our mind may not be sensitive to it, and may or may not register it, but that moment is getting recorded as a memory. It is like living life with a camcorder on all the time, and we can review the footage any time by rewinding it.

Every day, you take the same route to your office. One day, instead of driving, you join a carpool. Suddenly, you notice so much more on the way that you could not on other days because you were focused on driving. None of it probably matters to you, except the new cake shop, which you realize today has come up in the place of the grocery store, since you last saw it a few weeks ago. The memories about the grocery shop had triggered bad emotions every time you drove past this area because he had cheated you by giving you rotten bread, which he did not replace. But today it is different. Now you realize, seeing a cake shop this will save your time, next week when you would be buying a cake for your daughter when she comes home from the hostel. This triggers relief about finding a cake shop nearby and old memories and happiness about a good time with your daughter. Since you are being driven, you now have time to attend to these emotions and feel very enriched. You reach the office feeling very rich and content. You create a *belief* that if you are driven rather than driving, you are more content than before. So impression or memory exists in the subconscious and as per our need, we trigger our emotions which in turn create experiences. Experiences become *belief* and *belief* creates the need for the same experience again.

This creates a hard disk of various emotions, memories, impressions and *belief* in our emotional body. Every moment, the space around us is changing, evolving and impressions and memories are being created and old ones are being rewritten through experiences. New beliefs are written and old beliefs are removed. In the external world, we say that we must keep pace with changing times and become contemporary to the fast changing world. This is how the universe evolves with time and space and the same is true for the universe evolving inside us with time and space. Based on our experiences, we bring something into our consciousness. This changes our energies inside by replacing the old impressions or *belief* with the new one. The changes inside us now seek its manifestation in the external world. This is how we continue to seek harmony and stability within and without. This is a continuous and connected loop of the internal world and external manifestation which always seeks to be in harmony with each other.

The grocery shop, with which you had a bad experience of the shopkeeper cheating you, is not visible to you anymore. Anger is now replaced by a smile on your face because of the cake shop triggers memories about your daughter. And the nice experience with the shopkeeper who did extra thing to bake a cake for your daughter. The grocery shop is now located in the inner lane where the locals still interact with him and get fooled, but your space is cleared.

This is how in the universe and within the body, we create experiences. Though the old exists, you don't attract the same kind of situations unless you like to go inside the bylanes to visit the grocery shop which you can always do.

Healing is like this. Old trauma and memories are not deleted from your memory but sent in by lanes that you don't have a purpose to visit. It is now replaced with higher vibration experience and your spirit is now brighter – free from the dark. However, you can always visit the dark, nullify the effect of healing and go back to grocery shop and suffer again. Your only chance to avoid reversal is your wisdom and awareness about the episode of the past from which you have done your learning.

He was hardly 3 years old when he discovered that he loves to kick the ball, watching his sister playing football. He insisted that he also be allowed to play. For several days, he continued insisting on it but was not allowed due to his age. He did not wait for the academy but started to kick the ball all the time at home. He started watching football on TV and would ask his sister to play with him. He began to surround himself with football all the time.

Be it on TV, on the field, or video games. It didn't matter in what form football was available; he just wanted to be with the football. Within no time, he was tried by the academy. Playing with older boys, he would run behind the ball for forty-five minutes without even being able to touch the ball once. That did not stop him from running behind the ball. Once the game was over, as everyone packed, he would go and grab the ball and start kicking. The coach saw this passion and would come and play with him while others packed. Within a year, when he went for his first ever tournament, he was awarded the best player at the age of 5 playing under 8. The environment was created. His mother made sure she was watching the match with him on TV late at night. His father informed teachers not to push him into academics, and coaches would spend extra time and teach him difficult tricks and his sister will play at home and teach.

In his growing up years, not every day was a good day for him, and he would feel disheartened. His mother would not let him create a *belief* of whether he was good at it or not. She would gently get him back to the ball. Gradually, he learned that all he must do is to play football. He was sad the day he lost or when his favorite club lost a game. He would cry his heart out in pain but for a very brief moment and soon would be with the ball again to practice the tricks he learned while watching it on TV. This is how he continued connecting with the joy of being with football rather than feeling happy or sad of whether he won or lost. He was not allowed to create any *belief* out of his game except one – be with your joy and if that comes from playing football and learning football, then just keep doing it. This creates hunger in this child to continue to learn and get better with it. Each time, he loses, his joy is lost, hence he does not come back tired and rejected but full of energy to get that shot right and to restore joy. No motivation or encouragement is needed for this boy. Gradually, this child becomes good at anything that gives him joy and develops new ways to remain curious to explore being good at. When he discovered that mathematics is fun, he started to solve the mathematics level of kids older than him. Tomorrow, if he does not become a football player, he will discover what else makes him curious and will figure out ways to be good at it. Be it survival through a corporate job or teaching football. His spirit and soul are now aligned operating in the environment of curiosity and living with joy.

Since there is no *belief* here and no need for survival other than living with joy and pursuing what gives you joy, there is no karma attached with the act of playing. There are no or little emotions to manage. He remains with three states i.e. pain, *bliss* and curiosity. Pain for a brief moment when he loses, *bliss* when he plays which he does almost all the time and curious to find ways to play more. Hence, mind is absolute – free to remain focused on having access to joy and such a mind is then consciousness, which is filled with joy so anything he does has to become joy else he will not do it. If the same boy was born to a poor family, then he would have to probably struggle for survival while playing football. In such a case, he is born with some karma, which he needs to clear off while exhibiting his spirit.

This is what the reincarnation principle talks about – cause and effect. Experience a moment, create a *belief*, which causes karma, triggers emotions, obscures the spirit to flow and results in us going through experiences, which are necessary to clear that cause to experience the spirit. This is cause and effect.

A lot of people complain and wonder why good people have to suffer while nothing happens to bad people. Bad people do not allow their karmic layer to open up, and are focused on learning and acquiring wisdom through wrong deeds. They are connected with the dark and not light. May be in the next birth or towards the end of their lives when they have done it enough, they will drop their minds and that is when their karma may open up. On the other hand, good people are the ones, who are in reverence of the universe and are constantly on the path to clear off all their belief/karma from this life and various lives to quickly reach a stage where they have direct access to their spirit after cleansing. In this time and age of convergence and speed where the globe is shrinking, and we are all connected, effects of karma are far faster. Hence, clearing the planet from dark energies is rather fast. This means we do not really have to wait for next birth to clear off the karma, we are clearing in this birth and epidemic of *suffering* (distress, disorder and disease) is the validation of it.

Take another example: As a child, you take your pocket money and go to the neighbor's shop to buy some candy or ice cream. It is a routine, and you do it every day. Take one note of INR 50, buy your ice cream and the shopkeeper gives you change and the ice cream. One day, your mother counts the change and reminds you that the change you received was less. Depending upon how she handles it with you (scolds you, ridicules you, threatens you, warns you or educates you on the process to explain how to count money before leaving the shop), you will create one of the following beliefs:

1. I should be careful with my money. I will count it next time.

2. Shopkeeper has cheated me. I will teach him a lesson tomorrow by stealing candy.

3. My mother does not love me.

4. I am useless and worthless.

5. Cool, I will go to shop tomorrow, clarify and be smart next time. Mistakes do happen.

Of course, you could form any other *belief* as well. If the child here forms a negative *belief*, his joy to buy the ice cream is gone. He can become smarter by counting the money but now his obsession is to be right rather than feeling the joy that the process of buying the ice cream was giving him. He still enjoys the ice cream but his spirit is lost. Each time, he is curious; he would first try to be right rather than being joyful. He is smart now in our eyes, but he lost his curiosity potentially too early.

No negative emotion can sit for long in your spirit because that is not the true nature of any spirit. *Belief* (and not experiences) can only hamper and tone down or fracture your spirit for some time as long as fear for survival is active, thus becoming a source of emotions.

The layer where all the karma and *belief* with the corresponding emotions are stored is called the soul. Theoretically, your entire spirit, in its pure form is packed in your soul when it decides to be reborn to clear its most important karma. The most important *belief,* which needs to break away in one lifetime remains active in the soul and the rest of the karma remains dormant in the soul. If we are successful in purifying the spirit in one lifetime for the karma, we have been born for, then the dormant spirit may open up to offer you more opportunities to quicken your evolution, or else they remains dormant for the next lifetime. This is how our DNA or genes are structured, where the most of it remains dormant, and only a small part of it is active. It is like every child in kindergarten has hidden possibilities to do a PhD, which unravels as the child keeps moving through each class.

To better understand this, let us take the example of the Prime Minister of India, Mr. Modi. He was a tea-seller and before becoming Prime Minister, he was the Chief Minister of the state for three terms. Much before he became Chief Minister, he was a Member of Parliament for several years. From being a tea-seller to becoming an MP, was huge quantum jump, and if he wanted, he could just settle down and enjoy a normal stable, secure and respected life. He continued breaking his *belief* and being driven by passion to serve, he kept opening up his dormant *belief* to achieve more in one lifetime. Such cases are, where one can have courage to face fears and break their own limiting *belief* by expanding expression of the spirit. This is similar to DNA activation. DNA activation cannot be done by doing some spiritual technique but by pursuing your spirit and relentlessly experiencing it in service to humanity. Such spiritual practices are alarming and very dangerous.

It is possible for anyone to become Prime Minister without expansion of the Spirit and without activating DNA. Here you can pursue the purpose of the soul without expanding the spirit which is in serving humanity. It is the same difference between a startup Founder and career CEO.

For example if you are born in a Hindu family, morality of this religion is designed to ensure that a soul pursues its purpose in a safe environment within the confines of the Hindu religion. By doing so, its purpose is to view humanity through the teachings of the religion, and it will exhibit certain emotions by having experiences. The constraints taught by the religion, soon begin to contract the spirit in doing more and this is where you decide to open up to other religions by making friends or experiencing other religions by visiting church or the dargah to break a set of *belief* stored from previous births. Once you do that, you feel liberated and your spirit is expanded. This triggers a new set of emotions and experiences in your life and internally, you feel the sense of freedom.

The spirit of humanity is much bigger than the purpose of a soul born in a specific religion. The purpose of every such religion is to bring you in touch with the spirit. Each religion has taught the same, but some of us find it safe to remain confined to the boundaries of the religion, this limits the experience of the soul. Being safe is primitive living and is a controlled evolution. Religion is a *Belief* and just an example here. You can always have primitive living by remaining confined to your *belief.*

As a sportsman, when you make a mistake without the referee noticing, you have the choice to let it go or to pause and inform the referee. If you inform the referee, you are saying my own survival or the purpose of my soul to become a star player is far less important than the spirit of the game. So even if a billion fans get disappointed because you could not perform as per their expectation, they go home in reverence of you. Famous "hand of God" goal by Maradona did make Argentina win the match and potentially fulfilled the purpose of his soul by being the best player. The spirit of sportsmanship is although compromised and will haunt Maradona as and when he begins to turn inward.

Survival or the desperation to survive is that wall which isolates the spirit from the soul. Once that happens, it is like a car without a navigation system. Hence, it may continue to acquire more bad karma or eventually find a way to reach the purpose, but not without mending the way and causing damage to the soul's journey.

Knowing the purpose alone is not enough. It is very simple to know it by feeling your own fantasy or free expressions or by getting in touch with your negative emotions to realize what constraints your spirit. If constraints are removed, you will set out on the path of pursuing your purpose. If you really want to fulfil the purpose of life, first start to align with the spirit in which this purpose will be fulfilled. Like that boy, who would come home and crumple up a piece of paper and make a ball out of it to kick around. Like that girl who always goes for her dance glass several minutes before and is the last one to leave by participating in every aspect of the theatre and expressing her spirit though her role is just for 5 minutes. Once your spirit is expanded, purpose will emerge on its own. Spirit is that energy field in which if you arrive, purpose of life will unfold on its own effortlessly. Go to the playing field first before making a decision which sports you will play and what role you will have in the team.

EMOTIONAL BODY

There is only one state in which the spirit would always want to be; it is the state of *bliss*. Human experience on this planet of duality introduces another state where the spirit is comfortable being and that is the state of pain.

As a child, we only knew the state of *bliss* in everything we did. If we stopped to experience it for a moment, our spirit felt pain within. The state of *bliss* corresponds to wonderment. One remains in the state of wonderment of life and dances in tune with nature. It is the basic nature, which exists outside of us, and it is the basic nature granted to us within, when we are born. In wonderment, we merge with the nature (Universe) and become *one*. It is in this state of *bliss* that we have no desire or longing. If humanity remains in this state, there is no way we would evolve as a race on the planet because there is nothing to evolve to. But that is the basic nature of the spirit with which we are born, no matter how small or big the taste of this bliss lasts for each of us during our childhood. In our growing years, this is what we seek through various deeds and pursuits.

When spirit is mixed with the five elements to form a human body, it seems that the challenge is to experience the same *bliss* together with these five elements. Life in the physical realm or simply said, physical body has its own demands and commitment. The purpose of human life has to do with the life per se, and to deal with its challenges while pursuing bliss in its various forms. The purpose is to make us aware of its needs and through this; reach the state of *bliss*, not by ignoring the needs of the physical body or life in this realm. As nature takes its own course through us, various situations which force us to look at the physical reality, take us away from *bliss* for that moment of time. Taking us away from *bliss* is a way of nature to reflect to us the other side of duality, which is the state of pain. Pain is the process of purifying the five elements which we breath to arrive at *bliss*. There is no way, you can attain *bliss* without purifying the demons of these five elements and you will learn about them in the chapter energy body. Higher the *bliss*, deeper is the state of pain to do a balancing act to keep you in harmony with nature and to adhere to duality. Once pain and *bliss* both are effortless to attain, we dissolve the duality and enlightenment (awakening) happens. Duality only means purification in the properties of five elements. Once that is done, there is only one state.

Pain is a state in which we connect to mystery. In this state, we become a seeker and ask the questions – "Why this?", "Who am I?", "What is life?", "Who is God?", "What is it all about?". In *bliss*, we have no such questions. Hence, in *bliss* we become One with nature and in pain we seek nature. To rise above duality, which religion and all spiritual practices talk about is to feel the *bliss* in pain and pain in bliss. To feel the mystery in wonderment and wonderment in mystery. Both of them are the same state. To feel them, is to lift the veil of MAYA (illusion).

I lived in Delhi and in Zurich. Delhi temperatures can rise up to 50 degree Celsius in the summer and Zurich temp can go to -10 degree Celsius in the winter. If you touch the car's steering wheel in these two cases, it burns your hands and it feels like the same burning sensation. If you want to have a low budget experience, keep an ice cube on your palm and then a hot cup of tea. You will know the duality merges here without spending money.

The common force, which keeps us connected between these two states is curiosity. Curiosity drives you towards wonderment and pain leaves you with curiosity. It is in this state of curiosity when you pray or seek an answer that mystery unfolds and brings an insight to direct you. This is the reason why people who conduct prayers, chants and worship seek a solution to get their wishes fulfilled, their prayers do not work. For your prayers to be heard, you first need to be connected to the mystery to be able to communicate your question. You never have to wait for an answer to come to you but always have to raise your vibration by refining the question to arrive where answer already exist. You cannot reach a specific website and get the information without having connected with your broadband. Pain is that connector and curiosity is that driver, which brings us in touch with our answers.

Mystic has this curiosity and has felt the pain in the *suffering* of human life, he remains connected to mystery through meditation and comes back with replies for you. He is not a magician. When you approach him with a query, due to your faith in him, you are curious and that is how you connect to the mystery through the *Mystic*. He always has a powerful, dedicated internet link and through that, he accesses all the information from your spirit and emotional body and gives it to you. Much like you visit a cybercafé to surf the internet in the olden days because you do not have an internet connection at home.

The higher you stay in the state of *bliss*, the deeper you go into the state of pain, and the bigger is your consciousness. This is what spiritual practices talk about when they talk about the concept of enlightenment. Reaching such a high and deep state, comes from acceptance of life, and to accept is to have faith. Any other state, you experience yourself to be in, is the result of trying not to be either in pain or in *bliss*. This is due to the lack of acceptance, which actually is lack of faith in the universe or nature and is the *suffering*.

This non-acceptance triggers various emotions. Ayurveda has classified nine states (quantum states) of emotions, their correlations and how they can be transformed from one state to another state. Lack of faith is the mother of all emotions. You must have experienced playing with a child, like running behind them, pretending to catch them or tickle them on their stomach, they have the ability to laugh uncontrollably. Initially, you also laugh with the child and you discover your energies are lifted and you forget your stress. However, few more moments into the laughter with the child, you feel exhausted and out of touch with yourself. You are not able to touch the peak of *bliss* with the child or even if you do, in the initial stage, you are not able to sustain it for the duration the child is able to. It is because you have a *belief* that life is not *bliss*, or if you laugh a lot, you will have to cry the same. These are limiting *belief* we create for ourselves to feel safe, and these are programmed into us since eons. This is the moment when you do not have faith in the universe or in yourself, whichever way you like to express it, but both are the same.

The reverse is true as well. On the death of a loved one, you mourn and feel pain for some time, and you work hard to come out of it. You distract yourself and keep finding some work to occupy your mind. The idea is not to feel the pain but to begin to survive.

There were risks attached to being lost in your *bliss* or going deep in your pain. It potentially had reason to drift a person away from their responsibility, and that is why family and friends were scared. If you remain in pain for long, you may turn a *Mystic* or lose your mental balance or become mentally unstable, which will take you away from the responsibilities. Hence, some religious and cultural rituals are for thirteen days upon the death of a loved one. The purpose of this ritual is to restore faith in life and move on. People from the community come to help you express your emotions toward the loved one you have lost. They support you emotionally with love and compassion to allow you to feel your pain. They offer you help to let you know that you are not alone, and finally, through religious rituals and preaching, people help you become aware of the mystery that life is.

Once with the pain, it turns you curious about life and death, meaning of God and purpose of life. Once with the pain, you begin to have a better tolerance and acceptance of life and its situations.

The nature of deep pain is such that it detaches you from the world. If you are allowed to feel deep pain, your curiosity in mystery of life can grow so big that you may turn a *Mystic which is alarming for a Survivor in you.* Pain is transformative, and if you look at the biggest of the leaders, who have contributed to society in one way or another; they have gone through pain by accepting it.

On the other hand, if you can find *bliss* and stay with it, then you are complete in yourself. This is also a very alarming situation for our social and family institutions. If you are complete in yourself then a social and family fabric cannot be built around you. If you attain *bliss* within, then you do not need a spouse, family or religion, and if each one of us can feel complete, then institutions will crumble. The whole premise of the relationship is that we are not complete in ourselves. We need to be together to feel complete and find our *bliss* through each other, in each other, and for each other. So if you come back home and tell your spouse/partner that you had a good time with your friends, this can be threatening to your partner who feels the loss of space in your life. Your partner, much like you, is programmed that we are together to find *bliss* for each other, and this is an exclusive space both hold for each other.

Hence, every society, culture for many generations, has been trying to create a bandwidth of emotions, in which they would want people to operate. (Figure 7)

EMOTIONAL BODY

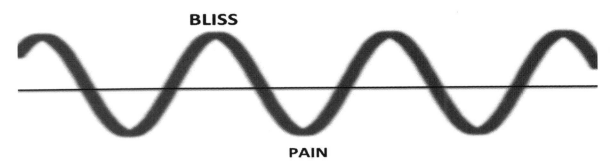

Figure 7 : Natura tendencey of every experience towards bliss or pain

But none of it was originally done to clamp your ability to feel *bliss* or pain. It was rather done to create a culture of interdependency and living together. The idea was to create togetherness and sensitivities towards each other and make living a better place by being meaningful in each other's life, or else, it becomes like a life of a *Mystic* who is comfortable with the pain and *bliss* within and have no need of others. They are not the people who participate in the evolution but are catalysts of the evolution. We have something to learn from them. If we can integrate the *Mystic* within, life will become effortless and full of richness.

No matter which culture or religion you come from, its customs and rituals traditionally ensured that we share everything from pain to *bliss* and success to failure. There was a culture, not long ago, where people were very comfortable sharing their guilt, shame or fear and yet they were respected for what they were. Joint families were meant to be a support system, and they always ensured that they do their best as humanly possible and for the rest, help you connect with the universe by preaching faith in life. So, if you are experiencing the pain of the loss of your father, in a joint family, many elder men would be sensitive to your pain, and in their own way, would help you transmute that pain to gradually help you move toward *bliss*. If you are filled with joy and *bliss* due to some success, families ensured sharing the fruits of success in one way or the other to get blessings and happiness of everyone in your success. The whole idea was not to trigger inadequacy in self when in pain and inadequacy in others when in *bliss* and treat life as a journey and equality rather than an accomplishment to reflect superiority/inferiority over others. The bandwidth created for the *Survivor* was for the reason that outside this frequency zone, they had a support system and rituals to accompany them through these extreme frequencies.

Religion further helped people with acceptance and pain, which meant acceptance of mystery. The word destiny was invented not to make people feel helpless in the outcome of their choices, but to accept the nature of life and dance in the mystery. Destiny turned out to be a tool, which converted *suffering* into pain and pain into acceptance of life, which unfolded into a new insight and new direction for the people to move toward *bliss* to experience their true spirit.

Such is not the case anymore. We live with strangers. The size of a family and ties of relationship have shrunk. Religion as a means of faith is long eroded, and gone are the festivities and rituals, which we celebrated within our community. Our entire emotional and spiritual support system has collapsed. We are programmed to remain within a bandwidth of frequency, beyond which we were being supported by the institutions we were in. Now in the absence of a support system or society, there is no safe bandwidth in which we can feel safe and well supported. We are left loose on our own and that is forcing us to create a self imposed bandwidth which we can manage and continue to feel safe in. This has resulted into shrinking our emotional expression further and from a stable normal bandwidth, we are now moving into flat and monotonous expressionless living. Hence, entertainment, drinking, sex or any other quick method, which can help us release our repressed emotions and give us the sight of *bliss* is becoming a big industry.

If you are in your forties like me, you would have noticed that, earlier, every morning, there used to be a big crowd outside the temple or church. Now, you can see the same crowd in the pubs and malls. This is the crisis our generation is facing. This is where we have a problem with health, happiness and relationships. In essence, we are facing a problem with our own selves, which is reflected in other pursuits. Birth of spirituality and compulsion to find a support system within is the key challenge of this generation and the next generations to come.

The emotional body is like a lubricant – the lubricant between the spirit and physical body. If we block this lubricant, we lose access to our spirit, and since spirit must seek its expression as per the law of nature, it creates scenarios, which gives us pain or reminds us of our emotional bodies. Diabetes reminds us to slow down and not push harder for survival because it cannot digest some truth through events of life. Cancer gives us pain in the nerves of an extreme order. This pain connects us back to mystery, as an expression of darkened spirit, which cannot be contained or suppressed anymore. In the symptoms of our *sufferings*, lies an emotion or emotional block, created by a *belief*, which if released through awareness makes *suffering* disappear. This is what you will learn through the third (NV HUNTING) technique. A technique through which you can liberate yourself from the karma and corresponding emotions stored inside, which are causing you *suffering*.

We have two choices now – either to rebuild a support system through a loving relationship of interdependency or to discover a support system within. In the first case, we know how we are failing miserably today because the tone of humanity has been set for an individual journey. The challenge with the second approach is that we do not know a process or mechanism through which we can turn inward. Even if we do, then we have no yardstick to know if we have found ourselves.

The solution lies in building a loving support system outside, by first turning inward to rediscover ourselves, and this exactly is the yardstick. People pursue spirituality as an escape mechanism because they feel they have lost it all, but the whole idea of spirituality is to get back to life. The idea is to discover same harmony and peace in the ecosystem as you have found within and that is how each one of us will contribute to the planet's evolution.

There is a difference between pain and *suffering*. You must have come across the quote, "Pain is inevitable and *suffering* is an option." This goes to confirm the fact that spirit will always tend to be either in pain or in *bliss*. There is no *suffering* as far as spirit is concerned and none of us are born to suffer, no matter how bad we may feel about ourselves or believe we have accumulated bad karma in the past.

Suffering is created by the decision to block the natural tendency of spirit to experience pain or *bliss*. This is done by the mind, which creates a *belief* that it is not safe to experience pain and there can be a million reasons to have this *belief*. Let us take the same example to understand it better. When a child is hurt in the leg, he will cry so loud that he holds his breath till pain disappears. The child here is feeling the pain and being complete in the moment by holding his breath. Once the pain is over, within a few moments, the child would be back to its original stable state and that is *bliss*. The child would not create any *belief* that his friends are bad or that he got hurt, or that God is unfair, or any such *belief* about being hurt. Without any *belief* or scar, the child goes back quickly to play with same friends and in the same environment. But if we stop the child from crying and tell him things like – boys do not cry or you are a brave boy, do not cry – he stops to cry but the pain is still there. Now, he has a mind which starts to work that pain is not good, and he would not be considered a good boy or a boy if he cries. Now the *suffering* starts. Heart wants to cry out and feel the pain and the mind says do not feel pain. He learns now to suppress the pain. This is *suffering*. The power, which the child has developed to keep his pain inside, is through a *belief* created by mind and this is called the Ego. The Ego is nothing but an instrument of the mind, which is used to keep emotions or hurt suppressed. If you have a strong ego, you are considered a brave and powerful person because no matter how difficult the situation is, you are not emotionally affected. This is how people see you. In reality, you are affected as much as a weak person is affected except that a so-called weak person decides to experience the emotion or does not have the power of the mind (EGO), strong enough to control emotions. If it is a compulsion to feel emotions due to the inability to control them, then it triggers hopelessness, and if it is a choice to experience emotions, then it is a function of consciousness due to awareness..

The hopelessness is loss of faith and this is where through mental power one has a chance to survive by connecting with the dark to avoid mental disorder or hopelessness.

Emotions have motions and are originated due to lack of faith. Lack of faith is the mother of all *belief* and *belief* is the reason behind emotions staying in the body. If not for *belief*, no matter how bad your experience is, as you feel the pain, pain will disappear and will leave you at your steady state with a larger consciousness, like the child who bounces back to the state of *bliss* after experiencing the pain fully. If you are in the state of peace right now, something happens and it gives you pain, if you allow yourself to experience the pain, you will bounce back to your state of peace. If you control it, it will take your peace away, and now you are *suffering*.

But this is not all, you have an added advantage if you allow yourself to experience the pain. Each time, you feel pain, it only goes deeper. The deeper it goes, higher it bounces you to the state of *bliss* and not just to your old steady state. In this process, it makes you more authentic by making you feel detached from others. You are wiser now. Gradually, your state of *bliss* is filled with larger consciousness and deeper wisdom through which you feel guided and aligned to your purpose. In this state, no disease or distress or disorder can exist in your body or mind or spirit. Women are gifted with this process by nature. They have the period of menstruation every month when they release their repressed emotions through pain. If no repression, then there is no pain during the menstruation period. They naturally turn inward by withdrawing from the worldly affairs during this period. They are accepted as nature by everyone and allowed to be themselves including not to have the compulsion to have sex. They largely stay with their emotions and attention is on the body. During these days when they have a higher sexual arousal, they transmute that into their spiritual energy which makes them connect with their deeper wisdom and their spirit. They are now living like a Mystic during this period every month. They need no meditation or spiritual practices to be authentic. They are a superior gender by design. This is the reason when the menstruation is delayed; they feel gripped by this unknown fear that something is not adequate with their well-being.

For a cure to take place, experience of pain is inevitable. The more you feel pain, *suffering* disappears, a higher steady state of *bliss* is attained. There is a difference between grief, sorrow and pain, while sorrow and the state of grief is still about feeling the loss or disappointment and still having some hope or expectation. Pain is a state in which realization has settled in about the loss. Experiencing the pain is acceptance of the loss. We live in a connected world. Each one of us is connected with another one. Within close relationships, we are more intensely connected and transmitting our energies to each other all the time and affecting them in good and bad ways. This is most visible in mother-child relationships and more so, if you have a special child. So I will take example from mothers of special children where we have brought changes in the child without working on the children and just by working on the mother. Pain is a container of energy. If we experience pain, our energies will not spill over to others. By making mothers accept pain through the three techniques, they have reversed ADHD, border line autism and many other distress situations in their children. Special children are locked with the energy of mothers and that happens mostly by mothers going through bad emotions and situations during their pregnancy.

If pain is not easy to experience, then try to move towards *bliss*. Experience the *bliss*. The easy known method to humanity to experience *bliss* is through sexual arousal. During that time, you acknowledge arousal and experience it within your body, your negative emotions begin to fall and lift you towards *bliss*. In this moment, as your desire grows, you begin to see hope, yearning to belong (merging to be one), a sense of adequacy leading you to have acceptance of self. Fantasy is hope and hope is faith. Now, if this arousal peaks and you witness it, it will give you pain and pleasure in the cycle before settling down to one of the two states. If you are comfortable with your sexuality, then there is a three step process through which you can expand the bandwidth and to experience *bliss* and pain as a healing mechanism. Step one is acknowledge that you have a desire. Step two is to experience it in your body while observing your breath and allow it to expand into your whole body. Step three is to absorb, transmute or release (masturbation). The third step is optional from the health and well-being perspective and often you arrive at it effortlessly and naturally. You shall acknowledge and experience in your whole body to spread the *bliss* and pain and will leave you in a very deep state of peace if absorbed. In fact it is a whole body scan as well. The part of the body where you do not feel any sensation when expanding the energy in the body is the indication that you are holding some belief inside which is blocking your flow. Women who do not feel the arousal in the breast are at the risk of attracting breast cancer. If you are not comfortable with sexuality then during the course of this treatment you will turn comfortable as the cure is not possible unless life force energy (pro creative energy) is not free from the belief.

By attaining the state of orgasm (*bliss*), you are beginning to vibrate higher and your steady state is now going up. As this grows, it increases the contentment through self-acceptance.

You will now not be able to spill over energies to your child or to relationships. This starts to restore the behaviour of the children back towards normal.

But there is a catch by just experiencing the pain or *bliss* does not work as a Cure. The reason is *belief*. You can experience your pain as often as you want, but you will find the pain comes back and that is because your *belief*, which caused *suffering* is still the same. This is the reason, many techniques, which bring you in touch with your emotions do not work as a cure and probably at best, help you feel less distressed. If you lost a relationship, you can experience pain of loss or pain of loneliness for several nights and cry your heart out, but as long as you hold the *belief* that you have lost something, pain will continue to emerge one way or another, and you will suffer if you try to manage it. Every experience is meant for a reason, and if we do not make learning out of it, our *belief* remains intact. There are techniques where they handle it at mind level to replace your old *belief* with a new one or a positive *belief*. This again works in making you a better *Survivor* but does not eradicate negative emotions held in your spirit by an old *belief*. It is just pushed into your subconscious and carries high probability to appear as disease. Therefore it is imperative that pain will always bring larger consciousness, deeper insights and wisdom about the purpose of such a pain and insights to lead you towards hope. If not, then you are still holding a *belief* and you are still experiencing sorrow and *suffering*.

But we do not need to do anything to arrive at our *belief* or pain to gain insight for transformation. Through the techniques, we become aware of the *belief*. Insight and wisdom, will come on its own leading into the expansion of consciousness. *Belief* breaks down on its own and is replaced not with another *belief*, but with wisdom about why a specific event was important in our life and what the learning was. This restores the faith in life, and as faith is restored, hope comes and negative emotions do not emerge, even if we are in the same situation again.

The law of nature is that if you do not hold on to an emotion and feel it fully, it will disappear within a few minutes like the child who was allowed to cry in pain while playing. It is against the law of nature for any emotion to stay in the body.

In principle, none of the emotions are required from a holistic perspective but in the physical realm, emotions are the language imbibed into the elements (five elements, which we are made of). It is a way to connect with the spirit to fulfill the task for which we are born.

This is what Buddhism talks about Madhya marg (middle path). Live in the moment. Feel the pain, if pain comes to you, laugh if you feel like it. Each of these will connect you with the spirit.

Nature of emotions is such that they either exist in the past or in the future and never in the present moment. The present moment is just a moment, filled with mystery and wonderment to be experienced. If there is no *belief* attached to the present experience, then the next moment will also be filled with mystery or wonderment. You often experience such moments briefly when you are on holiday and in nature. Such a moment will fill you with faith and will make you curious.

Worry, Anxiety, Panic: Emotions of the Future

We never worry about the past, but we worry about the future. Hence, this emotion belongs to the future. You are waiting for the school bus to arrive. It is three minutes late, you worry. You worry because you either do not trust the traffic conditions, or you do not have faith in your life. Although with your experience, you are aware that delays can happen, your basic nature is not to trust, again due to some *belief* or past experiences or the news you heard of a school bus accident the previous day in some country you cannot even spell the name of. Hence, you lose trust in the system or because your life has been full of so many unforeseen situations that you do not have faith in your life and you believe anything can go wrong at any time. These are your *belief*, which are triggered due to insufficient faith.

A few minutes later, your worry turns into anxiety. Anxiety is a higher frequency than worry. Worry is like a passive virus silently staying at the lower abdomen area eroding your excitement (*bliss*) of meeting your child. Gradually, as the state of joy of meeting your child begins to collapse, worry starts to rise as negative emotion and touches the peak in the form of anxiety. This is no more a passive response, and your joy has already collapsed and is now replaced by a negative *belief*. Till the time it was worry, your emotion remained an emotion. As it turned into anxiety, it could not be contained in an emotional layer and due to *belief*, it is now in your mental layer as well causing you anxiety of survival. It is now active by activating your mind to take some action. You feel unstable, and now you start to plan various actions, which you can take to ensure that you get the news about the whereabouts of the bus.

This is your ego. You believe you can take some action. Let some more time pass, if no information comes your way, you begin to turn hopeless, and your entire system feels like it's collapsing. You panic now. It is collapse of your Ego or your ability to survive.

All these emotions are a result of insufficient faith in the universe or trust in your life. Before moving further, let us understand faith and trust,

"Faith is trust in the unknown and trust is faith in the known."

You are in a loving relationship. You do not trust your partner, but you have faith in the relationship. You come from a background where you have seen a relationship working, or you have a belief that relationships is the way. You probably trust your love and faith in the relationship that one day, your partner will turn around. By having faith in the relationship, you are saying you believe in the relationship. But your partner is not so sensitive and not so trustworthy. You remain tolerant, patient and loving hoping and waiting that one day he/she will turn around. You continue to accept the relationship with its pain and *bliss* and would probably pursue some hobby or channelize your energies into something constructive.

However, what if you trust your partner but do not have faith in the relationship. You will turn insecure seeking the assurance, validation and approval in a good relationship. In spite of your partner doing everything for you, you will not be able to live in harmony and *bliss* with her/him. You probably have a background where people have always rejected you. If you are Indian, this is very common with the second girl child or you have low self-worth hence you do not feel comfortable with so much love coming from your partner and fear that someone better than you will take your partner from you. You trust your partner but you do not have faith that your relationship will last.

Let us take the example of the school bus. You have faith in yourself and you trust the traffic system. Let us say you live in Europe and not in India. In Europe, you have a credible public transport system and safety and security is the optimum. You trust the system, but if you do not have faith in yourself, even that is enough to give you anxiety. If you have faith in the universe and thus in your life, then even in Delhi, where trust in the system is rather low compared to in Zurich, you will not worry so much so soon.

Faith is, trusting the unknown. Future is unknown. Having faith means having faith in life, Universe (you may call it God). Trusting is having faith in the known. A person, a government, a system, you know you trust or do not trust.

When we lose faith, fear grips us for the next moment. Fear becomes the root of all negative emotions like worry anxiety, panic. This is where the mind (ego) depending upon how strong it is, is able to sustain the blow of these emotional states and survive. If it cannot, it sets up the ground for mental disorders.

The root cause of fear is the desire of the mind to defend and live with certainty. Hence, it plans so much for the future in order to avoid uncertainty of the future, which in its essence, is the basic nature of the future. So the more you look for certainty, the more fearful you become. If the mind is strong, you would do more planning and ways to control the future. This is the vicious circle, mind for survival is caught on and spirit is feeling squeezed.

Regret, Remorse, Repentance and Resentment: Emotions of the Past

These emotions from our past are stored in our emotional body and the mind can access these emotions at any point of time. Clearly, these emotions are based on your life experiences, and your *belief* created these emotions. You regret making the wrong choice in the past – like not pursuing sports and focusing on studies and career. You regret because you do not feel happy in the present moment due to the choices you made in the past. Remorse is different from regret. It is a feeling of regret with realization and carries the seed of reforming or correcting the mistake of the past, if judgment is removed from it. You regret that you played politics with your colleague and that killed his reputation making him lose his job. But you did it because you wanted to survive. However, you do not regret it till you are focused on survival because your *belief* that anything to survive is fine, does not allow you to access your emotional body in which there is regret. Once you retire, one day, it hits you and you feel the remorse of your wrong doing. You start teaching your children and others not to do such things. Hence, you are reformed. Reforming involves self-forgiveness, which comes on its own when we have a realization and accept the mistake. But if you start judging yourself for the mistake you made in the past, you repent doing it, and that triggers various emotions such as guilt, shame, unworthiness.

Resentment is all about feeling that someone has done you wrong. It is a feeling of being the victim and carrying the bitterness. It is the result of not owning your choices and having expectations from others.

All these emotions are triggered by *belief. Belief* is judgment. Unless you break the *belief*, there is no way, you can get rid of these emotions, and as long these emotions stay, whether you access them or not, they will continue to contaminate your spirit. There will be a day, when your spirit can not take it anymore, and it will surface in your body as disease or your landing up lonely, so that you can witness these choices and related negative emotions. This is what is happening to our generation now. Our spirit is seeking release for its expression in pure form because we have accumulated lot of repression and karma by not attending to our spirit. We are focused on "somehow" surviving and staying in the mind almost all the time. Love heals.

Fear, Guilt and Shame: Emotions of the Past

Every family, city, community and country has rules, called morality or values. They have a specific purpose – to create a more responsible *Survivor*. As a child, when I stole money from my father's pocket, it was an innocent act to me, so I did not feel guilty, till the thought of being caught with ice-cream came up. Hence, I first felt fear and that fear led me to feel shame, in case I was caught and it was made public to all family members. Over the next few days, nothing happened and I felt assured. That is where I began to feel guilty about it and thought of various other ways I would have quenched my need for ice cream. Morality is imposed on people to protect the value system.

Guilt is experienced by people when they break their own rules or morality as imposed by them on themselves. Making a promise to yourself to go for a walk in the morning to start a wellness program, or wanting to quit smoking, they feel guilty when they, in their own eyes, break their own rule or promise. In these cases, guilt does not become shame or fear as this is the internal process, but instead carries the potential of becoming regret, remorse or repentance.

If it remains as guilt, it erodes self-worth and your opinion about self begins to go down. If it persists, you feel more ashamed of yourself and turn hopeless, which is the brewing ground for depression and the beginnings of losing your mental balance. Hence, the confession box, offered by churches, were rightly designed to heal guilt and the job of the Pope was to transmute the hopelessness of the guilty into remorse, while offering assurance that he is accepted and not judged. Guilt, shame and fear are very deeply interconnected and one emotion gives rise to another one.

Note: Fear is the emotion that arises due to concern about the future but I had to mention it here due to its interconnectivity with guilt and shame. Besides construction of classifying the emotions in past and future is to help readers become literate about emotions and trigger an intellectual curiosity.

Placebo Effect and Healing:

Root of all negative emotions is insufficient faith. Fear is the first emotion of a *Survivor*, which comes due to lack of faith. To manage fear, it triggers various emotions and *belief* and leads to choices that are not authentic. Faith is hope and hope is a state in which all our negative emotions and *belief* begin to fall and a positive emotional state or higher frequency can be attained. Since the fall of religion a few centuries ago, as we began to hunt for security in the future, hope was replaced by a sense of certainty and was migrated from a state of being to mental stability pinning hopes in the form of the rational. If that certainty breaks, we turn hopeless. A lot of people, who felt certain that their property prices would only go up, when they lost their jobs, turned hopeless as all their plans to be certain fell apart. In the 2008 subprime crisis, people even committed suicide seeing no hope for the ability to bounce back. It is funny, people know that they have a private job, and it is not certain but they take huge loans from the bank for 20 years believing that they would feel secure and safe.

The placebo effect is not fake, but a real process of curing. It is not dependent on some sugar pill given externally, though that can be incidental as you place your faith in getting better through the pill. However, if you place faith in getting healed, you will get healed through whatever external process you adopt. What is important in healing and transformation is hope, which leads you to faith in self and the universe. When you have faith in the moment of hope, you begin to open up your emotional body. As you open up your emotional body, your mind begins to drop and negative emotions begin to leave your body free. This frees-up your mind of the *belief* and expands your consciousness. All of this happens to people at times without being aware, but it flows with their intent to get healed. Be careful as you read this. A lot of people believe that they have faith in some miracle or God and still die miserable and no cure works for them. In reality they own no responsibility for self and hold *belief.* They are driven by fear and not through wisdom. They carry ego that nothing can go wrong with them and they are rather angry when they say they have faith. Placebo is a very fine process where deep level faith exists and one may or may not be aware. A trigger like a sugar pill is an excuse for them to quickly drop all their *belief* and turn inward with faith. In fact you can say this book is all about how to make placebo effect work?

Placebo heals, but it needs some process or guidance or techniques, which makes faith work. The reason placebo is less probable to succeed is due to the rise in our ego. For faith needs ego to drop to allow access to your emotions, which have obscured the spirit like clouds do to the sun. This state of witnessing your karma, feeling your emotions is called a state of surrender. This puts us in a catch-22 situation. What shall come first? Drop of the ego or the restoration of faith. We would have no problem in having faith if that heals, but in our *suffering* it is very hard to trust faith. We will go to anybody who can solve our problems, and there's nothing like it if that gets solved without going anywhere. Hence, it is not correct to say we are very skeptic and hopeless and are blind about the scientific approach. For some reason, nothing has worked in the past, or it was misused by people whenever we placed trust in someone else or in faith. We turned to science in hope of a credible solution. Now that science is failing us, we are now becoming more hopeless looking for solutions outside and trying to find ways to find them inside. Hence, humanity as a whole is now ready to search for a solution which works for them every time, and they can fathom why and how. This is where this book is positioned. Not for blind believers at all, but for people who are ready to experiment and make their own realizations.

It is a very scary feeling to surrender. You begin to feel the fear of surviving as your definition of self, which you had crafted by hiding these emotions, begins to collapse. This is where this wisdom, that if you feel your emotions while observing your breath, shall come to rescue.

A classic example of faith comes from Indian mythological story of Meera Bai, a devotee of Lord Krishna who was given a cup of poison to test her faith towards her Lord. She drank it because she had absolutely no doubt in her devotion for the Lord. The poison did not do a thing to her.

In my seven years of working with people and helping them cure themselves, it was not very frequent but not uncommon to come across a family or a patient who had absolute faith in recovery or to bouncing back. Since almost every case was through reference, where they had seen recovery of someone, their trust in healing themselves was multiplied before coming to me. As they began to experience the cure, their trust turned into faith very quickly and such people have always scared me with their power of faith. They follow each word spoken by me so humor had no place. They were a delight to work with where effortless healing took place. In fact, they added a huge value to my research by helping me come up with new advanced techniques.

When you approach the treatment by practicing three techniques, be aware that you may feel hell for some time and if you stay with it and witness it, you shall see how it is changing your consciousness and healing you. All of this is carefully crafted in the techniques, and you can continue to remain skeptic but as long as you pursue these techniques, you will find that faith is developing on its own. This time your faith will be based on your experience as you witness relief and changes. Now this faith is not in anything outside you. You now do not need to have faith in science, logic, experiences and miracles of others, God and spirituality but in your experiences and in your commitment for your life purpose. You are now a spiritual being and turned inwards.

MENTAL BODY

"Mind has No Mind".

> **"Mind has no mind outside the need to survive. In its pure form, it is consciousness".**

People born with mental disabilities and child prodigies are two types of minds where very little mind can be developed to bring their awareness about physical reality albeit called normal, focused on survival. In case of mental disabilities, they are born with a fusion of the subconscious mind with the conscious mind and are pre-programmed to continue to experience certain states and emotions and feel stable and blissful. Outside these pre-programmed states, they have very little scope where they are open to any programming. They carry relatively weaker relationships with the physical world. Biological functions such as eating, sleeping, excretion and breathing are the only few functions for which they connect with the body and physical reality. Being God's own child, they remain in absolute *bliss* and pain.

A child prodigy is the same. In this case also, subconscious and conscious are integrated (not fused or pre-programmed) toward a vision and except very little connection to the physical reality, these children remain in the state of *bliss* pursuing their passion. If you do not intervene, they display the same tendency in their behavior as mentally disabled kids.

There is only one difference. In the first case, it is a compulsion and fusion is hardwired and in the second case it is a choice and integration is rather soft and fluid. There is a conscious choice to pursue a passion. This free will expands their aura so much that it brings *bliss* to everyone. For normal people falling in between the two, our journey is from compulsion to choice and for this reason, we have cultivated the mind in such a way that we pursue our passion and purpose for which we are born using free will. However, before that we have a duty to first take responsibility of our own lives, be on our own, in terms of our ability to survive and participate in the drama of life which says each one of us shall participate toward an organized evolution of humanity as a whole. For this, we built a set of *belief* by creating a need and organized various emotions and behavior which are acceptable within the framework set by respective culture in which we are born.

This is the reason why the mind has no mind beyond its purpose to help us survive in the physical form. While we are allowed to structure our definition of survival, that definition must comply to the norm of the culture or society in which we are growing up. If we take the example of the Indian caste system, traditionally, the mind of a Brahmin is not structured to being that of a warrior. It shall remain focused on growing the knowledge and acquiring wisdom like the ancestors did, and as written by the framework of religion and culture. If the child tries to pursue to learn the skills of a warrior, he is potentially trying to pursue a passion or curiosity, which would require him to break certain norms and rules. This normal child is then being aligned with the spirit pursuing to discover his purpose much like a child prodigy who is gifted with the same. This has huge implications first at an individual level to break free from the clutches of *belief* imposed and then at the family level. It is far more dangerous at the community level because now an example is being set, which if emulated by other Brahmin kids, would jeopardize the basic fabric of the community, and will change the course of evolution set for generations. There is also a fear and insecurity among parents as they feel helpless in supporting the child, who is deciding to do something for which they have no expertise to support the child, should he need the support. Fear of failure and a longer spell of owning the responsibility of the child while they are aging, forced parents to cultivate the mind of the child in such a way the child is able to do a basic minimum of what a child is capable of, so that the child can survive on his own, hence they encouraged their children to take the safest and certain route. Idea was to keep the child within the framework of certainty as much possible.A trader would encourage his son to become a trader than a painter and teacher would want his son to become a better teacher. This is safe and within control and it has very little respect to the wish and desire to pursue the purpose of life. Traditionally, there was no real need to develop the mind for survival as surviving was based on the trade you are involved in and since mostly it was about farming, which again was dependent on the nature, there was an increased incentive to look up at the sky and live with faith to mitigate the sense of uncertainty. People developed various ways to remain content within the means and hoped that the government, climate and priest were conducive to their survival and life continued to progress like this generation after generation. Hence there was nothing like cultivating mind only for survival. It was integrated with within conscious and subconscious.

Then, God played the dice and the Industrial Revolution happened. People discovered that survival can be guaranteed if they acquired the new skills. It made people choose certainly as it offered them choices by acquiring these new skills. The phrase, the sky is the limit, was then coined to offer hope and vision for people to discover their own infinite potential. The curiosity in discovering their own selves through religion, which was turning into a disappointment by then, found new direction to explore the mind and the world for the choices and possibilities it offered.

With all the good it has done for humanity, we are now dealing with the massive side effects of the Industrial Revolution, which is like a plague affecting the well-being of humanity across all religions, cultures, nationalities and finally age groups. We are under stress as a society in this globalized world. Below, are two diagrams (figure 8), which attempt to show you the difference between life before and after the Industrial Revolution through pie charts. Do not go by the size of the pie as there is no data here except your own lives, and you can adjust the size of the pie as per your truth. They are qualitative and not quantitative. You should be able to relate to the point I am making and understand where your majority of life force energy is going now to cause your suffering.

EVOLUTION SINCE INDUSTRIAL REVOLUTION

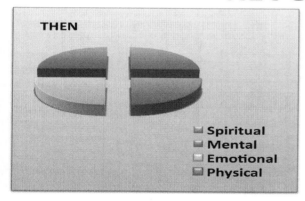
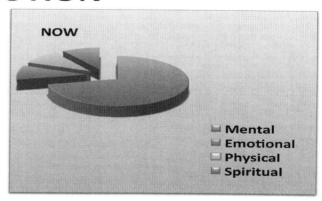

Figure 8 : Demonstration of difference in life now and before industrial revolution

Before the Industrial Revolution, uncertainty as a will of nature was acceptable, and yet life was a celebration after attaining certainty about basic survival with limited choices. People were together in their uncertainty because any natural intervention such as no rains, storms or flood affected all of them collectively.

Industrial revolution did two things. It first made survival uncertain unless they acquired new skills and second, it left people alone in their uncertainty. The binding force which brought communities and institutions of family together began to collapse and forced people to search for their own higher degree of certainty. This made humanity discard every other aspect of their life and strive to reach the sky by staying in their minds most of the time. Life is no more a celebration or a journey but ambition to feel secure and certain and this has caused an imbalance in the Spirit-Body-Mind. In many ways, we have fused our subconscious and consciousness to continue to remain in one state – a state of *suffering* to seek certainty and are disabled to experience anything else. So who is really mentally disabled?

Survival is not just related to making money and buying food, but also extends to emotional and spiritual survival, which has come under threat due to strained relationships with the self and its reflection in all our relationships.

Holistically speaking, the Industrial Revolution reflects the laws of nature. Our journey in life is to lose the innocence and *bliss* of childhood, become aware of the physical world, participate and contribute in the evolution, gain wisdom, retire, detach from the physical world and pass that wisdom to the next generation. This is what the Industrial Revolution has done to humanity. It has made each one of us responsible for the self and put us on our inner journey.

Insecurity, fear and needs, which defined the basic fabric of interdependency. Institutions of family and society were created to support these needs. In new age, we are going to build a community of being together for each other in each individual's own inner journey. This will form the new age institutions through compassion and wisdom.

We have come a long way in evolution since then. Now information is a commodity, and knowledge is no more a premium. We have participated in bringing everyone to a connected global community and are now looking at a massive convergence of communities and democratization of power through digital innovations. The dark has been been good at organizing together traditionally. Fear binds us, but this is the first time the light (good) is coming together and becoming a force. The work for the next generations now is about extracting wisdom through the infinite information and knowledge we have created in the last few decades. This is how humanity will find hope to accelerate evolution having suffered the side effects of the Industrial Revolution in transition in which you and I live. For any culture or civilization much like for individuals, to make a quantum jump in their living, it must go through a life cycle of ignorance to information, information to knowledge and knowledge to wisdom. Once it arrives at the wisdom, it triggers a tipping point for a quantum jump in the evolution of the consciousness.

The most beautiful aspect of wisdom is - it triggers on its own, selflessness and detachment and grows compassion, that cannot be blocked by anyone or anything. Fruits of wisdom can never be contained by a wise person for self. The very basic nature of wisdom is to treat the whole world as one within. We were ignorant about the apple falling from the tree, till Newton brought this information forward and landed up with the discovery, which became wisdom to cause a quantum jump in the consciousness of humanity. Of course, half of the global population is yet to participate and be integrated to the connected world. This is where the new-age government and organizations will find their business models and individuals like you and I will find our purpose.

However, in this book we deal with the side effects, which has affected the well-being of the people. If we do not reverse it, there is very little hope for humanity to be able to capitalize on its hard work of the last three hundred years or so.

The problem with the mind is that our mental capabilities are infinite and only our imagination is our limitation, we are trapped in the whirlpool of thoughts. The challenge in acquiring skills is that it has a lower shelf-life due to a rapid evolution in the digital era.

As a child, we are timeless and ageless. We live in the moment and do not understand the timetable of life. There is no day, and there is no night for us to cry, laugh and eat or to excrete unless it is cultivated in us by our parents. Cultivation of these habits is the cultivation of the mind. This triggers a movement of energies to be brought to reality toward an organized evolution by respecting the needs of the physical body for which the mind is programmed with *belief*. If the soul needs the spirit to be in *bliss*, then it has no option but to discover *bliss* in the needs of the physical body in which time to time the physical realm demands. This means then to leave the *bliss* and to take care of its needs. Organized evolution through various *belief*, a representation of rituals, morality, and values was intended that one can then experience *bliss* while fulfilling the needs of the physical body.

A child is either in *bliss* or in pain and in an ideal perfect scenario, going through both frequencies. A child stabilizes in a specific range of frequency closer to *bliss* unless interrupted by some memory of the past, due to which the child begins to either cry or laugh. The nature of our organized evolution is such that we must not let a child be extremely happy or in extreme pain. We get uncomfortable when someone is in pain. Pain being a transformative frequency, which brings detachment, is very risky for the ecosystem.

But not everything happened as per the holistic vision and wisdom, which existed with our ancestors thousands of years ago, and the gradual erosion in the wisdom was the natural outcome from one generation to the next generation as various cultures began to interfacing with each other across the globe. Post Industrial Revolution, wisdom actually began to be replaced by fear, and that is where damage has occurred to our well-being which is now being reflected in our health.

We have a choice to cultivate the mind through wisdom or through fear. We have learned from the examples of the child who is fascinated by the flame and from the child who is hurt on the leg, in previous chapters, how we inflict fear by killing the curiosity and then the natural instinct to experience pain to make the child be better as a *Survivor*. In this way, our mind is cultivated through induction of fear, which gave us a sense of inadequacy to acquire better skills to survive and excel. This got us trapped to stay in the mind. Since fear is an emotion, it is irrational and is beyond time, and we can call it a quantum state of vibration. As long as we are vibrating in this state, This will keep firing thoughts to search for faith in name of certainty and this is why a chase for excellence and to be better than others is an infinite irrational process followed by people who worshiped logic, science and technology in name of modernity. There is no way, we can obtain well-being unless we realize that first we need to deal with our fears and sense of inadequacy. This means accepting self where we are, which will give us faith and will reduce activity of the mind to trigger movement towards restoring Spirit-Body-Mind.

We are learning this through trial and error. We are becoming wiser about ourselves through mistakes when we find ourselves acutely lonely, relationship break ups and finally through diseases and various others forms of *sufferings*. Only in these moments of failures, are we forced to re-visit our *belief* about ourselves. More often than not, we are so badly trapped that even if we gain insight and wisdom, we are seldom able to come out of our misery which has been created by the mind. When Einstein said that problem can not be solved by the the mindset that created them means that fear driven mind even if it gains knowledge about the solution can not solve it unless the mind comes from the position of wisdom. This is where family and communities worked together to heal each other, solve the problem through wisdom and now we are turning inward to tap into the inner wisdom to do the same or by becoming a digital community and family to tap into insights and wisdom.

This exactly is the reason, being positive or positive thinking as advised often does not work. The whole premise of the mind is to regulate or control emotions. I am feeling insecure about my job, and I have all kinds of negative thoughts managing this fear of survival. My friends advise me to be positive and have faith. How would I change my insecurity by thinking positive? My fears do not change by thinking positive if at all I am capable of thinking positive in that state. All negative thoughts are result of this hopelessness which turned into fear and became insecurity. But if I had faith, then I would not feel insecure in the first place. To be positive, I can not do anything at the mind level, but by raising my vibration to arrive at hope, then positive thoughts will come on their own.

The fear-driven mind, in which we are trapped, cannot be healed by creating another *belief*. This will only make the mind more complex and will trap our energies further. If we have to deal with this, then we will have to deal with our fears. We cannot deal with the fears by directly taking fears head-on, but by moving towards wisdom. Wisdom is deep inside us, and that can be accessed by us by turning inwards, which is what is taught to you in this book. A process to shift your consciousness effortlessly towards wisdom.

It looks as if it is a huge task, but this is where the techniques will help you. It is an automatic process if you just pursue the techniques, then you will realize that your mind is now purified. During the time when you are practicing the techniques, allow your mind to continue to have its own negative patterns, thoughts and *belief*. Continue to add *bliss* to your daily routine through the techniques and gradually within week, you will begin to sense that you are incapable of thinking the way you used to think negatively or react in a specific situation.

In summary, there are two approaches, either fear-based or wisdom- based. Wisdom is always within us. It is a product of insight turning into awareness and by staying with awareness, knowledge transforms into wisdom on its own. To do this, we only need to connect with the mystery so insights begin to flow.

It does not downplay the importance of information and knowledge. You will always need all that knowledge you have acquired but application of knowledge for your good and for the larger good is having wisdom in which you will have to use your insights.

Let us further understand the implications of the mind through the example of the child who has a pain in the leg. The child is told boys don't cry and they are supposed to be brave. If the child has strong will power, which means a stronger need to survive which means he has to be now nice to parents and society – to show that he is brave, he will suppress his pain. This will make him immune and insensitive toward his pain and gradually towards emotions of others as well because he knows he has to be brave and so does everyone else. As an adult, his partner wants him to be gentle, caring and expressive, and this boy does not know how to express correctly. He only knows how to ask for his needs to be fulfilled.

Let us take another example from the other side to better understand the mind.

From the last chapter we know how you respond to the child who is trying to go into higher state of *bliss* crossing the boundary of *bliss* we operate upto. In reverse direction we feel again very insecure if the child tries to go into a deeper state of pain than we can handle. You fear that if you allow the child to feel this sadness, he will get into depression and will escape from his responsibilities. Hence, you do everything to distract the child from feeling sadness and find a way to engage his mind into something else with the intent to bring his focus on survival. Many more thoughts and *belief* are now invented to manage the emotion, and his sadness is trivialized. The way it happens to you in happiness that you feel tired beyond a point to sustain that higher frequency, you have the same problem to be with your child as he goes into deeper states of the sadness toward pain. Again, your own *belief* becomes a barrier to not let your child go into the frequency you cannot pull him out from. It is an unknown zone for you. Child will be alone if he goes into the pain deeper than the frequency at which you have put a limit for yourself and now want to pass on to the child the same limit so that you can be of help to him within a known or comfortable range of frequencies. It hurts your ego to see sadness in the child because you feel worthless if the child feels pain because of your *belief* that you are doing everything for the child, so how can he be sad to the point that you are helpless in helping the child? Since you grew up seeking certainty discarding faith, you want to make sure your child also gets the same and do not allow him to trust his own self or to teach him to have faith. Though the solution is very simple. If you hold the space for the child in that moment, child will go deep and will bounce back with insights.

This is the problem, which I explained above is erosion of wisdom. We do not share our experiences with our children. We do not share the mistakes we made. We do not share our learnings because we want to portray the image of being perfect. We pass on our *belief*, our limitation and our fear by forcing the child to follow our instructions and not have any experiences on their own and want the child to be a world leader. It is like dragging a car without the wheels into a formula one race.

Many years ago, a close friend was sharing how she is not happy with her marriage. She went on and finally said, "I have told my daughter not to get married as marriage does not bring happiness." Assuming she is right, and marriage was bad for her – which of course is not the case for all of us living in and out of marriage – she should have told her daughter about her journey, her expectations, her own mistakes in the relationship with a note like, "I hope, when you are in a relationship, you do not commit the same mistakes." She should have passed on the wisdom she acquired through the relationship and should have given her daughter confidence to pursue her choices by incorporating her own learning.

Now this daughter is *suffering*. Her nature wants her to be curious about relationships, and her *belief* from the mother is not to go for it. Now she is *suffering* when she meets a boy and and is attracted to him. Her instinct says he is good, but her mother has told her that relationships are not good. Assuming she decides to get into the relationship not out of love but out of compulsion, she remains cautious and reluctant to open her heart which does not allow her to be totally present in the relationship. It is now a compromise to live for survival which is safe and fills the minimum needs.

Every compromise means reducing hope. This means less curiosity. This would need extra *belief* to support such lower level of hope. This means that now mind needs to further work in managing new emotions. This means now you need more oxygen in your mind and stay more in mind but spirit very much wants to experience life. So either we develop shame or guilt or make it dark by hiding it and still doing it. This shrinks the amplitude within which we were vibrating before to be stable with new set of *belief* which are managing few more negative emotions inside. Gradually, this continues to shrink and we we turn flat, numb and feel bored with life and its status quo. In electrical engineering, in which I am qualified, it is called converting AC current to DC current. This state of flat frequency, when we want to break free from or when the baggage carried by the spirit is very high and wants to erupt for its expression, turns into bipolar disorder like a tuning fork being hit to the rubber pad. It is now vibrating at a high frequency zone of *bliss* and pain but without any control and free will. (See figure 9.)

AC TO DC STATE CONVERSION

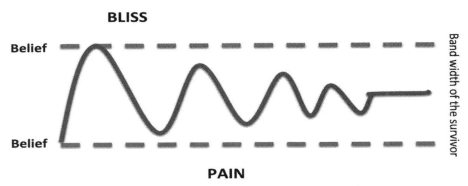

Figure 9 : How we are turning monotonous by not feeling safe to experience emotions

The reason why we have mental disorders spreading almost like an epidemic is because of this fear-based mind, which is increasingly occupied to keep our spirit (and emotions) under control which mind is not able to take anymore. This requires a very strong mind (EGO) to continuously manage the spirit or we can say that due to lack of support system the level of ego we developed so far is not able to keep the emotions under control anymore. The time and space in which we live now, humanity is continuously moving toward more free will to experience authenticity, unless one has a very strong ego, suppression of spirit is not supported by the energies and ecosystem in which we live. If our need to survive does not make sense or it goes down at any point of time, we discover that many emotions which were suppressed begin to surface. This is the reason, people keep inventing one work or another so that they are never free to face their own self. Through this, they are able to avoid mental disorders, but they fall trap to disease or distress because now the body is not able to contain it and through disease, it brings the attention on the issues faced by the spirit.

Mental disorder is a state in which behavior, thought or emotion occurs on its own, without any control of our mind, and it interferes with normal functioning of our lives. By this token, each one of us has a tendency towards a mental disorder as we do have certain situations in which some emotions are triggered on their own. The best and simplest example is a burst of anger, which is unexpected but happened and we regret later. If occurrences of such episodes grow in its intensity, periodicity and time interval, we will be labeled as *suffering* with mental disorder.

This is the reason, reversing mental disorders has been simplest with the techniques presented in this book. The most complex mental disorders have been brought under control within a week. As we restore the breathing and at times manually release the emotions stuck in the body to quicken the recovery to open up the breath, the mind begins to stabilize and release the repressed emotion, which happens on its own as breathing is restored. When emotions are released, then the mind, which has been extra occupied to keep them under control has no stress as there is nothing to manage now. It is like the CPU of mobile phone or computer where you have opened up many apps or tabs. Now, the processor needs to allocate its resources to keep those apps under control and due to this, resources are allocated to manage all these apps and is not available to register the experiences of the moment. Your attention span on any issue goes down as in the analogy of CPU, Its attention goes in managing the apps running in the background than being present in the present moment. This is the issue our children are facing – lack of focus. This is because they are managing a lot of apps in the background, such as not feeling loved, feeling insecure seeing parents fighting or feeling pressure of studies. This is burdening their spirit, which wants to be in *bliss*. The mind which is managing apps uses resources by consuming breath and leaving lesser amount available for the body.

Learning through fear helps a mind remain focused on survival as long as the need to survive is strong enough and learning through wisdom creates awareness about life including survival. Such awareness is the creation of consciousness. Hence, consciousness is larger than the mind and it still includes issues related to survival. Mathematically, the mind is a subset of consciousness. Consciousness is driven by wisdom, and the mind is driven by information and knowledge. The knowledge is a subset of wisdom.

The mind has no mind beyond its need to help us survive. It does not matter what the definition of survival is. For someone, INR 100 is enough to secure their survival. Therefore, this person will work toward that and for his brother it could be INR 1000, so he will work accordingly. They both have the same *belief*, hence their struggle is the same. At the energy level it is the same effort.

With time, our fear-based living continues to use a larger part of our mind to keep our true spirit through emotions under control. This causes wear and tear inside our body and triggers rapid aging. With resources in our hand, to break free from the monotonous bandwidth,we indulge either in entertainment to make our mind believe that we are good or we seek expression of our spirit, through alcohol, drugs, sex and seeking various relationships where we feel adequate. Both ways, we are counting our miles on the treadmill without travelling any distance.

The growing trend of such a mindset, is now surfacing in the form of dementia. When you feel you have survived enough, which means you have finished all your responsibilities for which you had cultivated your mind in the name of surviving, you no longer feel the need to keep emotions suppressed. Your mind is now obsolete in its function. This feeling of obsolescence and irrelevance which has creeped into you at your ripe age makes you seek some relevance by wandering in moments of the past which you did not live fully due to the pressure of survival. The present moment holds no promise, the future looks bleak and the sense of purpose is missing. Going back to old memories is juicy and gives a sense of adequacy. This is dementia. Parkinson's is when emotions are seeking expression and the mind is not letting them come but is weak enough to not be able to keep them suppressed, hence the body turns stiff and it shakes when you move. Release the pressure on emotions, offer a safe environment, and you shall find shaking of the body going away. Reversing Parkinson's is not even an issue. Try treatment processes (Section 3) for a week and see the difference without doing anything.

The cultivation of the mind, which is trained to survive is called ego. Ego is nothing but a program of your mind, which acts as a gatekeeper for your emotional body. This means that if there is an emotion, which is triggered by someone or a situation, which threatens your definition of survival, you will defend your point of view or your definition about yourself to feel stable.

If you tell me that I am not an honest person, and I believe I am an honest person, then this can hurt me and shatter my *belief* about myself. As this *belief* shakes, it will trigger so many emotions proving me wrong in my own eyes. All my life I defined myself as an honest person and it gave me great sense of adequacy, this actually has been my driver to survive. Your view about me clashes with my *belief* about myself. It now risks breaking down my existence.

I have many options to deal with this situation. I can take this as input and introspect, but for that I need to be wise enough and open to such a situation. I can outright defend myself and may even attack you in order to defend. I may run away from you and never see you again or tolerate what you said and show no reaction but to sulk in private. However, if I take your opinion seriously and it means a lot to me, I may lose my worthiness and keep drowning in my various emotions causing me depression. If so, I do not have an ego because I could not defend my survival. Everything else and everyone else matters to me more than me. If I defend myself, that means I have a good ego, and if I attack in defense, I have an over-inflated ego.

The higher the ego, the more you are out of touch with your inner-self and better at surviving, potentially at the expense of others. A lower or fragile ego means the inability to defend and that is where it is brewing ground for a mental disorder. You have a risk here that you may not be able to recover from the hurt and continue to question yourself. You may get stuck in the conflict between emotions and thoughts causing a deadlock of your energies and sucking all your life force energy affecting three pillars of well-being i.e. breathe, sleep and sexuality. If you can absorb and rationalize this input and bounce back with more learning from this episode, this is where role of your consciousness is coming to the forefront. This means other than surviving, your mind is sensitive about the grey and dark areas of your self as well as awareness that you are not perfect human being. this is the reason, we get deeply hurt in close and loving relationships because we are emotionally available to them and see no need to defend and define. The fights between brother and sister in the childhood are a beautiful example to reflect a trusting deep level of love and care for each other but hurting each other does not cause hurt or need to defend for long. They soon drop their ego because they have basic acceptance for each other unconditionally anyway.

This experience can give you a glimpse into how a fragile ego can trigger distress, and if the impact of such events is much bigger than your ability to defend it may lead into a disorder. If you have a well groomed ego to protect yourself, then you either have an issue with emotional distress or it holds a potential for disease one day.

It does not mean ego is good or bad. It is clear that you need ego to survive and defend yourselves. But like you do not sleep wearing your formal clothes, you do not wear your defensive guard all the time. You must have moments of reflection within and that needs ability to drop the ego and be very neutral to review yourself. When you are hurt by people, by all means go and defend yourself. Come home, introspect and heal that aspect. In a workshop, I teach people to make three circles. The outermost circle is your business or work environment, middle circle is your intimate family and friends, and the third one is your own inner-self. Your ego is very strong in the outermost circle. It is more flexible in the middle circle, and there is no ego when you face yourself. This way, you will only become more and more authentic.

Let us understand how the process of spirit works to defeat the mind in how it shows up. Take any of the examples that you have experienced, Fever, stomach ache or a headache, and I am not yet talking of the diabetes, cancer and thyroid. Let me take the example of a fever. You are doing an important task at work, and you have fever – a mild one. You begin to notice that your body is now out of sync with your mind. The speed at which you want to work, body is not supporting you, but because work is important, and you must finish by tomorrow, you continue to push through. In a few hours, it increases to 102/103F and now you are not able to even think the way you were thinking. You find it hard to continue to work. You delegate your duties and your attention is now on your body and the discomfort you are experiencing. Just few moments before this, you were so charged up with something so important, which is now not even in your thoughts any more. Now you are feeling overwhelmed by fever and only one thought or actually no thought but an emotion is being experienced as to how to get out of it.

A strong mind is not a strong mind any more if it is not in harmony with spirit. This is the relationship of the mind with health. When your consciousness remains limited to the mind and ignores the emotions and physical body and its needs, your spirit revolts. Since the spirit must find its way, it reminds you by bringing your attention to the body. This is what happens to people when they have chronic diseases like blood pressure and diabetes. Each moment, they are reminded to be conscious of their body but to be more precise to be conscious of their spirit, which is by now contaminated by belief and needs to be restored. High blood pressure means feeling guilty for being angry. Hence, it remains stuck in your blood, neither suppressed nor released.

There is only one purpose of distress, disorder and disease: It is supposed to bring you in touch with your spirit and bring you in touch with all the toxins in the form of *belief* and emotions, which have accumulated over a lifetime – actually several lifetimes. Since, this is a convergence age and the egocentric evolution has hit its peak and time is here now for good to get organized, we are seeing an epidemic of *suffering* (distress, disease and disorder) spreading across all age groups. We can not be demanding transparency and accountabilities from the governments and institutions without we ourselves first becoming authentic. Some are choosing to be and others are forced to look within as a result of their *sufferings*.

Consciousness is directly proportional to health. The larger your consciousness is, the better your health is. In fact, it is well-being all across the three layers. Consciousness being driven by wisdom will always include expression of spirit in its activities. If you ignore your consciousness and remain fixed in your mind, it finds a way to help you realize where you are at, and discomfort in the body is one of the ways in which it does that. This is why Ayurvedic system had lifestyle as one of the pillars of preventative medicine. In this lifestyle, when they spoke about aligning with nature, worshiping and Yoga, the purpose was to align the spirit, body and mind albeit meditation, to remain healthy and in union with nature before starting your day for survival.

Having understood the role of the mind and how it is developed, let us look at what consciousness and subconsciousness, and unconsciousness is. Consciousness is what you are aware of and not what you know. One day, you decide to buy a new car. This time it is Hyundai, a change from the Honda you drive now. As you step out of your house for work in your Honda, you notice Hyundai cars more than any other brands of car. You have just become more aware of Hyundai and your attention goes to the billboards of Hyundai. You begin to read about the specifications and features of the car on the internet. Suddenly, your consciousness is expanded, and your mind has thoughts about making a decision and manifesting this decision. Now your mind has an expanded view about cars. Let us further expand your consciousness by saying that you want to buy a new car, and you do not know which one is good. When you drive today on the same route, you discover various brands of cars, and you start to read about each one as well as compare technical details. Now you have a huge knowledge and using your insight, you shortlist a few and buy one brand. The knowledge about the rest of the cars is now gone into the subconscious.

Your computer has RAM. It has a certain capacity (let us say 16GB), and you have a 500GB hard disk. Your RAM is your consciousness. Your hard disk is your subconscious, and when you store your emails (mail server) on the cloud; that is unconsciousness. The moment you log into your mail account, all your data pops up from somewhere.

Unconsciousness is a huge ocean which stores all the wisdom and history since the origin for all humanity much like the mail clouds, which saves data for billions of people in one common place. So, origin of your soul and life before that is in its unconsciousness, and it is a mystery to the greatest of the seers to decode. Even if it is not, it is out of scope for our book as our concern is not to find a God but to find health.

The subconscious is where the data of your past from this birth as well as from all previous births is stored. It has all your *belief* stored, which actually forms your tendency and trajectory, and on the basis of your trajectory, you are reborn into a specific family for a specific task.

Consciousness, which is RAM has more to do with the present moment and physical reality. Depending upon what tabs are open on your browser, that is what you are aware of and that is what your mind is on in that moment. If you close a tab, then all activities of that tab are now gone in the hard disk (subconscious). You click another tab and your consciousness shifts to the information and data related to that page. If it reminds you of your old times and you like to look at a picture stored in your hard disk, you begin to access your subconscious and bring that into your consciousness. That is how we keep switching between the conscious and the subconscious and have the ability to read and write, edit our impressions, learnings and experiences. Nothing is fixed. Each time you access old memories, you may learn a bit more about it and that expands your consciousness by making you more aware of the hidden perspective about the same thing.

But the subconscious is always much larger than we think it is. There is very limited information we are able to bring from it and keep in our consciousness. We only know it for whatever information we can quickly recall – a few childhood memories, our trauma, trophies and first love, so to say. But if we want to find out more detailed information about what else is stored, we close the browser and go to the hard drive in the file manager tab and access each folder, files and so on.

Let us understand the functioning and correlation of consciousness and the subconscious a little better.

You had a good time with your friend some time ago and laughed a lot, taken some pictures and selfies. The next day you forgot all about it and went to work. These pictures are now in your hard disk. When you go to the photo app or gallery, you see the pictures, but not your word document which has the termination letter from your employer which is also stored on the same hard drive. So it depends what you wish to access from your subconscious.

Now, when you see pictures, the first impression is that it feels good to see smiles and laughter. Then you remember the joke and recall the whole event. Remembering the joke and recalling the event is also stored in the subconscious and you can access it without actually seeing the picture, but by visiting that space in that time, it automatically surfaces. This is the function of your conscious mind which is now staying in that space of the past and allowing all the memories to surface.

Now imagine this picture is with your first love with whom you have had a good time, but you had a nasty breakup later on. You happen to see this picture again, but the same picture does not bring a smile on your face and does not give you joy. Why? Because you created the *belief* that you were stupid to love him so much. He was a liar and so on. But this *belief* is not in that picture. It is by now in your conscious, which you have tagged later on with all the memories about him. So each time you recall any good memories with him, this tag called *belief* is invoked from the conscious and changes your emotions about your memories.

Now go one step further and see that picture thirty years later. It brings back the smile again. It brings the same tag of "being stupid to love him", but this time, none of it affects you. You are fifty and wiser and your consciousness has evolved. You have just one *belief* now. Teenage years were crazy. So many stupid things we did. Now you smile not with the picture but at yourself, and then you probably call him and you laugh about your stupidity.

In these years, your consciousness expanded, and your *belief* changed about life and that changed your view about memories or in other words, it changed your subconscious or your past. The subconscious is your heart and consciousness is the mind. It is yin and yang – male and female.

The consciousness of the person *suffering* (distress, disorder, disease) shrinks and remains focused on the *suffering*. Take the example of a fever – once it is high and you can function no more, the mind turns numb, and you only have one thing in your consciousness and that is that you want to feel better. This is the exact reason why expansion of consciousness is directly proportional to well-being and health.

The mind, which is focused on survival with time turns very complex and fragile. On one hand it has to work extra each passing day to keep spirit under control, on another hand, it has to continue to justify that it is stable and everything is fine. This is the reason, we are traveling more to break away from our mind to expand our consciousness or drinking more to numb the mind and feel some emotions or seek more entertainment to break free from the issues of survival and somehow trying to keep ourselves healthy.

Is there a way, rather than waiting to turn fifty or being caught by any form of *suffering*, we can expand our consciousness? If so, we not only prevent *suffering* but also become wiser and more joyful. Meditation is the way to do it.

Expansion of consciousness in our life means bringing subconscious to the conscious. This means becoming aware of everything in our past and the various emotions, trauma and *belief*. Access of the subconscious into the conscious can only happen when the mind is empty and is devoid of thoughts. That means we reach a stage where our mind has no thoughts, so that whatever is stored in the subconscious begins to surface and clears up the trauma and old *belief*. The techniques given in Section 3 makes it an effortless process.

ENERGY BODY

*E*very experience leads to some emotion, and if it is a negative experience, it will create discomfort. If this discomfort is not dealt with and is kept for too long, it will destabilize you. This is where the mind will come to try to manage this emotion and put you into survival mode. You will develop a *belief* such that you feel stable with the experience which means suppressing and containing it within unless a child who would feel pain and bounce back to *Bliss.* You are hurt in love. You will keep feeling hurt and restless till you develop a *belief* such as no one loves you or love is not for you or any other *belief* which makes you stable. To be stable means now you are comfortable with whatever emotions this *belief* gives you such as grief, self-pity and worthlessness. Every emotion has a frequency at which it vibrates, meaning the energy level at which it is at. This is what *belief* does. It creates an energy field within which you vibrate and then attracting incidences and people who validate this *belief.* Now you feel you are right and stable. This is the exact purpose of a *belief* to allow you to feel stable and keep you within a specific range of emotions in which you feel your existence and that you are right. Once you vibrate in specific zone of frequencies, you start to create to attract experiences which create a reality which resonates well with your vibratory zone. You never really question that other people who have gone through the same experience do not have the same reality. You never realize that they are different and better off because they do not have a limiting *belief* like you. I had a phobia of driving and felt like I could not drive a car. I asked myself just one question – how come for so many years; so many people are able to drive, but I can't? I broke that phobia though in a very dangerous ways. Of course, it was very dreadful to go through the process of breaking it. I did not know any techniques which now you have access to. Since then, I am very proud of my driving and feel very joyful for the long hours of driving which I have been able to do so in different countries.

The law of attraction then works to manifest only those experiences, which will validate your own internal vibratory planes. Any experience outside your *belief* system will make you unstable If it is positive experience, you will call it miracle. The miracle is nothing but a vibratory level manifestation which is beyond our level of vibratory level. For example, it is routine for us to see people walking out of our centre healthy within hours, so I can say miracles are routine for us though for the science presented here, it is just normal and routine and within the range of my *belief* system..

If you believe no one loves you and someone comes your way to show you love, you will feel unstable. After failing to run away, you would want to give up your *belief* but will constantly seek assurance and get the proof of love from the person. You will be in a loving relationship but not feel loved and will suffer due to conflict between your own *belief* versus your inability to deny love. Regardless, you either seek to be stable with your *belief*, or change a *belief* and seek stability with a new reality. This is why when at the mental level we make resolutions and decisions not backed by our *belief*, we struggle to manifest them. Breaking a *belief* requires gaining wisdom and learning the purpose of the event (you will do that effortlessly using the third technique – NV Hunting). The energy field created is driven by our *belief* and for many lifetimes, we have an endless list of *belief* which has limited our energy to not let us have access to our infinite potential to gain access to infinite energy within.

In reality we have multiple *belief*, some limiting (negative) and some liberating (positive), we continue to oscillate between that spectra of energy. For example, you are scaling up your business. Each time, you reach a new high, you find some obstacles or it crashes. You build again and it now is a pattern. Take another example, you come home after a very successful day at work, feeling motivated to spend quality time with the family and your spouse picks on you. In both the cases conflicting *belief* is in play. In the first case, you could have a *belief* in your capability to build a successful business or career and yet have a subconscious level *belief*, which is the fear of success. You feel you may lose a part of yourself if you become successful and you will not have time for yourself. In the second case, on one hand, you could have a *belief* that the family is important and you want to nurture it, on the other hand, there could be a subconscious *belief* such as; my happiness does not last long or no one appreciates me or I am lonely or no one loves me.

You can put aside this book for a moment and feel your own energy field by doing an experiment for a few minutes or for few days, depending upon how well you like to do it. The process is simple – list down all your needs. You know from the chapter *Origin of Belief* that 'need' is the mother of all *belief*, which originates from the lack of faith. This experiment is to bring our subconscious *belief* into awareness. It is the way to unlock infinite energy. Through this process, where you can sit on each *belief* everyday once for a few minutes, you will heal yourself so much that you probably will not need to read the rest of the book or learn any technique. So what is happening to you in the process?

By listing down your needs, you are clearing up huge subconscious memories, which comprise the unknown and known *belief* and most of them are in conflict with your conscious reality. I grew up like anyone else that after doing engineering, I will buy an apartment to live in, save tons of money and retire at forty and then lead a life of purpose. Very early on I took to entrepreneurship breaking one belief after another, but one belief was hanging loose and that was that I will have my own house. It was irrational because every few years I have changed city, countries and profession. All my friends had bought one and gradually even my employees had bought theirs. Even the jobless people, whom I coached into getting a job, soon had their own apartment. One day, I sat down with this *suffering*, which used to surface once in awhile and one day I let that need go. I saw a vision of being free at the cost of shifting apartments now and then. This liberated me – more acceptance came – which was way different from mainstream people. I started enjoying my money and invested in wiser instruments and had better returns than my friends who were paying a mortgage every month, who ended up in my workshop for transformation. I chose health, freedom and the future for my children over stability, pride and security. I was in any case of this *belief* but my subconscious caused so much stress, it conflicted with my consciousness. Now, I have unbound energy to pursue what I wish to without any internal conflict.

Let us say your *belief* is that life is tough and you need to work hard for your money. Start to feel what happens if you do not work hard. Observe your breath and feel it. Keep experiencing the various emotions that it brings up. Let us say the fear of dying, the shame that your family will consider you useless, a guilt that you are making your children suffer, all plans for the future being shattered, turning hopeless and so on. So, you feel fear, guilt, shame, worthlessness, hopelessness etc. Feel these emotions while observing your breath. These emotions have a frequency zone in which it keeps you vibrating and because of it, you continue to work hard for your money.

It may sound like you are turning into a *Mystic* by doing this. You are not wrong, but in reality, it is making you better at surviving. You can imagine through this process that now you cannot encounter any unfortunate situations in the future as there is nothing in your subconscious, which is seeking to manifest and bring attention to your consciousness. You will feel more empowered to pursue your need but without generating negative emotions or dark energy. You are now vibrating at a higher frequency. Start with food, then sex, money, love, appreciation, security in your old age, respect in society and so on. Define your need for survival without which you feel like you are dying or feel you are worthless. When you feel hungry, delay food and feel hungry for a few minutes, while observing the breath and watch what emotions and expectations arise that food fulfills for you. When you are hungry, you have just one thought – how to eat and survive but to survive, each one of us may have very different set of *belief*. This exactly, is the reason every culture or religion has a ritual of fasting. Fasting is a process through which we discover our hidden *belief* and attachment to life.

The other important aspect, traditionally, has been worshiping or praying. However for mystics, it is meditating. Faith is the highest quantum level and when we meditate, it raises our vibratory level. At a higher level, low level emotions and the corresponding *belief* hidden in the subconscious cannot exist as they cannot vibrate at a higher level and begin to show up in the consciousness. As we witness this *belief*, it clears the subconscious and expands our consciousness, making us wiser about the self. In addition to this, as *belief* breaks down and our energy field opens up, it heals the effect of karma. Karma is nothing but *belief* created and judgement made. This is why, your religion always said that come to God, and he only can heal your karma (sin), he will forgive you and liberate you. Spirituality said, expand your consciousness, you will be free from the cause and effect of karma. This is the process that happens internally and for that, you do not need to be in a church or a temple.

The mind as a regulator of emotions, by default, becomes the regulator of energy. Be fear driven or wisdom driven, mind can regulate anger into humor and humor can be turned into joy. You can arrive at wisdom through fear in a split moment. Take road rage. You get wild at someone. He comes out of his car with a gun. You apologise and come home and reflect on the value of your life which could have gone for something as stupid as lack of patience or tolerance. You become wiser that all of it is not worth your energy. Very often, we find elderly people being able to transmute their lower frequency emotions into higher frequency emotions, due to the wisdom acquired over the years. The transmutation of anger into *bliss* or mentally switching off anger and diverting your attention, are two very different things. In the first case, it is the path of surrender where you are first becoming aware of your *belief* and patterns, which expands your consciousness, and then through its acceptance you become aware how it holds your energy. As you become aware, you become wise and fears drop. In such scenarios, you can sense a quantum jump in your energies quite instantaneously. You will do all of this effortlessly by following the three techniques. As you read this chapter, start becoming aware of yourself.

In the second case, where you switch off reference to anger, remember anger is not gone but becomes a directionless emotion, which tends to surface anywhere or everywhere as a surprise. This is the path of will. Earlier, many mystics and now a great number of people who are seeking spirituality or becoming healers actually decide to leave the material world without resolving their karma to pursue *bliss*, assuming it is a better lifestyle than being in a corporation. When they do it, they, through their practice, do attain powers and *bliss* but as they begin to vibrate at a higher level, all their unresolved needs and greeds begin to surface. Being comfortable with their powers, now this becomes very difficult for them to heal internally and more difficult to hide, hence they develop the tendency to indulge in hoarding sex, money, power, and/or wanting to control people. Various healing modalities like NLP work on this principle. Disconnect reference to your negative emotion and lock it down by positive *belief*. By doing this, it shifts your frequency to higher plane and instantly you feel better and assume you are healed. But your negative emotions and the *Belief* is not gone and your mind now needs to handle lot more. This is why NLP and many such techniques are designed to limit your consciousness to select few things and remain focused on it. This is why you will see lot of debris in the ecosystem of such people while you will find them very sharp and successful at their career. This is a reflection of the dark, which they did not resolve. Dark is that you are aware that you have a need, but you do not wish to connect with the need but suppress it. It comes out irrationally. Hence, any spiritual practice, which people engage in, where they work consciously on suppressing their need for sex, love or family, create a hidden dark behavior, which surfaces the moment they begin to vibrate higher. They are, in other words, denying to connect with their pain by refusing their needs. They are ambitious about *bliss* and lack basic understanding of the law of nature. They are fear driven, moving towards mystery by denying or escaping from the needs of five elements.

This is why many healing modalities including meditation and Pranayama do not work as a cure though they are the cure. At its best they offer some relief to the stress, therefore are practised as prevention or lifestyle. This is degradation of sacred practices in value creation. When people meditate daily for hours and feel better, it is because they are able to shut their minds for some time, but their *belief* does not change, and they consciously do not want to face issues, which surface within when they meditate. With this approach driven by ambition, no cure can be a cure, including the one you hold in your hand right now. You would hear people meditating for two hours and the next moment, they are ready to treat their family and colleagues in a very insensitive manner, justifying that in a practical world, we must do this to survive.

Few people who transformed their *suffering* and found themselves guided to become healers interned with me to learn this science and become healers. They each did become a healer and very effective ones. To be a healer with us means to evolve and vibrate higher and expand your consciousness so much that there is nothing hidden as dark in your subconscious. When I would coach and show them the pattern of their life which needed to be addressed, they faced high resistance and stopped evolving. For them spirituality or sitting in meditation became a nice escape from their reality. This is good enough. They had already travelled a long distance in a very short time and now needed to be stable at this level, being aware that one day they will have to move forward by addressing the reality which they became aware of through this process. It should be easy for you to figure out who they would attract for offering transformation from here on? Those who can remind them of their own inner reality or who only want to transform as much as their healer has. Limitation of your healer actually becomes your limitation and that is why healers have to be on a continuous path to evolve.

Prayers, worshiping and meditation are another way to liberate ourselves from the clutches of *belief*. When we pray, we invoke faith. When we chant prayers, we regulate our breathing. Faith and then breathing starts to nullify our thoughts and our access to the spirit begins to flow, giving us a sense of divinity from within. The ultimate aim of all these techniques is to make the mind free of thoughts, access the subconscious, release emotions and merge with the spirit, which has unbound highest frequency of energy. The end game of spirituality is also in surrender (that happens on its own when you accept pain) to the mystery and becoming one with nature. However, unlike religion, spirituality is rooted in rational and conscious awareness as opposed to being fear-driven and having blind faith in case of religion.

All such rituals enhance your energy body also known as your aura. Before any reality can manifest into the physical reality, it begins to manifest in your energy field, and that if read by a *Mystic*, can forecast your future. I use this for forecasting disease or probability of unfortunate situations happening in the future. Your aura photo if read properly predicts potential disease much before your CT scan shows it to you. The good news is that anything if seen at the energy level, is easier to reverse quickly than if it manifests in physical form.

All emotions can be clubbed into seven base frequency ranges. They reflect the light or positive frequencies and opposite to them are the seven negative emotions. Since every emotion is generated from a belief, we can safely say that there are seven liberating *belief* and seven limiting *belief*. However, out of these seven *belief*, we will have an infinite number of belief and combination of them engineered which are trapping our energies. These seven quantum states of emotions are represented by the seven chakra system.

Relationship between elements, chakra system, LIGHT, ENERGY, MASS

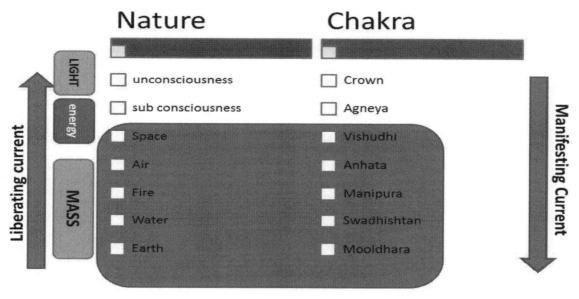

Figure 10

CHAKRA SYSTEM

*I*t is an interfacing layer acting as glue binding light and mass. A layer of energy which binds the spirit with the physical body and carries the imprint and code of the karmic journey, which we know as the soul tendency or "Sanskar." If we go by Einstein's equation E=MC, then C is light (we are light beings), M is mass (the physical body) and E is energy (this is represented by the seven chakra system). Each chakra as you can see from figure 11, has specific color, emotion, specific sound, specific frequency, and specific virtual location in the physical body. These seven chakras directly correspond to seven glands of the endocrine gland system. The seven glands are the physical form of seven chakras or the seven chakras are an energy representation of the seven physical glands. This is how Light, Energy and Mass are interconnected. Every experience creates an emotion and that emotion corresponds to a specific chakra and creates that level of energy in you. When you experience some emotion that will relate to a specific chakra. This will affect that specific gland in the body. If it is positive emotion, it will spin the chakra in positive direction and if it is negative emotion, then it will spin the chakra in opposite direction. This is how your well-being and health is directly connected to your lifestyle and experiences in life. All chakras spin together and are interconnected and are never in isolation. If one chakra starts to spin in an opposite direction, then it will have a tendency to turn other chakras also to spin in the opposite direction, if it is powerful enough. This is why, one event gives rise to one main specific emotion but is capable of bringing along other emotions as well.

For better understanding, *belief* create a frequency state. Call it a quantum level. Like a multistory building has many floors and as you go up, your view widens. Consciousness enlarges. Being at ground floor you can not see sunset and horizon, same way, if you vibrate at a lower state where fear is the emotion, you can not imagine *bliss* or experience the feeling of it. Emotions, karma, experiences can be said to be energy because that is what they generate. So, you have mass, energy and light which is E=MC.

Now take any experience and any emotion. Let us say, you experience fear, making you feel unsafe. This will correspond to the Mooldhara Chakra and will be reflected in the color of your aura in the red frequency range. This frequency of Mooldhara will affect all other chakras because they all are connected with each other and spin together. As the Mooldhara chakra begins to change frequency due to the emotion of fear, it starts to influence the speed and direction of other chakras. Let us say you did something wrong and now you are experiencing fear, and this fear leads you to guilt, which comes from the Swadhishtan chakra. From there it influences the Manipura chakra, triggering shame (threatening autonomy or survival). Its influence goes further up and you feel not being loved, and when it comes to Vishuddhi chakra (throat) you realize the truth about your mistake, and at the pineal gland it creates hopelessness or wisdom. Depending upon what you get from the pineal gland, you may form a belief in the crown chakra to either protect yourself or to confess your mistake. If you decide to hide and defend yourself, you start to spin all the chakras in the opposite direction. You invent a lie and now you need Manipura chakra to defend that lie in case you are caught. Let us say you have a strong ego and power to assert yourself, your Manipura chakra will get activated to keep these emotions under check to make you survive. You come home, and if you create a *belief* that you did the right thing by asserting yourself, you are now keeping your fear and guilt suppressed as this *belief* will not let these emotions come into your consciousness. You now need to hold this *belief* to survive. To do this, you need to feed it energy and hold some emotions like fear and guilt and not allow them to surface. This disturbs your breathing because your mind has extra work to do and consumes your breath (life force) and in turn the physics of five elements with your breath. This in turn affects secretion of hormones because they are nothing but mass representation of the 7 chakras and its energy levels. This disturbs the Ayurvedic, Vata, Pitta and Kapha combinations and changes the chemistry.

This change in hormones will now change the spectrum of emotions you feel and will shift the frequency range in which you operate. Can you see now that it will start to attract the same kind of experiences which will resonate well with your energy system? A new energy system which is caused by a new *belief or by defending* your mistake and hiding your guilt or shame.

In place of that, when you come home and realize the mistake you made, you learned not to repeat this. With this awareness, you will begin to spin the chakra in a positive direction and as you release shame, fear and guilt, love and compassion or pain will grow with the realization expanding your consciousness and that will shift the frequency to a higher level, restoring breathing to even deeper levels. As you vibrate higher, you will not have a tendency to make that mistake, which means you will not attract such situations in which you feel tempted to make a mistake because you now have expanded your consciousness.

All chakras spin together in both directions creating positive and negative emotions. A chakra, which is frequency of love is also the frequency of grief. Any change in one chakra frequency due to any experience, will affect the frequency of the other chakra. As that gets affected, it will generate another emotion, and if you create a *belief*, then you will create a pocket of those energies inside. Instead, if you make a realization, you will free up that energy in that specific chakra itself and will offer a higher vibratory level to the other chakras. For example, you shout at a child, he or she feels unloved, accepts it and it pains the child making them cry. He holds no *belief* to affect any other chakra. Your spouse comes and holds him and gives love and child is back to *bliss* with you both. No *belief* formed unless it is a pattern.

When you fall in love: Your heart is filled with love and your spirit begins to feel *bliss*. In this state, your mind begins to switch off any thoughts about survival and becomes pure consciousness filled with love. You begin to feel one with love and your consciousness is just love. This is the state of meditation except now you are one with nature through another human being rather than *bliss*, which you experience in the state of meditation internally on your own, feeling one with the divine. This is a state like that of a *Mystic* (not a *Survivor* anymore), who is lost in love/*bliss*. You begin to see beauty in everything and treat everyone with a smile. In this situation, it pushes the high vibratory energy in your lower three chakras to make them vibrate at the level of love. This takes away emotions from the Mooldhara for the need to survive. Fear, or hunger, from the Swadisthan for any guilt in expressing it, and the Manipura for any shame. Now all four chakras are vibrating at the same frequency. i.e. love. You lose touch with the body and feel love throughout.

It does the same with the three upper chakras to become one with nature. It pulls down the energy from the crown forming belief about faith in that love, hope through light, from Agneya to experience union, and from Vishuddhi for truth to make you feel love is real. The energy in all the chakras is now vibrating at one frequency. Your fantasy now is to merge with the lover, your insights are all about union with your lover, and this becomes your absolute truth in that moment. Any other form of reality such as assignment at work, physical reality like paying your bills, all dissolve or become vague. If you retain the energy here (almost all of us have experienced it at least for a few moments), you shall find that you lose differentiation between you, your lover, the universe and love. You just feel love. This is called becoming one with nature in spiritual parlance and that is why rational people say love is blind. This breaks all your *belief* about life, hurt, pain, regret, and you want to express all of it to your partner with a hope that it will now be cleared from your emotions. Trust, faith and hope are all pinned on this feeling of love or the partner. Now you are neither a *Mystic* nor a *Survivor* and you begin to merge in union and feel a sense of completeness. This is the feeling of wonderment and a very mystical phenomenon.

Then, God plays the dice. You break up and it is a shock. Heart chakra, which was spinning due to love, now begins to spin in the other direction giving you grief. As that happens, it starts to release energy in the other chakras, but in the opposite direction. Your faith in love, trust in relationship and love is truth is gone, and you feel life is meaningless. You feel unworthy (Manipura) and that leads to guilt that you made the wrong decision (Swadisthan), and lose the desire to survive (Mooladhara). Since this is a sudden rush of energy going back into all the chakras, it is a 180 degree shift in the emotions you experience, and you do not know how to handle this energy.

This is how your energies and your experiences are connected, and these energy levels are directly affecting the flow of hormones in your body. This is the reason why no medicine or treatment can be effective because your *belief* changes the chemistry of your body. At best, you can manage the symptoms you are experiencing. There are many cases where people claim that they took the medicine for their thyroid and that thyroid is cured for years now. The reason is that without them being aware, while taking the medicine, they were also releasing that *belief*, which had caused changes in their thyroid gland. Whenever you hear such a miracle done through any medicine system, if you go deeper into their life before and after the symptoms, you shall be able to find shifts in their consciousness and medicine just worked as a trigger like a placebo effect. Whenever you find allopathy or any medicine system becoming a cure, it is actually a real placebo effect.

Unconsciousness + Subconsciousness + 5 Elements (consciousness) = 7 Chakras

First five chakras represent the five elements, and Agneya is the seat of the subconscious through which we access our spirit via the karma and *belief* layer. This is the pineal gland or the third eye and is the guide for our inner journey. We have three eyes. The two eyes are to see the physical world and when we close them, we activate the pineal gland and open the third eye to receive insight, intuition and hidden wisdom. Through this, we see all past lives and our karma, and when we are in the state of meditation, our subconscious begins to open up and various past lives are seen in that moment, which in its essence means you are clearing the effect of those karmas and getting aligned to the light.

Crown chakra (unconsciousness) is the place where *belief* sits. This is the place where elders touch you to bless you with an intent that you release the *belief* and open up your energy and get liberated from karma. Through this chakra, you set the frequency range in which you vibrate and manifestation of that *belief* takes place. This is also the seat of wisdom. This is why Indians touch their elder's feet – to greet as a reflection of a drop in ego and surrender to their wisdom. A blessing on their head means a transmission of the same wisdom, which the elders have.

Unconsciousness, which we know as the light is also the dark. A situation, in which we see no hope, means we see no light and that leads to darkness. This is where the dark takes over to offer a *belief*, from the subconscious for survival. Whether it offers dark or light is all subject to our own karmic balance, which we carry over various lifetimes. Typical example is in Hollywood or Bollywood movies or the extreme case of Hitler. The hero loses his family, his respect and dignity in his police job, and realizes he has no hope. Rather than accepting this as his fate and turning inwards to discover why all such episodes were important, he decides to be supported by the dark and goes on to take revenge by killing people and taking the law in his hands. Hitler did the same by choosing the darkness to destroy the world. Since we feel powerless when hopeless, we do have these tendencies, and we take the support of the dark in manipulating relationships or hiding our wrong deeds, which makes us feel like we have the power to control our environment. This is what we are doing every day in our lives. We make our choices through the darker aspects of ourselves, and call it the practical world concerned with our survival. Unless we become aware of these practices, no cure will be effective and stable.

Unconsciousness or light is seen and felt by us in *Yog Nidra*, but in reality, you can see this in your well-being and in your ability to nurture planet earth in your work and love for yourself and the surroundings. A majority of the people who are working on their transformation are in the process of moving away from the darkness of the unconscious. They become aware of their dark tendencies of being fearful, insecure or nervous and they work on healing them. This is how subconscious is reducing and consciousness is expanding. Each time you meditate, you are moving away from the dark and becoming a light being.

Meditation can be done by anybody, daily. It is being done for thousands of years by mystics sitting in caves and meditating but that has not expedited the pace of evolution of the planet to a level it should have been by now. We had a *Mystic* on one hand with complete wisdom and a *Survivor* on the other with limited consciousness and a focus on surviving. There was a gap, which spirituality promised to fill. However, it did not have a credible mechanism for the masses to understand and practice at home. Through this book, I am attempting to do the same with all of you – to integrate the Mystic in you to make you better at surviving. This convergence of *Mystic* into a *Survivor* will expedite the whole process when each one of us operate through wisdom and not through fear.

The meditation alone is able to move you toward the light each time you meditate. You feel blissful but that may still not translate *bliss* into a physical reality. Your miseries and *sufferings* may still continue in the same way. You would see a lot of *Mystic* healers living very pathetic lives themselves though they are powerful healers or scholars. The reason is that they do not integrate their light with the five chakras or with the physical body. They have a *belief* on the lines of, physical body is perishable and life is meant for *suffering*. Or a *belief* like I am a special child of the God, birthed to discover divinity. Or I am looking for something more meaningful than what is given to everyone, or simply being ambitious or an escapist.

The purpose of meditation is to become aware. The awareness of the dark tendencies. Once you become aware, its power to influence you begins to diminish and gradually through authentic choices, the dark heals on its own. This is a lifestyle issue. This is a well-being issue, and this is what you are learning as The Cure.

Liberating Current and Manifesting Current:

Life or nature or the universe is flowing through these two currents, the liberating current and the manifesting current (figure 10), going in a circle. This is the flow of energy in the body. Take the case of a toddler to understand this concept. Toddler is in the state of *bliss* and lives in a world experiencing hope and light. Now when he feels hungry, his physical self puts a demand on the *bliss* to be interrupted, and he feels the pain of hunger and cries. He gets food and bounces back to *bliss*. Since this child is making no *belief*, he is not holding any part of nature inside him. Manifestation of his desire to be fed is by bringing down energy through the manifesting current. Once that is done, liberating currents carry the signal and bring him back to *bliss*. Liberating current and manifesting current, like a sea wave, come and go without changing your steady state unless you form a belief which then disturbs the flow. This goes on round the clock throughout our life.

Manifesting any reality in our life, starts with fantasy. Let us say, while growing up, you have a fantasy of becoming a mother or a billionaire. This means you are connected to the light and you hope beyond hope. Fantasy then becomes a vision as hope continues to build. Vision then turns into a desire and desire into an ambition. This is where your mind gets active to manifest itself into reality. For this fantasy to manifest itself as a reality, energy current needs to move from crown chakra to Mooldhara chakra passing through all chakras. This current, which is moving downwards, is called the manifesting current. This is different from the fantasy of a prodigy, who stays in *bliss* through his passion. Here this child does not make any ambition to manifest *bliss* through football. His fantasy is his reality and both these currents are one for him.

When such a child goes for a tournament and is kept as a substitute, he feels the pain of not being able to play for those moments, but his spirit keeps him in *bliss,* watching his team play and remains in a mode of curiosity to get a chance to play. But if this child decides to suffer by crying and getting angry with the coach? He loses the spirit to fulfill the purpose of his soul. i.e. to play. Here, manifesting currents are being blocked by *belief* in between at one of the chakras. This now starts to affect the fantasy and reality and are no longer integrated as one.

This is best understood by looking at infertility. In each of these cases, the woman fantasizes about being a mother. In her own formidable years, she may have formed a *belief* that being a mother means losing freedom or she may feel fearful about nurturing the child and make the child suffer the way she suffered in her childhood. This blocks the flow of the manifesting current and she feels hopeless. This was reflected in her desire for sex, which was also has dried up now. Her mind was saying that she wants to be a mother; so she did whatever the mind said by visiting various astrologers, IVF centers and whatever else she could do. Majority of such cases were resolved by breaking the deadlock of the currents stuck due to their fears and *belief* through techniques and processes listed in section three. Apart from that, they were asked to resume their normal sex life for their own pleasure and allow nature to take its own course. This restored their fantasy which was gripped by fears and *belief.* You can check yourself if your fantasy is not filled with light or it is filled with light and that will have a direct impact on manifestation of that fantasy.

The liberating current starts from the Mooldhara chakra to the crown carrying energies of your experiences to complete the cycle. If you made a *belief* based on an experience in your life, you will create a pocket of energy. This will dilute the flow of energy going into the crown to liberate you from this experience. You liked food in a restaurant and it was a wonderful experience. You made a *belief* that next time you want to have a wonderful experience through food you will come here. Liberating current is now interrupted and you are stuck with this belief. We do that in love very often and rather than making love liberate us, in order to hold on to our insecurity or partner or those good moments, we do not allow fantasy to create another creative experience.This is what you feel when you talk about forgiveness. Forgiveness means releasing the *belief* based on your experience and that releases that hurt from your specific chakra, where you held the energy and it completes the cycle of energy flow by acquiring wisdom. Forgiveness does not work by saying I have forgiven.

Similarly, when you start to feel detached from the needs in your life, the liberating current begins to intensify. This happens because you broke one *belief* (need is the origin of *belief*). In doing so, your faith is restored, which activates the crown and pineal gland and further the Vishuddhi chakra creating more breathing space. For example, you have this *belief* that you shall have the same lifestyle as you have now and for that you must work for X more years and save Y amount of money every month. You remain very adamant about it. One day, your teenage daughter asks a wise question, saying to you "Why are you not being in the moment and letting it impact your life in this way?". You decide that it is fine to save Y and even if it is less than Y, it is still OK. This breaks the *belief* and liberates your energy, bringing you more inner peace and making you feel like you have more time and space for yourself to live in the moment. Tell a child that rather than aiming for 95% marks in high school, aim for the best without changing the amount of effort needed. You can now see how much space and energy opens up. Suddenly, you start to breathe and live life, and your faith that life is beautiful, is restored.

However, what if an unfortunate situation, like the rape or death of a loved one, forces you to disconnect with the person? This forces you to block your heart, which is the regulator of both the currents. A high rush of energies, which happens all of a sudden in such cases remains stuck and divides you in two parts. The upper part has the manifesting current in the three chakras above Anahata and the lower part has the liberating current in the three chakras below Anahata. Your *belief* holds them and cuts the flow because these are high–intensity, quick and sudden events. In such moments of mild or intense distress, you can actually feel different temperatures in both parts of your body.

This causes distress due to the energy being stuck. Now no circulation is happening as life force energy is now trapped in the body. Hope is replaced with hopelessness and in this moment, support of dark comes in. If ego is strong, it will seek survival at any cost. If ego is fragile, it will drown in the whirlpool of negative emotions. Mind cannot handle such a high rush of emotions hence taking support from the dark, it begins to fill conscious, drowning in a whirlpool of negative emotions. Mind cannot handle such a high rush of emotions hence taking support from the dark, it begins to fill the consciousness with dark emotions. This is the state of despair moving towards disorder. Excessive energy in the pineal gland which is now dwelling in the dark does not let your mind function and also disturbs the healthy partition between subconscious and consciousness. It forms obsessive thoughts which as it happens causes loss of sleep leading into further uncontrolled communication between subconscious and conscious. At the same time, energy stuck in the lower chakra turns into addictive behaviour searching to reclaim the identity. Rape and death are still very extreme situations, but as a normal person, due to insecurity and insufficient faith or limiting *belief*, a lot of currents remain stuck in our various chakras during so many of our interactions we do in our normal life. This is where grounding these emotions every day is important or else it affects your sleep which then starts to affect the three pillars of well-being (breathe, sleep, sexuality)

Anahata chakra (heart) or love is the regulator of these two currents. Any experience in your life will affect love, hence disrupting the flow of the current. You steal money from your father's purse, it creates the fear (Mooladhara) that you may get caught. This fear makes you feel guilty (Swadisthan) of doing it. As you feel guilty, it makes you feel ashamed (Manipura) of yourself. This takes away self-love (Anahata). Now all four chakras are affected and have blocked the flow of manifesting current and liberating currents because energy needs to be fed to this *belief* and its corresponding emotions. In addition, now the mind needs to be strong enough to survive, while dealing with these emotions which need a lot of energy. All of it disturbs your breathing as the energy flows through breathing and appropriate hormones will be released on how much energy is held in which chakra.

A child who has a big ego, does not feel ashamed and justifies it instead, then it becomes his *belief* about life. Right or wrong, he does not equate it with self-love. Hence, the flow through the heart continues but the ego (Manipura) builds up to justify his act of stealing. This becomes a *belief* that stealing is cool, and he is still loved. Now, he will start to vibrate in this zone to attract either such opportunities, to validate that he will still be loved if he steals, or find ways to define himself to test if he would still be loved. Since he is surviving and still loved at the surface he can remain guilt-free and fearless as he learns how to survive and yet be accepted. While he does that, he is creating dark emotions (shame, guilt and fear) inside and storing it in his emotional body. Defending the act of stealing does not wipe out these emotions but only helps in pushing it into the subconscious. As he grows up, he falls in love. His heart opens up and that drops the need to defend self. This releases all the emotions of guilt, fear and shame held in Manipura because now love is given unconditionally and he does not need to validate or seek approval. This starts to remind him of his deeds. As he feels loved and accepted and his ego drops, he now has issues in accepting himself with his wrong deeds. He feels the need to confess and this is where we seek unconditional acceptance, or he denies the love by judging that he is not worthy of it due to shame in his deeds.

In reality, all these years he was playing with his dark emotions and validation of love which he was seeking. He has been *suffering*, switching between love and self-acceptance with dark emotions. This is the reason why we break away from unconditional or pure love when someone offers to create some safe boundaries. It is a very uncomfortable feeling.

We seek unconditional love all the time but outside our mother, wherever this is sought, it demands self acceptance and drops into our defense mechanism. Dropping ego threatens our survival with fear that if love goes away, how will you pull yourself up again.

Let's take another example; sex is linked with love. It is when we feel safe (Mooladhara), appreciated, respected, cared for, and feel loved. We begin to love the person and want to manifest love through sex seeking union, being one with nature, resulting in orgasm, which is the state of *bliss*. The purpose of love is to feel Oneness and that happens in the moment of orgasm for *survivor* or in the moment of devotion for a *Mystic*. But what happens in every relationship is that we begin to feel we are not loved enough. It could be situational, due to stress or just the true realization of it. We begin to block manifesting currents and suppress the desire for sex. Procreative energy, when blocked, turns destructive causing damage to the mental and emotional body, eventually leading to physical disease. This is akin to forcefully, fasting endlessly. In such cases, when we feel we are not loved, we begin to reverse manifesting currents back into the stream of liberating currents, and it all builds a reservoir in the pineal gland creating havoc in our mind and emotions. This becomes a loop in which all the energy continues to circulate. Manifesting currents as coming down gets blocked at heart which feels grief, and liberating currents are stuck at Swadhishtan by blocking sexual energy which by now is going in the reverse direction to become self destructive. In this state of hopelessness, again we form obsessive compulsive behaviour. Delinking love and sex is a vital component in attaining well-being.

If rather than feeling grief, you seek love outside your relationship, or you seek out to be more nice to friends and colleague, instead of actually forming a loving relationship. Soon you discover the same pattern. Again you feel you are not loved enough and the same pattern resurfaces. If you are not authentic and continue to seek security in the present relationship and love outside, you create guilt within yourself. You do touch *bliss* in this relationship but create dark energy inside. Now starts your *suffering*. You respect the sense of safety and security in the existing relationship. You respect that you have a need to fulfill, which you get from outside causing you distress. You are constantly busy in managing your *bliss* and security. Since you have access to Google, you start to justify your guilt by saying that the partner outside completes you as a soul mate or twin flame. But you are stuck due to kids. This makes you feel good about yourself – that you are such a kind soul, *suffering* in silence, but taking care of responsibility and sacrificing the divine union with your soul. Really? Give yourself a break and meditate the way it is taught to you in section three.

Love heals and rightly so. When you are vibrating at a high frequency, than lower frequency ranges like guilt, shame, and fear cannot remain inside you. Hence, you develop the tendency to share everything with your partner, to seek a release from it, otherwise you feel guilty. This is what love is supposed to do. Offer a loving environment and allow you to heal your past wounds. It allows you to be authentic because it creates an environment of acceptance and safety. Need to pretend does not hold merit now, so you drop your ego (*Manipura*) in love. As you release energy from the Manipura chakra, which was controlling your fear, shame and guilt, it now surfaces. If you do not release this energy, then you would want to hold on to this loving environment and yet keep your negative emotions under control. Suddenly, rather than feeling love, you are busy in managing love by controlling your partner or manipulating. Suddenly, the magic of love is over as you are not vibrating at the high frequency anymore but manipulating the love frequency to fulfill your needs of security. As you try to do that, partners feel love is not flowing and begin to distance themselves from each other by creating ego to defend himself/herself. As your partner withdraws, you feel empty because you have this need to manage love but now there is no love. You make do whatever you can to ensure that love continues to come to you from the partner so that you can continue to play in it. This creates *sufferings* in the relationship and is a prime driver for most. Now, there is no more love. That magic you had during orgasm is not there anymore.

But if you share everything, and you are still loved, it changes the *belief* about love and relationships and feels very empowering. This is what people are seeking out today through extramarital affairs and multiple relationships. Creating a dark environment in which we all are acceptable to each other the way we are. As a result we are not healing or growing our consciousness.

This is a little interesting phenomenon. Rise of the grey. Earlier generations either lived in dark or light. We create a shade of grey by designing an environment where we seek acceptance of our own negatives. By doing that, we are creating a grey consciousness. so to say. This will lower mortality levels or high virtues we had earlier. This is reducing overall authenticity on this planet. You can better understand how our value systems have gone down by now by accepting corruption in our country. Now even we are open to do it. It is interesting to note that how the hidden dark subconscious is brought out in our consciousness as grey and creating an environment to accept it and gradually begin to heal it.

In this time and space, where life is tuned for an inward journey, sharing a lot of you is not a good idea. Keeping it suppressed is causing *suffering* and making it grey is eroding *bliss* and overall purpose of life. Turning inward and transforming for self acceptance is the way forward to have acceptance for self and for others to create a harmonious and virtuous society. No one has so much energy in today's time to hold the space for another person for their excess baggage, hoping one day we will have a transformed relationship. Relationships need lean and clean structures to have a fair degree of individual space. Interaction and support offered to each other is now meant for the individual journey of transformation rather than the earlier model of collective evolution.

Let us turn the table. Sex in love is fine, but what if you end up getting intimate with someone and have sex. Since sex is linked to love, it shakes up your *belief* in yourself and you lose self-respect. You begin to now invent the love around this one night stand, which in its essence was never there from either side. This loop continues and causes *suffering* where liberating current and manifesting current begin to move in a loop.

It is a gross mistake to do chakra healing. Chakras spin on its own based on your *belief*. To heal a chakra, is to become aware of your *belief*. The best you can do through various methods often popular in the west is clear the lack or excess of energy for some time, but it oscillates back to where it was. Healing chakras for your symptoms is like cleaning your WC while the dirt is in the overhead tank. Each time you flush, the dirt will be visible to you.

Chakras are energy fields vibrating in seven frequency zones. The combination of seven chakras creates infinite patterns and frequency ranges. That is how we all have a unique life and unique experiences. While our uniqueness is visible in our unique faces, which are also unique, we all have a unique path. While we may have the same experiences, our *belief* would be different from the same experience.

Chakras shall not be studied like a zodiac sign for diagnosing the symptoms, as all are linked with each other. Take this example: You have a thyroid issue and you want to go research it on Google and read everything about the Throat Chakra. Then you go on YouTube and use chakra healing music. This will not work.

Thyroid is due to the suffocation of your space. This means that your husband asks you to go out for an Italian food, but you wanted to eat Chinese. You smiled and complied for Italian. This is not because you wanted to but because you wanted to feel secure. So when you agree, you kill your desire for Chinese. Emotions like 'no one cares for me' or 'women always have to sacrifice for their relationship' or 'if I speak my desire, my husband will judge me' crop up or you simply do not feel safe. In this moment, you may feel a lump in your throat, grief in your heart, a sinking feeling in your Manipura area because it is submission and not expression of autonomy. If you feel nice about yourself for the sacrifice you made, It helps you boost your ego (Manipura which was sinking now spins otherway) but suffocates your space (throat). If this decision was driven by the need to be nice, it means you fear rejection. If so then, it is the Mooladhara chakra which needs to be healed first to feel acceptance. If you are feeling unsafe to express yourself, then the Manipura chakra is the prime driver for your thyroid. If it is driven by being loved then it is the heart chakra and Swadhisthana. However, the solution is very simple. You tell your husband that you wanted to eat Chinese, but you are very happy to go for an Italian meal this time. This way you do not feel suffocated, negative emotions do not arise and on the contrary, it may trigger some sense of worthiness in you to be of value in the relationship and you end up nurturing patience.

Every experience would have one primary emotion – positive or negative. As per our *belief*, it will affect other chakra systems. The impact on that chakra will trigger some other emotions through another chakra. This is why two people with the same experience can feel different and create a different perception and create their own unique reality. This is why, various healing modalities, which only focus on healing emotions do not work as a cure and other healing modalities which focus on replacing a *belief* with another *belief* does not work as a cure. They are good to manage your symptoms but then why not use allopathy then?

CHAKRA SYSTEM

Chakra	Color	Sound	Emotions	Emotions	Endocrine
Sahasara	Violet	EEE/OM	Attachment	Detachment	Pineal
Agneya	Indigo	EYE/AAM	Illusion	Intuition	Pituitary
Vishudhi	Blue	AYE/HAM	Lie	Truth	Thyroid
Anhata	Green	AHH/YAM	Grief	Love	Thymus
Manipura	Yellow	OHH/RAM	Shame	Autonomy	Pancreas
Swadhishtan	Orange	OOO/VAM	Guilt	sexuality	Gonads
Mooldhara	Red	UH/LAM	Fear	Secure	Adrenal

Figure 11 : Relationship between, emotions and endocrine gland system

This energy field, which has colors and sound, is nothing but your aura. Your aura has all the information about your past, your probable future and your present state. This is why, when you walk into the company of a *Mystic*, he is able to sense or read your aura and make a prediction. The same was possible for your parents and grandparents – to just see your face, read the energy field and tell you how you have been or what challenges you are facing. A dirty red color will say to the *Mystic* that you are facing financial problems or having issues with your mother. A dull green will reflect your sorrow. These are just to help you understand in a very simplified way. However, this entire science is more accurate when felt or sensed using intuitive faculties.

One does not have to be very intuitive and wise. Your mothers and grandmothers over the years intuitively knew how to read the energy field without knowing that they were reading it. This is because they are always connected with your energy field, even when you are far away. They are far better than healers, as they are connected to you at a spirit and soul level. They have known the flow of your emotional body which is inherited by you from them. Hence, they are able to track the source of your emotions and able to give you suggestions on what steps to take in a specific situation. When you call your parents and say hello, just with the sound of your voice, they begin to get insights through your energy field, much before you say something verbally. Even after their death, they do not lose a connection with you, till you liberate them by healing those tendencies, which are running in the family. You can always block the flow of their wisdom by disconnecting with them but they can never disconnect with you. They hold an energy field space, and if you step out of it, they will continue to hold the space and through their prayers, they can try to include you in the space or wait till you fall back in the space again.

I grew up in Saharanpur, Uttar Pradesh, in the North of India, where I saw my mother, grandmother, taking the first freshly made bread (roti) out, circling it around us, and then offering it to the cow. This is how they used to cleanse the aura so that no bad energy was stuck in our energy field. In fact, in occult practices, those weird looking Tantriks with bones and a broom in their hands, used to move that around the head and the body with the idea of releasing any evil spirit energy stuck at the pineal gland. They even would touch or hold you with the palms at your temple area where the nerve for the pineal gland runs.

When a mother puts her baby to sleep on her lap, she taps on the temple to calm the pineal gland to make the child sleep by regulating the overactive mind. This is the pineal gland and you can feel that right now. This pineal gland, if hyperactive, (take your fingers to temple area to locate it on both sides and you will feel a pulsating nerve), the child will have problems in sleeping. In fact, this nerve is one of the symptoms I check in mental disorders cases or to check criminal tendency or addiction or anger or sleep disorder. A prediction of the future events by reading the energy field has been part of any culture since a long time, though such a prediction can never be 100% accurate because it only reflects a tendency at an energy level and is still not manifested. Before disease or well-being sets in the body, it reflects in your energy field. During the last seven years, every case without knowing much of its history, I have been able to diagnose the patterns and risk of an unfortunate situation or possibility of a disease in the near future. The understanding of the chakra system is the vital wisdom in forecasting such patterns. The good news is that since it is in an energy field, it can be reversed very quickly by practicing *Yog Nidra*, and it may not have to manifest at all. By practicing the three techniques, you are mitigating a risk of possible disease or unfortunate situations in any case by restoring your energy field to an optimal level in the *Yog Nidra* state. These techniques have been used by several healthy people too, to raise their vibration, attract abundance and richness in their lives. It is simple to understand this book. Anybody who practices these techniques is moving towards higher vibratory level. Some start from -10 to move to zero and some are at zero to reach at 10. Even if there is something negative stuck in your energy, such practices mitigate the risk by healing those negative energies and clear your path for higher vibratory levels. This is where we are back to lifestyle and its impact on well-being, which was the main pillar of Ayurveda (medicine and spirituality) and now even your allopathic doctors are saying,

"Take this medicine but change your lifestyle. Do Yoga, Pranayama, meditation, brisk walk, light food, no spice," and so on.

We have reversed many such relationships, which were on the verge of breaking up. The unique thing is that we did it without even working on both the partners. Just one person needed to come forward and practice the techniques. No coaching and no counseling are ever given to such a distressed person. By the time they start doing the third technique (NV Hunting), rather than blaming each other, they begin to realize their own flaws and ego. This transforms them, which in turns transforms the partner who has not visited us. As you read this book, do not expect for your partner to start practicing this. You start. Commit to a 6-week schedule and watch your relationship and your transformation into a new being. But it has always been very difficult to revive a relationship where couples have kept away from sex. Reason is simple, they have used the sexual energy (procreative energy) into destructive energy. And in place of love, they live with judgment, anger and hatred toward each other. If you are in one of those relationships, do not work on the relationship or yourself but first break the barrier toward sex which you have created. You will find your energies are turning towards positive and with the given techniques, you can revive the entire relationship.

We are light beings, The pineal gland is the only source inside us as light. Our eyes also see when light falls on them. So by nature, light is an internal process. But sound is the medium which is innate in us, and through sound, we can connect with the physical world and spirit. Sound is the connector which brings us to the light. This is why the ritual of chants in the Vedic tradition and Buddhism and carol singing or Ajan in Muslim religion is about generating those sounds which are specific to a chakra. Chant of Gayatri Mantra consisting of (tas wut va aae ni yum) has the seven sounds of seven chakras. When chanted, it harmonizes the chakra with each other and optimizes the frequency range. Try this out. **Om Ganpati Namo.**

See the effect you feel at the base (*Muladhara*) when you pronounce the word Ganpati. This chant is for the Lord Ganesha and is done to remove obstacles in worldly matters and help one manifest material success. Hence, this God is to be worshiped first before starting a new task or venture. Now if you chant Ganpati, it creates higher vibrations at *Mooldhara* chakra activating it to retain manifesting currents so that its energy field grows to remove any potential obstacles. Hence, Hindus worship this God before starting a new business or venture. So you really do not need the Ganesh idol or to be born in a Hindu family to take advantage of this powerful sound.

Chant the beej mantra sound of each chakra and you can feel yourself at the location of that chakra in your body. You can discover the emotion behind the hurt of a child by listening to the sound he creates while crying. The same wisdom can be gained about emotions of your partner while love making, from the sound he/she creates during love making and in orgasm.

At a physical level, you only need to understand two things. How the endocrine system functions and its connection with the central nervous system. If your endocrine glands are optimal, nothing should go wrong because oxygen is going into each cell. This will revive your immune system. This endocrine gland system is the physical form of energy body of the seven chakras. This is the connection and integration of the seven bodies.

PHYSICAL BODY – SLEEP, BREATH AND SEXUALITY

> **Stop counting the drops in the ocean, swim across it.**

There are amazing facts about the human body and you can Google them. For example, there are over 73.2 trillion cells in our bodies. 25 million cells are produced every second. A nerve impulse travels at a speed of over 400km/hr, a sneeze generates wind traveling at 166 km/hr, a cough at 100km/hr and a heart beats more than 100,000 times in a day. 2.5 million red blood cells are generated every second by the bone marrow. This list of amazing facts goes on.

All of these, work on their own without your intervention, and these facts and findings are a gift of science. What does it mean to you when you read such a marvel of engineering created by mystical forces? A perfect product, which has been functioning for several thousands of years in countless human bodies. More science discovers such data, more they are making humanity go toward wonderment and have faith in mystery.

Medical science looks at this data and assumes that when there is a disease or something is not functioning right in one organ or the other, It comes out with some chemical to locally intervene, which is bound to disturb the whole ecosystem of engineering and functioning inside the body. It disturbs the functioning of the body in all the cases. You can get some temporary relief by taking a medicine for headache and it works, but if you continue to externally take chemicals in the body, be aware that it will affect your entire engineering. Hence, allopathy comes across as a gift when it comes to diagnostics, acute cases, emergencies and surgery. Much like you have plumbers and electricians who fix a snag quickly, but when this turns chronic, you need engineers to come and look at the source of the problem. The design of the human internal functioning or the engineering process is not inside the human body or in the chemicals and cells. It requires you to study the design as a whole, which in the last chapters you have read. We have changed the chemistry in the human body within hours and not even weeks and months. This is the reason allopathy, though it never claimed that it had a cure, does not have a cure. They will tell you that your pancreas is not functioning. They will give you insulin but you ask them why your pancreas is not functioning while your neighbor's pancreas is fine, and they will tell you a story because there is no real answer with them. Their replies make no sense to you and sound the same which once middle men in the church/temple/mosque spoke when you asked, why are you *suffering*. This leads to giving you more fear than wisdom and more hopelessness rather than mechanisms or tools to restore your pancreas.

Your *belief* is driving your chemistry. Change your *belief* to change your reality.

But when a *Mystic*, or the Mystic in you, looks at this data, he bows down to the mystery, and in an instant, he feels a sense of well-being. This is the moment faith builds up, and in that moment, your consciousness is filled with wonderment and gratitude which automatically leads you towards *bliss*. If you can stay in this moment long enough observing your breath, it will lead you into *Yog Nidra*. Let me say it again that you arrive at the state of *Yog Nidra* (meditation) by observing your breath which makes your thoughts turn to zero and opens up access to your all layers into the physical body. Through this process, your oxygen is optimally going to each cell restoring your chemical makeup. The restoration of the internal processes in the body is at optimal level through the state of wonderment, hope and faith. *Bliss* and pain are cyclic in nature. Pain is the process through which you release all the toxicity from the body. This completes the cycle of *bliss* and pain, which is the cycle of optimal well-being.

The day science and spirituality begins to converge, as they are beginning to do so, humanity will begin to evolve at a far more rapid pace.

There are only a few things that can go wrong in a normal, healthy human body.

1. Specific organs stop to function or develop a snag.
2. There is an issue in some pipeline.
3. Feedback mechanism, which carries information to and fro from the cells to the central nervous system is obstructed.
4. Toxins are not releasing causing malfunction.

Let us look at some logic because we believe we have blind faith in science, and we discard anything which is not logical.

Any type of malfunction, which you witness in your body, be it distress, disorder or disease, is a function of blood not reaching the cells or specific cells, or is not carrying enough nutrition and oxygen. The central nervous system remains interactive with each cell in a closed loop feedback mechanism.

If this is true, which it is and we know from the science even if we do not go by common sense, then your 73.2 billion cells will continue to regenerate new cells. Old cells will die, become toxic and there is a system inside, which works to release the toxicity through various means. Within a reasonable framework, subject to normal living, it is all about oxygen and nutrition intake through food which governs the optimal functioning of the body. Each minute, it has to kill twenty-five million cells, and that means the immune system is functioning well. So even if food intake is not good enough, as long as oxygen intake is good, immune system will find a way to function at an optimal state. These toxins are then released by the body.

Let us look at other numbers which we all have known by now and it shall give you a deep insight into your body and dispel fears. The human body consists of minimum 65% water and 18% carbon and then you have a huge list of other metals and elements and chemicals. Out of which majority of them are elements like nitrogen and hydrogen. Metals are less than 1% of the total human body mass.

This means the body is an interplay of two major chemicals – water and carbon. Water as an element is represented by Swadhisthana chakra, responsible for emotions, which is the language of the spirit, which due to karmic effect would have dark energy as well. It is also the center of creativity, which is the life force energy and in other words, sexual energy. This means that no matter how clean your spirit is, it will always have dark energy in some proportion as long as human life exists.

Carbon is that dark energy and must be 18% in the body for a healthy person at any given time. With oxygen and carbon, light and dark are inside us. This is what religion and spirituality said; the universe is in you and you are in the universe, flowing through each other. You create negative emotions, carbon increases inside and toxins increase putting pressure on your immune system. You change to positive emotions, you restore oxygen, and move towards light. When the water element goes down toxins grow which means carbon grows. The water element is the function of the emotional body. Emotional body is a reflection of the Spirit. Any attempt made to regulate emotions and to keep them repressed requires an intervention of the mind. This means extra force to be applied all the time to keep an emotion inside. This needs a strong *belief* and that *belief* needs to be fed through oxygen, which otherwise was supposed to nourish your body. The more you stay in your mind, the more oxygen you consume and the less you have for the body. This we have already established in other chapters so far and is known to humanity since ancient times.

Based on the above concept, each case, no matter how terminal or chronic in nature, was led to restore chemical balance using breathing at our healing center. Medical reports corrected automatically after a few weeks of work on the patient. At the risk of sounding arrogant, but with the intent to instill confidence in you, I must share with you that there is no way an ICU patient has remained in the ICU for over five days, if I am in the ICU attending to them. I have personally gone in at a time when all medical parameters were bad and the patient was on a ventilator but conscious. They were out of hospital in a week and shifted to the normal ward for further recovery after being declared out of danger. I am not a magician. I know two of my friends, who took very little support from me, but worked on their loved ones and got their aging parents out of the ICU. There have been so many cases, where I was contacted after they had paid the fee for operation to the hospital and doctors were ready for surgery the next day for either amputation of the leg or for eye operation for glaucoma. With a very tiny window of almost twelve hours, I worked on them overnight and guided the caregiver to do two processes as listed in the section three. In case the patient is conscious, in addition to the two processes given to the caregivers, we asked the patient to observe the breath and keep attention at the toe which was to be amputated, in reference to the amputee case. The next morning when they visited the doctor for surgery, doctors refused to perform the operation, seeing the patient's healthy condition. In one case of amputation, a dear friend who had a lot of faith followed my instructions for his brother. The whole night they kept breathing (and doing what is explained in Section 3 - Treatment). The next day the doctor who was going to perform the amputation, refused to do it. The trick is how to increase blood supply to the toe, which is affected. Oxygen will travel where your attention is. If you breathe with attention on the affected toe, it will increase the flow of blood in that area. Of course, it is too good to reverse a decision for amputation overnight. This is where mastering the technique and following additional processes as listed in the treatment section helps accelerate healing and recovery. There are many stories from the last seven years, almost every week there was one such case. You can probably make out that this book is written with solid experience and conviction using science which works in each and every case.

Allopathy is a gift of science to the world. It is so beautiful to get your report and understand the nature of imbalances in the body. We are abusing this beautiful gift which does wonders when it comes to scanning, diagnostics, tests, surgery and life-saving situations. Acute cases are best handled with these drugs. Once disease is managed, it gives us a lot of scope to turn inward to reverse a *suffering* in the body on its own. We are making the same mistake with science which we once made with God. We are placing irrational faith in science now, and they are doing the same thing that middlemen of religion did – inflicting fear and controlling our lives.

We have encouraged humanity for making their choices and explore their potential. We have given them the much needed wings, but have caught their legs. We are eternally hopeful and curious people, who want to keep searching for our solutions, but we are handicapped by our *belief* and imposed morality. Our spirit is tired with our endless failures in finding its own authentic expression. We are curious and want to explore or implore, but we feel tired to walk the path into the unknown with faith in ourselves or the journey of our lives. We always want to belong to something or someone. We have made false promises to our children by giving them the impression of immortality due to which they face issues in accepting any unknown situation. When everything has to be known, which is against the law of nature, curiosity is getting killed and when we are not curious, our view is very myopic and motivation is very transactional. Curiosity about life connects us with divine energy, which is always ready to give us insight and guide us toward a meaningful life. We want a partner, a friend, a God, the parents, and government. Failed in search for solution through them, we now want medical science and technology to look after us. It has always surprised me that if all the wisdom was available with us for thousands of years, why have we not evolved to live a purposeful life? The reason is that we have always looked outside and placed faith in everything but ourselves. While our curiosity is authentic, solutions are not coming our way. It has only come to people who have turned inward, listened to their spirit and went ahead by placing faith in their insight.

When your kidney is not filtering, that means you are holding some grudges from some episode in your childhood, and you are unable to forgive. In all probability, it is an anger towards your mother. Work on releasing the grudges for a few days. Forget the section three. Follow these steps right now.

1. List down all episode of anger from childhood mainly towards mother.

2. Check and you will discover that you mind has discrete sections often having conflict in your thoughts.

3. Breathe this anger by observing your breath and feeling that anger.

4. Do that for few minutes till your anger disappears.

How do you feel now? You will feel calmer. You do that for a few days and go for your kidney test again and witness a very small change in your results. Is it not fascinating and empowering that you can be the master of your life? This is what it means to turn inward. Do you see that you hold immense power within to heal yourself? This is without even knowing the techniques which are listed in section three. Now you just need a small technique and a process to cure it fully. This is what it means to be curious and this is what it means to have faith in the unknown and trust your journey.

Let us take cancer. Healthy cells are generated in a specific organ or system which spreads to other parts eating away all the nutrition. It is uncontrollable. This is what we know as cancer. Right? Why would the central nervous system do it unless it registers a panic? Imagine if you are told that there is going to be war after a week and no groceries will be available after three days. You will panic and hoard all that you can. Why does an organ feels isolated is because it feels inadequate and unloved. Roots of cancer are in feeling unloved and again it comes from your childhood time. This is what the central nervous system is doing. It does it when it does not get a feedback signal from a specific part of the body. This part gets isolated for blood supply and that is where panic arises. Have you heard about heart cancer? It has all the blood. When I worked on infertility cases, we came across several cases where the uterus wall was thick or blood supply was very low or non-existent. Since I worked with the IVF center and all these patients were sent to me by the doctor for stress management to increase their fertility possibilities, I had access to their reports and feedback. Using the techniques mentioned in Section three, we used to restore blood supply back to normal within forty-eight hours. Since we worked alongside allopathy, it was so exciting to see how the uterus wall thickness shrunk to normal within two days. Had we left such cases unattended, it would be a sure case of cancer in the uterus in a few weeks time. So how do you reverse cancer? Use NV Swimming technique to improve the blood supply and use processes mentioned under the treatment section. Once feedback mechanism is restored, the central nervous system will know that a specific organ exists and will stop producing extra cells in the body. During the writing of this book in the last one year, several cancer cases who attended just two-day workshops have been on a constant recovery process from cancer with proven medical reports. All of them with the same techniques and processes as given in section 3.

Breath will not reach your body optimally if your mind is busy. Then it needs more oxygen which essentially is meant for the rest of your body. This means a hyperactive mind, as it is being fueled. Sleep means conscious mind is of zero thought, and it occurs when body feels the fatigue and is not able to think anymore. If the mind is active, your sleep is affected. As sleep is affected, your mind again has more chaos. This means you now need more oxygen for the mind. That means further reduction of supply of oxygen to the rest of your body's cells. As this happens, your entire life force energy would be absorbed and used by your thoughts. Your sexuality is now eroded. Your sexuality is nothing but a life force energy which you inhale with breaths.

Sleep, Breath and Sexuality – 3-Way Switch to Plug into Internal Engineering:

Every experience triggers emotions based on our *belief* and that creates thoughts which affects breathing. We know this by now. Once breathing is affected, thoughts continue to remain stuck and emotions continue to disturb us – except when you push them down to handle issues related to survival if you are a strong headed person. More and more life force energy is used to feed those emotions and thoughts trying to maintain your stability. You are going through bad relationships while working on an important assignment, you will know how draining it is to keep yourself stable and yet perform in your work. As the mind remains disturbed and engaged, it affects your sleep and that disturbs your sexual energy. This is the vicious cycle triggered by one bad experience, in which if you are caught. Internal engineering which is working inside your body regenerating cells and various other functions to keep you healthy is disturbed. Blood supply to your cells is reduced as now your mind has too many activities to be fed by oxygen, which is by now in any case less in supply because of your disturbed breath. The carbon component in the body grows, and you are toxic.

Whichever way, if you can keep three there parameters restored and optimal, no toxicity can stay in you. For seven years, every treatment done on patients meant restoring these three pillars.

There are cases like severe mental disorder and terminal cases or old age people who can not follow three techniques mentioned in the section three under the chapter "Healing". They require external intervention to mobilize the energy to release them from the trap of energy in which they are helpless. Treatment section has two processes given for this purpose which you as a caregiver can help your loved one break the deadlock of the energy and restore their breathing and sleep. Typically, it has been a trend that in the most distressful, terminal or chronic cases, the patient is unable to follow any of the instructions to do breathing, and this is where we do treatment as listed in Section three. In most severe cases, it takes about three to five days for us to help the patient restore their parameters and be able to follow instructions to learn the first technique. During these three to five days, the patient is either sleeping all the time or crying or eating a lot. After learning the first technique, the patient is in the driver's seat, and we take a back seat teaching them two more techniques. Through the techniques and coaching, we help them understand the cause, which is presented to you in all the previous chapters. By the end of the two weeks, most of the symptoms are over and by the end of three weeks, the patient begins to feel empowered and healthy to be able to go home and practice on his or her own. This is applicable from schizophrenia to cancer. Everything else in between requires much less time. Our objective is to restore these three parameters. This is what you shall look forward to when you work on yourselves or administer cure on your loved one who is *suffering*. Since, you are reading from the book, you may need a little more time to attain results. The good news is that now, the cure is in your hand, and it starts to work within hours to arrest the speed at which the *suffering* is growing in you. This is very empowering when you perform treatment techniques mentioned in Section three, you will be amazed that within hours, you can start to see the results, and you do not need any faith in anything but sincerity to do it properly and commit to the process. In fact, all of you are advised to start with the first process of the treatment section and experience the difference overnight.

We have known enough about breathing. A separate chapter has been written on it. In fact, the whole book is about breathing. Let us learn about sexuality, which is often confused with a sexual desire while sleep has often been taken for granted. We do not understand its significance and science as much as we do not understand the science of breathing.

Sexuality- Life Force Energy and Hemoglobin:

When we breathe, we breathe in the life force energy (Prana). It is difficult to logically describe what life force energy is. We feel it. It is like no one has seen air, or heat but we experience it. Biologically, breath, which mixes in the blood and reaches out to each cell and keeps us healthy is actually a life force energy. It is this sense of well-being, which we can then cultivate for our various pursuits.

Let us attempt to make it simple. The origin and start of the life force energy is through sexual union. Sexual energy, therefore, is called 'procreative' energy. We often fail to register that the same energy can be destructive energy if we are not aware of its nature and attributes. Life is like two sets of rivers – one masculine energy and one feminine energy.

These two rivers meet with each other to produce for either of the one. You and I just jump with our one lifetime into one of the two rivers. Both the rivers, with time are evolving, getting contaminated and then purifying and this goes on. Going by the reincarnation theory, a soul has been born in one family ecosystem several times and then the same soul has been born in so many different families in either of the river forms and it can be different in each birth. It carries the blueprints of wisdom and *belief* of multitude frequencies through all these experiences in its spirit. Since birth till death, life force energy, which flows through us, goes towards various pursuits, which are essential for our evolution. Our life force energy which we say is infinite and unbound, if it needs to be released to make it available for us here and now in this birth, then it must release its held up *belief* from those various life time in which it is stuck. It shall also open up by accessing the hidden wisdom which comes with unbounded energy. What you know as your present life force energy or the one which you gain through the techniques to cure yourself is not even the tip of the iceberg. What you have hidden in you or rather trapped within your innumerable *belief* system is a far bigger ocean of life force energy. Sexual energy, which is the base energy to ensure that evolution continues, thus acquires the central theme of living and is the tool through which you can access hidden life force energy and the techniques given after you have attained the cure, will help you unlock it.

It is common sense and seems like universal truth that each new male or female born shall be a better human being than the previous generation, or else, humanity will perish. Of course we have no idea why? What will happen if we all perish? We will perish in this lifetime so why all this talk about making the planet a better place but we know we must do it and this remains a mystical question about where we came from and where we are going.

EVOLUTION CYCLE OF LIFE FORCE ENERGY

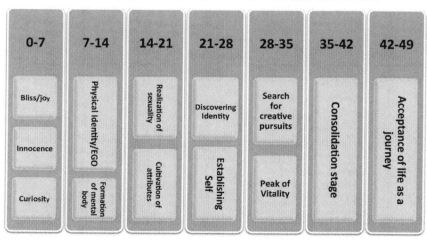

Figure 12

Life force energy, as shown in the diagram figure 12, moves with the nature of life from birth to death. First it goes toward creating the attributes of a specific gender you have chosen to be born as, then it goes in developing a child into an adult through various stages. Your creative pursuits and your choices each moment are consuming the life force energy. Without you knowing it, it is nurturing every thought or emotion, be it positive or negative. This is equal to your breath or oxygen being consumed by you at intent, insight, emotion and at thought level.

Broadly, after the age of seven, this life force energy begins to become procreative to define your physical identity and an attribute of your gender. By the time, you reach fourteen, it is available as raw sexual energy. During the teens, you discover that you have a journey ahead on your own and use this raw energy to cultivate various attributes, skills, making choices. From the age of twenty-one, it is time to establish in the physical world and contribute. It reaches its peak during the ages of twenty-eight to forty-two and then begins to stabilize. Post the age of forty-two, it works towards self realization, detachment and celebrating life and giving back to humanity. All through this cycle, sexual energy as sexual desire goes through various forms and intensity but continues to exist as a minimum base energy throughout. Sexual intercourse remains as a means to experience union and oneness, therefore, it holds an important aspect in our living.

When a soul decides to be born to cleanse itself, it makes a choice from the spectrum of frequencies it wants to deal with, in the next birth. It first chooses the gender through which it shall make all the experiences. Then it creates the roadmap or blueprint for that life. You can understand this concept better with the example of your GPS. You fix your journey from point A to point B. It shows you the map with optimal route and also shows you various points in between when you can exit the journey. If you exit, then it will reroute you again towards the destination. Same is the case with the journey of soul which knows its purpose and keeps giving you insights to re-route you towards it.

Since Spirit speaks through emotions, every experience will exhibit the emotions of same frequency. Life force energy, which we breathe, goes toward grooming the role of the gender, and in making the choices in your roadmap. Based on choices, leading into experiences, depending upon formation of *belief* or no *belief,* the life force energy is either absorbed or freed up as an expression of your spirit. Please see correlation of these three aspects.

Sexual energy as sexual desire is one small part in the whole life force energy spectrum of various frequencies but it is a base and essential frequency. The divide between sexual energy presenting itself as sexual desire and for other pursuits is very fluid. At any stage, we can use all of our energy in construction or destruction of any pursuits making us experience absolute devoid of any sexual desires or vice versa. In summary, here are the components of your life force energy:

1. Passive infinite energy trapped by *belief* in the subconscious or hidden in the wisdom waiting to explode in the consciousness.
2. Grooming you for the gender which you have selected in this lifetime.
3. Nurturing the attributes of your gender to enable you to create a container of your choices and purpose.
4. Sexual desire.

Please see the diagram below for the attributes of specific gender. There are three ways to experience sexual energy as sexual desire:

1. Experience it as sexual desire.
2. Suppress it.
3. Transmute it into procreative energy in various pursuits.
4. In first case, it has two aspects.
5. Need for sexual act just like any other species on the planet.
6. Using sexual desire for oneness with the lover which is in accordance with universal law where we seek our completion by merging with our partner.

Once again, the divide between these two desires are very fluid. We can use all our life force energy to fulfill our basic need or combine both need and oneness into one experience. We can also keep both separate and fulfill our basic need for sex and use need for oneness for various pursuits or feel this as pain or transmute for healing. If we suppress it, it goes to become destructive energy and this is where well-being and health are affected. The sexual desire which is a basic need, if that is denied or suppressed, that component of the sexual desire is what becomes destructive. Whether you get satisfaction or a feeling of union with your partner, it is nullified if the need is denied in the relationship. It is that which turns destructive and generates a lot of emotions. The solution lies in acknowledging the need, experiencing it within the body and then using it either for fulfilment of need, or oneness in love with your lover or for transmuting it for higher perspectives such as procreative energy. In the real world, you will do all of it and will feel balanced about yourself.

Transmuting sexual energy or life force energy from sexual desire to various pursuits happens all the time without our awareness and is rather a advanced level of task if performed with awareness. It is function of mind vs consciousness or fear vs wisdom. You are working on a creative project such as writing a book or painting or preparing to cook for some guests, you can discover how sexual desire in those moments begins to convert your desires into joy as you begin to get absorbed in your task. However, you shall be able to discover that once that task is complete, you have probably even more sexual desire back in place for the purpose of either need to be fulfilled or for seeking oneness. This shows you that life force energy is unbounded and unlimited and its forms are fluid.

Before you can decide to transmute sexual energy into spiritual energy as often taught by religion by giving shame and by spirituality as a greed for enlightenment, you will have to acknowledge its existence and you will have to create a lot of it in your Swadhishtan chakra and then transmute it with breath. In fact, through the first technique, it happens on its own if you are sensitive to it. However please note, if you block the flow and do not acknowledge the part where it is one's basic need, it turns destructive and this is where this chapter is addresses this issue from the perspective of health and well-being. You can see in each of the cases of *suffering* of any form, unknowingly, they have transmuted the energy because when some trauma occurred, they could not be aware of their sexual energy. So many girls and boys who suffer with infertility, depression and various other forms of distress in their teen and post teen age, have some negative experience around the age of fourteen, or before when they are beginning to have this huge flow of sexual desire building up. Another common finding, largely true in India, where a couple is in distress individually in a very happy and healthy relationship (yes, Indians can do it, they can be happy with you and still in distress because of you), women start to deny sexual desire for themselves when they do not feel a sense of oneness with their partner. I can not overemphasize that if everything is not good in your life with your partner or that is how it feels to you, like food, please take care of that basic need for sex while you discard its higher expressions. To do this, you only need to acknowledge your desire, experience it with breath and either release or just keep flowing in it. This aspect of your need is to be kept independent of a partner because if there is no partner, in suppression it becomes destructive and becomes an issue with well-being. By doing so, any negative experience does not get empowered and the mind does not require extra effort to manage the emotions and sleep will not be affected. This sexual desire as a basic need fulfilled on your own without a need for a partner (it is optional) is the most crucial link in keeping the three pillars of your well-being intact and work as prevention.

Sexuality is not as complex a topic as it has been made out by religion. They did it to control the power within you because if you feel empowered within and are able to decode the wisdom, you will not need them. That is still fine and we have almost arrived to a place where religion has a broad level reference in our life but the issue was to make society grow their interdependence. They had a valid reason to control sexuality in this regard in that pre-contraceptive era which holds no merit any more.

A myth has been around about masturbation or releasing sexual energy on your own, as a sin. When sin alone did not work, then fear was inflicted that you are wasting your life force energy by masturbating and that you will turn infertile or impotent. By now, I believe I do not need to give an explanation, having read all the chapters. Something which is infinite and is the life force energy flowing through you, can that be of a limited supply? The only possible logic is that if you feel the desire and you do not release on your own, then you will have a tendency to be dependent on your partner to satisfy your needs. This is perfect reason to grow interdependency.

Do not make a mistake to conclude that I am asking you to become independent by releasing your sexual energy with an objective of ignoring a relationship or turn insensitive towards your relationship. But sexual desire holds a maximum amount of complex *belief* in your subconscious. When you begin to witness it as described with breath, you will be unlocking your trapped energy and releasing through masturbation or absorbing it. You will actually do both. This will prevent suffering which is the objective of writing this. Your basic need as you feel fulfilled will move you to a higher plane for interdependence by making you more intimate with self and compassionate towards your partner.

Before sexuality can be talked about as sexual desire, there is significant aspect of life force energy which goes in creating a container for sexual energy. This is about grooming attributes of your femininity/masculinity. (Figure 13)

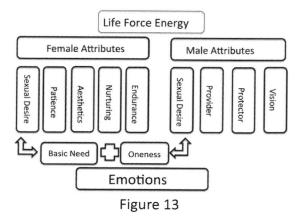

Figure 13

Through the diagram in figure 14 (on page 181), you can diagnose any of your issues. Since, women have been struggling seeking equality and empowerment and redefining the role of their gender, they are the ones igniting major shifts in their own definition and attributes. Let us understand through the above diagram, females and the issues they can experience. Men have been comfortable about their definition and its attributes. They are only recently feeling the disturbance in their attributes caused by the changing needs of the women in their definition. This is forcing them to redefine their own definition to do the balancing act in their nature.

1. Infertility: In each case of infertility that has been resolved, the root cause was a disconnection with mother. A few common triggers for such a disconnection are feeling rejected in the mother's womb (unplanned and unwanted pregnancy), being left alone during childhood (mother going to work or child being sent to hostel or grandparents), feeling that more importance and attention was given to male siblings, growing away from mothers, feeling disgusted as a child seeing a weak and helpless mother. In each of these triggers, girls grew up feeling disconnection to the river called femininity and decided to turn more masculine in their energies. For example, so many girls who came for the infertility treatment did not like the idea of femininity seeing the *suffering* of their mothers and adopted more male attributes (by discarding femininity), which created more male hormones in them. To be a mother is to first accept their femininity and its five attributes as shown above. Each of these scenarios are reflected in their emotions and through their emotions, it is easy to reveal the root cause of the problem.

2. PCOD/PCOS: When the woman discards the idea of her femininity and does not cultivate the attributes of patience and perseverance, this distorts her *belief*. Her sexual desires are also going more towards repression than actually acknowledging it and her emotions vibrate in a different zone. To be loved by a man, one needs to have attributes of a woman, if those attributes are not taken care of within, the relationship, as well as health suffers. PCOD/PCOS was rather an unheard phenomena two generations ago but today, seeing this disorder widespread, it seems it is normal to have irregular menstruation, fibroids and cysts. This is a clear symptom of non-acceptance of their femininity and its attributes. If you are one of those *suffering*, restoration is simple through the techniques. Give yourself three months to have a regular menstruation as you practice the techniques and processes in Section three.

3. Distress: Take a case of a normal healthy mother. this means she has strong femininity and her attributes are taken care of, and she has a regular menstruation cycle. By looking

at the set of negative emotions (true for male as well), you shall be able to find out that one of the five attributes has a problem and she has changed her belief around sexual desire from one of the three as mentioned above (one can always move from acceptance to repression and to transmutation). Hence, her experience of happiness is not eroded at the base level of femininity but at the procreative energy levels. This is directly reflected in her sexual desire, which is the vehicle for *bliss*. For example, she feels neglected by her partner or feels insecure by nature and demands some attention before she can open up emotionally, to experience her sexuality. If, attention is not provided, she locks her sexual desires and generates a lot of negative emotions. These negative emotions which then affect at least one of the five attributes of the woman, which will then affect her life force energy as sexual desire and then that will again feed more negative emotions and this cycle will continue.

Femininity is like a road, procreative energy is like a car and emotions are like a driver. No matter how skilful a driver you are, if the road has potholes, you are bound to experience a bumpy ride. No matter how good the road is, if your car is not functioning well, it will be a struggle through the journey.

The other way round is also true. Any experience, which generates negative emotions impacts your procreative energy which in turn imbalances one of the five main attributes impacting the definition of femininity and blocks the flow. Same is true for men. If someone bullies them, they suffer from their own definition of being a man and have huge emotions due to this issue. When they fear their job, they have a huge emotion in their inability to provide for their family. When somebody attacks their family, they have emotions around their inability to protect. They suffer in silence about their unworthiness when they are not able to provide a vision and wisdom to their children.

This is where the entire spectrum of issues fall at the core of our health – issues in acceptance of their femininity/masculinity with its attributes. The healthy women and mothers who suddenly feel at the loss of love and bonding with their men shall pay attention to one of the five attributes which are going down. For a man to remain attractive to the woman, the woman need to provide that strong magnetic field so that the man remains in that energy field. If you are losing on being woman enough which means missing at least one of the attributes, whereby not feeling completely whole within, the man will feel a less compelling need to be connected. In this situation, influence of your magnetic field is reducing resulting into a man feeling lessor drawn towards you. This is the same for men too, if they are missing any attribute, the woman will not feel the need to be connected either. You can sense this from the example of how you feel towards your partner after orgasm. You do not have a need to attract any more or your partner is not feeling attracted any more. At least for few hours. This is true for basic need driven encounters. When you both are in love and it is a sensual encounter, orgasm does not bring intimacy or take it away. It is just one high state of merging with each other. Women who are very fond of seeking equality, then they must know that orgasm is the only state in which men and women are equal and it flows in the relationship from here. It is not otherway round. They are at same vibratory level and one. All others times, we are two different genders with our own attributes and uniqueness.

Or put it otherway round. If you feel insecure in your relationship and like to turn inward for the reasons, check for lack in one of the five attributes which must be eroding your magnetic field due to which mutual attraction does not feel as compelling as it did before. Same is true for men to keep women attracted in their relationship. Men shall check their attributes and see if they are losing out on any one of them. To be a woman is to stay with a deep, innate, magnetic field in which the man has no option but to remain connected in order to feel the union. Motherhood in the women has a huge magnetic field for their sons, hence men even after growing up remain drawn to the mother. You can see from the example of men how they do not feel so strongly towards the mother where their mother is missing in one of the attributes reflecting in the energy field of motherhood, though as a women these attributes may still be well developed. It is simple to see that the magnetic field of the mother does not have that pull for the sons. This is where as a partner, the only way women can keep their men glued and loving to them is developing attributes strong enough. Such a woman is then a sensual woman. Sensuality is a fluid state held in the consciousness which in between the sexuality and spirituality, has well regulated emotionality flowing through it. Same is true for men.

In summary issues related to women's well-being are in acceptance of her femininity. A healthy woman, who struggles in her relationship with her partner, has lost her sensuality by losing out on one of the five attributes. When this happens her emotional spectrum shifts towards negative which impacts her sexual desire turning it from procreative to destructive. This is where a vicious loop begins to form. When she comes back to her femininity by restoring her attributes, she connects with her innate wisdom on its own and that creates a healthy magnetic field, in which her partner is drawn to automatically. Same is true for men.

For new mothers, as your need for the partner goes down at the expense of new-found motherhood, you begin to nurture your attributes more as a mother than as a woman, and this is where many healthy relationships begin to face problems. You can, of course, have attributes for both. This is the root cause behind women gaining weight after delivery when unknowingly, they choose motherhood over womanhood. The driver is insecurity. They don't feel insecure or lonely after giving birth finding their purpose in nurturing the child. They develop the tendency to discard the importance of a partner (and womanhood). A son offers a longer period and more unconditional sense of security to the mother than a husband could give to the woman in you.

Everything said above is classical programming above to which we respond unknowingly. A lot of it is under transformation but since very little is through awareness, we have invited more problems in our health and well-being and are far more distressed. For example, a girl who grows with strong feminine attributes and is independent and deeply connected to her journey is very sensual in her energy field. When such a woman becomes a mother, her deep wisdom and larger consciousness allows her to groom motherhood and womanhood all together with a sense of serving and purpose than for a sense of seeking security. Such women are not rare and is a fast growing population.

So how do we, male and female, both crack this deadlock of defining (femininity, masculinity), procreative energy with its attributes and emotions? There is no way you can directly work on your attributes and there is no way you can change your emotions. The easy way is to address the energy which is in your control and that is your sexual energy, and if that begins to open up, it will automatically bring emotions into the optimal range and also mitigate or heal the issues connected with the road (attributes) which has potholes.

Sleep, food and the desire for sex are basic necessities. We did not choose them. They are given to us by nature. Purpose of having these three parameters in balance is to strive for evolution and pursue our purpose of life. We have a sense of duty to keep these parameters stable. The form, quantity and methods through which we keep these parameters in harmony is not fixed and can be regulated.

Among the three, it is simple to handle sleep because the body does collapse on its own. Food too is easy to handle one way or the other. But regulation of sexual desire is in our hands, and this is where we have severe complexity in doing so for such a long time on the planet.

We have made progress with food by franchising it, and we have locked sexuality by institutionalizing it. Anybody can fulfill your need for food so that you survive but sex is not considered such a necessity. Though the morality around sex was created keeping it as a need for organized collective evolution in a pre-contraceptive era and that has made our life force energy and emotions all mixed up around this issue. The two parts of the sexual desire in which one is need and second is to seek union are bundled together rather than treated separately. We bundled it together, creating a product called partnership or marriage, and it made sense then but this is where we are facing issues with well being in our time and space.

In post-contraceptive era, we were trying to separate out these two things. From your health and well-being perspective, we were addressing here a role of sex in your health and well-being and not really addressing issues related to expression of spirit through it.

Like food is essential, sex is essential. But to think that only food from your mother will fulfill you is not the right *belief*. You can cook too. You can regulate your need to have food two times a day or just one time a day. Likewise for sex, it is linked with love, safety, security belonging and oneness. People deny even acknowledging existence of desire for sex on a small hint of not feeling loved or not feeling secure. This is where it begins to turn destructive and reflects darkness of your spirit to attract all negative emotions about yourself. I am talking about health and well-being here and not about pleasure and oneness.

Almost every one of us, grew up either being ashamed of our sexualtiy or were taught to suppress it. We were taught it has to be experienced only when there is a need to consume it through a partner. We are developing guilt around food and shame around sex, and we feel we are doing it for health and well-being. Really? With such massive negative *belief* and emotions?

Sexual energy which carries life force energy is your regulator to cultivate your attributes and through that it becomes the expression of your spirit. When you conceive something creative such as making a movie or writing a book or nurturing your garden or growing an idea into a startup company, it requires life force energy to be procreative at its best and uses a lot of your sexual energy to manifest your spirit to help your soul fulfill the purpose of your life. Therefore, it has a healing effect on your well-being.

Every human experience is either meant for *bliss* or for pain. Life force energy goes toward these states by default. After losing *bliss* as a child, as we grow up, we seek that *bliss* at different ages in different creative expressions. Act of lovemaking is one of the essential ways in which one seeks *bliss* by attaining the state of orgasm. It is taught to us that we shall seek that through a partner in a way of helping each other seek completion and union of their own male and female energies within. As partnerships are becoming complex and we are stressed out more than before, distortion has come in our expression of oneness through sexual acts from the health and well-being perspective. Rather than respecting the process and need for interdependency, we are turning dependent and respect for the process is missing due to ignorance about its deep impact on our well-being. The same procreative energy is used in meditation to attain *bliss* because this sexual energy can be transmuted for any procreative pursuit which offers the frequency of *bliss* or our ideas about *bliss*.

To experience *bliss* through sexual energy in whatever form is a three-step process. Step one is to acknowledge its existence in you, and this means removing all the *belief* and shame around it. Second is to experience it within the body because it is flowing all the time as you breathe. Third is to consume it as sex or transmute it in various creative pursuits. As far as health and well-being is concerned, which is the focus area of this book, you only need to do the first two steps. This is where religion played the game with us by asking us to consider it as a sin or suppress it or have shame around it. The reason is very simple. When you experience it within your body, it is hugely empowering. So much so that you actually need no one and you can feel complete within and in this process, you begin to gain so many insights that they guide you for the fulfilling of the purpose of life. The mistake is that the moment we feel the need, we very irrationally want to consume it. The moment, we feel upset or not loved in the relationship, we begin to suppress it. The moment we feel we want to be spiritual; we condemn sexual energy and refuse to acknowledge its existence in us. We do not realize that *bliss* through meditation or any other creative pursuit requires experience of sexual energy within and by witnessing it with breath, it holds the power to transmute and heal. It is life force energy and before it can be directed in any other form, it has to be felt and accepted. Sexual desire is built within and is fluid which can take any shape we want it to take for construction or destruction.

Transmuting through spiritual practices have been done by condemning sexual desire and through suppression and absenteeism, they have used spiritual techniques (largely and essentially mechanical forms of breathing and not the one you are learning). It is possible to attain bliss in meditation by suppressing sexual energy by using power of will and forcing sexual energy to transmute. Such a state of meditation does give you *bliss* but then *bliss* is felt by special children as well with its side effects being unconscious of their physical reality and *suffering* it causes to others in their life. Once they attain powers through such ways of being, showing control on the life force energy, their spirit which was kept under suppression now seeks expression, and this is where we see so many people on the spiritual path in a distorted way indulging in the sexual activities or having greed for physical manifestation such as power, money etc. Since they began with the *belief* that sex is shameful, after attaining the purpose of gaining powers, when the mind is not active in keeping control, they manifest this shame through their deeds and acts. It is like a plastic ball, which you push down in the water and keep buried. The moment you remove your hand, the ball bounces back with more force making it visible above the water.

Suppression is not the path. There is no spiritual energy which is intrinsic in us, but the state of *bliss* is. Intrinsic energy is sexual energy, which if handled holistically, grooms various attributes and creates fulfillment and contentment in living.

On the other hand, indulgence is not the path. Osho's vision was to allow people to experience sensuality and through that move them towards spirituality. He attempted to remove *belief and shame around it.* He hoped that soon, people would discover that *bliss* lasts longer in meditation than in an orgasm and would pursue holistic living. When *belief* around sexual desires are removed, it flows through your body making you feel very intimate and sensual which is the most healthy state to be in. It is neither sexual nor spiritual but somewhere in the middle being able to swiftly move up and down these two states. This is where he turned out to be wrong. People got stuck on indulging in sex. How long can you continue to have sex? Once you reach the orgasm, you will be empty and that state is the state of meditation. Since they also used various techniques of meditation namely dynamic meditation (which is what people try to do with power Yoga today), they could forget their *suffering* in double doses of *bliss*, and it did help them get uprooted from the normal, civilized society and its morality, but their consciousness did not grow. They were more like a kite stuck to the branch of a tree, which begins to feel the sense of flight with the wind but is stuck to the tree. His followers misunderstood. They thought sex was the medium for eternal *bliss* and got addicted to the indulgence. OSHO was much ahead of his time in this respect.

How can a spiritual practice for the purpose of seeking union and oneness within, find its way through indulgence? This was a very risky experiment by Osho, which had largely failed and his profound wisdom is so grossly misunderstood.

Witnessing is the way to deal with it. Buddhism taught this and Osho also had the same wisdom and taught this all his life that we should witness everything, and nature will take its own course for the higher purpose. But for some reason, witnessing sexual desire was not taught, and this is what you shall learn now as a powerful tool in your hand to free up your belief and open up life force energy so that each cell gets more oxygen.

Each time you observe your breath, you shall witness a rise in your sexual energy, and you can start to feel it flowing in the body. Initially your mind would want to consume it, and this is where you should keep breathing, and let it spread into the whole body. Or abort it and consume it but come back again. Do not fight with it.

As it grows, it will surface various emotions associated with good or bad experiences or the trauma and *belief* around it. Keep witnessing it and keep breathing. Gradually, it will either leave you in deep peace, *bliss* through orgasm or in deep pain. All three states are good enough to take away your *sufferings* and restore your breathing and well-being.

The more we stay out of touch with ourselves and remain in our minds, the more we feel deprived of feeling our own inner-self, and this creates the need to be loved far more than before. If attributes are not cultivated, it directly goes in the form of feeling sexual desire, and we feel we need a lot of sex. True, we all need it, but not as much as we feel we are deprived of it. You can test it yourself. When you are sitting with a partner and you feel sexually aroused, start a conversation and you shall realize that suddenly warmth, love and intimacy grows and the impulse and desire for sex reduces. Through the chakra system, you can explain that your energy from Swadisthan begins to move up to the Manipura, where you feel your identity in the form of being respected for what you are, to the heart chakra where the feeling of love grows and to the throat chakra, where you begin to now express your deeper level of truth. Then to the third eye where your insights flow and crown to de-addict you with the need to have impulsive sex. You may still have sex now, and you would find it more fulfilling as you nourish the energy in all chakras. This is where you have a cure for premature ejaculation. When you are emotionally very dry, you are desperate to reach the state of *bliss,* you rush all your life force energy to quickly reach orgasm and feel *bliss.* Another reason is that there is guilt or shame around the act of sex, and you just want to get rid of this act as quickly as possible. Yet another reason is that you feel compelled and controlled by aggression of the partner or fear of judgement by your partner. In such cases, if you are with another a person where you can be yourself and there is no desperation and you feel nourished emotionally, you shall find your premature ejaculation is healed.

The most important factor among women for bad health is repression of sexual energy. Their sexual desire is linked with first seeking safety, security, recognition and appreciation.

Depending upon the culture you are growing up in, this has been a traditional package through which a woman feels loved and their sexual energy begins to flow. In the absence of any of these parameters being fulfilled, they are programmed to shut their desire. Since it is linked with a contract with a man, they further believe that they are only supposed to experience sexual desire from their man which adds to the complexity. Hence, they land up repressing the sexual desire until and unless a conducive environment is found, which is becoming increasingly difficult and rare.

Shutting down your sexual desire is denying the life force energy to flow. Every mental disorder case where their mind has sticky and obsessive thoughts is due to the fact that unknowingly, they have a repressed sexual desire and that energy has gone back into the opposite polarity chakra (pineal gland), where it begins to turn into dark energy affecting the subconscious mind by eroding the healthy partition between the conscious and subconscious mind. Mental health is restored very quickly by restoring these three parameters (sleep, breath and sexuality). In fact, just by restoring the breathing, the rest falls in place on its own as they are all deeply linked with each other.

The recommendations for men and women are that they witness their sexual desire and breathe it. There is very little need for you to seek its release through masturbation. When needed, please go ahead. This is recommended even for people who believe they are in a sexually fulfilling relationship. Through witnessing, they discover that their dependency on the partner for emotional gratification goes down and that creates a lot of space of mutual respect and love for each other. The whole idea here is that it takes care of your well-being, which is linked with expression of the life force energy and sexual desire is the regulator, through which you can seek a higher degree of sense of completion within. Gradually, this technique of observing breath while in the state of arousal, leads you to become more intimate with yourself and the anti-aging process starts not only on your face and skin, but also internally in the organs. The key point here is that when you feel the desire, nurture it. Of course go ahead and consume it when you must, but first begin to experience your own life force energy within and have no *belief* around it. Increased life force energy flowing through your body directly adds to the haemoglobin levels in your blood.

TIP: Deep and rapid breathing pumps the energy in your navel followed by deep and slow breathing spreads this energy to your whole body. If you practice this cyclically, you will transform from being sexual to being sensual and from sensual to a spiritual being. Women feeling low or a different level of arousal or absence of arousal in the breasts, if when feeling aroused can bring the sensation of arousal to the breasts will decrease their chances of breast cancer. From a well-being point of view, you can sense the risk of any potential health issue in the future by seeing how sexual energy spreads in your whole body. If you feel it does not go to specific parts of the body, it means there is some emotional block there. Do nothing except as taught to you in the techniques and it shall restore balance. Do not equate it with a different level of sensitivity in a different part of the body as some health issue. There are three regions in the body, which have different levels of sensitivity when caressed or paid attention to.

Story is not very promising for men either. They grow up in the hands of their mothers, move over to the wife. Other than making money and being a provider, they outsource not just their emotional needs but even their emotions to women never realizing that they are hugely dependent on others to decide their happiness. They either remain dependent or if they become smart realizing their power as a provider they manipulate women to get their needs fulfilled. Traditionally, men experience emotions through their women or the right way to say that is that their emotions are kept in balance by their women. Their needs since childhood, are provided by the mother before they ask for it. This means that before a child realizes his need or feels the pain of not being given, it is provided for. Hence, for them sexual desire is a need which they feel shall be fulfilled. They realize their emotions only when their need for food and sex is fulfilled and that is the time their emotional bodies open up. Since they carry the pressure of being a protector and provider, they remain on guard all the time and expect needs to be fulfilled. This is the reason, when they say something to their daughter in a stern voice, she feels unsafe and feels the fear of not being provided for. Hence, in most cultures, men communicated their concerns to their daughters through their wives, and that is how father and daughter relationships have this graceful space between them where they endlessly continue to feel for each other. There is a big risk attached with men feeling emotions. If they are allowed to feel emotions such as when they feel for a community, country or for women, there have been wars. You can check yourself if your man starts to cry or when he feels insecure or panics about his job, what happens to you. You feel unstable and vulnerable and you have the fear of the unknown. Men's anger and emotional panic destabilizes women by triggering a fear of her existence. It is very common for women to hijack all negative emotions from the men to make him feel stable by taking on those negative emotions and experiencing it or ensuring that men never fall in that range where they feel a lot of emotions. Hence, it was meant to be a beautiful arrangement created by society and perfected over thousands of years to make man and woman support each other for their weak areas and complement each other.

But now the time has come for man and woman to explore higher levels of frequencies in their relationships – to help each other discover their purpose and individuality rather than relationships being based on fulfilling each other's needs. We all, therefore, are under pressure to understand it and bring that in our own self and then reflect this in our relationships.

SLEEP

Like a breath and life force energy, this is the third pillar of your life. It has been given to us but we have no control over it. However, similar to breathing and sexuality, we have not paid attention to its power and its role in our well-being and recovery.

Like breath and sexuality, if we try to control our sleep, it turns destructive to our well-being. These three natural phenomena are mystical in nature and the very basic essence of our living. We have no clue on how breathing takes place and why we feel sexually aroused or why we have the tendency to close our eyes naturally every night and have no clue next morning about where we went in the night. It is magical how by restoring three parameters, we have seen people getting cured in last seven years. Almost all of us have experienced the magic of the interplay of these three parameters in our adult life while making love at night.

You can witness the magic of mystery by fusion of sleep, breath and sexuality while with your lover in the night. In the process of love making, your eyes begin to shut, your thoughts begin to disappear and breath goes deep. It then modulates between slow and rapid but remains deep. With modulation of breath, you feel the joy spreading throughout the body. With almost negligible light around you, enabling you to turn inward, embracing your lover, in the state of trance and love, you can witness *bliss* with fusion of sleep, breath and sensuality in those moments. This is a very fine thing, and it is not about the intercourse or the need to have sex. It is a gradual and slow process. Such a moment is the moment in which sexuality, sensuality and spirituality fuse into each other and you feel one with your lover and one within. This is the moment in which wonderment and mystery become one and this is the moment in which pain and *bliss* are one. This is the moment which makes you feel like a complete human being, and if you can carry this spirit within through the day, you are filled with compassion and purpose in living. It is the same process for a *Mystic*, who experiences the same fusion within, without a partner by observing the breath and feeling the sexual energy transforming into sensuality by spreading in the body and dissolving all the dark within and attaining *bliss* and oneness within. The time at dawn is best suitable for supporting this fusion of unconscious, subconscious and consciousness. If you are in a loving relationship, you can now practice spirituality at dawn after spending night of a fusion with your lover. You are more fortunate to be able to do both as you have no belief around sexuality and spirituality but driven to experience *bliss*.

Sleep is a process much like the Cinderella story. She must return home by midnight or else the magic spell will end. Such is the case with sleep. We must return home to unconsciousness every night for specific hours or turn poor after the spell ends.

The purpose of the sleep is to clear the karma from the experiences done during the day and clear the consciousness of its impression and integrate the experiences with the subconsciousness and unconsciousness. It is an essential background task to be performed every day to take the backup of your experiences and validate them against the purpose of your living. If you have failed to acquire the wisdom through the day, subconsciousness intervenes by giving you dreams in the night or insights in the morning when you wake up. This is called guided living and supported life full of faith and surrender. This guidance is possible only if you follow the process of sleep, which means that your conscious mind shall be empty while going to bed.

By clearing your conscious mind of its thoughts, you confirm your faith in the unknown. This process alone is a symbol of your faith in the nature. This is enough and you really do not need to worship God. The purpose of your prayers and meditation is to be able to sleep in the night with faith in the tomorrow. This faith in unknown or tomorrow comes naturally if you have lived your day full of purpose through the day, which means an authentic life.

If your mind is not cleared of thoughts, and if your emotions are strongly held by the subconscious, you see dreams which are actually insights but mixed with various emotions and thoughts. You wake up with cryptic clues. For insights to be clear, your mind shall be empty before going to bed.

For a *Mystic*, there is never a dream because his sleep is never a sleep, but always in state of *Yog Nidra*, where insights are a regular stream which guide him with the next steps. Even when they attend to people, they remain in that state and speak whatever they catch in your energy being in such a high quantum state of *bliss*.

This is the reason, bedtime reading helps you unwind and get into zero thought state. It helps you clear your mind and brings you back to the present moment. It is a way to expand your consciousness. This is the reason couples engage in conversation at the end of the day to help each other clear their held up emotions by sharing. This is what love making or sex does, and this is what you do through meditation or prayers to clear your conscious and subconscious before going to sleep.

Some of you believe that you sleep very sound and yet you have *sufferings*. Since this contradicts with my diagnosis, I have gone deeper with them to do further research. Here is the truth. If you have sound sleep, there is no way you will have any health issues.

If people sleep sound and yet suffer, it means sleep is not sound. Generally people work very hard through the day. Keep emotions suppressed and over work their mind, so at night, the body cannot take the load of an overheated processor. As it gets ready to merge with unconscious, it crashes the mind and sound sleep comes. The body has its own process to seek its rejuvenation on a daily basis. When they wake up, they wake up with almost the same emotions and thoughts with which they had slept in the night. It is like a computer crash, when restarted, it shows the same programs, which were open in the tabs the night before.

Some of you are lucky that when you wake up, most of your thoughts and emotions are cleared, and you feel fresh enough to lead the day better than yesterday. This is because, somewhere at the inner level, your faith is intact and your trust in life is bigger than yesterday's experience. So you could be crashing in the night but due to your faith in life, it clears up all your thoughts on its own and leaves you fresh in the morning.

Sound sleep, which we look forward to for your well-being, is as follows:

1. When you wake up, you feel lost for a few moments, not knowing, who you are and where you are. Really a short moment like you had in your childhood.

2. Curiosity. Do you begin to feel curious to sleep several moments before actually going to bed. One of the finest sign of well-being.

   Sign of potential risk on your health

1. If you experience thoughts from the previous day or anxious thoughts about the day for the tasks, you are under mental stress, this is a sign of a tendency towards disorder.

2. If you experience a lot of negative emotions or events from the previous day? That means you have tendency towards distress.

In summary, sleep is a process in which your karma of the day from conscious and subconscious is taken into unconscious and you are fed back with life force energy filled with insights and wisdom to lead the next day. It also brings realizations and wisdom about your previous day and offer an opportunity to heal the karma of the previous day. This is possible only if your mind is empty before going to sleep so that it does not interfere with the working of the subconscious and unconscious on you during the night.

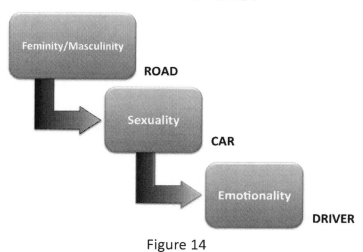

Figure 14

MEDITATION – THE CURE

*M*editation is *Yog* (not the Yoga as you know it) – *Yog* means union. In different cultures, time and space, it is defined as the union of the human with God, the union of Shiva and Shakti, union of the subtle with the gross, union of Yin and Yang, union of soul and body, union of heart and mind.

And when we meditate, we experience the ecstasy, the *bliss*, the silence, the light and the divinity. You have heard all of it. We have been hearing such narratives for ages and yet no one has been able to explain how to do it. Closing your eyes, listening to a guided voice on YouTube, or chanting, or attending a workshop; we have tried all of it. Even if we had reached the state of meditation, it felt good, we didn't know if tomorrow we would have the same results.

If it is a union, then what is separating us from our own divine inner-self? If we can remove that layer of separation, then we do not need to do anything and that state shall be the state of union, hence a state of meditation.

We can explain this with the help of a child prodigy like Messi, who has discovered *bliss* through football. Both his heart and mind are in football round the clock. He has no need for survival coded into it, and his parents have also not told him that he must focus on studying and become an engineer one day. This state in which you are complete and one, is the state of meditation. You stay in a state of *bliss* throughout. To be One with your nature is what meditation's objective is – a *Mystic* meditates in the cave and an artist plays his sitar. To be One means that a program in your subconscious and your conscious is the same. Each of us experiences the same when we fall in love. That is the state of meditation. We experience that we cook for our child or do gardening albeit not always and not consciously.

All these states in which you go beyond time and space and lose your sense of survival is the state of *bliss*/union/meditation. Our mind cultivated for survival is the barrier in connecting us to our inner-self. If this mind drops, then we are in the state of meditation.

Pranayama is a process to reach the state of meditation through balancing the electromagnetic field and making your mind devoid of any thoughts. Exercising is meant to mechanically push the breathing deep which in turn will force your mind to stop thinking (suspending) and brings attention to the body which will release held up emotions in the process of pushing breath deep. Yoga is meant to deliver the same. Through all of this, you seek to stay in union and that is possible only when the mind turns into a zero thought state for a few minutes. The entire process on the guided voice or any other method as listed above is not a state of meditation but a process to attain the state of meditation. So, if you practice Pranayama for an hour but reach zero thought state for three minutes, then you were in meditation for three minutes only.

Meditation is state of *Yog Nidra* (conscious sleep). It is a state of sleep in which you are conscious of it. In *Yog Nidra*, you will not be aware of your surroundings but if some disturbance happens in the surroundings, you will become aware of it and may come out of *Yog Nidra*.

It is a state you attain when you gain complete thoughtlessness. For you to reach that state, you need a process to empty your mind gradually through awareness,.where it turns into a zero thought state and merges with the subconscious (emotional body). The difficult thing about meditation is that your mind is not the same daily. It has been involved in the last twenty-four hours in managing some more emotions. Hence, you may have to be in a different timespan daily to arrive at the state of meditation. Even if it is the same, in the state of meditation as your emotional body begins to open up, you are bound to have a different experience almost daily, primarily because the infinite world opens up for you.

So meditation is the union of the conscious and subconscious in which the conscious mind loses all its existence related to survival and merges with the subconscious. You can say it is the union of the consciousness and the subconsciousness. You can also say it is the union of the heart and the mind. The most beautiful part about meditation is that it aligns you with the purpose of your life for which you are born.

We are born for a reason, and it is never in the *suffering* or the punishment. If we encounter difficult situations during our lifetime, it is because there is something to learn and clear karmic debt and that learning is vital to fulfill our purpose. This purpose of life is programmed in the subconscious and each time we make authentic choices, we come closer to it. In fact, if you take a closer look at yourself, you will discover that you already know what you want to do in life while in a different career. So, we all know where we flow naturally and where life will be blissful. Due to our insecurities, being a part of the conditioned mind, we fear taking the plunge to pursue it. So, when you reach the state of meditation, your conscious mind programming begins to dilute, and your purpose and authenticity begins to get written in your conscious mind. For the subconscious to be able to write something in the conscious mind, it needs the conscious mind to be empty and in a listening mode.

When you begin to meditate, with each day experience to stay in meditation, you begin to vibrate higher because, now, every day you are touching this *bliss* state. This grows your overall frequency levels to higher planes. As that happens, toxic emotions or toxins in your body which are vibrating at lower frequencies will have to leave your body and you feel aligned with your spirit. It is like you are a company running on a loss, but as you begin to meditate, you gain money reducing your losses everyday. Let us take the example of a relationship in which you have a lot of anger and frustration daily. It drains your energy each moment as this is a loss making situation for you. Now three things happen to you if you start to meditate and reach *Yog Nidra*:

1. It stops draining your energy, as you, now, have extra energy.
2. Disengages your mind from generating anger. So you may have same intense argument, but your anger will not last as long as it used to, and it will not be as intense.
3. You shall find positive emotions and hope coming to you. This is how simple meditation, as explained above, transforms you within three days.

Meditation is a simple process. State of meditation is a state in which consciousness and subconsciousness are one. This is only possible if your conscious mind has no thoughts. Let me repeat when the conscious mind has no thoughts. Breathing is inversely proportional to thoughts. Thoughts are created to regulate emotions. Emotions are the language of your spirit. Since the spirit seeks its expression through experiences, each moment is an experience generating emotions.

If you begin to observe your breath, your thoughts will start to drop. When thoughts are dropped, emotions, which the mind was controlling or regulating will surface. When you begin to experience emotions while observing the breath (because emotions will hold your breath, like thoughts did), those emotions will release the *belief* and will leave your body to align you with the spirit and light. This will expand your awareness about yourself. That state in which you arrive now feeling a trance is the state of *Yog Nidra*, also called meditation. Each time you do that, you are guided with insights. Your vital parameters and chemistry begins to restore as negativity or toxicity of emotions and toxic *belief* are beginning to clear up from the subconscious.

But it is not as simple as it sounds. As you begin to do it, your emotional trauma begins to open up in *Yog Nidra* or afterwards. So many memories, that you had kept under control through the mind, will now surface. Past lives will start to open up to cleanse the karma and your body will begin to change as it looses a lot of fear. Although this is the reason you're meditating, if you are not aware, you may create another fear and not really reach *Yog Nidra*.

The most beautiful aspect of meditation we have witnessed for seven years among thousands of people is - as your mind begins to switch off daily for a few minutes, it doesn't form a specific pattern of thinking anymore. So it actually begins to break your patterns of thinking, patterns of specific emotions and your reactions in specific situations, which you encounter daily, and it really surprises you and people around you that things are changing. At the energy level, not only with you but in your ecosystem, whomsoever you have had your energy entangled with, begins to get unstuck. So a loving relationship, in which you have begun to suffer, fades away and love surfaces, all by itself. You only meditate and change nothing in yourself.

It sounds unbelievable that meditation can be the cure. At best, you know meditation as a process to de-stress and gain vitality and peace for some moment. If you have read the previous chapters, you are right that meditation helps in releasing stress and gives peace which is the sign of well-being. So it makes meditation a very good preventive or maintenance tool or lifestyle activity. But if you persist the same, it becomes the Cure. In simple words, I just went a few steps deeper than you, where meditation became a Cure. So far, whatever form of meditation you have known and practiced has worked as an escape from *suffering* and has been more like an anesthesia.

So the simple ground rule is, if you begin to meditate for 20 minutes daily, as described above and you reach the *Yog Nidra* state for a few moments (you can reach this state only when the mind turns into zero thought state), within three weeks, you shall be able to experience a transformation in your life and your *suffering* will start to reduce or get eliminated. Many people who claim that they meditate for two hours daily, but continue to suffer with their problems, are not really meditating. This is how each case in seven years has been cured. The cure is in your hands. I can help you arrive at the cure, but to administer it, is in your hands.

The challenge in manifesting the cure through meditation is that observing breath is a difficult task because our minds are wired up. It becomes further complex if you are in distress, disorder or chronic disease because in all three states of *suffering*, your mind is not in a balanced state. This is exactly the reason you have this whole book and three techniques and two processes to bring any patient to a state that he gains reasonable control over their breath. Some of the data from our seven years shall help you understand the power of meditation as the cure.

1. She had blood cancer for 10 years and was on a truck load of medicines including daily doses of oral chemo and a big number of painkillers, when she attended the workshop in November, 2015. She used to experience pain in her bones round the clock. One week after the workshop, after practicing NV Swimming technique (breathing), she reported 80% reduction of pain in her bones. She was declared free of cancer in the next five months by her doctors after extensive tests and diagnosis. During this time, she visited me two times for a period of two and three weeks each, where she practiced all three techniques to make her state of meditation deeper and longer throughout the day.

2. When I work on an ICU patient or a chronic case of illness, I meditate for about thirty minutes every four hours and within a week on an average, the patient comes out of a critical situation. If I do this for six weeks as remote healing, no matter what *suffering* a patient has, the patient is able to go back to normal life and medical tests validate his healthy state.

3. When I conduct a healing week where more than 500 people across the globe attend, they all receive healing in about 30 minute-sessions and many are completely able to resolve their distress. This means that a few minutes of the state of *Yog Nidra* every day for a few weeks shall be enough to reverse any *suffering*. You only need to get better at observing your breath and keep walking every day towards the cure. This statement is coming with credible experience of succeeding in each kind of case. Therefore, it shall give you enough confidence to practice it.

4. Patients who are healthy and have lifestyle issues like depression, unhappiness, stress, diabetes, high BP, migraine, stuck in a bad relationship or job, trauma, PCOD, infertility have been able to resolve their *sufferings* by practicing NV Swimming for about twenty

minutes daily for three to six weeks. Out of twenty minutes, they attain a state of meditation for three to five minutes, on an average.

5. When patients *suffering* with any kind of chronic disease, disorders and/or distress, they attend one week (up to three weeks) of treatment at NV LIFE, they go through the process as mentioned in the treatment section and are taught three techniques as described in the same section. Within one week, no matter how chronic their situation is, they are able to pursue the techniques and gradually get out of their *sufferings* with disease or disorder over the next few weeks.

You will learn it in Section three of the book, which is dedicated to practicing processes and techniques to administer cure for yourself or your loved one. You may feel intimidated with the above data and feel like you are inadequate to create such results. Some of you may argue that it is because of my healing powers that such phenomenal results are achievable. Partially, you have a valid point but here are the reasons you can do it too.

1. Healing energy flows with intent. I have reached a stage where I do not even need to sit in meditation, healing happens with my intent and many a times, just when I am listening to your *suffering* over the phone or reading the chat. Hence, I have written this book with a very powerful intent that each of you who buys (not borrows) will receive healing. So while practicing the techniques, you have the same healing powers coming to you as any person who attended my program.

2. You have the luxury to gain wisdom through various chapters of this book while still under treatment as per the processes written in Section three. When I work on patients at my center, I do not even ask them or lecture them for the first three days till they gain back some energy. They remain lying down almost the whole day as per the processes written in the section three.

3. There has been more than enough cases where people came for treatment when they were in a disastrous state and in six weeks, not only were they healed but they also turned into healers themselves. Each of my patients, by practicing these techniques, have brought transformation in their situations. This means they have healed themselves. There is no way these techniques will fail you, but you can fail them by not practicing them.

4. This shall tell you the power of meditation and shall motivate you to practice meditation as the well-being and the cure for various types of *sufferings*. Please follow the process laid out. Meditation as you know so far is not the meditation and certainly not the cure.

Once you arrive at *Yog Nidra* using first technique, you will know the difference that you have not known in meditation.

5. We all have healing energy innate in us. It is nothing but our ability to remain in the state of *bliss.* The longer we can stay in *bliss*, the more power we have to heal ourselves or others. In section three, healing is described in detail. How you can become a healer for yourself or others, and you do not need any certification or special program for that.

6. You will always have online support from us. You can also attend workshops conducted in your city or take help from trained NV Life experts to move a step up.

Below is the diagram (figure 15) which shall show you how to monitor your progress towards the Cure.

Periodicity, Intensity and Time interval – are parameters to track progress

THE CURE– FIND YOUR COORDINATES

Figure 15

1. With your issues, you are in the quadrant between "fear" and "need". It does not mean you do not have moments of *bliss,* contentment and joy or negative dark emotions of the quadrant Fear – Wonderment.

2. The more you focus on your need (or greed), the more you get disconnected with mystery and wonderment. This disconnection means you are not driven by insights or guiding forces. This means insufficient faith. So, you may have planned your finances for retirement very well, but the future will always grow your worries because you lack faith and the reason for this is that you are disconnected with your inner-self.

3. On the X axis, you have *fear* and *wisdom*. The more you move towards your wisdom, the less fearful you shall be. So when you look at your finances, and are connected with mystery, you shall experience the wisdom coming to you that everything will be alright. After all, how much money would I need post retirement. All I need is health, peace and some money for myself and my wife. Now, you are aligned to the wisdom that we all will go one day. You trust yourself that you solved so many difficult situations that came into your life. But, if you are stuck with, *I do not trust the future, anything can happen*, or *I am alone, and no one will help*, or *I will be obsolete*, then you will have the growing need to plan for the future out of fear and you will be in the Fear – Need quadrant with *suffering* and struggle.

4. Need – Wisdom quadrant is the one where typically our previous generations lived, with a far stronger social fabric and larger families, which automatically acted as a mechanism to stay with the wisdom and ground fear for each other. Hence, at any moment, if someone was distressed, families, friends and societies would give a sense of wisdom, taking away the fear of being alone and pulling the person back into the contentment zone. So even if your disease was not healed or your misfortune was not changed, you lived and then died feeling loved, accepted and hence, content.

5. Wisdom – Wonderment Zone: This is where you need to reach daily for a few minutes with the first technique. This is where Messi lives, a *Mystic* lives and all those people who lead a purposeful life, living without the fear of tomorrow and without the need to survive. You can be here now too. Here you are cured for your *sufferings*. No *suffering* can stay when you are in *bliss*.

6. Fear – Wonderment Zone: It is easy for you to understand this zone, if I say it is all those people who perform black magic or people with a lot of spiritual power (often known as Tantrics, (though Tantric is a positive word) who control the lives of people. They have deep-rooted fear but they are detached from the world, therefore they do not feel any need for survival. But they are ambitious about gaining powers or practicing mysticism. Or they are normal people like you and me. As they gain wisdom, they gain power and as they gain power, they develop ego, tip into fear and suddenly they shift from Wisdom – Mysticism Zone to the Fear – Mysticism zone. But it is not reserved for those people alone. Each of you are infected with pessimism, negative thoughts, insufficient faith, lack of trust and filled with anger and desire for the power to harm others if possible. We control and disempower people for our own gains. We are jealous. All such frequencies are in this zone and your disease, disorder or distress has these frequencies manifested

in it. As you read these lines, do not try to come out of the dark zone. This is just to make you aware. We do nothing about this zone except becoming aware of such a zone in ourselves. We do not try to remove the darkness inside us. We move toward the light. Where there is light, dark cannot exist.

The Cure is to move from zone 1 to zone 2, and zone 2 to zone 3. Each time, you hit *Yog Nidra* for a few minutes, you go into *bliss*. This brings insights leading you towards wisdom and dropping your fears. This reduces your greed into need and moves you towards wonderment and mystery. As that happens, you are now making profits. On a technical note, you discover that your mind has dropped. Peace has started to stay the whole day and your symptoms are fading away. This happens on the day you are able to reach *Yog Nidra*. However, for individuals who have not got any health issues but working on well-being and inner peace, need to move towards contentment. Contentment and wisdom are like the chicken and the egg. They both help each other grow. Read the chapter on parenting and there is an exercise there. This exercise is a prerequisite for all participants in the workshop and everyone changes their reality after doing it for few times and arrives in the contentment zone. The more you do it, the more you tap into more wisdom and that starts to bring contentment. The joy of flying is not in flying but in knowing the ground, or else it becomes wandering. Hence, connecting to your roots and learning how far you have evolved from your parents offers you a sense of contentment, and this is what you learn from the chapter on parenting. It certainly does not clamp your degree of freedom but adds a navigator to your flying.

This is a movement you make through *Yog Nidra*. To arrive in *bliss* and that itself offers you insights, which turn into wisdom. Wisdom will dispel fears on its own. Wisdom will also take away greed and develop faith. Faith will create a sense of wonderment in you. As you practice every day, you are already moving in the quadrant of Wisdom – Wonderment. Do not try to cure your *suffering*. Move in this quadrant and *suffering* will disappear on its own.

A holy saint (say the Dalai Lama) and you are walking in the forest. A lion or snake comes in front of you. The Dalai Lama smiles and continues to walk while you are frightened and run back as fast as you can.

It's the same event but two different reactions. Nope!! Reactions are the same. The Dalai Lama also felt the same emotions of fear as you felt. However, in his case, he was able to ground his emotion in a microsecond and bounce back to his state of *bliss* without you or any camera capturing the reaction. So intensity of the emotion was the same but time interval was different. It is like a millionaire losing INR 10 versus a beggar who only had INR 10. The amount lost is the same but the impact is different.

Take the case of anger. It is common to all of us, and we experience it a few times in a day. As you begin to take this treatment, your anger will not vanish overnight. But its intensity, periodicity and time interval would start to reduce and you will discover that its intensity, periodicity and time interval are reducing on its own. So if earlier, you were angry 5 times in a day and 8 out of 10 in intensity, it lasted thirty minutes each time and each time you had used your willpower to recover from it to get back to normal. You shall discover that now you get angry only three times and it is four on a scale of ten and lasts only fifteen minutes and you do not have to do anything to get back to normal. This clearly means that your silence, peace and happiness are growing in intensity, periodicity and time interval. Thus, your health has started to restore on its own. As you practice more, this will only grow and you can track your progress toward well-being through these three parameters.

SECTION 3
TREATMENT, HEALING AND CURE

Suffering (Distress/ Disorder/ Disease) and Diagnosis
"Consciousness Is Directly Proportional to Health."

Consciousness and health have a direct relationship with each other. The bigger the consciousness, the better the health. As you begin to fall sick, your consciousness shrinks. We have almost no other thought or emotion outside of this *suffering*. We learned from the example of fever in the previous section how our mind collapses, and our attention remains at our body and emotions when the fever increases. To help you recall our learning, the reason we are attracting *suffering* is because this is how we are turning inward and connecting back to our spirit, which we have ignored by staying in our mind.

As you begin to reverse your *suffering* by practicing techniques in this section, you shall see your consciousness expanding. This means, becoming more aware of yourself, your tendencies, better acceptance of yourself, better comfort with your past. Better acceptance of your failure. You shall see more insight and more wisdom about yourself.

DISTRESS

Distress and stress are two different stages of non-harmonious states. Stress is a feeling of tension or pressure or simply put, burden. It can occur at any level of your being, i.e., physical, mental, emotional or spiritual.

Stress is a state where you feel like you are doing something beyond your capacity. Stress is not an issue unless it stays for a prolonged time interval and begins to erode into your overall happiness. You then probably feel either a bit down, tired, angry or irritated. If you are able to sleep peacefully while still under stress, your mind gets reset the next morning and you are able to think of ways and means to handle or eliminate it. You are still under control.

Distress is termed as extreme anxiety and often caused by either the major events in your life or a series of events resulting in a state of hopelessness or loss about a specific aspect of your life. For example, if you are not happy in your relationship, you will still continue to be optimistic about other aspects of your life such as job, raising kids etc., but this nagging feeling about your relationship remains inside you. It happens at an emotional level. Your mind is now working extra hard to try to contain or rationalize distress. Failure of a relationship or breakups, generate a whirlpool of emotions and though you are aware that your work shall not suffer, you discover that you have lost focus. You try your level best to somehow handle and manage your life. More often than not, you are able to keep your distress and your mind separate, though life is not fun anymore and you are left vulnerable in other situations.

Distress like any other negative emotion is due to lack of faith in the universe. If it is the failure of a relationship, causing distress, then it is because you do not see hope and feel disappointed. You feel disappointed because you had pinned all your faith in the relationship as a source of your happiness. Now as faith in life breaks due to failure of the relationship, your trust in self goes down causing distress. You are aware that there are so many options but the reason you find no energy to work toward the options is the frequency range in which your emotions have brought you down. Your *belief* comes in between. This is why, turning inward and having faith in self is the way. If a relationship breaks, you do not lose trust in life and move on.

The moment you are unable to contain or confine your distress, it starts to affect your mental body. The spilling over of emotions into your mind causes substantial toxic thinking or behavior and by now, it can be said that you are developing tendencies of mental disorder because your mind is not in control anymore and begins to confine you to only do things you need for bare minimum survival.

If you have a strong mind and keep distress suppressed, this is where it has potential to manifest as a disease with much distorted emotions surfacing at that time. The real challenge with distress is that you land up in a zone where you lose aspiration for life till something happens to you externally to restore your hope.

The bad news is that almost all of us are distressed at various levels. Not all situations of distress leads to disorder, but it does consume your life force energy, affecting your electromagnetic field. Thus aging and fatigue at various levels begins to set in with time. This is where our well-being is affected, which on one level has already affected your *bliss* and is now ready to affect your health.

DISORDERS

Mental Disorder is a disease at the mind level. It occurs when the mind is losing control while trying to manage distress. Mental disorder is a state where your behavior is not in your control. You are aware that life is big and full of choices. You know that you are loved but your emotional body in distress is so deep into hopelessness that you do not see light, and you drown into the darkness. More often than not, the root cause of mental disorder is in parenting – when events of life in our childhood and adolescence make us feel we are not loved enough. This is the quickest way to feel hopeless. In our formative years, if kids are brought up with love and acceptance, they are very unlikely to ever get into mental disorders in their adult life regardless of how impactful the events of adult life causes a state of hopelessness in them. Here are some of the early signs of mental disorders in healthy young people.

1. Death in the family on which the child had not cried. Often grandparents are the ones with whom they are attached.
2. Temperature of their forehead remains higher than temperature at the lower abdomen and at the feet.
3. Breathing is shallow and may be jerky.
4. Sleep is light or disrupted or full of high speed dreams, one after the other, leading to feeling exhausted upon waking up.
5. Seeing colors in the dream.
6. High temperature in the belly area, forehead and feet being cold. Child is holding lot of anger.

DISEASES

*I*t is easy to understand how diseases are formed if you have understood how distress and disorders are formed by now.

The fact is that pain is not acknowledged and the mind actually forms a *belief* about continuing to survive. It is a way for the spirit to force us by breaking down the engineering of the body to seek our attention. It is aggression and revolt by spirit. All of us have experienced some busy schedules for a few days, and we postpone our emotions such as playing with our kids or just relaxing, listening to music. We encounter stiffness in the body, fatigue and at times a running nose, cough etc. After the project is over, we get back to the normal routine, go for movie, may be grooming or massage or meditation, and we feel rich. The body gets back into shape. To simply say, repressed emotions surfacing as diseases is the over simplification of the concept, though the true but larger picture here is the mind not acknowledging the pain and denying the loss felt in the emotional body.

My observations from the last seven years:

I started working with mental disorders and then distress. For a very long time, I kept thinking disorders are easy to deal with. Distress is very easy in any case, and you will experience it when you follow the treatment schedule. I used to be scared about working on diseases till the day when I saw people who approached me with any disorder or distress healed their migraines, thyroid, blood pressure etc., while I was only healing the distress/disorder for which they came. Gradually, I understood the science and started teaching it in a workshop, I was very comfortable with any chronic diseases, and I finally got to help people with cancer. Then I began to feel that disorders were tough to deal with because after a while I encountered few cases of relapse. But this is half the truth. Here are the guidelines to decide how effective the cure will be and what is tough to heal.

1. You have a problem, but what is the problem you have with the problem? Check that. If you only like to talk about it and gain sympathy, then you just need a few friends, enough beer and maybe some extra sex but not the cure. In such cases, this book will actually help make you accept the problem and heal you as much as you like it to be. Few people after the workshop do not practice or practice only on a need basis what is taught, because in two days, they healed as much as they wanted to be healed, and then they move on. Here, you treat The Cure like a massage parlor. Job done and this is perfectly fine.

2. What is the incentive for you to get out of *suffering*? This is a huge reason to decide if a person with a mental disorder would want to reverse the disorder or not. The mental disorders are almost always an inability to face reality by force or by choice. Disorder is often an escape route not to take up responsibility. Curing their disorder leads them to take responsibility. Therefore, they would only get cured as much as a symptom of disorder does not bother them any more; such as lack of sleep, and/or where they begin to give up taking responsibility. Any schizophrenia patient, *suffering* with hallucination and/or delusion can stop having these symptoms within a week with the two processes defined in the treatment section (using cotton and circling on the navel). But you will find it hard to get him back to taking up responsibility of his life, if there is no incentive for him to earn his living. This is why I can be sure that western countries would reverse their disorder faster than Asians because they have a task to take up responsibility of their life. A sole bread earner for his family with a strong incentive to keep his job if *suffering* from Schizophrenia can be cured within a week. With the book, he can get cured in almost the same time with little support from the caregiver without my intervention.

3. Disorder and distress in young kids: Please do not use these techniques with them to start with. First mothers (and in some cases fathers as well) need to heal themselves as a large part of their *suffering* are either coming from the pregnancy period or during their early childhood. Of course, after working on yourself, start them with cotton in the right nostril as detailed out in the treatment section. We have seen very good results in children when they have been told to observe the breath. It is a fun thing for kids.

DIAGNOSTICS

Appearance of Symptoms

Less than one year   Less than 3 years   Less than 5 years   More than 7 years

C. Detailed Information

1)   List of common symptoms and a brief summary

_____

_____

_____

2)   Are you on medication? Yes/No

3)   For how long, have you been taking medication (number of years)? _____

4)   In a day's time:

    i. How many times do you experience these symptoms?

_____

_____

    ii. For how long do these symptoms last?

_____

_____

    iii. On an average, what is the intensity of the symptoms (on a scale of 1 to 10, 1 being the lowest and 10 being the highest)?

_____

_____

    iv. Is there any particular trigger for which the symptoms appear?

_____

_____

D. Mental-Emotional-Physical State

1)   How is your breath?

    Jerky   o

    Shallow   o

    Rapid   o

    Shallow and rapid   o

    Slow   o

Goes till chest	o
Goes till navel	o

2) Do you experience negative emotions since the onset of the symptoms? (tick as many as applicable)

Hopelessness	o
Nervousness	o
Worry	o
Anxiety	o
Anger	o
Grudge	o
Hurt	o
Trauma	o
Panic Attacks	o
Self-Pity	o

3) Mental State (tick as many as applicable):

- My mind is always occupied by one thought or the other.
- Even when I don't want to think about certain things, I feel compelled to think those same thought patterns.
- It is difficult to control thoughts.

4) Physical State (tick as many as applicable)

Temperature

a) Forehead is always/often warmer than lower abdomen region

b) Legs and hands feel cold

c) Navel and below navel areas feel colder

d) Lower back and shoulders are stiff and painful

Overall lack of energy in the body: Yes/No

How is your sleep quality?

Very sound	o
Light sleep	o
Disrupted sleep	o
Sleeplessness	o

Difficult to sleep   o

RAPID   o

Do you dream?

All the time   o

Never   o

Sometimes   o

Nightmares   o

Dreams appear one after another and in high speed   o

Do you see colors in your dreams (i.e., whatever images you see have colors in it)? Yes/No

After waking up in the morning, what kinds of thoughts do you experience?

Thoughts of previous night	o
Feels various emotions at waking up	o
Few moments of blankness (state of thoughtlessness)	o
Worry of future	o

What are your common patterns? (For e.g. I always land up being fooled by people, all my relationships break at same point, I start with enthusiasm and then I lose it in my new job)

_____

_____

Sexuality

I don't feel the desire	o
Low and mild	o
Obsessive	o
Normal healthy attitude and fulfillment	o

I trust my intuition

Always	o
Sometimes	o
Never	o
Regret that I didn't follow	o

E. Major Events of your life

a) Write about 3 major events of your life

    i. First Event

_____

_____

_____

    ii. Second Event

_____

_____

_____

    iii. Third Event

_____

_____

_____

F. My wish list from life (in different spheres of life):

b) Health

_____

_____

C) Material/Financial

_____

_____

d) Relationships

_____

_____

e) Spiritual

_____

_____

f) Social

_____

_____

How to understand diagnosis:

If you have gone through section two, you will be able to make your own analysis based on the parameters given below. Here are some quick facts:

Healthy person:

1. Body temperature increases slightly from head to toe.
2. Wake up feeling lost for just few short moments.
3. Breath goes below navel and is unobstructed.
4. Some level of curiosity about sleep and being in silence for few minutes before sleep.
5. Have normal sexual desire and reasonably comfortable about it.

Every other state means you have a task to work upon yourself. You shall come back to this diagnostics every week after starting to practice The Cure to check the improvement in these parameters. An improvement in these parameters is beginning of well-being, though you may still have symptoms of your *suffering*.

Special note: Seeing colors in dreams is not a very good sign, which shows up in an imbalance of the above parameters. These colors mean interference of subconscious with conscious mind. Often kids have this tendency. Just by using those two processes in the treatment section, this will restore by improving the sleep.

NOTE: This form will help you diagnose your distortion, to being well. We have used it extensively and it takes me less than three minutes to know your root cause in almost every case to predict your trajectory for recovering with The Cure. With information given in section one and section two, you shall be able to do learn to do the same after some practice.

CURE

1. **Everything is vibrating in the universe. Nothing is fixed, nor death and destiny.**

*Y*ou are angry and the next moment, you laugh at yourself and calm down. We face many such situations where we move from one emotional state to another effortlessly or through will power. This is what quantum physics says. Nothing is fixed and everything is vibrating. The entire science of treatment which you have read in this book is based on this principle of quantum physics. This means your tables, chairs, appliances, your body, and of course, your relationships and bank balance – everything in this universe is vibrating and nothing is fixed. If this is true, it is simple to assume that your *suffering* is also not fixed. Cure or happiness in your life is also not fixed. If that is true, then destiny is also not fixed, but you have a choice, and your choices lead to one of your probable destinies. It is like a maze we solved during childhood to find the right exit door, based on the choices we made. Every choice leads us to more choices or limits our potential choices and narrows it down to one specific outcome, which we resigned ourselves to and accepted as fate or destiny.

This is the starting point of the cure. Your *suffering* is not fixed. No cancer or schizophrenia is fixed. It can be reversed. These are just states at which you are vibrating, and if you vibrate longer in such states, you feel stable with your *suffering*. It is like a traffic cop on the noisy junction getting accustomed to the noise, but that is not his fixed state. Place him in the garden and his vibratory level will change. Discovery of a mechanism of breathing is that vehicle that can move you from *suffering* to *bliss* and make you vibrate higher where lower frequencies cannot catch you. Therefore, the disease, which is an outcome of that lower frequency zone in which you stayed long enough, does not exist on a higher plane anymore. The Cure, in reality is about vibrating higher and staying at higher vibratory levels.

You can discover your vibratory level by listing down the emotions your *suffering* brings about in you. For example, anger or disappointment in case of high blood pressure, fatigue and helplessness in case of diabetes. Every disease is one quantum state, which curtails your degree of freedom or choices and forces you to have a conscious awareness about that specific emotion, which has been long repressed.

When you start this treatment, you start to vibrate higher toward *bliss*, which on its own begins to heal those low frequency emotions. When you are in love, you are vibrating higher, lower emotions such as anger, hopelessness or unworthiness do not come to you though they do exist in your emotional body. As *bliss* begins to spread in your whole being, lower frequency states become unstable as your entire being (spirit) now wants to move toward joy or *bliss*. This section is about how to vibrate higher and stay there by practising the techniques.

Since NV LIFE was born out of ICU cases where doctors had given up on two multi-organ failure cases, let us understand why death is certain but not fixed.

Any critical or terminally ill patient has reached an energy level where his/her entire system is ready to collapse due to the series of choices made over a period of time. The patient has not chosen consciously to die but has now reached a stage where dying is easier than the ability to generate such large quantum energy to turn around. It is like a company strapped of cash, choosing to go bankrupt if the huge capital cannot be infused. Since the patient cannot tap into his infinite energy source or receive it from external sources, as options begin to close, dying becomes the default choice. Such a decision is not a choice but a compulsion.

However, if it is possible to provide extra power, there are possibilities for him to vibrate higher and realize that it is possible to revive himself. In this higher state rescued from the lowest state of no hope, the patient still has a choice of whether he wants to die or come back to life. This is what I landed up doing – helped the patient in the ICU get extra power to make a decision to come back or go. I just offered a choice. It is possible to do this and in many cases where doctors had given up, people have revived without any healer like me because they are mystically able to tap into the infinite power of their own spirit. The family plays an important role in reviving the patient. I am aware of such families who without any external help, have unknowingly followed the same principle and revived their loved ones.

So death and destiny are not fixed. That is why different people have a different life span. It is the number of breaths which we are designed to have.

2. Imbalance in the male and female energies (electromagnetic field) causes disease/distress/disorder.

The electromagnetic field is dynamic in nature and is subject to fluctuation with breathing. Breathing is the function of our emotions. We breathe differently in different emotional states, hence disturbing our electromagnetic state. If an emotional state stays for long in our body, we begin to get stable in that state where disturbed breathing becomes a norm. Since emotions alter our breathing, altered breathing alters our emotions to seek stability as per the law of nature.

3. Every experience is either meant to take us towards *bliss* or towards pain.

Every experience is meant to take us towards either *bliss* or pain. We suffer because we try to control the natural outcome of the experience gravitating towards either *bliss* or pain. If we release control of our ego, *suffering* will go, and we will either move towards *bliss* or pain. This will stabilize our consciousness at our stable state. Regardless of our experience giving us pain, gradually our stable state would only move toward *bliss*. Pain offers insights and wisdom to guide us towards the purpose which is the manifestation of *bliss*. Our attempt to control the experience disrupts our electromagnetic field by disturbing our breathing.

4. Need is the origin of *belief*.

The need to survive is the origin of all *belief* emerging from the lack of faith. As *belief* is formed, the need to control our experiences grows to seek certainty. A movement toward being a *Mystic* is the path to reverse *suffering*.

5. Any emotion felt in our body, if witnessed and felt fully, shall leave our body in a few minutes.

If you allow any emotion to be surfaced while observing your breath, it will leave your body on its own in a few minutes and will align you with your spirit. This is "The healing".

6. Breathing is inversely proportional to thoughts.

Belief develops our mind. Mind has no mind except for survival. This grows the gap between the subconscious and conscious mind and the spirit (emotions) feels trapped in this process. Our definition of survival creates a need to control an experience.

Thoughts and emotions, held inside, require a life force energy, which is being consumed from breathing without our awareness. When we begin to observe breathing, it starts to disempower the thoughts and that will release held up emotions.

7. The problem with the problem is that it does not allow us to stay focused on the problem.

You probably want to read this statement a few times and grasp it. This statement is what will make a healer out of you.

When you pay attention to a problem, you will discover that rather than staying with the problem, it generates various emotions and/or thoughts and drifts your attention away from the problem. The reason we are not able to solve a problem is that we cannot keep our attention at the problem. If we can, we find a way to solve the problem, or we are guided to solve the problem. We are able to solve problems which are important to our survival such as being unemployed. Since this remains in your consciousness almost all the time, you do find a solution. This is also the law of manifestation. You work on a project. It requires you to take twenty steps before you can manifest the reality. The art of manifestation is to only keep attention at the next step. Complete it, and then move to next step.

8. Merging the past into the present is the secret to LIVE in the NOW.

We can stay attentive in the moment if our mind does not swing between past and future. The more it goes in the past, the more it erodes the hope for the future. The only way to live in the present is to merge the past in the present without its joy and sorrow. This will effortlessly hold the vision of the purpose and will exhibit the spirit guiding through insights and wisdom, moment to moment.

9. Breathing is the only link between life and mystery.

Breathing carries the code (purpose of life) in our subconscious. It being an autonomous process requires no attention. When breathing is brought to our attention, it begins to decode the purpose. It comes in the form of realization, intuition or insight. This leads to synchronicity, which becomes the guiding force. Observing the breath leads us to drop into the conscious mind and that enables sleep and optimal life force energy (sexuality). Sleep is the state in which fusion of conscious, subconscious and unconscious happens. This is oneness in spiritual parlance.

10. *YOG NIDRA* is the union of the Spirit-Body-Mind- The Cure

Union of Spirit with matter is the state of meditation (*Yog Nidra*). To be able to arrive in this state, conscious mind shall become thoughtless. It happens when you observe your breathing. When conscious mind becomes thoughtless, it merges with the subconscious. Subconscious has emotions which now begin to surface and conscious mind witnesses as they leave the body free of them. Expansion of the larger consciousness is the natural outcome of this process. These emotions are held due to *belief*; hence it heals our karmic layer which is blocking exhibition of the spirit. As we arrive at *Yog Nidra*, the integration of the spirit with matter happens and insights about purpose of life begins to empower the consciousness as expression of spirit. This is The Cure.

THE SCIENCE OF CURE

*A*ny imbalance or disharmony, acute or chronic has been reversed based on the following principle, which this book consists of but comes to you here in summary.

1. Disharmony is caused by a disturbance in the electromagnetic field.

2. Electromagnetic field (Yin and Yang) is changed by disturbance in breathing.

3. Breathing is inversely proposal to thoughts.

4. Thoughts are created to regulate/suppress emotions.

5. Emotions are created by our experiences.

6. Experiences are manifested based on *belief*.

7. *Belief* is created by the environment as chosen by us.

8. Environment/parents are chosen by us based on our karmic journey for cleansing.

9. Every experience is an opportunity to release old patterns and karmic debt.

10. Cure is the realization of the true expression of our spirit for which we have been born.

Based on the above points, the chemistry in your body changes.

1. Disturbance in breathing causes less oxygen in your blood stream.

2. Less oxygen in the blood causes toxicity in your body.

3. The immune system is weakened due to a higher toxicity.

4. It affects the flow of hormones in your blood.

5. Hypothalamus is connected with the central nervous system and registers whether there is stress or not, internally or externally, and results in the respective hormones being produced in the body.

From this you can see that the breath and the chemistry of the body are very much connected as explained in the Medicine and Spirituality chapter. You arrive at this state of *Yog Nidra*, when the thoughts are zero and held up emotions are released. It is the same optimal state of *bliss* a child lives in. In this state your breathing is deep and slow and oxygenation of the body at a cellular level is optimal. The brain has no function, other than restoring the body and its engineering to its optimal level. When the optimal level of oxygen reaches every cell, they have no option to release the toxins, and the immune system is restored. In this state, hormones from the endocrine gland system, flowing into the seven glands, are optimal. If you continue to be in this state, as a child is always, all unwanted emotions which can disturb hormonal balance, will not happen. The Cure, is nothing but an optimal immune system and optimal supply of hormones in the body.

HEALING VS TREATMENT VS CURE

The Cure is a state of balance or union of spirit matter or Spirit-Mind-Body. Hence the cure is always within you. You are the Cure. No one else can ever cure you. Any process or technique used in restoring you to this state of balance to manifest the state of Cure can be called treatment. The purpose of treatment is to trigger healing.

Our treatment section is specifically intended to enable the healing process to trigger it at all levels. It is designed to shake up energies and trigger restoration almost effortlessly. In fact, in several situations, treatment processes alone is the Cure. This Section is specifically designed for a caregiver who can, within minutes, start the process to arrest the speed at which *suffering* is growing. For example, someone is in massive distress and kind of suicidal, you can start the process and within hours you can see the difference. You can compare them to ICU emergency services though they are much more effective than that. Some of you may find it hard to learn the techniques given in the Section *Healing* for the following reasons:

1. You have tried various ways of breathing and your knowledge will interfere in following the instructions given.

2. You realize after reading the instructions that I am saying something different and would want to try it out but because you are very intelligent, you will try to innovate the techniques without even experiencing it. Some of us have problems in following the instructions and we like it "my way".

3. Stress level is so high that when you begin to do the techniques as instructed, you will not be able to pursue it because your mind will distract you. This is the single reason, large enough for people to take some time to learn it. This is where

the treatment process is recommended as the first step for a few days before learning first technique.

4. If you have a disorder, disease or are distressed, it is very hard to pursue the techniques on your own as the first step. Start with the treatment process first.

5. Terminal cases of *suffering.*

Exactly for this reason, we have the treatment section, which effortlessly regulates your breathing and triggers healing in you. Once you are there, pursue the techniques given in the chapter "Healing". The key driving factors to influence healing are as follows:

1. **Acceptance:** Accept what you feel. Do not fight. You are angry, accept that you are angry. You feel guilty of being angry, accept that you are guilty.

2. **Receiver:** Receptivity of the patient, and it does not depend upon his faith in the healer or in the healing modality, but in being curious and open to transform himself. To be open, means to witness the effect healing is bringing. Initially, it may give you restlessness and fear. These emotions are surfacing to leave you. Allow this to happen.

3. **Trust:** Trust the process. Your experience is your validation.

4. **Intention to get healed:** Check your intention and not your desire to be cured. You may feel resistance to be healed beyond a point and may find comfort in your *suffering.*

5. **Faith, curiosity and hope:** You do not need any one of them to start the treatment. You can start the treatment section and follow the instructions. As you begin to experience the difference, your faith, hope and curiosity will rise and then you will get more involved

6. **Ego:** This is the demon you need to become aware of. Your mind will trick you and keep you busy by finding excuses to not to pursue healing. Each day you heal yourself, you will feel that the effect of ego is going down.

Discipline, Sincerity and Commitment:

It is an observation that many a times, people who fail to see the results in arriving at a cure, lack one of the three attributes in pursuing it. They will be committed in carrying out the process as described in the *Treatment* and *Healing* sections but will not be disciplined about it. They will change their schedule every day to finish everything else first and when they have no energy left, they like to commit themselves to it. This affects their intent to heal.

The far more common observation is that they will be disciplined and committed but not sincere. They will go by the schedule and just do it as if they have come for some blood test or for some scan as for an allopathic treatment. This is due to their lack of attention. If your mind is occupied, you put cotton in the right nostril (as shown in *Treatment*), then it will interfere with your thoughts and will suffocate you. If you are addicted to thinking, your natural reaction will be to remove the cotton and resume your obsession. The whole idea is to break thoughts and this is where you need to be sincere about it.

You are disciplined and sincere but you have multiple priorities, hence you are not consistent with the process. This will not bring you the desired results though you will feel the healing effect. This is due to the lack of awareness about your *sufferings*. You must remain committed at least till you reach the critical mass and techniques become effortless or so addictive that you automatically begin to adjust your schedule to include these techniques in the core of your day.

Intention, Attention, Awareness

Dr. Deepak Chopra in his book, *Quantum Healing*, gives an account of various patients who got cured by his intervention. In his summary, he mentions that he does not know what really works in one case and does not work in another. He concludes that "Intention, Attention and Awareness are the ingredients in enabling healing." But how do you make medicine out of it or create a process that can be given to people as a medicine. Let us examine how this statement is the soul of any cure because it is. In seven years, this statement was given to people in every workshop and the entire cure, which you have read in this book it is essentially an expansion of these three words, which determines if you would be cured fully or not.

A disease or *suffering* is a way of the universe telling you that you are not doing something right with your life. This is how the universe is bringing your life to your attention. You are successful and happy and one day you discover, you have diabetes. Suddenly, your attention turns to your body, which you have been ignoring. Once it comes to your attention, you begin to become aware of its behavior and patterns and its impact on your life. Then comes your intent – What is your intent to cure it? If you accept it as a way of life, clearly you have no intent to cure it. But those who have the intent to cure have not let diabetes grow in the body. They remain aware of their problem, pay attention to their daily schedule and keep discovering various situations internally as well as externally, which have an impact on their well-being Universe is making them become aware of themselves. An inward journey albeit forced upon. There are people who alter their lifestyle in order to quarantine impact of this disease and refuse to suffer. They just refuse to accept that they are hopeless in the face of disease and by altering the lifestyle; they are able to contain the disease and begin to maintain inner and outer balance in their life.

Reverse the logic. You are in a loving relationship in which a few things are not creating harmony and peace. Check what your intent is. You are aware that something is not working in your relationship. Take a simple example of your partner's habit, which irritates you daily. What is your intent? You are emotionally affected and expect him/her to leave that habit. You are aware, it comes to your attention, but since it clashes with your habits or *belief* you are rather upset than having the intent to resolve it within.

Energy flows with intent, not with decision. With decision, you use your willpower to channelize energy toward your goal. Your intent is to sleep but your decision is to work. Your intent is to remain employed and feel secure financially but your decision is to quit and start on your own? What happens?

"When your intention is to transfer loving energy there is no way you can fail ... because in the subtle realms' intention is action" – Leonard Laskow in his book Healing With Love.

Your energy flows with your intent. You intent to buy a new car (let us say HONDA) while you drive a Hyundai (second hand, six years old, badly dented and locking system is broken and you have to go to the passenger side to put the key in and open and then come back to driving side to start the car – by the way, this is my car). Like a routine, you leave in your car today for work and you are surprised that you notice so many Honda cars today. You had taken this route daily but never noticed before. So, you have the intent for a Honda, and it catches your attention. Now, if you conclude that you do not have money or you postpone your idea of buying a car for a year, intent is killed and you do not see so many Honda cars. But the power of any intent is such that you still do not stop seeing Honda cars on the road. It fades with time or probably never fades as karma is already created, and it is imprinted in your subconscious.

But as you continue to pay attention to the Honda due to your intent, you become aware of the car in more details. You probably read more reviews, and then you discover that your neighbor, whom you have seen so many times in the lift, is holding the Honda car keys in his hand and you start talking. So, you become aware of the presence of Honda cars around you. Intent now turns into the desire to own it and then you pull in all your resources to manifest it one day. This is how you manifest the Cure.

In seven years, I have met only desperate people. Desperate to get well and they promise me that they will do anything and everything to get well. I make an internal assessment on how much he is willing to get better and on that I attempt to search for an answer to one question – Agreed that you have a problem, but tell me what is the problem you have with the problem? If it is a case of OCD, then they say, "I cannot sleep and I am tired of my thoughts.". So here the problem is not that he wants to experience the bliss of living, it is that he is tired of his compulsive behavior. Hence, when parents say they want him to complete engineering and that he is a genius, well that is not what the patient feels. Completing engineering, being on his own and taking charge of his life is not his problem. So the patient will follow anything till he gets to sleep and the thoughts are gone (often within a week). Post that, he just wants to sleep. So when sleep is disturbed, he picks up one of the techniques again and does so much that it restores his sleep. The Cure is done. He is not dependent on others but he is not independent yet. He does not want to be. He wants to experience free will and not commit himself to survival and the rat-race. Now as parents, this is not acceptable to you. You are cursing yourself and angry about such a fate. Right, so you have a problem, please enroll yourself for the treatment.

Assuming that you have a noble intent to heal your cancer or relationship or anger and you are aware that you do not like it and you have a problem with this problem, how would that heal now? You need to now pay attention. When you pay attention, you will discover that you are not able to keep attention on your anger or cancer. It triggers emotions. Feel those emotions while breathing. Do it again. Keep doing it and pursue the insights you begin to get. Nurture the insights. Your consciousness begins to expand now. You will already start to feel better by now. Of course, now that you have the processes in this Section, you do not need to do this. It will happen on its own now.

This is exactly what Deepak Chopra magically wrote with three words and now his profound wisdom hidden in these words has become a cure with techniques, processes and science.

HEALING

What is Healing?

"Time is the biggest healer," is the myth which was once a truth. If it is true then the theory of karma and reincarnation is wrong and with time every soul would be born in *bliss* and will only grow more blissful in each lifetime.

As a rejoinder to this statement, we hear, "Let us move on, it will heal by itself." This statement has merit in it for people becoming good at dealing with their lives and those getting better at surviving. If you experience trauma, there is no way its impact has left you. You may decide to move on and that would mean mentally becoming capable enough to not let you get affected by such events as you go on living. But the impact and memory of that experience is still present in your emotional body (subconscious), and you have learned not to access that part of your memory. In later stages of your life, when the need to move on dies down, these wounds begin to surface. In reality, they have not healed, but you have learned to manage them. You have learned to avoid such situations as much as possible. So if you are abused during your childhood, even in the most loving relationships, while growing up, you are cautious. If you grew up with an insecurity seeing your parents fight, a harsh tone in your own relationship scares you that you are failing in your relationship. But you have learned to move on as you were told time is a healer. Is it? Is this life?

Time is a healer for a wisdom-driven mind and not for a fear-driven mind. Let us move on means let us move on with faith in life. Over the years, as your consciousness expands, you begin to see life in a larger context, it begins to subconsciously heal the *belief* attached to such negative events of the past and that heals. But, today, we lead a largely fear-driven life and we are not good at having faith or feeling loved and secure in our ecosystem. Therefore time is no more a healer for us.

If we go by the concept of spirituality – everything happens for a reason, everything has a meaning to it for us to learn and evolve from, and the only way you can heal yourself is by evolving – you evolve your consciousness around that event so much that you feel liberated from the clutches of that trauma. If you are abused, then you discover why you attracted such an event, and how this tendency of seeking attention at any cost, unknowingly attracted people to use you for their need by fulfilling your need for attention. You discover how your need is a handicap in your life where you are always dependent on others for love and appreciation, else you feel rejected. Your awareness about yourself and your vulnerability is enough to evolve you to a higher level. Now trauma does not feel like trauma but like a gift from the universe to teach you a lesson, to equip you, and to pursue your life's purpose. You may further reform others, educate others, but that is secondary. You have now moved one plane higher. The realization that you need love and appreciation and feeling pain of rejection can transform you to be a stage dancer. Learn to feel emotion as emotion and live them rather than repressing them in the body and seeking manifestation in a toxic manner. This movement is by being aware, and this is what is called growing consciousness in spirituality. Quantum physics says that you can move to a higher plane by raising your vibration. Likewise, you shall see that wounds on your emotional body open up one after the other, and it appears as if it is a never-ending process to heal. Once you finish all of it from this birth, you begin to face tendencies from previous lifetimes. It even goes more complex in life if you are constantly evolving yourself to higher levels by breaking your limitations and *belief*. You may begin to feel that you are getting stuck though there is nothing in your conscious you can find that shall affect you. It is very simple to think that you could be having such tendencies as a roadblock coming from your previous lifetimes, but the hard part is to realize that it is coming from your ancestors or both. It is easy to work on your past lives but how to work on your ancestral tendencies?

Healing is all about evolution, growth in consciousness and alignment toward an effortless, abundant life. If this is true then healing is like breathing, which shall run effortlessly and it shall not happen that we are moving around on the street with the ventilator on. This means, we cannot be dependent on an external person for healing though we may tap into them time to time at crucial turning points in our lives just like looking up at a map to help us navigate.

If life is all about evolution and growth in our consciousness, then there is no way the universe could have left this in the hands of a few people so that we remain slaves and dependent on them to be healed. This is in contradiction to nature and to assume so, we either do not understand the laws of nature or think that God is dumb, and we are his flawed design.

Since ancient times, this wisdom to heal was available with every household, and they had their own ways in every culture to heal various issues. Then it all got hijacked by a handful of people who started to tell us how to heal with pills or money or divine light without telling us what healing is. We are seeing the same trend with food. Now multinational companies (MNCs) tell us what is good for us and we are giving away our wisdom to some MNC, which have found out (faking it) that 2.30009876543% fat in milk will keep you slim. You blindly believe all this in the name of science over the wisdom of your body. Food is going to be the next big industry to enslave people after religion, technology and pharma. Where will MNCs tear apart wisdom of our women and make them slaves to such stupid data? You moved away from religion and its middle man to pursue logic, rational living and science, and now you are a slave to the so called scientists and its middlemen who exploit you for their gain. Neither you trusted your self then, nor you trust now. Have you really evolved?

Healing, like breathing, is innate to us. It is happening on its own as breathing happens. Since, we are not looking inward, we are not aware. In addition, our lifestyle has changed so much that our distortions or imbalances are far bigger than our ability to heal them. Hence, the word healing is confusing. If we have a wound on the physical body and it is cured in a few days, we say we are healed. If we are distressed and a healer gives us some relief through one of the many healing modalities, we feel we are healed till it surfaces again in some other form. It is the same issue – non-acceptance of ourselves and our desire to quickly move on. We do not wish to learn from our experiences, which in its essence is healing or at least the beginning of healing.

In simple words, healing is just a positive energy, which can be triggered by the external environment or due to a shift in your conscious. But it is flowing in you all the time and has now caught your attention. You need to get out of your mind to experience it internally and discover the triggers, which blocks the flow of healing. To stay with the mind and not know that healing is happening is like not being aware that your back pocket has enough money to buy you lunch, and you are begging on the street to buy food.

Any frequency which is a level above the frequency you are vibrating at, is healing and each time you vibrate higher than where you were, it feels nice, thus healed. Feeling nicer is feeling healed. You sit under the tree and you feel calmer, you feel healed. You come back after long hours of work and peep into the sleeping child's bedroom. Seeing the child blissfully asleep, your fatigue vanishes, you are healed. When you visit a temple or a church or go into the forest, it gives *bliss*, you are healed. Anything which brings you closer to experience your spirit, you are healed.

In all these cases, the process to feel better requires that you move out of your mental body and become aware of your surroundings, which directly impacts your emotional body. Your consciousness feels enlarged rather than just being stuck on your survival issues held by your mind. So by definition, it is a positive energy, which lifts your own vibrations to a higher state. Please note, it is your own energy, which is vibrating higher now, and it is not some divine energy or a great healer's energy, which you have acquired. External healer or a temple, a tree or child's face is just a healing environment in which you tune into and it triggers a healing mechanism to start functioning. It also does not mean that the role of an external healer or situation, which brings this higher frequency in you, is insignificant. In fact, you shall have more such people and situations around you who lift your vibration up all the time.

The difference between you and Jesus (the biggest healer mankind has seen so far) is that all internal forces are aligned in case of Jesus, whereas in our case they are not; just like every iron is capable of being a magnet if one can align all its molecules in one direction.

The reason you have distress/disease/disorder is because your internal forces are not aligned. You can say, they were aligned and one day, you got disoriented. These forces are not a chemical imbalance in your body. That imbalance at a chemical level is actually the result of the nonaligned forces within. Alignment is the alignment of your emotions, mind and body, which you have learned by now is the state of *Yog Nidra*.

The reason you need healing is because you have fallen from the *bliss* of your childhood. After all, you were in *bliss* and you were healthy one day. The healing is all about attaining that state of *bliss* and then sustaining it. I am talking about *bliss* for a few minutes daily, which is enough to handle any health problem over a period of six weeks. The bigger your losses are, the more you need to live in *bliss*. This is what we have done in seven years with each person. Brought everyone to live in *bliss*, and they made this a daily habit through the three techniques. So, as far as health and well-being is concerned, no matter what your *suffering* is, all you need is these three techniques to restore your well-being and thus your health through *bliss*. It all starts with observing the breath. This *bliss* is the light. This *bliss* is hope, and this *bliss* is the state of alignment – alignment of spirit, body and mind.

This is what a healer attempts to do to you regardless of the technique or modalities he uses. He will make some difference in any case. Since most of the healing modalities you know are not designed as a cure, any cure coming out of such healing modalities is incidental. They are designed more for spiritual quests or to attempt to bring you in harmony with self for a specific issue. By that token, they are all very successful and serve the purpose of helping you evolve. But if your losses are large, as said before you need to have *bliss* for a longer duration, and that shall evolve your consciousness about self. That is where the healer and various healing modalities begin to have limitations in solving the most complex issues of your disease or distress on sustainable basis.

For example, when any patient comes to our center, we do not spend any time listening to their story. The more critical the patient is, the lesser time we spend in listening to him or diagnosing him. We directly put him under treatment to restore his breath and within hours, the patient begins to feel the difference. You will learn how to start treatment as a caregiver in the treatment section. Healing happens by making a person observe their breath. In the workshop, they become comfortable with techniques within two days, and with practice, they master it within weeks. Now you have lifelong tools to heal yourself. Very critical cases take 1 to 3 weeks to get comfortable to be able to start triggering healing within. But why did I write this book in so many pages? It's because I want you to understand that healing is within you, and it has its science. What are the barriers you may face in curing yourself?

In the healing center I ran, which was supported by interns, we created the energy field daily in such a way that anyone who walked in, began to vibrate higher and was healed. In several cases, people would find the shift in their consciousness by spending some time. Once, the mother of a special child spent two hours with me for consultation, while her son played out in the other room under a caregiver. The child got healed from two negative tendencies. The mother called on the way back to her home to report this magic.

I expected that she would go for treatment, and we would get a chance to heal the special child. But she never came back. It led us to discover an insight that hope can scare people. For many years, she lived without hope and she had accepted her situation with her child. She was searching for a solution assuming that there was no solution. This helped her justify that she left no stone unturned for her son. Such miracles, she had heard in mythology or had known to exist with some saint in the forest. But how can that happen in a 400 sq. ft office type of set up? This shook her *belief*, which was probably added by the fact that I dressed up and came across as a regular guy, the way I am. This was not an isolated case. There are several such cases which helped us understand human behavior in depth to administer the cure.

As you read this story, you will have the tendency to discount this lady. Do not do that. You have the same elements in you. You will heal only the wounds you cannot handle and once those are gone, you would want to lead your life with your old *belief*. For example, the day you master the first technique (on average 1 to 3 weeks – NV SWIM) you would discover that you are at peace, the struggle in your relationships are gone, insights are coming and you feel guided. Suddenly, you look younger and everyone around you compliments you and you are, in general, a few notches more positive and that makes you feel good about yourself. All these are side effects experienced in your health and well-being, and this book is all about attaining health as a side effect of you wanting to pursue *bliss*. You can, by now, even get your blood test done, and you will find overall improvement in almost all parameters. All these are felt by everyone who continues with the first technique daily for 3 to 6 weeks. So healing is happening to you each day as you attain *bliss*. You may not wish to pursue further evolution and stabilize here itself for some time before starting to do more techniques or starting to handle deeper issues of your life, which begin to surface now. This is perfectly fine. Respect your choice.

Take an example. Once you get the first technique right and start to get *Yog Nidra*, your power of focus grows and then there is one advance step given, which actually cures diabetes within a week. The CEO of a large construction company, who was a regular client to get his daughter cured from acute schizophrenia, was put on the three techniques to cleanse his energies so that his daughter begins to come back to normal, as she always found fault with her parents and blamed them for her condition. This is very normal for schizophrenic patients. He had high BP and diabetes and his wife had thyroid. As he learned the advanced step of the technique, within 3 days, his sugar level became normal. The next few days, it started to reduce further forcing him to eat sugar. He found life in this technique by eating sugar like normal people. Each night he would do this technique to keep his sugar level balanced and then eating sugar. One could argue that this would have ignited his interest in the techniques further to resolve diabetes, but he chose to have fun. It was very heartening for him to feel empowered that when the world was struggling to keep their sugar under check, he was the master and decided how to play with it by doing the technique to reduce the sugar levels and then indulge in eating sweets.

Exactly for this reason, this book is coming to you. Learn that you can heal yourself. Learn that you have the power to make choices to be in *bliss*, in misery or be stable. Learn that whenever you like to evolve further or understand your life little deeper, you have this book and the techniques. You really do not need to go anywhere else. But, you must. Go out and experiment with other techniques, learn and become skillful and then you will know what is powerful for you and works for you. Unless you experiment with yourself, your consciousness will not evolve.

On other hand, as mentioned above, this is the only a barrier in the success of this treatment with you. It is a very scary feeling that we can heal ourselves. After initial excitement of relief from pain or symptoms, it hits you that you are actually complete within yourself and that you are alone and you are responsible for your life. This is disturbing for many because it conflicts with the *belief* of a *Survivor* that we are social animals, and we are interdependent. It conflicts with your *belief* that you will be loved and taken care of. Since your childhood, you are programmed by your parents, relatives, friends, society, law and governments that you will be taken care of. We are programed to always search outward with hope and upward when there's no hope, but we never turned inward where there is hope, solution and infinite love. You are not to be blamed because you were never told how to turn inward. This exactly is what you are learning now. With this book in your hand, you can now turn inward, power will move with your intent.

So, how would you believe me that just a few minutes of staying in *bliss* for a few weeks (called *Yog Nidra*) is enough to liberate you from your *suffering* of all kinds? Is there any science of invoking healing? Is it something which will work for anyone and everyone? Can anyone learn it? Do we need to learn more techniques and modalities? Will it work all the time and in every situation?

The answer is yes for all your questions and power will now come into your hands. How to heal yourself, you know how now. You only need to know why and how this is healing and if there is any science in these nurturing healing powers?

Please move on to the next chapter to learn about it. I'd like to make a special request for those who are very serious to pursue health, well-being and spirituality to read the next chapter a few times and contemplate the teachings. This chapter has all the secrets you need to know about healing and transformation, and I have tried making it very simple for you to understand.

THE SCIENCE OF HEALING

How to Tap Into Innate Healing Power.

> *The problem with the problem is that it does not allow us to stay focused on the problem.*

The Mystic, Artist, Scientist and Technologist – they are the people, who always remained connected with mystery through the *bliss* and pain of it. They had very little respect for the need to survive (read origin of *belief* chapter). *Mystic* remained in *bliss* but did not know how to help us attain the same. In his company, whenever we meditated or prayed, due to his aura being so big, it automatically lifted our vibratory level resulting into connecting with the layers of mystery. This leads to either an insight or cleansed our aura, which solved our problem. We felt that it is the blessings of the *Mystic*, in who resides God and we are nobody. Certainly, *Mystic* or that temple, church or mosque did the trick of raising your vibration but same could be done by you working in your kitchen by observing the breath without any external help.

Artist is a person, who connects with mystery, nurtures the insight and then paints, sings or creates the same *bliss* in his creation. On seeing this, without doing anything, we begin to feel the *bliss* or that deep pain. The art form connects to something deep inside us and invokes expression of our spirit, and we do not even need to learn how to observe the breath or meditation. This is the reason, art has no price. A selected few who could tune into that classical music or appreciate that painting, are able to value the *bliss* communicated in that art form.

Scientists like Newton or Einstein came and decoded the mystery and generations after, that began to have a paradigm shift in the consciousness of humanity. No *bliss* per se, but mass level consciousness shift is brought by scientists who remain connected to the mystery of life.

Technologists like Messi, Bill Gates and founders of various start-ups like Google come and without any discrimination to the vibratory level at which we are, they are able to either take us to bliss like Messi does in 90 minutes or take away our struggle or *suffering* enabling us to vibrate higher. Messi is an artist or a *Mystic*, and he uses the mathematics to find that unique algorithm which feels impossible to everyone to score leaving us in wonderment and *bliss*. In a 90-minute game, the ball comes to him around 10 times. If you leave the ball with him for 18 seconds, there is very little chance that it is not a goal and that lifts a billion people into the state of *bliss* right away. Do you know any *Mystic* or even Jesus who could do that to such large audience few times in 90 minutes? Only technology like Google or a mobile can do that. It just lifts your vibration when you search on Google or switch phones to connect with people and heal your loneliness. Insights come if we are connected to the mystery of life. There are two paths: 'Path of Will' and 'Path of Surrender'. We are on the path of surrender. I want a job in a MNC, no matter what, is driven by the path of Will, and I want a job which helps me grow in all aspects and where I enjoy working and contributing while learning is the path of surrender. In the first case, you land up in a MNC with a rotten boss and a bad profile, and in second case, you land up in a startup where there is innovation and life is fun everyday.

Likewise, in the healing world, there are a lot of modalities and even forms of meditation where people are asked to focus on specific issues or specific Gods or imagine some color of light. In all these cases, you are using your conscious, mental capabilities to channel your energies into a specific object or issue. This is not healing and this does not work. It gives you the impression that it has worked. Why? When you use your willpower to focus on a specific issue, you internally reorganize all your emotions to get quarantined so that they do not affect you. Often you are told to speak a positive *belief* through which such emotions can be managed inside. Now rather than emotions, which are affecting you by surfacing in your daily routine, they are zipped and programmed in the subconscious by another belief. It may be good for your survival but more damaging for wellbeing. It is like rather than having food on the kitchen slab, you wrap it and put it in the freezer.

Coming back to healing using the path of surrender, this is where the second principle of NV LIFE comes into play. For healing to take place, you must be able to hold that issue in your attention (not by trying to focus) for long enough. Healing energy flows where attention is.

Essentially it is life force energy which is being directed to the issue and by doing so, you are vibrating higher. You are not killing the lower frequency to experience higher vibration. This means you are not searching for light, but by paying attention you are bursting through the clouds for the sun to come through. Light exists inside us all the time, and we never have to imagine or search for it. It is not about stopping to spend but about generating more cash. This requires your mind to be in zero state because you cannot have your mind drift into various thoughts. Through the practice of *Yog Nidra,* you will witness that your mind effortlessly remains with issues and distractions do not happen.

You must have heard from various healers that they are just a medium for infinite, beautiful, white light. They are right in saying so, though you may question if your healer is actually humble in saying it or it is also an ego where they flaunt being spiritual enough to be a channel. To heal, you need to keep attention on your issue and it shall not trigger any thought or emotion. Let us take the example: you have a problem that you do not have a harmonious relationship. Problem is not that you are not being loved but that you do not feel you are being loved. Now bring your attention to "not being loved" rather than why he does not love you. If you think he is the problem, it will trigger a lot of thoughts and emotions and will not allow you to keep the issue in your attention on the real problem (not feeling loved). So observe your breath and feel not being loved.

Pause for a minute, close the book and check your ability to heal your issues as of today. Do this experiment. Close your eyes and begin to observe your breathing. Now bring attention to one of your issues. Any issue, but just one. You will discover that it triggers thoughts and emotions and that it drifts your attention from the issue to something else in the pool of emotions or web of thoughts and will probably bring you to some other issue. But if you can, you will find this issue is now bearable, and if you do it long enough, this issue will be resolved. Now do the same thing after two hours or so. Take the same issue and the same process. See if it still disturbs you as much as before. This is healed by that much.

This is the secret of healing. You really need no techniques or modalities to heal a patient. All you need to do is very simple. Connect with the mystery, insights will begin to flow. To connect with the mystery, you will need to be in *Yog Nidra*. To be in *Yog Nidra*, your thoughts needs to be zero and for that you shall be able to observe your breathing. All the three techniques I have listed here as a cure are not really cures but techniques to connect you with the cure within i.e., *Yog Nidra*. The cure is inside you. It does not matter how many times I repeat this point in the book, it is worth it so that you do not get distracted by the rest of the content. In any moment of confusion, trying to practice the cure as guided here, rather than searching for clarification or support, just sit with your confusion and start observing the breath, and you shall reach clarity. Remember, every problem has the seed of solution if you can hold the problem in your attention while observing your breath. Agreed, you need to have enough practice but it is now far easier, cheaper and effective than licking the boots of people in the name of being loved and accepted and yet get kicked hard? Each time you do it, you will find something from the subconscious surfacing. This means unknowingly, some karma or belief was holding your attention. As you keep clearing it, you will find your ability to go deep into *Yog Nidra* for longer durations is happening and your healing powers are growing because now unknowingly there are lesser distractions in the subconscious and now total power is directed to the issues from all seven layers.

If you are already a healer with one modality or another, you will now feel that this information of science of healing (read below) is potentially contradicting your own knowledge and investment you made for so many years. Not really. Here is the solution. Let us say, you are a Reiki healer. Now start practicing Reiki while practicing *Yoga Nidra*, and other techniques. You will be amazed how powerful the Reiki becomes. Gradually, you will lose the differentiation between Reiki healing and healing. The conflict in you is dissolved. It is another thing that as soon as you practice your healing modality on this science, you do not need to do it. It is like standing in an empty bus. Why not just sit down and relax! The destination will arrive on its own. The only place where healers will face problems in pursuing the science of healing as described here is the ones who use willpower based techniques such as making people focus on light or do visualization or the ones practicing giving suggestions or NLP. It will be hard for them to leave the old habit of keeping the mind active. I am saying just opposite i.e. turn thoughtless by observing your breath.

You can see that each one of us has healing powers. I witnessed that in several of my patients, who were once cured, it showed a potential to become healers for others. I led a few students to practice becoming healers. There are many stories with us where a patient under absolute distress will turn into a healer in six weeks. Each of them found their own unique qualities as a healer. One of my healers could actually be more accurate than an MRI to spot the problem in a specific organ. Another one had capabilities to find out hidden information, which a patient or a family had hidden from us. Another healer could locate lost jewelry in the house or if stolen by a relative or locating the lost man who lost his way home and even taking over his energies and guiding him back home just like a GPS and all of it in remote setting without knowing even the name of the patient. There was this healer who could actually absorb all of your pain and leave you feeling stupid because you thought you have unbearable pain, and she would just absorb all of it. None of these are miracles. These were routine things. It hardly takes a minute or two for my healer to do it. If these are miracles, than miracles have been routine for us every day several times.

None of these are my capabilities as a healer. I cannot find out about your boyfriend and inform your husband. I can rarely see an organ which is malfunctioning in your body. While in the state of *Yog Nidra* and working on patients, I have been revealed so many ways to heal a patient that if I wanted, I could actually write a book on healing techniques and by developing them as tools for specific issues. This was MAYA and a trap. Such information has always been hidden by me from all my students because the whole idea is that once they are in *Yog Nidra*, they will discover the same themselves which is relevant to their life journey and suits their *belief* system. I have just one *belief* with which I approach any healing i.e., I do not believe your misery is your destiny. I do not believe human life is for *suffering*. I believe each of us has the potential to experience bliss and pursue life through wisdom. Can I show them that state and let them choose their path for bliss or misery? This book does attempt to do exactly that.

If I have to give you a sample of my healing, then it is simple. If I am clear that you will be cured then you can try as much as you want to go against it, you will be cured of the issue you are facing. It is not due to my healing powers but for my absolute faith and *belief* that I landed up developing healing powers. I know your blood report result much before you give it for testing. I can actually see how in the next three weeks, your recovery will unfold and where you will face obstacles and barriers. My daughter uses these powers for her benefit. She goes for the exam and I hold her energy so that she does not get nervous and her best can come out. I even know at what minute, she got nervous because I am holding her energy. I will know who in your family will interfere in your recovery unknowingly and neutralize the effect of it on you to create the healing environment for you to vibrate higher. Of course, there is much more to what I see in the journey of your soul and your patterns, which I keep cleaning up for your recovery. For example, I do nothing to cut the effect of black magic on you. It heals on its own. There have been many cases where the patient reported that they were *suffering* due to black magic done on them, which they tried getting cured by various Tantriks who refused to cut it saying it is powerful and fatal and they cannot cut it and I have done that in minutes. A family friend who got into distress because his wife found out about his affair, approached me to be healed as his wife also started the program with me. I thought he is honest and wants to come out of it and get back with his family. I got him on a daily remote healing for forty-two days. Each day I did healing on him, I felt he was not receiving, but my *belief* about him did not allow me to trust myself. I thought I am not doing it properly. His reports everyday would have a lot of fancy narrations, which confirmed he is receiving well. This conflict continued each day for around twenty days, and I was not happy internally. Next day, I spent some extra time to pursue *Yog Nidra* before starting on him. I saw clearly that he was outside my ring of healing energy and for some reason, I started pulling him in. So much so, that I landed up making it an issue and for few moments, I dragged him inside the circle. Please note, this is happening in *Yog Nidra* and in remote healing. My friend was a few kilometers away. While dragging him half way in, an insight came that I am using my will. I dropped it then and there. Completed my session and came out. That day he reported that when he got out of session, he found his upper half of the body at a forty-five degree angle to his lower body, and he was amazed how it happened as he had laid down straight in his bed. You probably want to know why he was not healed for twenty days. Because he was not honest. He was just polite with his wife, and he continued having an affair in those days. It occurred to me very late that when it takes me just a few sessions to get an ICU patient out, then why three weeks of serious healing did not bring the result for such trivia issue of distress?

Fascinating! Right? Sure, it may be, and I also enjoyed the power but kept it a secret because I want you to focus on the inner path, which will heal you from any such effects rather than create an ambition to gain such power. These powers will come to you on their own when you are ready for them. You neither need a course or practice under a Guru. You only need to stay in Yog Nidra for long enough, daily, which will reveal all that you shall require at that specific time. Accept it as a gift and move on.

Each of you who will practice these techniques will have these powers in your own way, which will be unique to you, but you will kill it the moment you create ego about it. With this background, let us get back to understanding the science so that you know why it will work for anyone and each of us.

When you wish to push a car, it is not possible to apply full force, unless you hold your breath. With holding the breath, comes full power. It is the same case with lifting two buckets of water in both hands. Unless you hold your breath, you will not be able to lift buckets for long.

When you pay attention to the problem (pushing the car and lifting bucket in this case), holding your breath happens automatically. This gives you full power to do the task. This means that if you are determined to do a task, holding your breath will happen, your attention on the problem will be absolute, and all other thoughts will die down for that moment.

In a ninety minute game, when Messi scores a goal, it creates *bliss* for more than a billion people. He attempts the same in ninety minutes probably around ten times on average every nine minutes. This state of *bliss* is equal to an orgasmic state. Do you see the power of this person who can cause more than billion orgasms every nine minutes? Sachin Tendulkar holds his breath when the bowler starts on his run up. He is able to do it for the whole day for all the balls he faces. When these players or artists are not really with the ball or performing, they remain in the game, keeping their attention on it and reading the game (keeping attention) to apply that unique algorithm or mathematical calculation, which creates a blissful experience for the audience. This is what I do when I am handling a critical case. I remain connected to the energy field round the clock while I could consciously be roaming around in the house doing various things. This is possible because my spirit is with the case. It is about passion.

Singers hold their breath when they peak in their performance and so does the photographer. A shooter or commando does so while taking aim to observe absolute focus, concentration and power.

It is evident that if we regulate our breath (slow it down) or hold our breath, it is directly proportional to power, focus and concentration. This also means that when we hold our breath, all our thoughts disappear and only one thought remains, where we intend to have our attention to be.

It is simple to understand why it happens. When you hold your breath, you contain all the life force energy and block the flow of life. It is against the law of nature. Now, your entire being works toward making you survive. If you have fixed your survival with shooting the ball into the goalpost or you are lost in your joy of singing and reaching that high in your notes, then your entire life force energy goes in that direction to manifest it. That is what it means to have total focus, power and concentration.

This is not akin to only these people, but all of us experience it many times during the day. When someone gives you a surprise by tapping you from the back or a shock or when you are very angry or when you are filled with joy. In each of these states, your breath pauses or becomes very rapid or slow.

Since breathing is autonomous (where the brain is not actively required to participate), we do not pay attention and even if we do, since we do not know the impact of breathing on our well-being, we ignore this as trivia or obvious phenomena.

Emotions or thoughts, which we experience, are functions of our spirit and our life force energy flows through breathing. Since our emotions or thoughts are a manifestation of our lives, when we experience them, we involuntarily fuel them by our life force energy going with them and powering them. In other words, oxygen or life flows with our emotions and thoughts. The basic function of oxygen (or life force energy or breathing) is to first mix in the blood, reach each cell and tap into the intelligence of it to trigger inner wisdom apart from keeping the body in harmony and balance.

So when people say, do not think negatively and be positive, the reason it does not work is that you are constantly empowering negative thoughts to control emotions under them and each breath gives some life force energy first to your thoughts and then remaining comes to the body. More thoughts you create around negative thoughts, more you empower negative thoughts and less oxygen is available to the body and you feel drained. You want to let negative thoughts or emotions go, you need to stop feeding them by observing the breath and more specifically by practicing the first technique. Within a week, negative thoughts, do not get power and die down leaving you with positive thoughts as spirit begins to express itself. So is the case with your sexual energy and sleep. It, being life force energy, begins to power your negative emotions and that is how it becomes destructive from procreative energy.

So the trick is not to operate at the mind level at all. The trick is to grow the power of observing the breath which will automatically shift your frequency from the negative to the positive zone.

Let us take an example. You are standing at the drainage area, which has a foul smell. How would you now convert that into a positive smell? Using perfume? But you are still standing there and the source of smell is continuous. Would you continue to use the perfume? For how long? Would you want to take up maintenance of that drain pipe so that you do not get a foul smell? What if that drain pipe is a past trauma? Or existing boss or spouse? You are adamant that you are standing at the right place and either you shall be given perfume (sympathy) to bear it or you want your healer or Guru to fix your boss or spouse so that he does not give you a foul smell. You have a problem, not them. Your relationship is stinking for you and not for them. So who needs healing? Move towards the garden by observing your breath.

The reverse is also true. When you experience an emotion, it may pause, hold or slow down your breath. Take an example of a small child who is hurt in the playground or has fallen off the bed. She cries so much that the mother starts rubbing the back to move the pain and ground it to help the child catch its breath faster by grounding the pain faster. Each of us who has seen kids falling off the bed onto a marble floor have witnessed this phenomenon. So, when a child feels extreme pain, her total attention goes in experiencing it. Involuntarily, she holds her breath to be total present in that moment. Within a few short moments, the child's pain is gone and the next moment, the child is up and running, playing with the same friends without judging them.

The essence of life is here and healing happens on its own. Pay attention because everything you need to discover and how to do it is here:

1. This means that the child does not create any *belief* and goes back to playing with kids or starts to laugh reaching *bliss* again. The child lives in the moment of pain and attends to it fully till it disappears. This is what Buddha taught us – to live in the moment. This is the trick. Live in that moment of pain and feel it fully.

2. If you do that, like this child, you have no *belief* or judgment about the event and pain does not become trauma or a bad memory, but wisdom to take care to not get hurt again or fall. She does not blame her friends or situations or her destiny.

This is the law of nature that if you stay with pain and feel it fully, pain will leave you. So all these talks about holding pain for so many years is because you have judged it.

From a healing point of view, you shall be able to gather that there is something very profound happening here. The law of nature says that if you allow any emotion to occur and you witness it without judgment or holding your breath, that emotion will leave you, and you will fall back to your natural state of joy or bliss automatically. This is exactly what you will learn with the third technique (NV Hunting) to heal all past trauma.

The secret is that as you are turning thoughtless, your ability to keep attention on any issue will grow. Now, if you bring your old trauma in your attention, your mind will not distract you to something else. In this moment, if you begin to observe your breath, then this trauma, which is actually holding a lot of your life force energy, will release the energy and restore your breath and the trauma will disappear. Now you know how to heal childhood abuse or even physical pain and how to pursue the inner journey and dissolve judgment and *belief* regarding the same. Let us say it again here for clarity.

A child gets hurt while playing. This is an experience causing pain. Involuntarily, the child begins to feel it fully. This results into holding the breath, again very involuntarily. Once, felt fully, the pain leaves her, and she is back with her *bliss* to play with kids but now wiser to avoid getting closer to that stone which hurt her.

How would you learn healing from her? You have past trauma, *belief* held inside. You are holding lot of energy and lot of life force energy there. You need ability to keep that in your attention if you have to recall. As you recall, you will find that you are holding your breath again. If you release your breath by observing it and feeling that trauma and if your mind does not drift you away to something else, this trauma will go and will leave you with insight, wisdom or purpose. You learn that in the third technique in detail in any case.

In order to experience the orgasm fully, we involuntarily hold our breath and turn thoughtless. This gives us the feeling of *bliss*. It is again as natural a phenomenon as pain is. These are the two states given to humanity naturally, and no training is required. If you carefully examine life on the planet, every experience we choose or are subjected to, we strive to attain *bliss* and when we fail, it leads toward pain. Disappointments, tragedies, calamities, allowing us to experience pain, success, money, relationships and fame, leading us to experience *bliss*. It is dependent on our sensitivity that a lower level of *bliss* may be enough for one person, and it may not be enough for the other. If we continue to grow our sensitivity (inverse of *belief*), we will continue to touch a higher frequency in both states. These two states are the duality often spoken in a spiritual parlance. In reality, they both feel the same and the day we experience it, we dissolve duality and this expands the consciousness which directly means health.

Each time you allow *bliss* to expand within you, you will merge with wonderment. You dissolve every question and become one with nature. You are the universe in this moment and the universe is you. You feel whole, complete and one.

Imagine a malfunction, accidental, intentional or coincidental. In the concert, just before peaking, the mike switches off. During an orgasm, the phone rings or while scoring a goal, you fall. What happens to the *bliss* which is being built inside but not being experienced? It is now stuck in you. You work hard to ground it or feel settled. Imagine that you are badly hurt like this girl child whose father scolded her not to cry. Imagine this state of *suffering*. These infinite accidents are our *belief which we have held inside us since lifetimes which is not letting us feel our pain or bliss.*

We have *bliss* inside but are unable to experience it, and we have pain inside but we are not allowed to express it. A huge power of your mind is required to contain and control it. Your mind says it is not happening or that you are not allowed, and your heart wants to experience it. This is the state of *suffering* (figure 16). *Suffering* is not pain but a struggle to contain the pain within and not knowing if you are allowed or not allowed to experience it

BLISS AND PAIN – Naturally Gifted

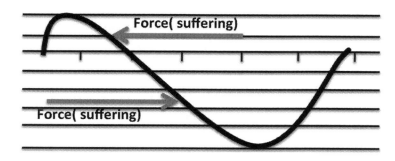

Figure 16 : Applying belief to control the nature of experience-Suffering

RELATIONSHIP

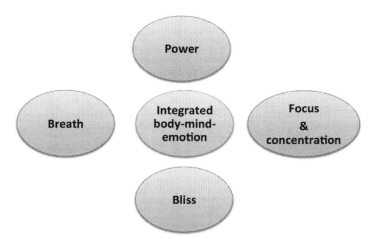

Figure 17 : Relationship of deep breath with power of focus and healign

Summary: If you look at various examples then you will discover that there exists a relationship of breath with power, focus, *bliss* and pain. This, in itself is a binding force which binds your spirit, body and mind. (Figure 17)

Your journey to higher levels of consciousness or your journey toward curing your ailments starts with observing the breath and getting better at it.

As you observe breath, it gets deeper. As it gets deeper, you begin to take less than 15 breaths per minute. As you reach 8 breaths per minute, you reach state of *Yog Nidra*. Deep and long breath is closest to holding the breath. As this happens, negative emotions leave you. Mind does not have enough work to manage the emotions. Unnecessary thoughts do not come. This grows your power to pay attention to the issues, which you shall address. This clearly grows your intimacy with self. This reduces your dependence on others. Now your relationships are changed because you are not as dependent as you were before. As this happens, you begin to attract higher and richer experiences with the same ecosystem or a new environment comes your way. Now, the law of attraction is working. You are also feeling guided. Inner confidence is high that you are taken care of.

This is not just theory that I am giving you. Everyone attains this state, by and large, within three weeks and most of them actually attain it with just the first technique and with just thirty minutes of practice.

This book is all about developing this ability. It is like preparing to have a gun, and once you have the gun, only then can you fire a bullet. Your ability to observe breath is that gun. Invest in making this gun of a high quality. This will give you the ability to keep the attention on your problem, and that would trigger the healing.

The reason it may still not work for you or cure you could be because the speed at which disease is spread, you are not yet powerful enough to overcome it on a daily basis. So if disease is equal to losing INR 100 daily, your power to heal is equal to saving only 1 rupee per day, and you may not feel like anything is happening to you with these techniques. The treatment section multiplies your saving power, and if you intensify that, you will reach a critical mass shortly to be able to arrest the momentum of *suffering* and soon reverse it. Having external help from healers like us will probably do that within hours. This is the reason, all the estimates I have given are the ones I have personally been mentoring, teaching and supporting. You may take more time, but you have the cure in your hands now. The good news is that the first phase of cure is not dependent on any one. Within one week, it will make you feel a difference. This will motivate you to become more sincere. There is no panic and no spending time, money and energy outside, in search of it. Start now. The cure is in your hands.

Treatment for Terminal, Chronic and Acute Cases

NOTE:

- This Section is specifically created to handle cases in your family where you feel helpless with your family members *suffering* with acute, chronic or terminal situations and you feel there is no hope left. You can revive your family members now without any external help. Aging parents where no medicine is working on them, a cancer patient in acute pain and doctors have given up, a schizophrenic brother or ADHD or autistic child. Within one week, without doing much, you can start to see the difference in their well-being, and this shall encourage you to continue to read the science in Section 1 & 2 and start to practice the techniques given in next chapter to go deep to experience the CURE.

- This is the starting point for you as well. No matter how healthy you are, if you are curious, you also start and see the effect of it on you.

- If you are a caregiver, first start with yourself. Your energies need to start lifting first. Then start with your patient at home.

It is recommended that you stay with this process for three days for yourself before starting to practice healing techniques unless your patient is very critical and you must start right away. In that case, start on yourself as well at the same time.

This shall not be used on friends, relatives or professionally outside in an ambition to become a healer or generate income. If you would like to help a friend, ask them to buy this book and let their family members help cases in their homes.

Allow yourself to first read the whole book, practice the techniques and evolve before working on others. In seven years of my research, I have seen that each of us have a healer within us. I witnessed great potential in many patients but that was to be used for them to heal themselves. There were few who became very effective healers to the extent that they were better than me in many ways. However, they all failed in their inner growth and their growing ego started harming them. If you have gone through the book, you will know in seven years, I have made efforts to tone down a healer in me and find a way to trigger a healer in others. This book is as a result of the same effort. Becoming a healer is not at all an easy job. The only way to be a healer is to arrive at a quantum level that healing chooses you and that is lot of sadhana (meditation). You can do the treatment at home as a housewife or as a parent on your family member without getting into the intricate details of the healing process and mechanism. The processes I have explained here are enough to bring about the cure in almost every case to reverse the worsening of the situation and stabilize the patient. You will be amazed to know that within these processes, lies the cure of most cases of mental disorders, infertility and various distress situations and addictions without even practicing the three techniques.

The reason I impose restrictions is very simple. If you start doing it today as a treatment on others for money or to help others without money, you will be driven by ego and not compassion, and this will drain you. It is so simple and economical to buy a book and self-treat at home. This book is the complete cure and the cheapest form of medicine one can ever buy. Your blood tests are even more expensive than the cost of this book. So why risk your own energy levels and yet, I encourage all of you to consider becoming a practitioner. With this book, you have online support on our Facebook page, and we will also be conducting workshops to help you go deeper with The Cure. You will also have remote healing sessions to help you expedite the cure. You will have more information about it on www.nvlife.net. We will also be training people to become wellbeing experts to work on others and take this up as a profession. Yet, I must make an exception to those gifted people who would read this book and divine will guide and support them to take this work forward in much bigger way. If just one line I read in a book can bring me so far, then I believe each one of you hold the same and more promise and potential in you.

PREPARATION FOR TREATMENT:

1. Create a healing environment. Allocate a room. Clean it up and take out the TV and unnecessary storage from the cupboard. Keep a bare minimum of things in the room as is possible for your situation.

2. Light the lamp. We use organic tea light-lamps. Use any oil (pure ghee) lamp or tealight-lamp from the market or just light a candle. Do not look for perfect objects, but start to move towards treatment and gradually keep enhancing the environment.

3. Use a diffuser, place camphor at the top and pour water. Ensure that water is always there, or else the camphor may catch fire or burn very fast leaving an unbearable smell. In place of camphor, you can use aromatic oil as well.

4. Light as many lamps as you feel gives you a warm and soothing effect in the room. However, before sleeping, patients shall have a minimum of one lamp lit.

5. Clean sheets on the bed. Comfortable mattresses and ideally no pillow for the patient. If the patient must use something, the thinnest possible pillow shall do.

6. Patient shall lay down straight. Hands unfolded and by the side. Of course, patient can turn sides and have free movement of the body during sleep or for sleep.

NOTE: These are guidelines and the ideal scenario. None of these shall delay treating your patient or suffocating the patient with rules. Use your intuition and have faith in your intent than in these rituals. Start now than delaying it.

Symptoms of the patients to be monitored as a sign of progress:

1. Check temperature of the body at 3 places. Forehead, lower abdomen and feet. In a healthy balanced body, temperature goes up a bit from forehead to feet. In several cases where you feel patient is not responding to any medicine or treatment, you shall find one of the following scenario:

    a) Lower abdomen is warmer compared to the forehead and feet. This means the energies are not circulating and are stuck in the lower abdomen. Largely, it shall be grudge, anger and resentment or addictive behavior as a symptom.

    b) The forehead is the warmest of all and the lower abdomen is the coldest. In addition to this, locate a nerve in the temple on both sides. You shall find that both or one side of the nerve is protruding and pulsating rapidly. You can compare it with the pulse rate of the nerve in your temple to know the difference. This means that the patient is mentally disturbed and will not let oxygen into the body. In fact, you shall always check this condition and in this condition, no major operation or surgery shall be performed as the patient will not respond and get the desired results. Chemo can backfire in this condition simply because in this state, any medicine you take sucks the energy in the brain and there are more chances of deterioration than recovery.

    c) As you progress, you shall see feet becoming warmer. It is sign of recovery.

2. Check breathing by bringing your finger below the nose.

    1. In most critical cases, the patient breathes out through both nostrils at the same time. Often, one side is thicker and the other side throws out thin air. We breathe through both nostrils only in 3 conditions. Deep state of meditation, before dying (it seems no one dies breathing out last from one nostril) and in case of acute disease. Hence, if your patient is breathing out from both nostrils, he is losing his life force energy

faster than normal. In this state, doctors always have to multiply the dose to bring parameters under control.

2. If it is only through one nostril, check breathing every 2/3 hours in a day, you may find that only one nostril is operational, and it is not switching sides every 90 minutes (45 minutes for the child) as per the *Swarn Yog* science for balancing the electromagnetic field. This means *suffering* is set in. If it is switching nostrils, this is good news. Your *suffering* is not that chronic.

NOTE: Temperature and breathing can be monitoring and collaborated in combination, and you shall be able to find the correlation of both the parameters by tracking the progress of your patient. Create your own local wisdom, and I refrain to give you the matrix here, which I fear may complex the whole thing in this Section because the purpose is to quickly get you to start doing treatment on your patient and not give you so much background information. Your objective in this Section is to first set the recovery process. The positive outcome from this is the best way to make you wiser. Hence, do not even worry if you can light the lamp or clean up the room or not. Do not even bother if you recorded breathing or temperature or not. These are nice to have things and not must-haves. This is only to help you start monitoring the difference and to increase your awareness. You need none of it. You want effectiveness of the treatment first. So you can learn it a little later as well. First, get down to initiating the treatment.

Treatment Processes
Process One: Balancing the electromagnetic field:

By now, having read a few pages of this book, you will know that balancing the electromagnetic field is the cure and this has been explained so many times in this book. Essence of the book is all about balancing the electromagnetic field of the patient, which flows through breathing. For a healthy person, breathing alternates from each nostril every 90 minutes. Your job is to get your patient to achieve it, as he is far from that state and cannot do it on his own. His entire spirit, body and mind's balance is broken down. It is like a wrecked car and this treatment is like a crane service to lift him out of the valley and get him to the garage.

HOW (see figure 18):

1. By default, you are first supposed to grow a magnetic field. You can do that by inserting some cotton in the right nostril and making the patient breath through the left nostril. This is the way to turn inward, and you shall refrain from talking on the phone, watching

TV or having conversations. Reading, listening to soft music, observing breath, painting, sketching etc., are encouraged but the ideal, perfect scenario is to lie down and sleep with cotton in the right nostril. First, get better, and then you have your whole life for such activities. The only exception to this rule is paralysis, where we need to see which side of the body is paralyzed.

2. Keep the cotton in the right nostril all the time including while sleeping, except when the patient goes to the washroom or has a guest. The ideal scenario is when the patient is in his bed and in the company of family or alone.

3. Everyone in last 7 years has gone to sleep with cotton during the treatment weeks. I use it on days I feel exhausted. If it remains in the nostril till morning, it tells me how much I was burned out. In normal course, my nose has a burning sensation within minutes to show optimal and balanced state.

4. If cotton falls off during the sleep, do not worry about putting it back. Just sleep and trust the process that it was supposed to happen only for those many hours.

5. If it suffocates, take cotton out. Do not make the patient breathe through the mouth.

6. Again, try it after some time and keep doing it to grow the duration with cotton in the right nostril.

7. Do not force and get desperate. Gradually, his system will restore and will be able to use it almost round the clock.

8. Ensure cotton is airtight, which means no oxygen is flowing through right nostril.

9. Cotton shall be stuck in the middle of the nose so well that it cannot be sucked up or visible from outside. See figure 18.

10. This is the evolutionary process. Much like the whole book and all its techniques. You need consistency and not will power. Whatever little success you get on the first day, your task is to build on it each day.

Process: Keep cotton in right nostril. Lay down and observe breathing.

Usage of Cotton

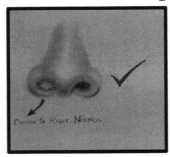
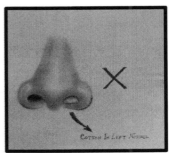

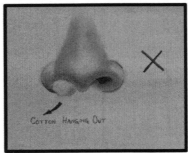

Figure 18

Duration of Use of Cotton:

As you know it is not healthy to block one nostril, but every problem carries the seed of the solution and blocking the nostril in an unhealthy person brings back the health. It is safest to keep using cotton in the right nostril and the day you are healthy, you will see that it is suffocating you or you will feel a burning sensation in your right nostril. This means you have reached an optimal level. Stop using cotton and enjoy good health. Periodically, every now and then, when you feel drained or have a bad day, use cotton in the right nostril and sleep. It is a nice lifelong tool in your hands.

Practical Issues:

This appears very simple but people create a lot of fuss and there are cases where they have genuine issues in keeping cotton in the right nostril. Have patience. This alone is enough as a technique to start reversing the symptoms and create well-being. So, all your efforts shall be to somehow implement it without forcing. After a lot of patience and failure to implement this, you may want to speak loud and be firm. Do that. It always works.

Following are the reasons for resistance:

1. No matter what the condition of your patient is and whatever the disease or disorder the patient is *suffering* with, the mind is obsessed with thoughts. By putting cotton in

the right nostril, you are deepening the breathing, and that is disrupting the thought process, hence the patient feels irritated. You do not lose your cool at all. It is a function of maximum 72 hours and your patient will ask for cotton to be applied.

2. Running nose and cotton getting wet: Change the cotton after a few minutes.

3. Blocked nose: Left nose will get blocked. This is all internal resistance. Again do the next process to open up the left nostril. Of course, let your patient clean it up and then again after a while, put the cotton in.

4. Phobia/Fear/Claustrophobic: These are all resistances to healing. Have patience and give the patient some time. Try again after another 30 minutes.

Failure in implementing it: If you have tried all the tricks and cotton is not working. This means that the patient has a major energy block through you. Start using cotton on yourself to raise your vibration first. Seek out someone else in the family whose receptivity with the patient is much higher.

Mental Disorder Cases:

You will find that in the case of mentally disabled children or autistic children, you would need a lot of patience and you may actually fail. In the case of schizophrenia, this itself if kept for a week will reduce hallucinations and delusions by 80% and in most non-chronic cases, this is enough to heal all your symptoms over three weeks. OCD patients will have problem keeping cotton and will require a lot of patience. However, your task is to find a way to implement it. People with mental disorders have maximum resistance from family members and do not trust them for anything. If you have a patient with schizophrenia, first you will have to use cotton for days and weeks and then you have a good chance of recovery of your patient.

Paralysis (Stroke):

This technique combined with the next technique 'Spinning' has the potential to remove the clot, if you can execute it within two hours of a person getting a stroke. I would dream to see this technique being used some day by hospitals on their patients upon arrival. However, mostly family or friends are the first ones to know, this is best suitable if you apply it on your family member who has just experienced a stroke. Of course, the same is applicable for people who are in a chronic condition after a stroke or when your patient is in the ICU and doctors are taking days to revive the patient. You can get a patient out in two weeks, on his feet, out of the hospital using these processes if you can commit yourself day and night to implement it while doctors are doing their work in the ICU on your patient. Of course, we have done it a few times.

Stroke on the Left Side of the Body:

This means that the left side is paralyzed – partially or fully. This means breathing is happening through the right nostril, and depending upon how severe the paralysis attack is, it may or may not happen through the left nostril at all. If you are within hours of the patient getting a stroke, do not use cotton as the patient is already in a difficult state, just use your thumb to block the nostril, which is operating i.e., the right side. Do it for 2 seconds and release, and then keep doing it in short spurts. You may be surprised that the left side of the body is responding. Patient might vomit, and that is tremendously good news. As the patient gains some strength, you can increase the duration for which you press your thumb on the right nostril. Be gradual and very gentle as the patient is in a tough situation and is only breathing through the nostril, which you are blocking.

In case of paralysis in the right side, do the same with the left nostril.

Do you understand why? In case of paralysis in the left side, female energy has collapsed and hence the patient is breathing only male energy and that we breathe through the right nostril (left brain) and vice versa for side of paralysis.

Use of Cotton in the Left Nostril:

1. Use it for a very limited time and under supervision. If it causes vibrations or headaches, or heats your body, remove it. You do not need it. This is an energy booster and if female energy (magnetic field) is not strong and stable (then growing the male energy by blocking the cotton in the left nostril will make the patient feel imbalanced and unstable. I rarely advise patients to use it. Almost in all cases, you do not need it and you certainly do not need it till you have done enough of cotton in the right nostril and have recovered from your *suffering*. My recommendations in exceptional cases is to use it every 4 hours for a few short minutes and quickly switch back to placing cotton in the right nostril.

WARNING:

1. There is a certain degree of intuition and experience needed to be able to use cotton in the left nostril. It is advised that you stick to using cotton in the right nostril (except in case of paralysis, which is as advised in the Section above). Patient comfort and his feedback is a prime driver for the usage and duration of the cotton. In a day or two you

will become an expert in handling it. Best is that you use cotton at night, while going to sleep to experience it.

2. Do not attempt on your healthy children below 7 years of age. Encourage your teenagers to use it.

Some applications:

My daughter goes to the examination hall with cotton in the right nostril, and this gives her the ability to automatically breath deeply and have patience. But when it is a logical subject such as mathematics, she uses it in the left nostril for some time. Girls with PCOD, people with anger, anxiety, sleep issue; this will automatically sort you within a week. Schizophrenia is cured only through this for hallucination and delusion within one week. Of course, it is a much larger issue but the patient feels relieved because he/she is now sleeping and the mind is restoring itself back to normal. This also clears up sleep disorder.

Energizing the Cotton:

What you read so far is all logic and science developed on the principle of *Swarn Yog*. But we connected it to mystery and healing. I give out cotton, personally, after energizing it. That means, creating intent and clearing the energy of the patient to accelerate momentum. In addition, it helped the patient believe that he is being taken care of and for the right reasons, as faith is the prime driver of healing. You can do the same, and see the difference yourself when you just logically use cotton. The next time you use cotton, use it after energizing the cotton with prayer. You can energize the cotton by chanting prayers. Like NV FISH, these prayers are another thing received in meditation and has been healing anyone who chanted it with total faith. You shall also be able to soon have an audio version of it on YouTube. However, do not bother about it. Learn it yourself. This Section of the book will help you begin to trust the universe, your insights and at the same time, see logic and science while you help yourself or your patients to go through a recovery process.

Process for Energizing Cotton:

1. Chant the prayer understanding the meaning of it. Prayer is given below with English translation.

2. Chant it while breathing out. Say each line while breathing out (while exhaling).

3. You inhale and chant the first line while breathing out. Then you breathe again and chant while breathing out. Your attention remains on breathing all the time, as much possible.

4. Keep this cotton at a sacred place – your place of worship or your meditation room or even on your bedside-table.

5. Do not touch and use it for any other purpose and no one else shall use this cotton except the intended person it is meant to be.

6. After around an hour, it is ready to use.

मुक्त कर दे हे प्रभु तू मुझे मेरे ही अभिशाप से,
रो रही है चेतना मेरी अनंत काल से एक बार और मृत्यु इस
जीवन में हो जाएगी मेरी कर्म मेरे यह ना कहें,
एक मौका और दे प्रभु!!

Free Me O' Universe, from my own curse

My soul has been bleating since eternity

Once again death will conquer me

I pray, my karma shall not burden my soul to be born again for the same

Narration: We curse ourselves and we judge ourselves. Our *belief* is the curse on our spirit. We are born to clear all the *belief*, which is blocking us from realizing the purpose of life. If we do not clear the *belief*, we shall be born again to the same task. Therefore, this prayer seeks divine intervention to ask for that strength, which clears up all our karma/belief and aligns us with the purpose of life in this lifetime only.

Process Two: Spinning the Chakra (Circling):

This process of moving energy works more powerfully than any advanced medical technology to bring the consciousness of the patient. Though it is safe to administer, it is the subject to a lot of expertise. As a caregiver, it affects your energy almost in the same way that it affects the energy of the patient, and hence you may find yourself quite incapable of performing this process. Though I have simplified this ancient *Kriya Yoga* technique, caution needs to be exercised. It is a mechanical way to restore the life force energy with the intent to free up the trapped mind. It shall not be overused. The receiver is the best judge when to stop it. use intuition while performing it.

Clockwise Spin:

1. Circle around the navel in the clockwise direction. Start with the wall of the navel and then grow the circle.

2. You can do it with one finger or a palm or switch from one way to another but keep it clockwise and use your intuition.

3. Do it with your right hand while sitting on the right side of the patient.

4. You may want to hold the right hand of the patient with your left hand. This helps complete the circle of energy flow.

5. Do it while observing your breath and sitting straight with the intent to serve, and you shall be in a composed state. Ideally, do it after you have done NV SWIM technique and reached Yog Nidra.

6. Do not do it more than 3-4 times a day in case of terminal patient and not more than once for any other case. But ask your patient each time if he/she likes to receive it.

7. Do not do it for more than a few days in any case as a regular practice.

8. 10-12 minutes is often enough, however, ask the patient for his comfort.

9. Ask your patient to continue observing the breath with their eyes closed.

10. Patient may or may not have cotton in the right nostril while you perform it.

11. Be aware, your own energies are spinning and you may pass out into deep sleep after doing it for a while. This is good for you as well.

Purpose: The purpose is to move down the person's life force energy, which is stuck in the mind and is not flowing freely in the body. When you do that on children, you are actually interfering with nature. Hence, once or twice a week in case of autistic children is enough and shall be discontinued for some time before starting to do it again. In some cases, especially on a healthy person, it may arouse them sexually. In some cases, it may trigger a hidden, deep trauma. In almost all cases, and almost all times, its known effects are discomfort in the beginning, some sensations in the body and in the legs and then the patient turning thoughtless and calm and falling into sleep for a while.

This alone is a powerful technique in most infertility cases to trigger fertility in the women. This brings lot of oxygen and blood in the reproductive organs.

The Science: This is one of the finest pieces of deep wisdom. If you are *suffering*, and it is not going away, that means your *suffering* is more powerful than your ability to heal it. Who nurtured it? YOU! How? By empowering it to grow and by giving your life force energy. This means your sleep, breath and sexuality have gone into nurturing it without you being aware of it. This is a classic example to see the importance of the life force energy turning destructive. By spinning the Swadhishtan chakra clockwise, you are bringing back life force energy to flow in the body in a procreative way. When you do it, whatever it is holding it, will free that up – typically, trauma, belief, negative emotions, sleep, deep breath and sexual arousal. This is huge and very powerful but you must remain aware that for you to spin something as turnaround from destructive to constructive, you require a huge reservoir of energy within you and that will also spin. If you are the reason held by your patient for his/her *suffering*, you will find that your patient has resistance in accepting from you. In that case have patience and continue yourself with the first process and keep your patient on the first process and allow some time to heal his/her repulsion toward you. This process is to be done by the opposite sex for the best results because that completes the circuit of male and female energy flow.

Exception: Do not do it on addicts, especially the anger and sex addicts. This may further intensify their craving for addiction. Instead, do clockwise for a few minutes and then anticlockwise and again clockwise. Keep spinning the energy up and down to disperse their life force energy through the body, which is stuck in this region due to which they have the addiction. It is the same for special children. Disperse it by doing clockwise and then anticlockwise.

Mental disorder: Safest way for all cases of mental disorder (depression, OCD, Bipolar, schizophrenia) is to spin clockwise because the idea is to empty their mind, but in some cases an anticlockwise spin may be required. Try it out and you will know after a few attempts, which one gives you the best results, and your patient in any case will tell you what is giving them relief.

This is an extremely powerful technique and process that has been perfected over a period of time. Do not be fooled by its simplicity, as it is very potent, and can result in emotional release. Therefore, it is to be used with *caution*, be intuitive in how you do utilise it, and own your responsibility with it. Please use only when needed as the results can be profound. Each time you perform this process, immediately lay down with cotton in the right nostril and observe breath and allow sleep if it comes. Do not skip this every time you go through circling.

Additional Notes:

This Section is the hardest for me to write. I feel very responsible in passing on these processes or mechanisms, which are lethal in their results. I am aware that you are far from being sensitive to realize what powers are coming into your hands but the process of empowerment must start somewhere, and you shall learn through experiments and take ownership of your intent and acts.

I do this because I see no hope for terminal, acute and chronic cases. This process is really like a ventilator for a terminal case and its results are very quick for us to see. I did it because no amount of resources and connections to the best medical facility is working for you. I pass this on to you because I have trained many common people with great results. For some of the people who began to learn to heal with me, it has worked wonderfully. It is simple and easy and quick in results, hence, it is best suited for terminal and hopeless cases. We have rescued so many hopeless cases in the ICU of the most expensive hospitals where doctors had given up and have asked the family to prepare for any news. They are the same doctors who have then made nice power points after a few days to show their success stories after we revived their patients.

Often, such practices are passed on after years of training people and checking that they are ready for it. I see humanity in sheer desperation right now. Let me give you an example, which has been happening for the last 10 days as I am on this chapter.

1. 3 weeks ago, this lady discovered that her husband, son (12) and daughter (3) had a fever and when it did not subside, so they sought help. Doctors diagnosed her husband with pneumonia and started treatment. Long story short, the husband died after 10 days in the ICU and the son and daughter were in the ICU for the same fever. 10 days later, the doctors did not know what medicine to prescribe because nothing was working. The daughter was still better but the son was critical when they reached me. I did remote healing sessions for a day, and we saw an improvement. We discovered that the child had a high temperature in the lower abdomen. The feet and forehead were cold. His mother was advised to place cotton in his right nostril for the first 72 hours and then on the fourth day, swap with the left for some time and so on daily. The mother did the clockwise spin a few times. By the fifth day, he was off medicine and had no fever and in another 5 days, he was discharged.

See, the reason I feel so compelled to pass this knowledge to you, is that if you take out my one remote healing session on the child, you and I are at the same level. I have written this book with the intent that all of you gain the same and more power as me. If you practice these 3 techniques as given in the next chapter, I see no reason why you will not become what I am. Of course it comes with time and practice. Also, it comes only by practicing, not by having the ambition to become powerful. It is indeed a lot of self-discipline and meditation and that also comes when you start observing breathing and following every insight and not your mind.

2. An infertile couple where a man was diagnosed with a low sperm count and erectile dysfunction is now blessed with a baby boy. The wife just kept him on cotton and did Spinning for a few weeks every night.

3. Every mental disorder case (non-aggressive type) can be cured very quickly – within days or weeks. Do it on schizophrenia, OCD and depression. I experimented with this process on mental disorder cases and then expanded its use to terminal and acute cases.

4. Doctors had kept the operation theater ready for this 55-year-old man, who had high diabetes, to amputate his toe and we only had 24 hours to remotely work on the patient to delay the amputation of his toe. Apart from remotely healing him for the night his wife continued doing Spinning a few times in the night while patient was on cotton and was asked to observe breath with attention on the toe. With little persuasion and second opinion from another doctor, we were able to delay amputation and in the next 3 weeks eliminate it. The patient is back on his feet now.

Ideal Scenario to Administer this Treatment:

1. Start with cotton in the right nostril in all cases except paralysis.

2. In the case of paralysis, follow the process given in the in the *Paralysis (stroke)* Section in this chapter given above.

3. Start to give yourself the same treatment to move your energy up. As a caregiver, you need this treatment more than your patient does.

4. Do this for 72 hours before experimenting with Spinning and cotton with the patient.

5. Start to practice the NV SWIM technique and get comfortable with your ability to observe your breath. This will emotionally begin to isolate your energies, which could interfere with your patient when you start to Spin his chakra.

6. If possible, get some therapist or healer to do this on your patient. I have got it done for one patient by their maid.

7. It shall be done by male on female and female on male to complete the energy circuit. It may not be effective on the same gender, however, in case of emergency, for a short time it can be done till you find a suitable person to do it.

8. Always pay the person from outside, you get to do this. Keep filling up energy of that person so that he/she can continue to give it to your patient and he/she does not pass own negative karma to your patient unknowingly.

9. Keep taking feedback from the patient to adjust your spinning pace, circling the size as the patient will tell you where he/she needs touch to move energy from.

10. If the patient falls asleep during the process, this is the best result. If patient feels sensations in legs, this is very great news. If patients reveals some memory or explodes due to trauma, it is great healing and if it arouses the patient, make them feel comfortable about it and ask them to observe their breathing. You may want to slow down and leave the patient alone.

Best outcomes:

1. the objective of this process is to free up the mind which has trapped life force energy and breathing is not optimal. You shall be able to see the difference in the breathing of the patient. It will start to go deeper. This is the reason you are doing it.

2. You will find your patient falling into sleep or *Yog nidra*. Perfect scene.

3. You can validate the results by patient feeling lot of sensations in the legs. This means, he has started grounding held up emotions. This alone is a very big sign of recovery.

4. Temperature will be restored, growing as you move from head to toes.

1.1 Law of Secrecy

While your treatment is on, follow the law of secrecy for first 3 weeks of starting the treatment and healing

- Do not speak in detail about the progress you are making.

- Contain the positive energy as it begins to build up within you, instead of rushing to share.

- Sharing may attract negative energies or may dilute your intent to heal.

1.2 Do's and Don'ts During Treatment

While your treatment is on:

- Follow a moderate lifestyle.

- Allocate fixed time for each of the 3 techniques. For NV Swimming, you can associate it with bathing. Whenever you take a bath, the first thing you do is NV Swimming. Similarly,

NV Fishing can be done just after lunch and NV Hunting just before going to sleep.

- Practice silence as much as possible.

- Be regular in your practices. Keep a separate notebook for writing all your experiences.

- Maintain a progress tracker.

- Don't start teaching it to others. It might cause more damage to you than benefit. Ask such people to do it on their own by buying the book.

- Do not speak about the treatment or the relief among wider friends and family till you reach an energy level where you do not dissipate positivity, which you are acquiring at an energy level each day in the treatment. Be very brief about yourself.

- Do not take the extra burden of work. In fact, try to cut down on anything non-essential. It is time to turn inward and repair self rather than race.

Changes Witnessed During Treatment and Healing as a Sign of Recovery

Science of Effectiveness of Cure

As you begin these processes, you will experience various changes in your body. During the treatment, our Emotional-Mental-Physical body shows many symptoms, and our role is to just allow ourselves to experience them. If you begin to experience any of these symptoms, it is a sign that you are on the path of recovery. The list includes –

- Nausea/Vomit

- Body Pain

- Shift in body temperature – Feel Heat and cold many times in a day

- Heat flashes

- Sensations in different parts of the body

- Shift in energy levels (in a day, you feel energetic and then energy dips all of a sudden)

- Mood swings

- Crying for no apparent reason

- No feelings/Feeling numb

- Frequent change in emotional state – Emotions like anger, irritation, sadness appearing many times during the day.

- All these symptoms will come and go practically every day after some time. Initially, you may not feel anything because your emotional body is frozen and it takes time to melt the ice.

How to Prepare for Treatment/Healing

To prepare yourself for the treatment, follow these simple steps:

- Wear loose, comfortable clothes.

- Lie down straight on the bed/mattress in a comfortable posture. Make sure your hands and legs are on your side and not crossed.

- Begin to observe your breath.

- Continue to observe breath. Your mind will interfere and will take away your attention from observing your breath. But as soon as you realize that the mind is wandering into thoughts, bring your attention to observing your breath.

Treatment on Healthy People:

Almost in all cases when people feel relief within days, they ask us questions like, "How do I bring my spouse to you?" The reply is, do not do that. Allow some days to pass by and as your spouse sees you transforming, there is no way he/she will not start the process.

You can do the same. Spare children below 12. Do not interfere with their nature if there is no need for treatment. They shall be put on step one of NV SWIM and that shall be made a habit when they go to bed. Within days, you will be amazed to see their power of focus and change in their behavior. They will happily observe their breath if you make it a game for them, but may always need you to remind them. For example, we asked kids to observe their breath and tell us what emotions they experience? Now, this is a fun thing for them and they love this game.

Do the same with your spouse. Keep working on yourself and your spouse will want to try it out. You can do wonders to reduce and eliminate the stress of your busy spouse by doing these processes. Corporate executives are often stressed out and age faster. You can see from their body language that they are not really happy. Put them on cotton gently, and do a clockwise spin as and when you feel like it. This will grow your intimacy, arrest their aging and will provide very deep sleep to your spouse. You shall find your partner becoming sensitive towards you.

Summary: Using cotton in the right nostril is actually for anybody and everybody to start experiencing healing except paralysis where I have given clear guidelines. Spinning chakra clockwise is great for mental disorder, aged people, and terminal cases. For people with addictive behavior such as special children, ADHD, anger etc., you shall spin it clockwise and then anticlockwise. While being a healer to others in your family, you must first raise your own energy level by first working on yourself and pursuing the techniques given in the next chapter and precautions given above. However, the best way to use Spinning chakra is to be interactive with the receiver and seek feedback and adjust accordingly either the large circle or small, clockwise or anticlockwise. You need to own the responsibility of these processes, as I would not be responsible in any way. These are very sacred processes, and I have written so many pages to reflect the importance of owning responsibility.

HEALING TECHNIQUES

NV Swimming

Breathing is the only link between life and mystery. It is an autonomous process, which means it happens on its own without our awareness. When breathing is brought into awareness by paying attention to it, it begins to decode the mysteries of our lives. This is the only way any *Mystic* can receive all the revelations and insight and you will receive them too.

The subconscious mind (emotional body) carries a code, which has a matrix of your current life and it seems to be a mystery to all of us. The conscious mind is conditioned to work toward survival and suppress our insights coming from our subconscious. We can listen to our subconscious only if we shut our conscious mind. This technique is all about aligning the conscious and subconscious, thereby speaking the same language, having the same power of focus and making the law of attraction work for you. Before insights can come to you from the subconscious to the conscious mind, significant garbage or baggage will surface through this technique. The best part is that you do not need to do anything to heal that emotional baggage which is now surfacing but use this technique, and the garbage will clear on its own. Sometimes it will surface and will come in your awareness and sometimes, it will just get grounded, leaving your subconscious clear. It is like when you open a tap, which has not been in use for several years, it gives out dirty water before it begins to flow with pure water.

The purpose of this technique is to clear the conscious mind from programming, which creates thoughts on its own and arrives at the zero thought state. The state of *Yog Nidra* arrives on its own if we reach the zero thought state. We shall reach that state by following this technique, which starts with observing the breath and then ensuring all thoughts are diminished. If we can do that, then the subconscious code will start to write into the conscious mind, or they will start to become one like when you see a child prodigy. This means no form of *suffering* can last because no one has *suffering* written in the code. If it is written, it is for the purpose of winning over it and learning to feel empowered. In this time and space, if this technique has reached you, it means you are destined to liberate yourself from your *suffering*.

As far as Cure is concerned, this technique with its advanced version is the cure for any form of *suffering* (distress/disorder/disease). The other two techniques are to ensure that your patterns are broken, the root cause is healed, and you do not fall back into the same pattern of *suffering* in the future. Starting from BP, thyroid, infertility, bone related issues and cancer to unhappiness, relationship issues, parenting and mental disorders. The only issue is that you may find it hard to apply on patients with mental disorders. For that, you are advised to put your patient on treatment (as described in the last Section) for a week or so to stabilize their minds. Later, gradually apply these techniques on your patient at home. If you are using treatment together with this technique, it speeds up the recovery process miraculously. "How to develop the ability to observe breath for a longer duration each day than before is the prime objective of this technique as a cure. Everything else will happen on its own, if we can do that daily for a few weeks.

Note:

These are specific scenarios with seven years of practice. Not everyone will face this but everyone should read more to gather more knowledge on this subject.

1. You will want to discount this technique because you have been taught breathing by several people or institutions. No one told you that breathing is the cure for your *suffering* though. I am the only one saying that you can cure it with breathing. Hence, please leave your knowledge of breathing like Pranayama, Vipassana or any other technique aside and be open to trying it exactly the way it is described here. Several healers and spiritual seekers, who have come to us with their knowledge, after trying this, understood why it worked and all those techniques did not.

2. If you have a mental disorder like a sleep disorder, depression, bipolar disorder, schizophrenia or any other, you will find it hard to practice this technique. As written above, please go to last Section *Treatment* – that alone is enough to get you out of mental disorder to a very large extent and in some, not so critical cases, full recovery. Once stable, start these three techniques gradually.

3. It is normal for your thoughts to distract you from breathing as you try to observe breathing. You will have the tendency to call it off and see this as a failure. Please be aware that the 3-step process is designed and perfected for all types of people over a period of time. They went through all these challenges and we got everyone hooked on to it. It is a matter of practice and each day you will get better at it. Also, please understand that this itself is the Cure, so if it takes you several days, it is fine. Once you get it, there is no looking outside for help. You would have discovered the secret for your joy and liberation. It is normal that you will not be able to observe breath for more than a few seconds, and you will always have to come back to remind yourself to observe during early days. But this alone will start to bring a sense of peace in you. You will only get better each day as you practice.

4. As soon as you become aware that your attention has diverted from observing breath, bring back your attention to observe the breath. Do that a few times, and you will be happy to discover that your mind is not playing havoc any more as intensely as it used to before. This you can expect to attain the first day itself, within an hour.

5. You will find that some thoughts are very sticky, and do not go away. Great news. You are aware of what is bothering you. Do not be hard on yourself. This awareness and acceptance of your mental state has now eroded the power of these sticky thoughts. The next day will be better. These sticky thoughts are often hurt or trauma in your emotional body and there is thought around it which is stuck in your mind to keep it under control. In a healthy, normal person, you find it at the bottom of all your thoughts, which means that once you start to observe breathing and reach the second or third stage, when almost all others thoughts cease to exist, this sticky thought will surface.

6. There are thoughts, which advise you to break this breathing process and call it quits. This is due to your mind being trained to remain invested in *suffering*. Do not listen to it and yet do not be hard on yourself. Quit by listening to it, but do it again in a few minutes or hours or the next day. This is how you can trick your mind effortlessly.

7. There are thoughts that are not sticky, but very tempting and juicy. You enjoy such thoughts. You do not want to leave them and resume observing your breath. Such thoughts are often related to sexual fantasies but not limited to it. Even thoughts connected to 'self-pity' can be juicy. Many a time, if you fail in this technique, releasing your sexual energy through masturbation or having sex helps you clean it up. The best way to do this

technique is after you feel fulfilled for any need, which might distract you. This is only in the beginning. You can sense from all the above points that I am asking you to somehow find a crack in your existing energy system by finding a way to start observing the breath. Once you get it right and I would say, in a week, you are hooked lifelong. Each time you feel like giving up, go back to the treatment processes to improve your mental stability and then come back again.

Caution: The common mistake people make is that they make a decision in enthusiasm and set a target that they will attain *Yog Nidra*. The moment you decide that you will observe your breath, you have this as a thought. This thought will not let any other thought occur, but this is where you will fail in making breathing a Cure. You will start to do breathing as it is taught elsewhere. Yes, this will help you somewhat to relax but will not lead you to the cure.

Let me remind you again that I have written so many pages only to teach you the ability to observe your breath. Do not make a mistake of thinking it is a simple thing. It needs lot of patience.

When people tell me, "Sir, I am committed for three weeks, as you said. I will get cured," it is true that they follow with commitment, but they take my word as a prescription written by a doctor and pills from the medical store. They are committed, but they are not *sincere* about the process. Many people come to the center, lie down and sleep, thinking I will come and cure them. So pay attention to the process. Avoid any fixation to result and outcome. If your process is right, there are no questions about not benefiting from it.

How to Approach:

1. Follow the instructions as guidelines and not as a rule.
2. Do not have any fixation in your mind in terms of achieving anything.
3. Be disciplined: Do it at a specific time in the day. Each of us has made it a routine to do it after bathing as the first thing. This means if you delay your bath by a few minutes or hours over the weekend, it does not create any stress as this is linked to an event and not to a specific time. If you are in a hurry in the morning, you can do it at any specific time of your convenience. Housewives often do it after kids go to school, home is in order and they have an hour or two for themselves. The working people like to do it after coming home. Patients at home or in bed, shall do all the time they can. They take a bath before dinner and do this technique. Choose your time. I insist that you do it after bathing, but that is not a must but a recommendation for the best practices.

4. Memorize these 3 steps. Do all 3 steps separately once to get the hang of it.

5. Use your intuition and trust your experience. Check them against the validation points given at the end of the technique to know how successful you were. If not, do not worry, do it again the next day. Within days, you will get it right and like everyone else, you too will be addicted to the good it does to you.

Technique:

It is a three-step process. (Figure 20)

a) Observe your breath

b) Deep breathing

c) Hold your breath

As you move from step one to step 2, you will discover that your thoughts are reducing. By the time you reach the third step, a few thoughts will remain. You will be calm and with the breath. Third step is the process, which will kill any thought. As you hold your breath, this is the stage of death, and when it comes to death and life, all other thoughts disappear. As all thoughts disappear, you have no option but to be in *Yog Nidra*. This means you never have to aim or target for achieving *Yog Nidra*, the state of *bliss* and cure. If you do the process right, you will arrive.

The reason, it is named *Swim* is because it is just like swimming. Here you make your breath swim in your whole body and have nothing to compete with it. The whole idea is to take more time for one breath, which clearly means it automatically has more oxygen in a breath. This happens on its own thoughts begin to diminish. If you are practicing it after reading the theory then you can now understand that even you do forceful breathing as taught at several places, it does not cure because by forcing to oxygenate your each cell to receive more oxygen may happen for some time but the emotions and *belief*, which are blocked by the flow are still not healed, hence as you get tired with forceful breathing and you sleep, you will feel relaxed. That is done for wellness, and this is done for well-being and as a cure.

It brings you back to taking just first step and being aware of the 3-step process. Be very swift to move from one step to another using intuition or insight and not a thought like – okay, now let us go to the next step. This will reduce the number of breaths per minute, which is what *Swarn Yog* teaches us.

What is *Yog Nidra*?

It is called *conscious sleep*. It is a state in which your body is at complete rest and your mind is at zero thought state. It is like the state of a child who lives in bliss as he has no mind, and yet to be programmed for survival. This state is a gateway to the deeper layers of *bliss* and as you start to have very limited thoughts, over a period of time, you shall discover that you are going deep into meditation (state of samadhi), which mystics in Himalayas live in, round the clock. This is the state through which, on its own, your subconscious is cleansing you and getting you healed from the karmic debt you are carrying since many lifetimes. Restoration of health, which happens on its own, is a very small gain with this process. You can say that you have access to very sacred techniques, which were hidden by *Mystics* and only taught through rigorous screening of the students. As said, gaining back your well-being or health is just a side effect you get in any case you start to practice these sacred techniques.

Now onwards, you do not have to worry about addictions, attachments, law of attraction, past life karma, patterns and how to control negative thoughts. You are now becoming a healer for yourself. You do not need any modalities after this though you may learn a few more and use them on the top of it. To give you an example, when I work on ICU patients, I stay in this state for 10 minutes or so, a few times a day, for a few days, and that is enough to make them progress towards health. I do not even need to know the name and location of the patient because, cosmically, we all are connected and energy flows with intent. It is like we all have a unique IP address and a healer has access to all such IPs.

Experience During *Yog Nidra*:

One will remain conscious of the surroundings. Any movement around you in this state will be known to you as you have not yet gone to sleep.

How do you know you are in *Yog Nidra*?

You will have one of the following experiences during this state:

- Images or faces of people you cannot relate to in this lifetime. These are the images coming from your past life and clearing your subconscious from any of its karmic debts.

- Light, various colors, often very bright. Patients with mental disorders may experience darkness and gradually find the small light coming. This means they are now moving from the darkness to the light and getting healed.

- Sound: One of the many sounds of the universe, which you can hear internally when the body and mind reach the state of absolute rest. It is one of the rare things to happen and is considered very sacred in spiritual practices.

- Video: Yes, it is normal that you will see a video, which is nothing but one of your past life. This will expand your consciousness, and it will liberate you from the karmic debt. For example, if you have been feeling rejected in this life, you may see video each time you are in *Yog Nidra* past lives in which you have felt the same in different ways. You may also see how you have rejected so many people. This means now your tendency to feel rejected is now getting healed.

- Symbols and mythological images.

- Most of the time, people get into deep sleep for moments while being in *Yog Nidra* and come back. Many a times, you do not see any of the things as listed above, but you come out feeling something was happening, and it is normal that you may not feel anything at all but come out very peaceful. Each day is a different day.

Experience After *Yog Nidra*:

You will feel thoughtless and clueless after *Yog Nidra* for a few moments and if you do not rush, you would just want to be like this for several moments. This is your state of peace and your comfort with your own self which is growing. Enjoy this moment.

How to Prepare for the Technique:

- Always do it lying down. Never in a sitting position.

- Wear loose clothes. Ideally, no clothes if you have your privacy.

- No leather-wear on the body and ideally, no spectacles and jewelry.

- Lie down straight on your back.

- Legs straight and should not be crossed.

- Ensure no breathing happens through the mouth.

- Hands by the side always, not on the chest or below the head. If so, your mind is active. Hands by the side, is the body language of surrender and agreeing to relax.

Stage One: Observe Breathing

- Observe your breathing. Stay with the oxygen as it goes in and goes out. This is what it means to observe your breath. Do not try to change your breathing. Here you are just observing the way it is happening. As you begin to bring attention on breathing, thoughts will distract you. This is where you need a very gentle effort to bring back your attention on observing each time your mind drifts.

- You will discover the nature of your breath and will be surprised that you are not doing cyclic or deep breathing. It will have all types of patterns. Random, jerky, shallow, rapid. Just witness them and keep observing.

- This may lead you to loosen your body. Adjust your body if needed during this time, like a musician does with an instrument before starting to play.

- Observe if any part of your body feels stiff. If so, just become aware and your body would want to loosen up on its own. You stay only with observing the breath. Rest all will happen on its own.

Duration: There are no rules but guidelines. Follow intuition. We have often seen people within 7 to 10 minutes reach a stage where thoughts are less and mind is less cluttered. You have a general sense of calmness, and this is where you swiftly move to the next step.

Tips: Observing breathing means to stay with the process of breathing. This means, paying attention to the oxygen as it goes into the nostril and then inside your lungs and diaphragm. It is about feeling the flow of oxygen as and where it moves during breathing in and breathing out. As you observe, you will find that breathing is changing the pattern at times. Allow it.

Stage Two: Deep Breathing

Warning: Do not perform deep breathing mechanically by inflating your chest and filling your stomach with oxygen. This kind of breathing is done by using the power of your mind while we are saying we shall arrive at a stage of no mind. Deep breathing means slower breathing rate and that itself increases the intake of oxygen. You can only do it if you are aware of your breathing rate which happens in first step. You need to do nothing to arrive on this stage. This is why, in the beginning, I have written please memorize the 3 steps. You may not want to come to this stage also and enjoy just observing for several days. In simple words If you are breathing in and out in 4 seconds, now do the same in let us say 5 seconds or so. In each subsequent cycle, it will begin to go deeper making your cycle longer. Once again, do not try to take extra oxygen. Be gentle in swiftly making the process longer than before.

How to Perform Deep Breathing:

- Our objective is to decrease the rate of breath. This alone is enough to give us more oxygen per breath, which actually means more oxygen for the body and that happens only when the mind is comparatively more empty. Hence, as you were performing breathing in step one, now gently, just slow this process down. This means that if earlier you were taking 1 second to breathe in, now you are probably taking 1.5 seconds to breathe and in each cycle, it will only improve your time duration for breathing in. This will automatically result in the increased time duration for breathing out. But all of it is an intuitive process. Once you start doing it, you will get the hang of it. Do not try to activate your mind to start counting seconds at any step of this technique or any technique in this book. We do not need to be obsessed to take more oxygen in every breath. As your emotions begin to free up and mind turns thoughtless, this alone will free up the path and more oxygen is already going in.

- While doing it, you may feel tired and just want to do a few rapid breaths. Do that. After that you may want to just observe your breath for a few moments to gain back some energy. Do that and when you feel ready, swiftly come back to this step. Do not take pressure that you have to continuously slow down the breathing in each cycle. You will only get better at it gradually. It is normal that you may go back to the first step in between and then come back to this step. Remember, it is NV SWIM and use your intuition to go back and forth as felt by you at that time. Listen to your own insights, and do not get obsessed with steps.

Stage Three: Hold

- Continue breathing like in step 2, but begin to hold your breath in your stomach for a few seconds. Be gentle. Do not push yourself for holding your breath for a longer duration.

- In each cycle, your capacity will grow.

- Each time you hold and then breathe out, it is bound to give you some fatigue. Before you start to hold again, catch on your breath by doing step 1 and/or step 2. This way, you will still be with the process while being gentle with yourself which is the essence of this process.

- By now, your thoughts are almost gone and hardly any thought would remain unless very sticky.

- You may discover that in between you are falling off to sleep (*Yog Nidra* state). The *Yog Nidra* may not happen at the end but intermittently. This is normal. It is due to the fact that as soon as your mind turns empty, your mind feels insecure and unsafe, pulls up a thought to remain active and you are awakened out of *Yog Nidra* in between the process.

In a normal, ideal and healthy situation, which you shall also start to have soon after some practice, you shall find that *Yog Nidra* happens only at the end and with good practice, you will find that you are able to reach *Yog Nidra* without reaching the third step.

For example, I do not know when was the last time I did all three steps. I only need to start observing the breath and within minutes I reach *Yog Nidra* and sometimes in sleep mode and come back to *Yog Nidra*. This is also true for many of the practitioners within few weeks of their practicing. So, it is not really just me with several years of practice, but almost anyone of you with some practice can reach that stage. Yes there are days when I have to follow all three steps to empty my mind.

Allow yourself to be in the state of *Yog Nidra*, generally, it lasts for 5 to 10 minutes. Unless, you are very tired, it may go longer but then that would be proper sleep and not *Yog Nidra*. Allow yourself to be in this state. When you feel ready, get up and sit for a few moments.

Duration: There are no rules again. But we have seen that beginners take around 30 minutes and within a week they are able to reach *Yog Nidra* in about 18 minutes. It is very normal that from *Yog Nidra* you will fall into a deep sleep. This is because now your body needs to rejuvenate and the fatigue must go. You shall allow yourself at least an hour for this technique and shall not have any engagement fixed exactly after an hour for the first few weeks of practice. Once you are good at it and your body fatigue is over, you shall be able to come out of it in 30 minutes. Also, do not put an alarm clock on or set a time.

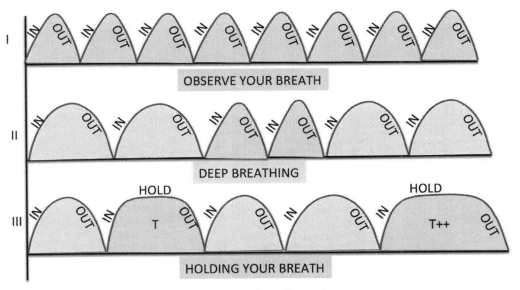

Figure 19 : NV Swimming – 3 steps

NOTE:

Once you are good at it, you can use it for anything. You are in a difficult meeting with your boss. Start to observe your breath while talking. You are on the phone with a friend, who affects you negatively, start observing breath, while listening to her/him. None of these can then affect your energy. You have back pain, start observing your breath while feeling the pain by keeping your attention at that place. As you do it, it will reveal the root cause, which caused the pain. When you observe the breath with attention on any specific problem, that problem begins to dissolve and life force energy goes where your attention is and healing flows with the intent.

Take another case of a woman who had issues with her son's ADHD/Autism. As part of our treatment, we first work on mothers to clear their energies, which are gone into the child. After this, there is very little work to be done on a child that mothers often do once they have learned these techniques. Now the situation is that they have only one son, and she runs from morning till evening from one special school to another. Clearly, she wants to make sure that her child gets the best, and she does that 6 days a week. She even eats lunch in the car when the child is in the school. She is waiting outside, ready to take him for another type of therapy. What do you expect when she does NV FISH – her whole being to be involved in just taking care of her son, her pain, her fears and anger? No, after the first round, we see her stuck in a loop of thoughts around how she felt rejected as a girl child – missing out on romance, sex, and obsessed with desire for attention. Do you see, when your heart and mind are not involved in solving the problem, how can you solve it? This is what NV FISH does. Within one month, this lady got rid of all therapy. She learned to lead her life with NV techniques and saved INR 90000 per month, which she was spending on various therapies and began to accept her son, who also showed a radical difference in his behavior by now.

We have heard that the mind is the most powerful tool, and we can pull infinite power from the subconscious mind to manifest any reality. With these examples, you shall be able to discover that there is a process through which you can do the magic a *Mystic* does with intense sadhana (meditation) by first shaping up the conscious mind, making it devoid of any thought, cleaning up the subconscious mind, and then having a connect between the two that is so strong that he can direct the conscious mind with his intent to access the infinite power within.

NV FISH cleans up your mind and ensures that no unwanted thoughts or emotions corrupt the mind so that the power of focus grows effortlessly without programming the mind using some NLP or hypnosis. Programming the mind using such techniques is like holding sand in the hand.

Let us get back to the technique. It is like fishing. We fish a thought here and reach *Yog Nidra*. So we throw the net in the water and wait without waiting. We are aware that when the fish is caught, we will know. So we pull the fish out of the net and then throw the net in the waters again. We do not go after the fish, which jumped out of the net into the water again.

We do this process 7 times. By the time we reach the fourth stage, *Yog Nidra* comes for most of us, and we really need not do 7 steps to reach *Yog Nidra*.

Like NV SWIM, we also have an objective to reach *Yog Nidra*, if it happens after the fourth, seventh or even the tenth stage. The objective here is to keep going deeper into the layers of the mind and that happens on its own and reaches the gateway of the subconscious (*Yog Nidra*). You shall be able to see the impact of it the next day when you do NV SWIM. Quality of your experience will be higher because your mind is cleared up.

One of the biggest advantages of this technique is that it takes away the influence of the subconscious from the conscious, and you operate from a deeper layer of wisdom rather than operating from the top of your head and being reactive. Hence, worrying, panic attacks, anxiety and anger disorders, which all of us have to some degree, vanish. But the biggest advantage it has on your body is that as your mind cleans up, it functions optimally to regulate blood and oxygen in your body. The purified mind is not consuming extra energy for those stray, intense and suppressed thoughts anymore, which were residing in the inner layers of the conscious mind. Do you see how this helps you as a Cure?

Did you notice that I am not even talking about curing you? I am in a way, not even relating to your problem if the purpose of reading this book is to gain health. I do not care if you have health issues of one type or other. I want you to make *bliss* a habit. If that happens, your vibratory level will not let you have any *sufferings*. This is how every case was cured – by making them focus on the process of recovery while the problem still persists.

Guidelines and Checklist:

There are no rules but guidelines. Having seen thousands of fishing reports of my students/patients and seeing fishing reports daily for several weeks for many students, here are some observations:

1. The first round shall often show you thoughts related to urgency. Like sending an email or preparing to cook for kids. The second round shall be deeper in the normal case where you hit into your long-term aspiration like attending PTM next week or birthday next week or a wedding to be attended.

2. The third and fourth round shall actually take you into the emotional body, as by now the conscious mind tuned for survival is diminishing.

3. The fifth, sixth, and seventh round shall actually be an access to past lives, trance, deep-rooted trauma or just pure light. This is how the seven layers of human body can be accessed through seven rounds. This is an ideal and perfect scenario, and it does not exist

with any one of us in this manner. In reality, we have these layers jumbled up into each other and exactly this is what you are attempting to clean up.

On these guidelines, here are the actual findings:

1. People come for the problem, but you will find that in all seven rounds, it does not feature anywhere. This is fine because now they know what their problem is.

2. You may find the first round itself going into the subconscious or some mystical journey. This means, as explained above with an example, that the subconscious mind is driving the person, and this person does not have their feet on the ground.

3. Corporate workers and people with big responsibilities, who are stressed, may discover almost all rounds filled with a task list.

4. People with mental disorders shall discover that they have obsessive thoughts, which appears in each round.

5. People with distress will reach, after a round or two, their trauma and hurt will remain there for a long time.

6. The most fascinating thing is that you may not have any thoughts or feelings, but you will feel some pain, sensation or discomfort in your body. It is so beautiful to learn how your emotions are stored in the body, crippling it down. Yes, be assured that by experiencing this pain, it is now on its way out of your body, leaving you healthier.

7. In the case of obsessive or compulsive thoughts (maybe you are *suffering* with OCD or distress), do not worry about resolving them. They will not go through this technique overnight and the third one (NV HUNT) is designed for the same.

Each day, your fishing report shall change and that would mean that your mind is purifying. Do not judge yourself when you see your fishing report. Do not be scared to see how dirty your thoughts are. Do not judge that you are bad person having such thoughts. Of course you are and that is why you are reading the book to transform from a bad to a good person (if you like to use this terminology of good and bad).

Preparation:

- Take a pen and paper. You will have to record a few findings. Ideally, start a diary. If you do not feel comfortable maintaining a dairy, do it on a fresh paper every day and tear it off after completing the process. Ideally, maintain a record. You will be amazed to discover significant insights about yourself after you have done fishing for some time. It is easy to take a picture of your report and save it privately. New-age people like to use their mobile phones rather than pen and paper. Please go ahead. It is better you do it than creating some resistance. People of my generation shall use pen and paper no matter how proficient they are with typing. I am skeptical that they will get entangled with screensaver and making few clicks and checking messages in between.

- Create a peaceful and quiet environment for the meditation process. It can be outdoors in an open space or inside a room. Create an ambience a candle, incense or an aromatherapy diffuser. Avoid music.

- Sit in a meditation posture, preferably Siddhasana with hands on your lap (not on the knees. See figure 20). If you have any physical discomfort, do it while sitting on the chair. It's important that you are in a relaxed state and your body is not strained.

- For best results, I always advised my students to do it for 3 weeks nonstop. But first try it out for a day or two to see how it goes, and if does not go well with you then commit yourself more sincerely. If it goes well, then continue for several weeks.

- It requires around forty-five minutes. The longer the better.

- Ideally, fix a time (rather an event after which you will do it). Dusk (gaudhuli) is ideal. Retired people do it at 4 pm after they have taken a nap. Housewives do it in the afternoon and many people like to do it in the evening after tea.

- Ensure you commit yourself to a fixed time, daily. If your mind says you want to be flexible about the timings, it means that you are not yet ready. Persuade yourself for one week to do it and by then, you would have enough energy to break the patterns of your mind.

- Avoid doing it as the last thing of the day. By now, you are already tired and will doze off within the first round itself. But if you cannot find any other time, then this is better than not doing it. At least with your intention, your energy will start to build up and cleanse your mind.

- Do not start this technique on the day one. Everyone does it after at least one week of doing NV SWIM because it requires you to have fair expertise in the ability to observe breath.

Technique :

Observe your breath and keep bringing the attention to your rectum (root chakra, base) and do it for 7 rounds or till you reach *Yog Nidra*, whichever comes early.

- Close your eyes. Observe your breath for a few moments.

- Observing it, you may want to adjust your posture, clear your throat, itch your nose etc. You may remember to put the phone on silent, latch the door and other such routine chores. Do it. Finish all of it and get ready to start now.

- Now for the next 2-3 minutes or so sitting in the position as shown in figure 20, continue to observe your breath and gently try to pay attention to your root. You will find it very hard. Do not try to take any pressure. As and when you remember during the process, keep bringing your attention back to the root. By doing so, your breath will go where your attention is and will help you breathe deeper, and effortlessly.

- After 2-3 minutes, open your eyes and write down your thoughts, feelings etc. Whatever thoughts you remember after opening your eyes (make it brief, in one line. It is not like writing a diary, you don't have to be elaborate).

- Close your eyes again. Spend a few moments observing your breath and attention at the base and keep doing it. And as you feel ready, after 2 to 4 minutes, open your eyes and record the thoughts you remember after opening your eyes.

- Do this 7 times in the 45 minute duration.

Sitting Posture for NV Fishing

Figure 20

NOTE:

The feedback we heard from few people is that they have no thoughts. These are often the corporate middle and top management people because they created a thought that they have to observe their thoughts, and this does not allow them to observe breath or let any other thought come. Some get very fearful of their mind and do not want any "dirty" thoughts to come, so they block it. Obviously if they keep this as a thought then they are not doing the process i.e., observing the breath. Some indulge in making a selection of thoughts. They shall probably go and have a buffet lunch than doing fishing here. Abort this technique in such cases and go back to the first technique and treatment processes. You are not yet ready. Of course come back and try after few hours or next day.

This technique is all about observing your breath and not observing your thoughts. Thoughts will flow like fish fall in the net. And when you pull out the net, some fish may jump out to the water. Likewise, when you open your eyes, you may find it hard to recall some of the thoughts. Do not waste your energy in such activity. Simple task is to just write down whatever you remember were the thoughts or feelings or findings during that round and get back quickly. It is also normal that in one round you may be blank. If so, pay attention to the technique and remind yourself to do it sincerely by remaining with the process of observing the breath.

The *bliss* experienced in this technique is far deeper and tempting than the first technique. You will never forget the taste of this *bliss* if you do it properly and within three weeks of your doing it, you may experience it several times.

It is possible that this process may trigger some old trauma. You might go out of control and want to break the process to have an emotional breakdown. Please do that. Attend to the breakdown because the purpose of this technique is to keep clearing the baggage hidden inside and now that it has surfaced, please attend to it. In a less dramatic situation, you may find some old memory surface but will be fine continuing. This is the ideal situation to heal it. Keep feeling that emotion while observing your breath. By now, if you have read part one of the book, you are aware that this is the only way healing works.

Do not be obsessed about each round lasting 2 to 3 minutes. This is a pure guideline, and I have never seen myself or anyone attain it. There is no need for such a stiff plan. As you begin to go deeper, each round will last longer. In fact, you will feel like you have lost your sense of time. This technique is all about going from mind to emotional body to touch your spirit. Hence, losing sense of time and traveling into vast space is very normal and yet a very profound experience.

NV HUNTING

Introduction:

This technique has the fastest result, and I have often considered it equal to surgery or call it surgical strike on your trauma. This technique is used in clearing the baggage of the past, which actually becomes the root cause of your patterns of *suffering* or disease. In the first technique, we worked on merging the subconscious and conscious. In the second technique, we worked on cleansing the mind (conscious), and in this technique, we work on cleansing the emotions (subconscious). Hence, as we do the first technique, we speed up the whole process of union of Spirit-Body-Mind. Like we swim in our breath, we fish our thoughts and hunt down our hidden emotions.

Spiritually, this technique is the only spiritual practice one shall have to live in the now. So much has been talked about the power of now and every preacher tells you to live in the now, but no one actually told us how to. This technique will automatically liberate you from your past emotions (not memories) and leave you in the now.

Living in the now does not mean that you forget your past. You all know that it has never worked. The harder you try, the more powerful it becomes and by now, if you have read Section 1 & 2 of this book, you would know how old memories and baggage results in *suffering* and disease. Besides, one can never live by cutting off from the past because your roots and origin lie there. If you are a business executive, you know the importance of data, which helps you see the trend and forecast with more precision. It's the same with all of you. Every bit of wisdom that we need as a guiding force is hidden in our experiences. Rather than learning from them the reasons and purpose of such episodes in our life, due to our *belief*, we create emotions and judgment. Let us understand how to live in the now.

1. Our mind drifts into good bad and ugly memories of the past. It drifts into the past all the time because we are not content with our present. The only time, we live in the now is when we perceive it to be in dire need of survival like an incomplete assignment or fear of the loss of a job. This too, we'd rather do in a habitual way rather than be total in that moment.

2. When we delve into good memories of the past, after a while, that also leaves us sad and less hopeful for the future because it was a good memory of the past compared to the present, which is not beautiful. Hence, the future looks rather grim. So even the good memory leaves a negative effect.

3. When we delve into bad or ugly, we feel less and less optimistic about making the present beautiful as this brings a sense of hopelessness.

4. The more we delve into the past, the more we swing into the future. It is like a pendulum. Traveling in the future fills us with worries and fears leading to insecurities, after which we want to control and hoard everything we can. Right from relationships, people and society, and wealth to seek certainty. The law of nature says the future is unknown. We are now at conflict with nature. It does not imply that we do not plan a future or consider a few scenarios and safeguard ourselves as much possible but with faith and vision and not with fear of tomorrow.

This becomes a vicious circle, due to which the modern society keeps inventing ways to keep you engaged and entertained to explore new things so that you do not turn inward but remain occupied with outward oriented activities. They capitalize on your fear for tomorrow and desperation to live today and hoard security by making you indulge in such products and services. You are driven by common knowledge available in the market, which no one is able to practice including your friends who teach you all the time. The phrase, "Forget the past, you only have one life. The world is open and full of choices, let us enjoy." Enjoy what? What one life do you have? Do you have a life without being with your essence? Agreed all of them are nice tools to somehow survive, but the question now is, are we surviving? We are feeling trapped or sick in our own choices. Is life really so worthy that you are so desperate to live? Is dying not a better choice than *suffering* and being desperate?

While the task is very simple, the only way we can live in the now is by expanding our consciousness to the extent that the past and the future, both merge in that moment. This is the only why, to feel complete and in union with nature. The purpose of being in the future is never to know the future. The desire to know the future comes from the insecurity due to the past experiences or greed to acquire more. Purpose of dwelling in the past and even the most traumatic experience is not really to feel the misery and turn hopeless but because those events have had that impact and carry that wisdom about life that our consciousness, by design, likes to visit them to learn from them. The entire wisdom that you would ever need to make choices in your present life is rooted in your past experiences. The universe conspired through those events to leave you all the clues you would ever need in your life as information, knowledge or wisdom to arrive on a better choice and to see your future possibilities, hence a direction and purpose is hidden in your past events. This is why mystical teachings say, you are the universe or the universe is flowing through you. This means for your purpose of life, the universe has already given you all the wisdom you need. You will learn through this technique how to decode the wisdom hidden in you. This is the same technique unknowingly used by secret service agents or investigative agents to decode the secret behind a specific crime and many of you have also used it unknowingly without knowing that there could be a process and science in doing so.

This technique is derived from the Sutra written in scripture – "*Vigyan Bhairav Tantra*" – which says if you reverse your life memories starting from today, till you were born, you can undo any pattern, be free from the debt of karma and get liberated. On this one line, I spent many years of my youth. I read OSHO who has translated this sacred 4000–year-old book with the promise to teach those 112 techniques written in the scripture., but OSHO also wrote three lines to explain this Sutra. I landed up developing it as a technique, process and science. In addition, I discovered that this technique is anti-aging. You can take a selfie before starting and then take a selfie again after three weeks and do this technique daily before sleeping for 5 min and allow yourself to fall to sleep while doing so. Simple? Can it get better than that? See the difference yourself.

I read this Sutra when I was 25 years old. During that time, I would attempt to understand it in my free time. What you receive here as a technique is actually a result of many years of experimentation. This technique was hardest to implement and went through significant evolution in the last four years working on so many cases.

Let us take some scenarios to better understand the impact of this technique:

1. This woman grew up believing she was closer to her mother than her father and always felt that it was her mother who made sacrifices and brought her up. She would have nothing against her father except that she would not feel the importance of her father as much as she felt for her mother. Post this technique, her life changed when she discovered how

her father personally took care of her, empowered his mother and silently taught her the most meaningful lessons apart from discovering how much her father actually loved her, which was subtle and non-verbal. She could feel it now. The nature of realization is such that it comes across as the truth. Your own truth. There is no way anyone can convince you against it. This piece of wisdom was hidden in the events of her life, which she had failed to capture before. Can you see how her whole life changed with just one such realization?

2. He lost his mother at a very young age. He was angry with God. In search of answers, he began experimenting with life and relationships and learned so much by reading and debating that he grew up with anger and a sleep disorder. His faith was broken. In every relationship and endeavor where he felt comfortable and loved, he found a reason to turn aloof not finding his mother there. He found his success, in money, wealth and fame worthless and aborted them in his quest for home. He grew up believing he was aloof and no one loved him. Post NV HUNT, he discovered why his mother had to leave him, and how all these experiments with life taught him his patterns and he discovered his quest for something deeper. He began to feel the pain and was beginning to feel detached. His anger toward the universe was healed, and each time he used this technique, he found wisdom and became clear of his purpose. He felt tremendous love within and began to give unconditionally and turned into a healer. A few years later, this man wrote this book, which you hold in your hand now.

Examples are many. Such miracles are routine for us at NV LIFE. You will learn to do the same now. Be excited. At the risk of sounding egoistic, let me tell you that even the mystics take ages to meditate and many births to come to such a realization, which ordinary people like you and me can do within hours with these techniques. I am talking about people who have no background in spirituality, coming for a workshop and going back with a higher degree of consciousness.

Coming back to how to forget the past and live in the now. You understand by now that you never needed to forget the past, and the only way you can be free from the ill-effects of the past, is by bringing the past into the present moment. If you do so, the future will also exist in this moment. Simple to understand that if the past is integrated into the moment, then the swing of the pendulum creates the future, and will also stay in the present moment as it swings.

But if it was so simple then everybody would have done it. It actually is as simple as it sounds or I make it sound for you. Here is how:

1. We have learned from Section 1 & 2 that consciousness is like RAM, subconsciousness is a hard disk and unconsciousness is cloud storage. Here subconsciousness means memories of the past, and here for this technique and actually everywhere, we have kept our definition valid only for this birth. Hence, we are not arguing if there is any reincarnation or rebirth, which some of you coming from different *belief* may conflict with. We are not a spiritual book but a health book and our purpose is to take these techniques as a medicine and not as religious or spiritual practice. It is more than enough for us to stay in this birth for the purpose of curing ourselves.

2. We also know we have no problem with our memories because we do visit them and keep them with us and are still surviving. The problem is that we have an opinion about them, and we do not know how to look at our life or heal our trauma.

3. Our problem is that our emotions are attached with them. Our problem is the belief attached to that. So, if you happen to recall the trauma of abuse, then our issue is not abuse, but the emotions that the event generated and corresponding *belief* we created with the event which disturbs us. If these emotions and *belief* can be released, then remembering the past turns into intimacy with the self rather than the past haunting us. This exactly is the purpose of this technique.

4. In essence, we are saying that if we hunt our emotions out and resolve the *belief* attached to these events then our hard disk (subconscious), which is huge, can fit into our RAM (conscious) and become one. This is how the past can be merged into the present, and this is how you can change your past by releasing the emotions and resolving the *belief*. So, your memories are rather purer and more sacred, and you begin to love and accept yourself and turn intimate. This has a huge impact on your relationship with yourselves and hence with others. Did you notice those of you who are on the path of your inner journey, having a very elated light experience are actually not intimate with yourselves till you clear this past? You have been fooling yourself so far though your intent has been very noble and shall be respected. Now you will become effortless in being intimate with the self and there will be no inner journey for you. You will have just one integrated journey with whole of your being present at the moment.

5. Did you notice, this has already resolved one of the biggest issues we have not understood and every spiritual teaching has been advising us to do for centuries; expand your

consciousness and become light. As your subconscious is merged with the consciousness, you expand your consciousness and from Section 1 & 2, you understand how 'expanded consciousness is directly proportional to health.' This means, we are not yet talking about how past trauma and emotions affect your health to cause you *suffering*. As you do this technique, consciousness expands because it liberates you from the *belief* and emotion, which was causing you *suffering*. It is bound to leave your body healthy and free of toxins.

We have two profound examples, from the history and mythology, of this technique by people who would have unknowingly applied it. It seems that when Buddha meditated under the tree for enlightenment, he went through his 500 births. As he reviewed his past lives, which ran automatically as a divine intervention, he began to see patterns of his soul and got liberated from the effect of his karma. That left him with the expanded consciousness with immense wisdom. This technique migrated him from detachment to enlightenment. So, when we do the same technique on our current lives and for the time spent in the mother's womb, we have all the wisdom in our consciousness required to lead our life, which is full of guidance, wisdom and well-supported by the universe.

To be able to arrive at such a situation where such profound divine intervention takes place, Buddha went through extreme pain after witnessing three events in a day. Witnessing these three events, feeling extreme pain which caused him detachment with worldly desires and left him with one profound curiosity "Who am I" by asking why do we suffer?

Do you see the magic of pain? It connects you with mystery. It takes away *suffering*. It leaves you with one profound question and the power to seek. Post that, Buddha never suffered and gradually only lived in *bliss*.

Another example we have from mythology is from Lord Krishna helping Arjun get liberated to fight for the cause. Krishna had to coach him on the journey of the soul and the theory of karma. In addition to this, he had to show Arjun, his various past lives. This was to reflect that we are supposed to do our duties and each birth has a purpose. Krishna even had to show him his true form as Lord Avatar and the various forms he could take – He made such massive travel in time and space of past and future to show Arjun the big picture and expand his consciousness, who was stuck in his emotions and attachment to his cousins. This was conceptually the same as NV HUNT, except that it was led by an external person to expand the consciousness of Arjun.

The Technique:

Reverse your past. Start with the end and go to the beginning. This means if you wish to do NV HUNT on your last 5 hours from 2 pm to 7 pm – consisting of 10 activities, which we call 10 experiences, each of these experiences will have emotions, beliefs and thoughts. Your job is to visit these 5 hours from 7 pm till 2 pm in reverse order. It is like the reverse button being pressed on a movie that you are watching. But reverse is in slow motion to capture finer details hidden in them. So if you are watching a wedding and the couple is accepting each other and leaving for a honeymoon, now you will see how they are un-wedding each other. Simple?

Key Points:

1. When you reverse time, your task is to observe your emotions. The idea here is to gather information that is hidden or the emotion created but not lived. For example, if I reverse my last activity say, changing into night clothes, I discover that the color is my favorite, and the cloth is soft and recall that it was a new one kept in my cupboard by my wife to give me a surprise. This means I discovered how much my wife cares for me. I felt none of these emotions when I routinely wore that dress and slept.

2. All of this information may come to you in one session or when you repeat such sessions again in the future. It comes on its own. You never have to mentally try to dig it out. The trick is to be able to stay in that time and space. All the information is always hidden in that time and space of that moment when it occurred. It is like zooming into a part of the picture and seeing more minute details or like taking a second and living it for a few minutes. It will reveal what it must or what your consciousness is ready to absorb as of today.

3. To be able to do that, you need the following:

   a) Ability of your mind to launch you in that time and space. So if you say, I want to reverse my seventh birthday. My mind shall be able to launch me there.

   b) Ability of your mind to stay in that time and space while the information is unfolding. This means that your mind does not drift into any other time and space or activity when the information unfolds

   c) To be able to do that, mind acts like a rocket launcher, which has launched your consciousness into that time and space, and now the only function of your mind is to capture the information.

d) It can be done so successfully if your mind has the power of focus. Power of focus will come from the ability to observe your breathing, and it will further strengthen with NV FISH so that the subconscious influences do not act as a distraction. This is why this is the last technique. People are advised to do it after at least one week of practicing NV SWIM and then NV FISH.

e) It is not necessary that you remember all the memories and only then you can do HUNTING. All you have to do is follow the process as listed below. Have your intent and launch yourself in that time and space. Whatever information needs to come, will come to your consciousness. It is so normal for you to not remember anything from your first few years of life. It is of absolute importance that you hunt on those first seven years when all the *belief* were formed. The trick is to trust the process and follow your intent. Just visit that period and stay there. Even if no information from that time period is revealed, you will have this sense that you are far more at peace and something shifted within you.

Summary: NV HUNTING is traveling to a specific time and space and staying there. To do that we need some control over our minds. We can then direct our consciousness to that space and our minds shall not take us away from it during the process. This means that we shift from the mental body to the emotional body and attend to it in totality, which is the path to connect with our spirit. This is how, when you attend to those emotions of the past, which are often a negative spectrum of emotions (mainly hurt, regret, pain, fear, shame, guilt, rejection, and feeling unloved), they get released from your emotional body. This leaves your spirit cleaned up and moves toward the light because your spirit is never dirty with such emotions except for the fact that through various experiences due to your *belief*, you accumulate them and these emotions act like a dark cloud, which do not let the sun shine. So, in reality, we never move to light. We are light beings. We only need to clear the clouds for the sun to shine through us.

Process of NV HUNT:

You can do HUNTING on three things from your past.

1. Events

2. Relationships

3. Emotions

Events will have relationships – if not with human beings then with nature. For example, being at the zoo and rescuing yourself from a tiger or fear created by being in the dark and dense forests. Events will have people, relationships and thus emotions. Emotions are created out of events and events would have relationships, in any case. Essentially, everything is an experience and every experience will have emotions and *belief*. However, based on our experiences with a several thousand cases, we have simpler and easier ways to approach our entire past.

Warning: By now, either you are very excited to do it or most likely very scared and skeptical. You spent an entire lifetime to store these emotions in such a way that you never have to recall them. Allow these feelings to sink in and take your time to come back and read it again and again, till you get comfortable doing it. Till then get better with the first two techniques, which will grow your confidence.

How to approach the past with NV HUNTING:

1. Major events of your life act like the biggest barriers in accessing information of the past. For example, if you experienced some abuse at the age of 10, you will discover that it becomes very difficult to access your childhood before that. Hence, if you try to attempt doing HUNT on your childhood, this event will haunt you.

2. The best way is to first do it on major events – like abuse, death of parents, and breakups in relationships.

3. By doing so, major obstacles in accessing your past are over and now the next easy thing is to do it on your parents.

4. If you do it on your parents, you are doing it on relationships. You find a lot of hurt in it which does not let you go through an entire relationship. Create an event out of this relationship where you find major hurt and perform HUNT on that event. For example, consider you grew up seeing your parents fight and your family shifted to a new house. You were 7 and this fight continued till you went to hostel at age 10. For three years you remained in a disturbed childhood. Now you want to do HUNT on these specific three years. When you start to reverse from age 10 till age 7, you find, it is not happening. This is because their major fights do not let you reverse an entire situation. You would know 3 or 5 such episodes where they fought very intensely or where the impact on you was very deep. Create those fights as an event, and then one-by-one, start performing HUNT on those events. Once done, then continue HUNT on all three years.

1. It is difficult to perform HUNT on emotions in the beginning because we do not have a large consciousness to be able to directly open up emotions. It is like you need a container to empty the dirty water, which is flooded on your washroom floor. It is easy to do, through relationships and events. For example, if you are 45 years old and you have the tendency to worry, and you want to root out worry from your life using this technique. You start to perform HUNT on 'worry' and you will find that to recall 45 years of relationships and events, which triggered 'worry' is very overwhelming for you to handle. Hence, do emotions at the end once your consciousness has grown and your emotional body is rather regulated and mind is reasonably stable.

2. Do not force yourself to recall everything from the event. It is not possible and certainly not required. Your task is to be in a specific time and space and the purpose is to cleanse your emotions and *belief*. It will happen on its own as you stay in that space. You only need a few memories in your consciousness, which will help you navigate to reach and stay in that space.

3. It is not difficult for many of you to visit a mother's womb. Of course you know nothing from memory. To do that, you can start to reverse from your childhood and keep going backward. You will arrive in your mother's womb and learn what all *belief* or fear your mother has been passed on to you. People often come back with details, which when they share with their mother, surprise them. This is because such details had never been shared by the mother with anyone. It doesn't necessarily have to be significant; it could even be a small thing like the mother not liking a guest coming home when she was five months pregnant with you.

4. People do not have the recollection at all for ages 7 and below. They probably recollect one or two vague memories. This is good enough. In such cases, start from the age you can recall and keep going backward. This will open up memories of age 7 and below, bit by bit. Or you can recall your seventh birthday, the dress you wore, the city you lived in, the school you attended, your friends and your teachers. As you do that, some memories will open up and that is good enough to get going. But do all these after you have finished HUNT on your conscious years.

5. It is possible that you choose an event and that triggers another event and your consciousness shifts to that. This is the moment when your spirit is guiding you to first attend the more important event. Hence, abandon your plan to do HUNT on your chosen event and go with the flow.

Preparation for the Process:

1. Defrost before frying: When you do it on heavy events or a part of a relationship with many jumbled memories, it is recommended that you first start writing down whatever comes to you in a free flow manner. For example, death of parent(s) and breaking up. They are so heavy that if you start to perform HUNTING, emotions will overflow and not let you cleanse. Your mind will indulge in experiencing the trauma while the task of the mind is to witness. Hence, writing the event helps you defrost your frozen emotions and then you can fry.

2. It is not important that you write in every case.

3. The best practice for the major events is to allocate a few hours. Start writing in the afternoon. This fills your consciousness with the trauma or memory, which was frozen inside. This will surely need a lot of tissue papers by the side. Live with these emotions for a couple of hours and by evening, HUNT. As said, it is like performing surgery. One shot, and you are liberated for a lifetime. Often, people do it on the weekends.

Steps of the Process:

1. Wear loose clothes and lay down. Start to observe your breathing.

2. Do that for a few minutes.

3. Now, continue to observe your breath like in step one of NV SWIM and NV FISH and begin reversing.

4. In case of death, you do not reverse. You stay with the news. For example, you heard on your phone that your mother died. All you need to do is stay in that moment while observing the breath because in that tiny moment, when you heard the news, infinite intense emotions are triggered, but since you had the rush to catch a flight, you could not live those emotions. As you stay in that moment, those emotions will erupt.

5. Keep your attention on observing the breath while reversing. You may drift a bit because emotions will come and take away your attention for a while. This is fine. Get back to doing it.

6. Do not be in a hurry. Stay in that moment that you are reversing. You will find that you got involved in those emotions, and you could not observe breathing. It is normal. As soon you remember it, start to observe and witness the emotions. Witness it; it is happening on its own as long as you are observing your breath. Observing the breath is the process of detachment.

7. Do not rush in coming out. You may experience a heavy head or feel more miserable or like something is stuck in your chest or in some other part of the body. Stay in this state.

8. Always finish this process by step one of NV SWIM. This is to help you ground all emotions and come out clean. If you do not do that, it would be like opening up the stomach for operation and getting up from the operation table without stitching it back.

9. Fill up the worksheets given at the end of this chapter. this will help you a lot.

Summary of the technique: NV HUNT:

1. Observe your breath (always do it lying down). Start reversing the duration from end to start of a specific event on which you wish to hunt. If it is abuse, then that event could be just a few minutes. Start from the end till the beginning. If it is on your mother who died 10 years ago when you were 37, then you had 37 years of a relationship plus the event of her death. First clear the death event as described above and then make packets of 37 years (ideally do it in a cluster of of 7 years) and start reversing the relationship through various events for that duration. While doing it keep observing the breath.

How do you know you have done it right?

5 validation points will help you know if you have done it properly or you need to do the same again.

1. Memory does not disturb you: You will experience that you do not need to recall that memory. It is now in your conscious, but it has no emotion that will disturb you. It may still have emotions. For example, if you worked on the death of your mother, it does not disturb you but you may still experience some wetness in the eyes. This is beautiful to have as this makes you intimate with yourself in acceptance.

2. Wisdom: You will discover that you have got wisdom or insight, which you did not have about that event.

3. Intimacy: This is my favorite outcome of all. I would love to see myself turning more intimate with myself and growing the beauty of solitude by transforming my aloofness and detachment.

4. Purpose: You shall discover the purpose behind why that event happened. It is equal to learning. Like the child discovered that the death of his mother at an early age meant he should develop strength in the rational mind and become a reformist. He would search for his mother in every endeavor and suffer not finding her in them. So, he would abort.

Now his search for a mother in any endeavour is not there, and he is able to have a healthy relationship with life.

Note: NV HUNT is never over, I even do it now. In each workshop, as participants did it on their respective issues, I would land up doing the same thing again. The same issues of my past throw me another insight or wisdom each time. In the process of writing this technique over the last four days for this book, HUNTING got triggered on the journey of my life. I could see myself from this day back to when I was born, on how I have made compromises in every relationship for my need to be needed and loved. It flashed in front of me like we see in movies. Though most of it has healed inside of me in the last 7 years, it did not stop me from falling to the patterns every now and then.

Anti-aging with NV HUNT:

The simple way to get a hang of this technique and its benefits effortlessly is to perform NV HUNT on your day. So go to bed a few minutes before your scheduled time. Start observing your breath. Reverse your day from the last activity of the day to the first activity when you woke up. Allow sleep to take over while you are still in the process and trust that only this much of the process was supposed to take place consciously. In some cases, you may find that your sleep is gone, and you have very high–intensity thoughts for the next 2 to 3 hours. In that situation, do not try to force yourself to sleep, but continue with your thoughts. Once completed, you will feel sleepy and be amazed to discover that with less hours of sleep, you are far fresher and more energized than any other day. This may happen only for a few days, or else the routine is that people fall asleep during the process and still find anti-aging happen. This anti-aging happens not just to your face but also to your organs and internal systems. There are tests medical practitioners conduct to find out what the age of your organs like your kidney or heart actually are. After a few weeks, you can get it tested to be pleasantly surprised that your organs are now younger than before.

But there is a deeper and more profound reason to do this every night. This liberates you from creating any karma, cause and effect circle. As you liberate your daily karma and associated emotions, you shall find that you are not forming patterns. Take a case where you are going through a difficult time with your boss or your spouse. You had something unpleasant during the day. You perform HUNT at night, and it stops building up emotions from the day. Now you will not be reactive, and this itself will start to impact your relationship and surprise your partner on how you have the capacity to be cool and positive while in such a situation comparing it to their previous experiences with you. So, we are not creating karma to have an effect on it in the future. We are being liberated toward a higher frequency daily and will begin to attract abundance.

Workbook: Please make use of the workbook to fill up the charts and make HUNT easy and effective. My favorite is the chart of emotions. When you fill that for negative emotions, it will become clear to you what your key negative emotion is – the one that attracted all other negative emotions. So if we directly can conduct HUNT on those emotions, all others shall fall apart to show us our true vibrant spirit.

NV- Hunting- Worksheet

- **Worry**

Worry is a low frequency, continuous latent emotion. It is more of a feminine energy and is triggered by uncertainty. Roots of certainty lie in the mind. Worry affects focus and attention to other issues in life and brings down the overall energy and happiness levels.

List down situations which trigger this emotion:

a. _____

b. _____

c. _____

- **Insecurity**

Worry, as it grows, gives birth to insecurity and this is where it adds to the male energy to take action to work toward security. Insecurity is often triggered by the lack of trust.

List down situations which trigger this emotion:

a. _____

b. _____

c. _____

- **Anxiety**

When fear is added to worry, it becomes anxiety. Anxiety is often triggered when a negative outcome of the event in the future is thought of and that is not acceptable.

List down situations which trigger this emotion:

a. _____

b. _____

c. _____

- **Hopelessness/Apathy**

List down situations which trigger this emotion:

a. _____

b. _____

c. _____

Emotions from the past

- **Guilt:** Lack of acceptance of self and high moral expectations from self.

List down situations which trigger this emotion:

a. _____

b. _____

c. _____

- **Shame**

List down situations which trigger this emotion:

a. _____

b. _____

c. _____

- **Jealousy**

Non-acceptance of failure and feeling of lack (inadequacy) in self, mirrored by success and abundant in others.

List down situations which trigger this emotion:

a. _____

b. _____

c. _____

- **Void/Emptiness**

This is often the case with people who are chasing their dreams. When they achieve something, they discover they have a void. They are not able to celebrate life often. It is rooted in rejection and lack of worthiness often stemming from childhood.

List down situations which trigger this emotion:

a. _____

b. _____

c. _____

- **Self-pity: Poor Me**

  List down situations which trigger this emotion:

a. _____

b. _____

C. _____

- **Loneliness/Aloofness**

Loneliness is the inability to find connections with the surroundings or the creative self and aloofness is a perception that the world is not ready for us.

List down situations which trigger this emotion:

a. _____

b. _____

c. _____

- **Grief/Sorrow**

An event of the past is far bigger than our hope for the future.

List down situations which trigger this emotion:

a. _____

b. _____

c. _____

List 3 major events of your life which brought about a turning point in your life. Describe them in short, how that impacted you. How it changed your *belief* about life and try to work on the negative events here.

Event One

_____

_____

_____

Impact:

_____

_____

_____

_____

_____

_____

Event Two

_____

_____

_____

Impact:

_____

_____

_____

_____

_____

Event Three

_____

_____

_____

Impact:

_____

_____

_____

_____

_____

Identify major emotions, which ruled the specific period of your life. There could be more than one emotion. The focus here is on negative emotions.

S.No.	Emotions	Age group 0-7	Age group 7-14	Age group 14-21	Age group 21-28	Age group 28-35	Age group 35-42	Age group 42-49	Age group 49-56
1	Worry								
2	Anxiety								
3	Fear								
4	Phobia								
5	Insecurity								
6	Guilt								
7	Shame								
8	Unworthiness								
9	Hurt								
10	Pain								
11	Grief								
12	Sorrow								
13	Aloofness								
14	Hopelessness								
15	Not being loved								
16	Emptiness								
17	Anger								
18	Jealousy								

Identify major emotions which ruled a specific period of your life. There could be more than one emotion. The focus here is on positive emotions.

S.No	Emotions	Age group 0-7	Age group 7-14	Age group 14-21	Age group 21-28	Age group 28-35	Age group 35-42	Age group 42-49	Age group 49-56
1.	Appreciation								
2.	Gratitude								
3	Faith								
4	Trust								
5	Worthiness								
6	Love								
7	Happiness								
8	Joy								
9	Peace								
10.	Light								

Create your bio for the duration of your entire life. Remain focused on the emotional journey and how each and every episode of your life triggered emotions.

7-0 age group

_____

_____

_____

_____

_____

_____

_____

_____

14-7 age group

_____

_____

_____

_____

_____

_____

_____

_____

Age 21-14

_____

_____

_____

_____

_____

_____

_____

Age 28-21

_____

_____

_____

_____

_____

_____

Age 35-28

_____

_____

_____

_____

_____

_____

_____

Age 42-35

_____

_____

_____

_____

_____

_____

_____

Age 49-42

_____

_____

_____

_____

_____

_____

List down key learning/insights from all the year here:

_____

_____

_____

_____

_____

_____

Advance stages of the techniques:

We call it an online twenty-four by seven version. Once you practice these techniques for six weeks, you can do these techniques any time and make them a part of you and your life. You can begin to practise them by observing your breath, whether in between the meetings, or while driving. Begin to witness the pattern of the thoughts, catch an emotion or memory, and start to witness it by observing the breath. Pause several times during the day to do this, as existence exists in the moment of pause.

THE CURE IS IN YOUR HANDS

*Y*ou are "THE CURE". The Cure is inside you. With this book, it is in your hands now. You have known what factors can make cure work for you faster and what can slow down or not work for you at all. You shall also be able to discover, after experiencing the techniques and realizing the cure, that health or your well-being was an excuse, this process is actually allowing you to become very intimate with yourself, giving you peace and a sense of connectivity with self. This is actually the science of spirituality, which comes to you as a cure for your well-being and health.

The treatment in this book is proven to be precise and accurate in curing issues faced at an emotional, mental and physical level over the years. The results are predictable and instant. Often one week of practice is enough for you to experience the transformation. It is a systematic and scientific process, it works for all. There is no way it can fail you unless you fail them by not learning the process. Your only challenge is to learn the techniques right and commit yourself for doing so.

Having said that, it is true that some people struggle a lot to get it right even after my repeated intervention. These techniques look easy and they are, but since it is journey in which you are breaking free from your habits and *belief*, at times, it takes strong intent to want transformation for yourself to break such habits and patterns. Through the techniques, it becomes smoother if you allow the process to take its own course. Please avoid any targets. Get the process and techniques right. Healing is an instant phenomenon. A shift in your consciousness is enough to turn the biggest of *sufferings* into *bliss*. Commit to the process and stay attentive to learning the techniques correctly. Cure is the automatic result of it and cannot not be the way for you if you get the technique right.

Your issues are not your reality. They are a result of vibrating at a lower frequency platform to which they belong and not you. You are not your cancer or you are not your depression. You just have this as an issue in your life to deal with. When you move up to a higher platform, such issues cannot reach you. So if you stand near a dustbin, you will be able to smell it, but if you sit in a rose garden, you get the aroma. These techniques are exactly the same. They do not fight the bad smell of the dustbin but bring you into the rose garden. You can always come back to the dustbin and again have the same smell. So the cure is also not fixed. The beauty is that coming to the dustbin is now your choice, so even if you suffer in your choice, your awareness will lead you to acceptance and empowerment as *suffering* is a choice now and not a compulsion, therefore, it is not a *suffering* any more.

In my view, this is empowering. You have a choice now to suffer or to stay in *bliss*. You are not dependent on anyone anymore, and you now have no one else to blame for your *suffering.* Choose wisely now because whatever you choose, your energies will flow for its manifestation now onwards. The cure is in your hands now.

SECTION 4
CASE STUDIES

INDEX

1. AN ENGINEER IN HIS TWENTIES WITH CARPAL TUNNEL SYNDROME.

I am an engineer and being in front of the computer all day during my work, I had started developing a lot of ailments ranging from migraines to carpal tunnel syndrome. Other than this, I was not able to cope very well with the demanding and unappreciative work atmosphere in my job, which led me to be unhappy most of the time that I was in office.

Going through all of this, I was in India during August 2016 on medical leave for pain in my wrist (Carpal tunnel syndrome). I had a tough time even rotating my right wrist, which was debilitating and I was here to get receive treatment. During this leave, my father who was posted in Jaipur at the time was informed of a seminar by Mr. Naveen Varshneya.

Just out of curiosity (looking at it in hindsight I guess somebody somewhere pulled a thread), my parents and I attended the system. I was impressed by the simplicity of what was explained by Naveen and the enormity of the outputs. Since my mother was also going through tough times of her own after my grandmother passed away, we decided to meet Naveen for a one-on-one session where he advised me to attend the NV Life workshop.

The first day I attended the workshop, I was skeptical and a little lost at what Naveen was explaining to us, but I was definitely relaxed after doing the exercises that he outlined. The second day was when I became a believer. After a few exercises, Naveen asked us to go into a hunting session, and he asked me to specifically focus on the pain in my hand. I tried my best to stay focused on my hand and after a few minutes, I could feel an ethereal hand (something like a shadow of my hand), extending out of my wrist and the pain going along with it. Then suddenly the ethereal part vanished and the pain along with it. I was able to use my hand freely, and I was pleasantly surprised.

After this, I have been doing the exercises regularly, and I find NV Fishing to be my personal favorite. I could within 2 weeks after the workshop notice a difference in my attitude to life. I loved going into a session of NV Fishing and introspect all the problems I think I had. They started to get diminished into minor inconveniences and slowly, I became at peace with myself and my problems. I learned that the solution to all my problems lies within me and all I have to do is search. I know that I have a long way to go and a lot of things to learn in my life, but I know for certain that NV Life will push me through and allow me to savor the happy moments of my life and for that, I thank Naveen. I have come to realize that the emotional ups and downs of my life are of my own making, and I can always choose the happier path. My takeaway from NV Life is, "Search within myself, find and get rid of all the things pulling me down and bask in the glory of my awesome life."

2. 73-YEAR-OLD SCHIZOPHRENIC WOMAN.

Medical history:

1. During the summer of 1976, she was in Patna and her family observed some abnormal behavior patterns in her.

2. She was taken to a village for a change. In the village, the changed behavior became apparent with a sudden rise in her thought patterns suggesting fear, guilt and rage.

3. She used to fear from the possibility of her death and the death of her dear ones — her kids and husband.

4. In one incident, on seeing one of her dear ones sleeping with a quilt that happened to be covering his head, she started crying assuming that the person was no more. In another incident, she started believing that people were making plans against her, and that people may kill or harm her.

5. Incidents like these went on for about 6 months, after which, she was taken to a psychiatrist.

6. As a result, eventually, she was given an electric shock treatment along with heavy doses of medicine, and she was advised to visit the doctor on a regular basis.

7. Her condition did not improve. In 2010, her doctor was changed with the hope that her condition would improve further, but she relapsed. She started hearing voices, which spoke to her. Considering those voices, which generally spoke of things against her, to be real, she started having a problem in her everyday life.

Observations:

1. During her initial years post marriage, she was unable to cope with the pressure of the expectations of a joint family and of her in-laws. As a result, she started believing that nobody was taking care of her.

2. This gave rise to a deep-rooted desire of being taken care of.

3. This desire took the shape of fear, guilt and sometimes rage that was in turn converted into hearing voices and other hallucinations.

4. With frequent visits to doctors, surrounded by well wishers and medications, the need to continue with the new support system was strengthened, which ultimately made the body dependent upon drugs to the extent of addiction.

5. Continuing medications for 35 years worsened the anxiety and instilled a strong *belief* that there was no health and no sleep without medicines.

Symptoms:

1. Audio and visual hallucinations
2. Fear
3. Rough skin
4. Complete lack of sleep
5. Anxiety
6. Memory lapse

Treatment method:

She was treated remotely. The patient and her family hadn't met me till the completion of the treatment. Her son had contacted me after seeing a few of my posts on Facebook.

After about a week of remote healing, she reported that there was an improvement in her energy level, and she finally got sleep. Her overall attentiveness increased, and she regained control on memory. Her only wish was to be able to live without medicine, which was fulfilled one day when she finally got off the medications she had been taking for 35 years after 2 weeks of treatment.

After the treatment, she stayed with her son in Delhi who anchored her recovery for 5 months. She was celebrating life every day and gaining better health. Her son (M) managed the project very efficiently which, according to us, is one of the finest examples of family support as a caregiver. Family support in schizophrenia specifically, or any mental disorder in general, is crucial. During these 5 months, few remote healing sessions were conducted, and she enjoyed great health, no medications and very good sleep every day.

Later, her son (M) had to leave for the USA, and she was sent to her hometown where she lived with her elder son and daughter-in-law. This was where she was forced to take medications by her elder son.

The reason why she was forced to do so was stated by her son (M):

"Let me explain the situation in which she started taking medicine. As mentioned, she enjoyed a med-free life for 4-5 months. At the time, she was living with me. I had to go abroad for 4 months so my elder brother took her with him to our native town, Patna. Post treatment, Mom's nature changed to the extent that we were all surprised. She was no more a person who used to be during her medication days. Now she would give a befitting reply to whoever says anything to her and she now had her own opinion and some amount of short temper as well. This didn't go well with her caretakers. They took her to the psychiatrist and started with the medication again, despite knowing that she slept well at night. I was told by her caretakers, my brother and his wife, that she had relapsed because of which she was taken to the doctor. They made sure mom wasn't available to talk to me. During those few chances when she spoke to me she told me whatever my brother wanted her to tell me. She confessed this later on when I got a chance to confront her.

Last month I became aware of the fact that she frequently visited the eldest brother's family (who lives in the neighborhood, since the eldest brother has passed away) and didn't return for days at a stretch. She didn't take those medicines with her either. Earlier, when she was on medication, she couldn't sleep even at night without her pills. But now, she can do well without those medications for days. So she was prescribed a medication, but was not taking the medicines and looked for opportunity to go away from my brother's house for days together. For a few months after she was forced to take medicines, I was kept in the dark completely."

Remarks by NV LIFE:

This case was done in the year 2011. It was one of the first few cases since we started in year 2010. Even then, we knew that schizophrenia or mental disorder is rooted in intentional or unintentional family behavior acting as the biggest trigger if not the cause. Her recovery was not possible in 42 days without her son having pure intent to help his mother heal, and his skills in observing minute behavior changes and creating a supportive environment for healing to take place. This was done when he knew very little about me, and I had done very little work on mental disorders. Having led the recovery, he is keen to share his experience to help other families, and he can be reached at monte.karlo@gmail.com.

Treatment process:

1. It was a remote treatment, till the treatment ended after 42 days. Naveen had not seen my mother, and I had never met Naveen. He lived in Bangalore, and my mother and I lived in Delhi.

2. Each day at a specific time, healing would start and my task was to give daily reports on her behavior to Naveen.

3. Healing process meant that she had to lie down in her room with eyes closed and listen to healing chakra music, which was provided by Naveen.

4. There was absolutely no break in the 42 days of treatment. Not a single day was missed, unless there was a reason. In that case, the time of the healing changed but not the frequency; that was kept consistent.

5. After 42 days, therapy was done weekly, on Sundays. This was done with the intention that the therapy support system is removed gradually.

6. Medications were not removed abruptly. They were removed only if instructed by the medical doctor and even that was done gradually.

7. Time to time, generally weekly, photograph was to be mailed to Naveen.

3. A CIVIL SERVANT IN HER FORTIES, WHO REGAINED HER PANACHE WITH BREATHING.

At the beginning of this year (not a bright start to the year, though), one of my friends told me about Naveen Varshneya (founder of NV Life) and the kind of work he is into. Last year, somewhere in the middle, Maa, the anchor of my being, chose to leave her mortal body behind. This was very upsetting.

Fights, disagreements, altercations and arguments became almost a regular phenomenon at home (hubby and a daughter in the inner circle and in-laws on the peripheral outer) and at work. I started feeling kind of depressed. I actually started living in the *belief* that my life had no meaning and purpose, but the thought of my only daughter held me back to the thread of life.

I also had to deal with a very bad knee-injury with my Anterior Cruciate Ligament (ACL) completely tearing. Frantically, I headed to Apollo Hospitals, Delhi and the top-class doctor (commercially ambitious) strictly but grimly advised a major surgery as soon as possible for both the legs to treat bone deformity.

The turnaround as planned (by Universe, guided by Maa):

Then, one day, I happened to visit my friend, she told me about the NV Life workshop being conducted the next month. I enrolled myself into it. The words Naveen said to me were, "Your knee will heal during the workshop." I wasn't so sure and thought to myself, "Hopefully!"

The W-Days:

Saturday, the first day of the workshop: I reached the venue well-in-time, telling myself to receive everything with an open mind (it should actually be with a shut mind, after NV Life experience). The venue exuded strange warmth, which was so engulfing and welcoming; a certain air of positivity and comfort gripped me, as I took a place on the ground mat with a backrest (#BodilyComfortsAreImportant). I did the homework at the end of the first day as instructed during the workshop and felt the emotion of anger while doing so, which helped me (I guess) reduce the intensity of pain felt.

On the second day (the last day of the workshop), I was experiencing gastritis, acidity and constipation, which eased after he worked on me. At the end of the workshop, I felt layers of burden being lifted.

The road ahead:

In this journey of 2 and half months, I have attended 2 workshops. Each workshop has a different flavor, direction and outcome according to the frequencies, mainly of the participants, the place and the organizers, as I see. If someone asks me today to rate my experience with NV Life, I think (feel more), my soul would certainly jump out and say, "Hey... thank you for getting in touch with me, I waited for you too long but never mind, it's always better late than never. Stay with me, I am there to help you, wherever you are and whatever you are in. Remain with me, connected, for I am the treasure you look for, to become wiser, healthier and prettier."

How does NV Life figure here, in this impeccable connection of the body, mind and soul?

Through very simple and basic techniques of observing our breath, the outer self (the body) connects with the inner-self (the soul) by breaking the barrier of the omnipotent mind. NV Life techniques are very easy to follow and can be done anytime, anywhere without any external requirement. It just needs a sincere intent of doing it regularly in a way that it becomes an innate part of us and our hard-pressed lifestyles. For me, it's like a charging station, where I need to plug in daily or sometimes twice/thrice in a day, depending on the usage of life-battery in terms of struggles (more emotional than physical, as is with most of us), worries, fears, over-thinking, doubts etc. To see each day with sufficient zeal and motive to carry on, without suppressing my feelings/emotions for the sake of external world and without exceeding the inner limits of the baggage carried.

It's not that NV Life promises me a bed of roses always; but now it has made me aware of the thorns around and the purpose of those thorns in my life.

"The best part about NV Life?

Every Morning

I have a new opportunity

To become a

Real (and hopefully, happier) version

Of Myself"

Reaping the harvest:

A top-class knee surgeon, based in Delhi pronounces that the ACL tear in my knee is not an issue at all, and the early degeneration of knees (for which I was advised major surgery in both the limbs) due to bone deformity can be easily tackled with medication. I now am able to run on treadmill at 10 km/hr without any discomfort, which was unthinkable, even with the so-called healthy knee joints, before the injury.

Migraine was another health concern I had since I was a child. Now I rarely experience this after having started NV Life.

The immense potential of I, me, myself (minus the EGO):

NV Life, what I see, feel and experience, helps us connect with one's own oasis i.e., the light within the inner being to draw the kind of power, strength, wisdom, joy and courage, which is an effervescent panacea to all ills. We have pro-created and reproduced with the multiplier effect. Now it is really up to us (sincere intent, will and commitment) to help ourselves by following the NV Life guide on the path of self-journey.

The destination worth waiting for:

It's time that we really understand and come around to take charge of our lives first (we are so habituated to live it up for others), assume responsibility for the choices and decisions we make, accept ourselves as we are (good, bad, pretty, ugly as we understand in worldly terms) and be in love with ourselves forever.

I live hopefully now, waiting in silence and exuberating, for the universe to play out something to enliven the words of L. R. Knost

"Do not be dismayed by the brokenness of the world,

All things break. And all things can be mended.

Not with time, as they say, but with intention.

So go. Love intentionally, extravagantly, unconditionally,

The broken world waits in darkness for the light that is YOU."

Dedicated to Naveen Varshneya: May you grow exponentially and infinitely to illuminate the darkness with the light within each one of us.

Thanks!

4. A SPECIAL EDUCATOR WITH A SPECIAL CHILD.

*M*y joining of NV Life was not just a coincidence or an accident. I was forced into it. Thanks to a lady who had experienced NV Life and cured herself from 9 years of cancer. When she started with NV Life and found it effective she spoke with Naveen about my son, a 17-year-old special needs child who was exhibiting major behavioral and medical concerns those days. I, being a rationalist was not interested in yet another line of treatment or therapy for my son. We were already going through one of toughest phases of our lives, handling a teenager who could not speak to express what he was going through. A series of medical examinations and tests did not yield any results, but were only adding to the agony and pain of my son, my husband and I. My husband and I had already spent months of sleepless nights in handling my son's violent and aggressive behavior. He would just get up in the middle of the night screaming and shouting. Throwing things, banging his head were a few things he did.

I was an easy target for him. Pulling my hair real bad had become a way of his venting out his frustration. In the process of managing him, I was bitten by him umpteen number of times. My husband's strength would get exhausted in physically managing my son when he would go completely out of control.

The heads in the school where I was working have been very empathetic and supportive about the challenges I faced. Yet, I was expected to do justice to my work. Many a times, my husband had to either take off from office, or he would be going late due to my son's condition at home. The husband of the lady who had introduced me to Naveen and his work and my husband were in the same office at that time, and he was completely aware about the scenario at home. In fact, being my husband's director, he extended full support. But then, he could do only so much. The atmosphere and environment in the house started affecting my younger daughter who would seek quality time from us but got neglected instead. It started reflecting in her performance at school.

Then, toward mid-December 2015, I was introduced to NV Life by that lady. As mentioned earlier, I was not at all interested. On speaking with her, she told me that Naveen was confident of getting the violent behavior under control if nothing else.

At that point of time, when to us it appeared to be an unending process, my husband went ahead and made the payment for the workshop which was to be held in Jan 2016. I was really upset and told my husband that if he was so keen he himself must have attended the workshop. But then came a message from Naveen that if it's for a son, then it's preferred the mother attends. I was furious but was left with no choice. Finally, on the day of workshop I reached the venue, I was upset and irritated at the fact that I was being pushed into something I was least interested in.

There, I meet Naveen who asked me to focus on myself, and this added to my agony as I was there for my son and not myself. He said things flow from me to my son and my response was... it's a vicious circle. To which he simply said ... 'we will break it' and walked away.

Phew! He didn't even hear me out and I was further upset. But still good sense prevailed, and I heard him with full focus during the workshop.

As it proceeded my doubts started clearing. My queries were getting answered without me actually asking them. The misunderstandings were being put to rest as Naveen proceeded with the workshop explaining each technique patiently. Each one of us was at liberty to sit, stand or sleep even while explanations were on. I was amused at this. Such a comfortable atmosphere – I hadn't experienced in any other workshop, ever.

As we proceeded through each technique, I was feeling better. After the end of day one, I thought we would be given a series of do's and don'ts but once again things were different. One could eat or drink anything. The only limitation was to restrict yourself from a social gathering since healing process was on, which was understood. Next day, I walked up to Naveen during the tea break and confessed that I had come to the workshop unwilling with a rigid mindset... and he simply said... "I know, it was very evident." That was the time I promised him that I shall try my best to follow the path he had shown and to my surprise by the end of the workshop, I was glad I attended and had decided to follow the techniques for the sake of my son if nothing else. After coming back home from the workshop, I cried my heart out for almost an hour. I just cried until felt better and relaxed.

One month down the line, when we visited my son's psychiatrist on a regular visit, his medicines were cut down from 3 times a day to once a day. In that one month, I had done all the techniques with great dedication. I realized this was actually working. Slowly and gradually, as the days passed, my son improved. In fact, I started feeling good about myself and wanted to take care of myself. The atmosphere in the house got better. I realized I had become really calm. No more shouting in the house, no unnecessary screaming and effect was evident... my son was smiling again. He had started playing baby games, which we would play earlier. He had started understanding things. My daughter who got ignored all this while started getting her due attention. There was positivity all around.

Few months into NV Life, I felt regression in my son's behavior. OMG! I did not want to go down that path again. I quickly got in touch with our coach Naveen and told him everything. He just asked me to do "hunting" and told me that I had become complacent. He was right. So I picked up, again. And during the process I realized that every time I was disturbed, it would show in my son's behavior. In fact, a few months ago, my son threw a major tantrum in the morning and while I was trying to manage him, he pulled my hair in the opposite direction and bit me. I was devastated. I had to go to work, which I did, and cried secretly whenever my mind was a little free. By evening, I had decided to quit NV Life thinking, "This is enough, I can't take this anymore." But words like observe your breath, be with your breathing, kept ringing at the back of my mind, and I did that. I chose to share it on the NV Life group on WhatsApp. It still gives me goosebumps while I write this; the support that I got from everyone was phenomenal. Within minutes of my sharing the agony and pain, the veterans of NV Life guided me on what to do and the rest just held me. By the end of the next day, Naveen pitched in and guided me further. I actually understood that if a mother is the earth the child is the plant, and any disturbance on the earth will cause double the disturbance in the plant.

It's been over a year since the workshop, and I am really glad I attended it. I have learned to handle myself in a much better a way during the times when I would actually get stressed. The constant guidance on the WhatsApp group has helped me change the way I think. The knowledge and insight gained by following the principles of NV Life has stood me in good stead in my role as the counselor and special educator of my school. It is easier for me to communicate and convince the parents who come to me. Following the techniques without bringing my mind into it, has brought about a positive impact on the entire family. And my cute son is once again settled.

I have covered a long distance and still have a long distance to cover.

My heartfelt thanks to the lady who introduced me, to her husband for guiding us to NV Life, and to the members in the NV Life for just being there, without being judgmental. My gratitude to the creator for giving me the opportunity to be mentored by none other than Naveen, in whose every word there is only guidance for the highest good.

And of course, a huge "Thank You" to Naveen for changing my perspective toward life and toward my son.

5. ANXIETY RESOLVED OF 30-YEAR-OLD MALE, CEO OF A SPORTS COMPANY.

I have tremendous gratitude to Naveen Varshneya, as his "Science of Life" technology has not only ensured that I remain empowered even during the most challenging times of my life, it has allowed me to stay connected to my true purpose of living.

Naveen entered my life over 6 years ago by chance, but since then all of our interactions and the work we have been doing together seem more like destiny. We first met on the sidelines of a football pitch in Delhi where I was watching his prodigy footballer son, only 6 years old at the time, impress a team of Spanish coaches. Back then, I was the director of a global sports agency and, on that day, I was overseeing the execution of an international partnership I had recently architected between one of the top football clubs in the world and an Indian organization. Although the partnership was a landmark initiative for Indian sport as well as one of the highlights of my career since moving to India from the United States to pursue my dream of developing football in India, there was a certain emptiness inside that I couldn't quite understand. It was as if my mind, body and soul were not aligned leaving me feeling insecure and anxious internally even when my external environment seemed complete.

After a brief conversation about Naveen's son and his development as a footballer, we started speaking about his work that was focused on connecting science and spirituality to heal and transform people's lives. This was a topic that I was fascinated by, but had little experience in. I shared a bit about my life and accepted his invitation to do a Skype session the following week, as he came across as a knowledgeable and genuine person.

Prior to the Skype session, Naveen had me answer some questions about my life, which ensured that I spent some quality time alone, self-reflecting in order to kick-start the healing and transformation process. The Skype session lasted an hour and by the end of it, I felt like I was speaking to someone who had known me my entire life. Just by reading my energy and listening to me speak, he was able to identify a series of patterns and "blind spots", especially in the areas of self-worth and relationships that have been running my life for a number of years – areas that have never come up even after years of self-development work.

We ended the session, and I agreed to start his 40-day "Science of Life" program, which included breathing exercises, journaling, distance healing sessions in the evening and regular interactions with Naveen over the phone and through WhatsApp. What I immediately appreciated about his approach was that Naveen was not trying to "fix me" through words, he was merely instructing me to heal and empower myself through focused breathing while he remained the support structure in the background.

At first, of course, the thought of committing to 40 days seemed challenging, however, I quickly realized that the "Science of Life" techniques, while deeply impactful, do not take too much time out of one's day, which is important especially for someone like me who is constantly on the phone, at the office or traveling for business.

So for the next 40 days, I committed to working on myself using the "Science of Life" technology and the results were extraordinary. I found that just through focused breathing, I was lighter, more accepting of myself and others and generally feeling more alive. Although Naveen was in Bangalore, and I was in Delhi, I always felt his presence during those 40 days, supporting and championing me along as well as giving me a gentle kick in the backside when required. By the last session, I was not only a transformed person full of love and self-confidence, I had mastered the tools to ensure I could remain that way even during the most difficult of times. Also, by the last session I had decided that I was stuck with Naveen, and he was stuck with me, whether he liked it or not. What I didn't realize at the time, though, was that during those 40 days, I had only scratched the surface in discovering the power of Naveen Varshneya and his 'Science of Life' technology.

I continued to stay connected to Naveen through attending his multi-day workshops, visiting his healing center in Bangalore, regular phone calls and, of course, through daily practice of his focused breathing techniques NV Swimming, NV Fishing and NV Hunting. After many interactions, I've come to understand that these seemingly simple breathing techniques have come out of the result of a lifetime of spiritual and scientific study by a deeply intelligent and compassionate person. I also came to understand and can confidently say that Naveen has a unique ability to read people's energies from near or far and provide exactly the guidance required. There were days when I would call him during times of crisis and feel so clear-headed after getting off the phone with him or, even more incredible, there were times when he called me out of the blue exactly when I needed support because as he said, "I'm now on his radar at all times."

Over the years, I've introduced my parents, wife, closest friends and colleagues to Naveen, and he has successfully assessed each of them and created a structure for them to heal and empower themselves through his breathing techniques. The feedback about Naveen is always the same as those closest in my life feel, he "sees right through me" and "says exactly what I needed to hear, but not necessarily what I wanted to hear." Also, those who commit to practicing his breathing techniques on a daily basis experience profound results in all areas of their lives. They thank me profusely afterwards for introducing them to Naveen.

Looking back now, I can say that meeting Naveen and being introduced to 'Science of Life' has been a miracle. His presence, guidance and breathing techniques are permanently running in the background of my life ensuring that I stay connected to myself, my loved ones and my soul's purpose in this lifetime. Thanks to the 'Science of Life,' I am now a happily married man, CEO of a major sports organization, and actively involved in my personal and social interests.

But my appreciation toward this work has little to do with the positive aspects of my life at present. What I'll be eternally grateful for is that thanks to the divine intervention that brought Naveen Varshneya and the 'Science of Life' into my world, I now have the understanding, tools and ability to experience bliss on a regular basis no matter what's going on in my external environment.

Finally, the sports management meeting yesterday afternoon went really well. Your advice was spot on as always.

6. HER TRYST WITH BREAST CANCER SURGERY, A 43-YEAR-OLD LADY.

Before I start writing about my experience with NV Life and Naveen, I'd like to give a background picture about my life at that stage. I'll begin by using the often used cliché that my life changed last year in September, 2015. I was diagnosed with breast cancer during this time and was told I was a diabetic. I was lucky that it was detected in the initial stages, but I had multiple tumors so I underwent radical mastectomy followed by chemo. I had seen cancer in my family often enough, so I thought I was ready to deal with it. What I wasn't prepared for was the constant pain of the surgery, the side effects of the chemo and hormone therapy i.e., insomnia, unrelenting pain in my bones, drug induced cholesterol as well as weight gain. The hormone therapy was inducing menopause symptoms, so there were mood swings and hot flushes, which further added to my insomnia. Medications weren't helping.

I thought alternative therapies would help, so I started homeopathy as well as Ayurveda medicines. I was suggested meditation, and I did go for it but I wasn't in a receptive frame of mind, so I felt it wasn't for me. I thought that I just had to accept my situation and hope things would work themselves out.

My husband has been my rock during this tough period. He was the one that got me to attend the workshop in Jaipur. Let me say, unlike other participants who attended the workshop, I did not join willingly. My husband had heard about NV Life from his colleagues and especially about a lady who had managed to overcome her blood cancer through NV Life. He told me about the workshop that was going to be held in Jaipur as well as this lady's case, I wasn't convinced! Then, he dropped the surprise that he had signed me up for it, and I was livid at him for being so underhand!

Anyway, on the first day of the workshop my husband dragged one very unwilling wife to this workshop. I was convinced that nothing would work for me. I still remember the day I met Naveen with my husband, and we told him my problems. I told him that if I could sleep, my body would be able to deal with my problems, and this vicious cycle of pain and insomnia would break, and I'd be able to deal with my problems better. Naveen promised me that he was certain that he could help me sleep better.

The workshop was an eye-opener in more ways than one. When Naveen said that healing was in our hands I just couldn't fathom how. As the workshop progressed, I realized how much emotional baggage I had carried around for years. I didn't even realize that I had not accepted my illness and the trauma that I had undergone, I thought I had dealt with it so well. Helping me face my emotional problems like losing my mother to cancer at 9 and realizing how angry I had been with her all these years for leaving me. I am generally a non-confrontational person and tend not to deal with situations or people that hurt me. Even if someone hurts me, I keep it to myself and let it fester within. I constantly worry and stress about situations as well as people I care about.

So the workshop was enlightening, and the breathing techniques helped me confront my worries and fears. I realized it felt as if a huge weight had been lifted. I was dying to tell my husband about my experience but was advised against sharing my experiences at that early stage of my journey. My surprise was the next morning, when I realized I had indeed slept more than my 2-3 hours (even after taking sleeping pills). I had managed to sleep 5 hours! I was also taken aback when an incident happened in the morning, which normally would have got me all riled up, and I just couldn't summon up any anger! I was so calm inside. After the second day of the workshop, the pain had left my bones especially in my legs. I was feeling light emotionally and physically and felt human after months. My husband was thrilled when I thanked him that he had made me attend the workshop. I have realized now, how my health, well-being, happiness and pain management lies in my hands, and I am thrilled with being able to lose some weight. So I'd like to thank Naveen for putting me on this path of self-realization. I'd finally like to add it has not been easy, and one has to put in an effort for oneself. So I wish NV Life and Naveen the very best in their future endeavors in helping and educating many others like me, as people will benefit from this.

7. OBSESSIVE COMPULSIVE DISORDER TURNING INTO HIS PURPOSE OF LIFE WITH NV LIFE.

*I*n few days, I realized that I needed psychiatric help, and I somehow visited the psychiatrist in Apollo Chennai Hospital. I was detected with Generalized Anxiety Disorder (GAD) with features of Obsessive Compulsive Disorder (OCD). I started taking the medications and had to visit doctors periodically. This was a painful process, and it took more than a year to get over the damage caused by this rejection. The medicines stabilized me to some extent, but I never got peace of mind or the feeling of happiness or bliss.

I then started working in the UK, but my health issues and symptoms prevailed there, and my symptoms were getting aggravated day by day. Again, it was reflecting very badly on my performance at work, and I could hardly do my daily routine. After around 8 months of my stay in the UK, I was sent back to India due to my miserable health condition.

So here I was with my parents in Kolkata. My dream of going and working in a foreign land had been fulfilled. I should be full of happiness and feel accomplished. However, on the contrary, I was in the most hopeless and miserable state.

My dad took me to the psychiatrist again, and he prescribed me a long-term antidepressant medication. I started taking the medicine and slowly gained a little stability but as usual, I did not get my peace of mind.

It was at this time that a college friend told me about a Treatment Center in Bangalore called NV Life and how it can help resolve my health issues. He said that the treatment mode was not based on medicine but on breathing techniques and meditation. He also said that his sister's health and family issues were resolved by NV Life, and that I could trust it, and added that Naveen Varshneya was the founder of this center, which was started in in 2010. This was the first time I heard about NV Life. He advised me to carry on with my medication prescribed by my psychiatrist and treat NV Life as a backup plan if my health issue persists.

I went through the NV Life website and FB page and read through the articles and testimonies of other patients. I found it very interesting and promising.

My First Visit to NV Life, Bangalore:

Soon I planned and visited the NV Life Center in Bangalore around August 2013. I still remember the moment when I entered the Center. The whole Center was full of smell and aura of camphor. Few Lamps were lit and decorated with beautiful flowers which had a beautiful fragrance and a peaceful silence, which is where I first met Naveen. My case history was taken and the treatment began. I still remember the first thing he told me which was that he still hadn't gone through my case history or talked with his Co Healer. He went through the journey and tendency (sanskar) of my soul, and said, that the root cause of my issue was that I had not done anything for my heart or soul. I did not understand these words and I somehow started feeling that he was fake. But I had no other option but to surrender to this treatment process as I had already paid them and by then I was at the end of long dark tunnel and I and I was stuck and did not see any other way out.

After lunch break Naveen was on the balcony of the center and he asked me whether I could see any change in myself. I bluntly replied no and said this was not magic that in few hours I would feel any change. He agreed with me then. After lunch they explained the science of breathing and why is it so important to understand this in connection with our health and well-being. I kept listening with rapt attention. I learned that with faster and shallow breathing we move away from health and age faster. The slower and deeper we breathe we move toward health and aging process is slowed down, and that our thoughts are inversely proportional to our breath, i.e. if we start observing our breath the thoughts start to fade away and if thoughts creep in we are out of focus from our breathing. These sounded like interesting concepts and increased my curiosity but I had no clue how this wisdom would heal my *suffering* and cure my disorder.

The next day I was told to lie down and to attend a healing session. I just needed to lie down and observe my breath. Soothing music was played and it was a 40 min session. For the first 3 to 4 days of treatment I could not see or feel much of a difference in my symptoms and the way I felt, until the fifth day. The frequency, intensity and time interval of negative thoughts and negative emotions like fear, guilt or anger were reducing. For the first time in the last 14 years I was able to focus on any particular activity I was doing without me thinking about the past or the future. For the first time in 14 years I was experiencing happiness and contentment. On the 6th day I was advised to have a consultation with my doctor to decide on the next steps regarding the medication as well as follow my intuition, as there was no hurry to stop the medication.

In next few days I was taught 3 techniques called NV Swimming, NV Fishing and NV Hunting. NV Swimming was to make my breath deeper and slower and to reach a state called Yog Nidra. After each NV Swimming session I was feeling peaceful and relaxed, and I was considerably less anxious and worried. With each NV Fishing session I was getting more and more aware of my authentic self and was going deeper into my thoughts.

By the end of 2 weeks treatment in NV Life Bangalore I felt almost all my symptoms of OCD and depression were gone and was feeling peaceful inside. After that, I was asked to return home and for next 2 to 4 months where my treatment was done remotely while I was at home in Kolkata. I received remote healing sessions twice for one month and the frequency of the sessions was lowered with time. Each day I was making progress and I was able to experience bliss and happiness after 2 decades.

With due course, I had a relationship and eventually our marriage date was fixed for the year after, even though Naveen had said that it was not advisable to. I also got transferred to another city. Slowly the pressure of marriage was creeping in and all my symptoms like anxiety, depression, vomiting started creeping in. My health started deteriorating again and I had to come back to my home at Kolkata. Again I was put on a long-term medication prescribed by psychiatrist.

My Second Visit to NV Life, Bangalore

After I got a little stability after taking medicine for few weeks I had to go to NV Life Bangalore for the second time. This was around November 2014, which was around a year after my first visit there. There I was told that the main reason of my *suffering* was the pressure of having a relationship and of marriage. I was advised that my priority was my recovery from my chronic mental disorder and I did not have enough capacity at that time to handle the pressure of marriage.

I had to undergo an intense treatment process for next 16 days in Bangalore during which, apart from zeroing in on the symptoms, I learned the root causes of my chronic mental disorder and *suffering.* I had a problem in following my heart and accepting the way I was. This was a huge learning and after I went back from the Center my love toward Music and Photography increased. The next year i.e. year 2015, was the best time of my life till then and I was full of energy and happiness. My performance at work also was best during this time and I beat my annual performance appraisal over a period of 9 years.

My Third Visit to NV Life, Bangalore

Meanwhile I got involved in a new relationship with and by the beginning of 2016 the relationship turned sour. This had a negative impact on my emotional status and triggered fear and anxiety in me again. I practiced the NV Life techniques which helped to regain my stability to some extent. Also I started taking remote healing sessions from a Non-NV Life healer. To my surprise my health started deteriorating more and more each day.

By April 2016 my health went to worst level and again I had to visit NV Life Center, Bangalore. My treatment continues, and I have left my job to follow my heart as a sketch artist, as that was the root of my issues, that I wasn't following my heart's desires.

8. A LADY LEARNS TO CONNECT WITH SELF, OPENING TO LOVE, SIDE EFFECT - WEIGHT LOSS.

*T*here comes a time in life when you are walking with a crowd, and you feel you are walking alone. You are talking but no one is listening, you are sleeping and yet you feel you haven't slept in years. Tears don't stop rolling down your cheeks, you begin to slump under the burden of your own emotions. You tell yourself to move on, and yet you are standing at the same place year after year, you know time is running out and you stand all motionless. People you lived with don't see you anymore, they don't hear you, and they don't know if you are still around. Twenty years of my life had just gone by, they just felt wasted, I gave everything to this one relationship, and it gave me back cold, harsh rejection. It felt like someone threw a glass of chilled water on my face in the midst of harsh winters. Everything just came to a standstill, there was an oscitancy that echoed my inner void, a hollow sound that reverberated my inner emptiness, The Sounds of Silence. They clawed at my existence, constantly chirping, I didn't want to hear it, but it was my Truth.

I was drowning in the vortex of my emotions, I was dying. My body was *suffering* already with undiagnosed depression, obesity, memory loss, slurring speech, nerves problem (losing sensitivity to touch), thyroid, medication for hormones that did more damage than help, PCOD, skin allergies and a cough that wasn't leaving me for a year. When I came to know about NV Life, I did not go for medical reasons, they were not on my mind! I was undertaking this journey to find myself. The best part of my first conversation with Naveen was that I remember telling him that I needed to find forgiveness within me to heal open wounds so that I could move on! I have moved on, and I am healed today on so many levels, all my physical ailments of the body are a thing of the past, but this has been a revealing journey! It is only about you! From beginning to the end, it is only you! He asked me to come to Bangalore for the workshop, and at that point, I instantly agreed that night that I became a victim of physical abuse. In the morning, I called Naveen from the doctor's place and said, "Maybe I will come some other time, right now I can't even lift my neck," and I also had a wound on my eyelid. He suggested that I sit down wherever I was and not move for 10 to 15 minutes. A huge shift happened in my energy while talking to the doctor, my cervical pain disappeared. I began cracking jokes with the doctor, and I immediately called Naveen back and said, "Tomorrow morning I am on my way."

When I reached his center and looked at him, I heard my inner voice telling me I was at the right place. I wanted to speak volumes and open a thesis of my life, but there was something in him that told me, "I know why you are here." He never made me feel like I had to explain anything at all. I had the curiosity to know why this happened to me after 20 years and Naveen told me this was a case of twin flames, post the workshop during the metamorphosis, my inner being was at the helm of finding my own twin flame. This is Naveen's most unique feature; he gives you exactly what you seek. And this twin flame feature got me very intimate with myself. All I did was the techniques, my life was only with my inner-self. One fine day, I found the answer within myself. That day, I absorbed every word of Naveen's, and I realized there was only one flame that resides within you. Love itself is within you and one is complete only within oneself. That day and today I never question my master, and I have never looked back.

My first revelation in the workshop was an eye-opener, not only did I not know myself, I was not clear of what I wanted, and I realized I did not have enough love within me for myself. The second day killed any amount of 'I' that was within and revealed several aspects of myself that wasn't a part of self-awareness. It was like a true mirror of my life, and my relationships – a rude and shocking awakening to my complete being and existence. In 48 hours, my life had taken a 360 degree turn, and my life was in my grasp. I had stopped being a victim of my own succinct emotions. The ephemerality of my darkness was subjected to my conscious awareness, and this desperate measure brought in the apocalypse of my life. One most important aspect of NV Life is Faith. You need to have complete and absolute faith, and it purely works on your intent. Fortunately, that was the only thing left in me.

The most beautiful part of the journey is the conversion, and it happens effortlessly. Naveen himself is a transitional energy, his persona and presence itself is healing. His terseness, ironically, is a sharp opener, and his brevity, the soul of wit. There is a Chinese tea that comes in the shape of a small ball when you pour hot water, it very slowly opens to reveal a beautiful, dried flower, and the tea is very calming. It is a moment of wonderment and curiosity and that is exactly how an hour of healing session with Naveen can be. His energy demystifies your 'I' to reveal who you are, and if you stay with the curiosity, it reveals everything about who you are meant to be. During my transition period, I came across one very important aspect of NV Life. To explain it as concisely as I can; I have been a fair reader all my life, my knowledge on religious books has been limited to my choice of books. I could never understand why in a temple or a place of worship it was important that you recite prayers in a chorus, especially if the meaning was not well explained. I could not learn it by heart, would be a wrong statement. I just didn't want to learn like a parrot, I wanted the meaning and understanding. As my journey began inward with NV Life techniques, my understanding of the childhood prayers started enlightening my inner curiosity, and I started to decipher the meaning of unspoken words. Rumi's poetry to Baba Farid's hymns in the Guru Granth, to understand the essence of what Jesus was teaching it all started reflecting inside me. They all teach you the path to inner light, and here we are experiencing that inner light. My transformation was not only about the loss of a relationship; that is what I sought my master for, it eventually healed childhood trauma, loss of loved ones, inner turmoil, failures, but it helped me on my karmic journey toward the ultimate seeking of light within self. In the process, I lost 36 kg in 9 months, cured my physical self of ailments and got back all that I thought I had lost. All this conversion as I mentioned earlier, happened effortlessly. Naveen brought me back to life, brought back my faith in the universe and everything around me. He helped me transform my anger, fear, guilt, shame, temper, ego and arrogance to love, compassion and joy. He has helped me acquire balance in my life force and energy and helped me be myself. My heartfelt gratitude to Naveen and NV Life.

9. A 49-YEAR-OLD LADY LOOKING FOR THE PURPOSE OF HER EXISTENCE, AN ENTREPRENEUR NOW.

*M*y personal web of feelings was trapping me, and I felt I could never feel that freedom ever again. A sense of being shut off in the captivity of my own thoughts was strangling me, and the suffocation of my own dilemma was imprisoning my expressions. Will I ever be free to feel the love I so deserve? Will I ever be free from my own miseries? I felt like I was floating because I could no longer feel the grounded reality of my existence. Help comes when you seek it, and it did come in various forms of modalities, as I learned to breathe and meditate I was beginning to feel what was wrong in my understanding of my reality, but it was a distant actuality that these alternatives would give me a solution I sought so desperately.

Failing verity of your close relations is a striking fact, and I couldn't accept that people close to me were blind to my existence and my being there was just factual. Through a wonderful person, I was introduced to Naveen Varshneya and my first session of healing was without meeting him in person. If the universe was aiding me then this was it. I was shocked that all my confusions came into my mind with a deep clarity in this healing session. I was transferred to a forgotten era and got reconnected to my roots without Naveen knowing me personally or having ever met me. I was eager for the second healing session and fortunately it was a healing with ancestors, visions of an era gone by tales of grandfathers came floating, and I was in the midst of my web that was getting clear with time.

Once I had the good fortune of attending Naveen's workshop and healing, he solved my misery in the third session and taught me techniques that could clear an ancestral curse and karmic debts. I may have traveled a long path through Isha Yoga to Theta healing and Affirmations but Naveen was my savior. Not only did I heal past karma, but I was able to deal with the loss of precious family members and the responsibilities they left behind. My personal relations started to heal and the love and respect I deserve has come to me effortlessly. Love, appreciation and compassion, is what a woman wants, and I received it through NV Life. My immense gratitude to Naveen for being who he is, and may his blessings always be there in my life. All it takes is faith, and I have immense faith and thanksgiving toward NV Life.

10. A 32-YEAR-OLD MAN OVERCOMING 2 DECADES OF ADDICTION.

*T*o introduce myself, I am a NV Life Scientist, and I'm not the only one. There are many, and there will be many more to come.

You may have wondered after seeing a smiley in the title and thought, "How, on earth, can someone smile after losing a job?"

"I am stuck up. Life sucks. Life is boring I feel suffocated."

These were my daily mantras, and I sincerely chanted them every day. I never saw any growth in the company I was working for, but I possibly couldn't take the risk of quitting without even having another offer in hand. But then going to that office, every day, was becoming more of a burden.

However, after attending one of the NV Life workshops a few months ago, I came out of this major problem which honestly, was a big relief after many years of *suffering*. Later, I started practicing another technique, called NV Fishing. Within a few days, I began to get better clarity. The voice was clear to me now. It said, "Quit your job, for Heaven's sake!" and that's exactly what I did the next day without any offer in my hands and began to serve the notice period. Of course, it shook me up a bit at times, but there was a sense of assurance within which I didn't allow anything to disturb me for longer than a few seconds. Unfortunately, there was pressure from friends and family, which kept mounting and a sudden tragic death at home brought more responsibilities on my shoulder.

So, here I was serving my notice period, friends calling me a 'fool', an added responsibility and having continuous rejected interviews. However, I was still feeling assured within.

I attended more than 20 interviews where I didn't succeed, and my inner critic started bothering me, "You've lost a good job." I asked myself if I had made the wrong decision. How come the messages I received in my meditation went wrong? In this state of total chaos, externally and total peace inward, I did what I knew I could do best. I kept doing NV Fishing more seriously. The more I practiced the calmer and the more confident I became. Life became clearer. One day, I wrote down what I expected from a new job and from my environment: Friendly boss, learning each day, friendly environment, closer to home etc.

Soon, one night before my next interview, I had a dream where I clearly heard a voice say, "Congratulations! You got the job." I woke up, got ready and went for the scheduled interview and by evening I had the job exactly the way I had written in my wish list. I can't express my gratitude to Naveen. My intention of sharing this experience is not to motivate you to resign your job or do something weird without any clarity. I just want to tell you that you can do wonders, and it is just your choice to choose *suffering* or not. Isn't it that simple?

Imagine you have a vehicle that doesn't need fuel at all and you can travel wherever you wish. NV Life techniques are the same: it is like a vehicle. Once you own it, you own it for life. It all depends on how deep you want to travel.

11. HER CONQUEST OVER 10 YEARS WITH BLOOD CANCER THROUGH BREATHING.

"*I* have a high fever and my throat is choking, what am I supposed to do? It started during the workshop and is still going on. Strangely I feel a lot of calm inside", I said over the phone.

"Send me your selfie immediately", he replied.

"Sure, in a few minutes", was my answer.

"I see health but a lot of pain in your eyes"….a long pause…." Let me see." Keep breathing", he continued to say to me.

"Yes, all my long bones hurt. I take about 9-10 painkillers a day".

Popping a combiflam I thought – how could he sense my pain? My world took me as a very strong woman and most of them believed that cancer doesn't bother me. "You have lovely hair and skin, cancer has touched you nowhere, you look happy and healthy". I wish I could lay my deep wounds in front of them… There was no one for me, "It's my battle, why should I let others, my loved ones, go through this pain", my mind conferred.

A dreaded night, as usual, with Thalidomide, Dexamethasone and pain killers and I knew I would see another morning in my life. It had been like this for past 9 years. Every day, a new day, in pain, but alive and I was thankful.

11th Nov 2015, 9.13 am, read the screen of my mobile phone. There was a WhatsApp message from Mr. Varshneya." Recall a 'chilling fear' episode in your life, a fear of death, fear of a ghost may be. Breathe into it and come back to me". It was quite strange, I could not understand what he meant and what he wanted.

The curiosity within forced me to defrost a few 'chilling fear' experiences on a piece of paper. I was quite surprised to realize that dying with cancer wasn't fearful to me. I got into "NV Hunting' and started going into the events which I thought would have resulted in this chilling fear in me. With every breath my awareness got deeper and to my shock I became aware of an event which was not at all there in my mind. I guess it's your consciousness which is awake guiding you when you need it the most. The event came and when I came out of my breathing session, I had a huge pain in all my long bones and felt as if they were frozen with crushed ice injected in them. I couldn't take the pain and the chill in my bones. I was shivering!!! I messaged Mr. Varshneya to let him know that this was happening, and he replied, "If you can take the pain for next 3 hours without pain killers, you will be without pain for the rest of your life. But just in case you can't, take a painkiller and sleep. I am continuing to work on you". I could sense the meaning in his deep voice, "Breathe through the pain Lady," he said.

I kept taking the pain, felt shivers all over my body and in some time dozed off. When I woke up after a few hours, I felt my body felt as light as a feather, totally calm and with no pain or shivers at all. It was truly amazing, my bones had never felt so healthy and my painkillers saw the dustbin. Since that day I have not had the need to take any painkillers.

While moving down the stairs after my presentation in Radisson, Delhi in September 2006, I fell and shattered my arms and legs. That's how my nearly one-decade-long cancer journey began in October 2006.

Diagnosed with stage 4-B multiple myeloma, I had numerous lytic bone lesions—a common problem for patients with this form of cancer in which the bone appears to have been eaten away. I had a huge Plasmacytoma at the left side of the base of my skull.

For the first 5 years, my M-spike—a measure doctors use to assess whether a patient's multiple myeloma is responding to treatment—bounced up and down. But the cancer never went into remission.

Those with cancer are always being encouraged by others to think positive. There is also this theory that negative thoughts and emotions, or stress, make you susceptible to cancer. So, I gathered all my willpower and started fighting these ever increasing plasma cells in my body. As expected, I was not complaining, cooperative and resistant to expressing emotions, particularly anger and hostility. I kept my pain to myself and approached every alternative therapy I could lay my hands on. They did allow me to be calm for a while but could not take the monster away. The chemotherapy spread all over my organs and with each day passing, I started giving up. I was exhausted, in great pain, required frequent blood transfusions and a regular intake of Thalidomide and Dexamethasone along with endless other medicines and supplements to keep my frail body going. I had to live for my son who was a toddler then.

Biopsies, chemotherapies, radiations, platelets and blood transfusions kept the sensations in my body alive – the sensations of pain.

Then, I was introduced to NV Life through my husband's boss's wife. The workshop was my eye-opener. In a few minutes of my being there, I kind of started unlearning all that I had acquired as alternate healing therapies. I started connecting to my breath. Few hours into the workshop I developed high fever and my body started aching. My tear ducts became overactive and I couldn't control the water oozing out of my eyes. Everyone in the workshop got worried about me. A lady, in fact told Mr. Varshneya that he should see and help me as soon as possible. And to my and her surprise he said," Don't worry, I am working on her.". The look in his eyes just spelled "FAITH" for me. I had HOPE following me since then.

NV Swimming, Fishing and Hunting opened a new world to me. The act of closing out the world and being in both myself and my breath was completely unique. Never before had I experienced such calmness and balance. I have used these processes daily ever since. The results were instant, but the techniques weren't all that easy to follow. While Swimming bought calm and peace, Hunting tore me apart causing havoc physically and emotionally. But there was always a positive outcome to it … giving me hope every day.

I had a 5-week intensive treatment at NV Life Research and Treatment Center where Mr. Naveen Varshneya took me under his guidance and protection. Three days into the treatment both my Hb (Hemoglobin) levels, and my TSH (Thyroid-Stimulating Hormone) came back to normal.

Mr. Varshneya was magically able to awaken all the pain inside me bit by bit, before he slowly and softly put it back to sleep during his coaching sessions, which were so soothing to my aching heart. He became my mirror; one that had the power to reflect every virtue and flaw in me without glorifying or demeaning my inner-self, allowing my ego to crumble during this whole process.

In addition to the breathing techniques, I was also introduced to changing my *belief* regarding my food habits, likes-dislikes and my perspective toward most life situations. This was quite transformative and got me closer to my inner-self. And along the journey, I learned how I had put obstacles in the flow of my life force energy with anger, grudges, rejection and just feeling unloved.

Within 4 and half months all my reports came back as negative, and I was declared cancer-free by my allopathic doctors, although Mr. Varshneya still felt the vulnerability of my health. I was kept in isolation from the outer world, even from my parents and sisters for about 8 months. I remained with my breath and silence. It was the sweetest escape from a harsh, fake world. This period helped me embrace simplicity and cleared my messy mind. Every experience I had was richer, more joyful and came in its very first form just like initial creation; very humbling. I could take one look at the authentic nature of the universe and feel so secure and content like I was still in my mother's womb not having a single concern in the world. The techniques kept redefining my sense of security.

From being cancer-free to handling the side effects of chemotherapy, it was another huge journey. Repairing hole in the heart, getting kidneys to optimum condition, leveling the oxygen in the blood, cysts in the uterus and cervix – all of this happened in the past 19 months. My relationship issues got sorted with each breath and **Yog Nidra** on their own, as my being was in alignment with my core, my inner-self.

I consider my journey with chronic life threatening illness, as well as several traumas to be quite successful thus far. You might think acceptance, strength, determination, and fortitude aren't easy feats, and you are absolutely correct. It has taken me a long time, and a lot of inside work to get to a point in my life where my pain (emotional and physical), don't dictate my life's path. I view them as minor obstacles (which are only challenges) in a life full of many bigger obstacles. I've learned not to wallow in self-pity; however, I've learned how important it is to grieve loss/pain as I'm reacting and adjusting to many different situations that have/are taking place. It's healthy, but can feel like an emotional roller-coaster that has included periods of numbness, anger, denial, sadness, and more. However, if I didn't allow myself to grieve, my emotional pain could get pent up inside, eventually boiling over and becoming destructive; therefore, I practice expressing my feelings of grief through healthy emotional outlets.

Thank you, Mr. Naveen Varshneya for sewing back my clipped wings and enabling me to fly again. Thank you for the fix, and thank you for the lightness. Thank you for keeping the promise of unconditional acceptance and for building some fine self-infrastructure inside of me; you have become attached to everything valuable in me and every good deed that ever comes to my mind. Thank you for the most beautiful heart-shaped footprints you have left all over my identity. I followed them and rarely fell. Thank you for the safety net that held me whenever those rare falls visited.

In the realms of logic, you might be only a messenger, a guide, a mentor or even a good friend but my inner child would like to let its imagination loose and believe the face of God to be yours, for it doesn't come kinder than this.

12. 29-YEAR-OLD LADY, PCOD CASE. TODAY, A MOTHER OF TWINS.

Being diagnosed with PCOD, Poly Cystic Ovary Disease, after a miscarriage in your late twenties and then trying to have a baby, can be quite a blow. Emotional turmoil is at its height, and when at a family function, you get asked questions like – When are you giving us a little one? A tiny pang that you feel inside makes you want to have a baby sooner than later, but the stress it causes further adds to the infertility. Fighting with my inner turmoil, the vicious circle of stressing over having a baby and of course, the insecurities you feel when you see your friends either flaunting a baby bump or a little infant in their arms, led me to want to work on myself.

A common friend, who I happened to meet out of the blue, suggested NV Life and told me to meet Mr. Naveen Varshneya (my mentor and my guide). He said NV has a way of fixing things, healing people by focusing on breathing. It sounded too good to be true, but then desperate situations allow you to take quick impulsive decisions that can be life-changing, and that is exactly what happened to me.

I attended a workshop organized by Naveen on 21 February 2015. A two-day workshop through which he teaches you various NV Life techniques that primarily focuses on breathing. At the end of the workshop he said, "It's only a matter of time, you will be a mother."

The workshop gave me new hope and more importantly showed me many facets of life I hadn't bothered to observe. I started making amazing strides in my health, and my happiness quotient just lifted as I continued to practice every day.

As the days passed, the techniques started helping me focus and enjoy more in the now, which was a welcome change. As predicted by Naveen, in March 2015, I learned that I was going to be a mother.

My first visit to the doctor for a scan revealed that I was pregnant with twins. My husband and I were ecstatic. Our happiness knew no bounds, but it was also the beginning of one of the most trying times as the pregnancy progressed.

Today my girls are 9 months old, but from day one of being told that I was going to be a twin-mom, till they were born, Naveen and NV Life techniques are what I have to thank.

The moment my gynecologist saw our scans, he told us it was a double whammy and that meant it would not be an easy pregnancy, especially because they were monozygotic and mono-amniotic twins (same egg and same sac). But he mentioned that in the third month scan, if we are able to see a tiny membrane between the 2 fetuses, they will be di-amniotic, which gives us more hope, as mono-amniotic twins come with a lot of issues.

So the work Naveen started through his remote healing was on making sure that we have that sac and each baby has its own sac to develop. Every day we would have one remote healing session and each day during Yog Nidra, we would encounter various issues that would have to be addressed.

Just before the third month scan, while I was resting one evening, I suddenly felt a bad pain in my stomach, and before I could reach my phone, Naveen was already calling me. He said, "Lie down." I just followed his instructions, but the next 30 minutes was a nightmare, the pain I felt was out of the world. I was screaming at the top of my voice, my mother-in-law looked very tense while I was holding her and screaming. I could sense a huge energy whirl around my stomach, and as if there were 2 hands holding my babies in place. When the pain subsided, I just couldn't get up out of fear and when Naveen called and told me – he felt that the babies were slipping away, I knew it in my heart, he had saved them.

This made us even more careful, my family made it a point to only talk positive things around me and not discuss anything that might remotely stress me out. My conviction in NV Life became stronger.

The third month scan came with a welcome relief of the membrane separating the babies, a big milestone was achieved, but it also came with a news of lower heart rate in both babies – one lower than the other. So the next task was to bring them up to health as the week progressed for the fifth month scan.

The heart rates were normal in the fifth month scan and from that month, Naveen began working with me with the intention of healing my relationship with my babies on a karmic level. The entire pregnancy was nothing short of a miracle, and every day I see my little girls, it is a constant reminder for me.

On the day of my baby shower, I encountered a major nerve cramping pain all over my limbs. That is when Naveen switched his techniques and taught me how to focus on the pain to heal. Also round the clock, no matter where Naveen was, he was keyed in on me and even the slightest discomfort I would feel here at my home. He would know in his home or center or even in the UK, while he was traveling. It was as if my little ones and I had an uncongested wireless direct line to Naveen, and we could message him to help us anytime, anywhere.

Every time I would get severe cramps – even as much as 17-18 times a day, we would focus on the pain and allow it to heal. Naveen believed that working on that could heal karmas of the babies to be born and allow them a cleaner slate with regard to entering this world.

Finally, during my 32nd week my gynecologist suggested that we go for a decided C-section between my 38th and 39th week. He mentioned that it is not often that we allow twin pregnancies to continue longer, but as my babies and I were showing good progress through all the check-ups, he was sure we could make it a little post my 38th week. Dates were decided as 11th November.

I was full-blown pregnant, doing anything was difficult and even lying down for sessions of meditation was becoming a challenge. So closer to the delivery, we stopped doing any fixed sessions. I was put on a 24 hour energy watch, as my family and I were preparing for the 11th. On the 10th, late in the evening, I started to experience contractions. The most interesting thing about them was that I was not in any pain, but they were contractions for sure. I informed my doctor, and he said if the contractions become too close, then I should rush to the hospital, or else come to the hospital as planned the following early morning.

On 11th November, Diwali day, amidst festive decorations, we reached the hospital early in the morning. At 9.30 am, when the duty doctor came to check on me and noticed the contractions, she was puzzled about how there was no pain, yet definite contractions. I was immediately prepped for delivery, and at 10.41 with a 19 second difference, we gave birth to 2 healthy, little baby girls.

Focused breathing, focused NV Life techniques, even new techniques that were identified as the pregnancy progressed and most importantly, with the constant work from Naveen and other NV Life team members, my life today is filled with the cooing and gurgling and smiles of 2 little angels that have brightened my life and given my family a new life. I have lived this miracle from the moment I entered my first workshop with NV Life and continue to ardently follow the techniques I have been taught at NV Life.

13. AN ARCHITECT RECOVERS FROM ANXIETY AND DEPRESSION.

The central tenet of NV Life, like in medicine, is that the body heals itself. The role of NV Life, like that of a medical practitioner, is to help create the optimal environment where self-healing can occur. As humans, we are affected by external forces as well as our internal climate - that being our internal dialogs and emotions. Our fears, anxieties and traumas on one side, and our hope, happiness and bliss on the other are states that we move between in response to impulses internally and externally. How we choose to behave toward ourselves and interact with people and the world around us is often directly influenced by the condition of our inner state.

Naveen and I crossed paths at a point where I found myself overwhelmed with emotions from experiences that I had not been able to put to bed. In short, I found myself in a state of anxious hopelessness. I felt as though I had no choice in how the world affected me or what options I had for being in the world. My headspace felt as though it was under siege from all angles. I was in possession of a mind filled with un-constructive thoughts which lead to destructive actions and a renewed sense of being stuck and helplessly blocked. Looking back was as painful as was looking forward. Moving through life was tremendously strenuous. What was worse is that no tangible solution seemed within reach. I could see a way forward, but it was for others, not me.

As Naveen is fond of saying, "It seems the problem with the problem is that you don't see the problem." This, in words described perfectly the hopelessness and resignation I think many of us feel when we are overwhelmed with life's challenges – past, present and future. I distracted myself to the point where I had no chance of dealing with the source of my own distresses. In this state of mind, like many, I also presumed that my "predicament," like me, was unique. This unhelpful mindset alone isolated me from searching for a way forward. Only until I felt the internal pitch of my emotions reaching unbearable levels, did I engage my head to sincerely search for a way through. In hindsight, it is fair to say, that each one of us is indeed unique, but many of the challenges we face on our way are very much shared by the virtue of being human.

Naveen describes himself as a technologist, rather than a Guru, a philosopher or an artist. His work has synthesized various known methods - drawn from eastern and western understanding of mental and bodily health - into several exercises that address the challenges many, if not all of us, will face at some point in our lives: to process and heal traumatic events. In its essence, his methods seek to restore us to a childlike, unselfconscious state. In this state we can give ourselves the permission to observe, share and communicate our emotions. He enables you to heal yourself, by first creating a space where painful feelings induced by trauma can be observed and interpreted honestly and sincerely, rather than judged, diverted or compensated. To begin to do this, our mind has to be present in the present tense. The core exercise that creates an anchor in the present is becoming aware of one's own breath and the practice of Yoga Nidra, or yogic sleep: the lucid dreaming state of consciousness between waking and sleeping that we experience as we fall asleep each day.

But because the mind, like the body suffers distresses and traumas to varying degrees at different points in life, this takes some trying. Our outlook on life and our ensuing actions often dominate our entire experience of our own lives and by extension the lives of those around us. To insulate us from our mental distresses, our mind has learned, also through experience, many coping mechanisms that mitigate our internal strife. Moreover, it is the conscious mind that blocks our emotions and our self-healing. Events in my own life, especially traumatic ones, became fixtures in my mind which made me become very adept at mitigating, compensating and distracting myself from the emotions that were welling up inside. These emotions were inevitably painful, and as such, to be avoided by whatever means necessary. I, like I am sure many other people, avoided myself. A litmus test for a stored well of distress and trauma for me was my lack of ability to sit still and be reflective. I could not abide my own company. Rather than face up to much of my own anguish, I sublimated any conscious contact with myself through plenty of work and other forms of restless busy-ness.

What Naveen and NV Life began to show me is how to shift my awareness. We began by examining all the different sources and layers of distress that had built up in my life from my childhood onward. We re-examined unhelpful *belief* and conclusions like attitudes toward my parents and other formative events that left deep tracks in my conscious mind. We created a matrix of strong emotions - positive as well as negative. This matrix in turn showed, not only how the various categories of traumas and elations influenced my own behavior and outlook, but it also decoded the various patterns that shaped my own experiences of life and the motivations behind some of the choices I made.

Naveen teaches and explains much else, but the key for me was experiencing what it felt like to observe myself without distracting myself – witnessing my own distress, allowing feelings of pain and distress to surface without judgment or interference from my own head. Once I was able to observe the rising and falling waves of my own breath, the experience of being able to unlock my own healing began. I was able to begin to wonder how it all came about. Centering myself like this created the space for self-healing. And from my previous state of mind, that in itself felt like a welcome accomplishment!

The practice of Yoga Nidra, or swimming as Naveen refers to it, sets the stage for further healing work to occur. In fact, it is probably at this point where the real work and the inward journey departs from. All the healing and unburdening happens here. Here is where the space in the mind is recovered to be used for living rather than ruminating over the past or fearing the uncertainty of the future. The ego or the comparing and jealous mind are put to rest. Our own conscious mind is how we are an obstacle to ourselves.

The exercises Naveen teaches create a practice concentrating on reconnecting and maintaining a strong connection between our mind and body. What I particularly appreciated about the set of thoughts, techniques and experiences is the humanity and acceptance of human nature as it exists. NV Life helps attain a deeper level of insight into the constellation of energies and forces which shape our lives. The exercises allowed me to witness and experience my pain without haste or the need to suppress it. As the practice progresses, moving between the inner world and the outer becomes a sort of oscillation between the 2.

Gradually, as emotions and old feelings are released and dissipate, the environment and the emotions that held sway change their meaning.

NV Life teaches you step-by-step how to become aware and how it feels to heal. This was the most important for me because the experience of cleansing, of letting the ego or conscious mind go, and of feeling the dissipating of trauma was key to being able to later help myself and to continue the practice. Sometimes, a very quiet voice announces the beginnings of a major shift in life. Naveen's is such a voice that points you - your body and your mind - to connect and become lighter. NV Life works with the energies and tendencies inherent in human nature and aligns them with without suppressing them or subjecting them to an external moral code. NV Life taught me through experience how a small shift in the space of the present, can have a lasting and freeing impact on my idea of the future. Learning how to be content in the present was a great stepping stone to the next. Out of contentment grows the optimism and a glad anticipation of the future. It replaces dread with hope. Hope itself is a great fuel for curiosity and creativity.

I would recommend the workshop for anyone who feels overburdened with grief or is immobilized by the presence of distressing or hurtful events in their day-to-day life. Learning how the mind can heal itself and how to create the conditions for this to occur is certainly worthwhile in shaping the days and years to come. It is an inward journey I fiercely resisted initially, but since getting underway, I've gladly embarked on it and have embraced its strange insights as much as I've appreciated feeling emotionally much lighter through it. It is not a journey I have found particularly easy at points, but which worthwhile journey ever was plain sailing?

ABOUT MYSELF

I trained as an architect at the University of Edinburgh where I received a Master of Arts and a Master of Architecture. I went on to work in Edinburgh, London, Basel, Zurich, New York and Canada, practicing and teaching with renowned firms and institutions. I was involved with several high-profile projects and clients in different parts of the globe. My work takes me to many different continents covering large-scale cultural complexes, private residences for ambassadors and presidents, and smaller more modest, but still very interesting projects. Despite the high-profile nature of the work and the many demands I attempted to be equal to, attending NV Life provided valuable insights and great assistance as I tried to be equal to many of the challenges my work brings despite often feeling overwhelmed with the emotional demands of my mind that I left unattended.

14. AN INCISIONAL HERNIA CASE, 33-YEAR-OLD WOMAN OUT OF PAIN.

NV Life is truly magical. This is what comes to my mind when I hear of it or think of it. I had been in severe pain pre and post a surgery. Incisional hernia is what I was diagnosed with after a lot of confusion among the surgeons and gynecologists. Initially, they were suspecting it to be scar endometriosis too, which was later ruled out. The pain was not only troublesome, but also disturbing. I had to deal with it — was the statement I would get on approaching any medical expert. But to live with a certain pain 24/7 requires a lot of mental, emotional as well as physical strength. My daily activities were being affected, and there was a lack of peace within myself. Internally, I felt I had such negative thoughts, all around the theme that I would never get back to normal.

Then I got to know about the MAGICAL NV Life. It was very kind of Naveen to have given me his precious time despite his busy schedule with his book which tremendously helped me. The intensity and duration of my pain showed changes and gradually it became bearable. I was fortunate to have attended his workshop too which further helped me. From his workshop, I learned how just by observing one's breath one can gain peace and health simultaneously. Though it's a very tough thing to reduce our thoughts and observe the breath, yet with constant sincerity and effort, it's possible to do so for at least some time. The results are that it can feel refreshed, peaceful and so good internally after practicing these breathing techniques.

As of now, I believe I'm cured to quite an extent and by following the techniques taught to me during the brief span of time at the workshop, I shall soon bid goodbye to the pain I was in for the last almost 20 months.

Thanks to Naveen and NV Life for helping me out.

15. A 46-YEAR-OLD MALE WITH ACHILLES' HEEL.

When I finished NV Swimming this morning, and having spent roughly 40 minutes in Yoga Nidra, I became one with my own breathing. Random imagery floated in front of my mind's eyes, some with real world patterns in them and some completely abstract, yet perhaps for the first time in my adult life, I was not trying to interpret them. It had taken me nearly 5 months to reach a stage where my mind was taking a long overdue rest albeit for a brief period of 30-40 minutes a day.

It was not always like this, nor did I think it was possible for me to suspend chronic and furious mental activity that I had come to believe was a great asset. I always thought it helped me arrive at solutions that were better and at a pace that was faster. At the same time, I recognized that this very trait was my Achilles' heel. The constantly whirring mind was often a minefield of fears, insecurities and anxiety. The consequence of this was even deeper thinking, which only worsened the situation or numbed my mind through intoxication. Even at the most intense phase of the intoxicated stupor, I was aware that I was only applying balm to the symptom. Occasionally, the dependence would reach a peak, followed by more intense trips of guilt and finally a suspension of all indulgences. The cycle was as predictable as unbreakable. I had read around these mental states, and I was convinced that a particularly trying childhood and testing economic condition in which I grew up were the root causes.

With an equal measure of interest in science and the mystical, I had explored Pranayama and Dhyana (concentration). My proficiency with Asanas since childhood had prepared me physically for an attempt at Dhyana. To my chagrin, I never managed more than a few seconds of mental inactivity. All in all, I had concluded that my condition was mine to adjust to. It is something I had to manage, since it couldn't be eliminated. I had behind me roughly 15 years of intense effort to reach a peace of mind, all in vain. This is when I met Naveen.

I was introduced to him a by a friend who knew him in an entirely different context. This friend along with 2 others had resolved to help me come out of my deep distress during a particularly trying period, which also involved an ailment and the death of my father. They had known me for some time and labeled me as being fiercely independent and one who was fanatically scientific and rational. I, of course, fitted this description to the tee, since over a period of time, I had come to be deeply skeptical of the religious mumbo jumbo including the religion I was born into. This distrust included disciplines of medical and physical well-being, which perhaps didn't owe its existence to the religion itself – at least the way I understood it.

I had seen Naveen around and had known him loosely as a healer. I was both intrigued and amused by the description, but didn't think much about it. But faced with a distress for the nth time and determined to find a lasting solution, I heeded the suggestion and surprised the other 2 friends. I had arrived at this decision using a simple logic. I had employed my (supposedly above average) intelligence to seek solutions to my problems for many years, all resulting in nothing but total failure. All efforts of mine had only resulted in the repetition of an identical cycle. With this inglorious past, I had no right to judge other methods. More importantly, someone close to me and wishing my welfare had decided to place his faith in a method despite knowing me, that in itself deserved an honest try from me.

With this I met Naveen, only to learn that he wanted me to breathe! Ordinarily, something like this would have attracted enviably inventive insults from me, but I had decided to suspend decision! I was then initiated into remote healing. My rational mind asked several questions including, "How does the energy that flows into me know my address?" etc. Again, I had decided to participate in the ritual regardless of my lack of *belief*. Naveen warned me of a bunch of unsavory physical discomforts, none of which I experienced. All in all, the first 2 weeks were following a set of procedures and staying determined on my path. I got out of the negative spiral, but I had done this several times before, hence I didn't immediately attribute any of the changes to the procedure itself, but more to the discipline that I had followed. I, of course, acknowledged that the rituals had a huge role in helping me maintain the discipline.

Once I began NV Swimming, I began facing difficulties with the volume and frequency of my thoughts. For the first few sessions, I tried to curb them, but they bounced back with even greater vigor. During one of the sessions, I decided to experiment with breathing methods as a way to find something to keep me occupied. It was merely directing my thoughts at a single coherent object. In that session, I discovered diaphragm breathing. I then progressed to a deeper concentration by likening my breath to a snake. From randomly scattered thoughts, I had graduated to thoughts in a single area. It was far from what Naveen had advised, but it was a step forward for me, which I was desperately looking for.

I was quietly happy that I had managed to reduce the unruliness of the mind. After this, I went through a phase where I mistook the purpose of NV Swimming to be perfecting the act of breathing. Needless to say, I tied my breath in knots and often ended up being breathless. It took me 2 months to realize (as opposed to understand) that the purpose of NV Swimming was Yoga Nidra. It was very important that I realized this myself rather than being taught because nothing builds conviction like one's own discovery.

Once I realized the underlying purpose, it became easy for me to surrender myself to the flow of breath and get lost in its observation. When I began to experience brief periods of Yoga Nidra, my conviction in other methods strengthened too. Most notably, the use of cotton went up in regularity. At this time, I began to notice significant changes in my reflexive reactions to people and stimuli. I was astonished to notice both calm and confidence in my thought and demeanor. I was able to fend off challenges and criticism and in many cases convert people into my school of thought with scarcely a disturbance of inner peace. An earlier me would have been palpably agitated and perhaps alienated my audience even while delivering a decision that was based on impeccable knowledge and sound logic. From this moment on, it was easy for me to double down on the path. Having said this, I continue to be skeptical of some things, for e.g., I am still not convinced of remote healing. But my scientific temper compels me to acknowledge and accept the evidence of my own success.

Toward this end, I have experimented with variations of cotton usage to check the change in my inner-self. I must say my conviction has only increased with each experiment. I continue to make an effort, rejecting nothing but accepting only what I have personally experienced. I am making progress every day.

16. DENGUE – ICU CASE

*I*t was 26th December 2009. I was busy with an event at my college as a member of the organizing committee. My 22-year-old son had cough and fever since 25th December. He took a Crocin tablet and rested. But on the night of the 26th, when I returned from college, I noticed that he had a high fever of 103°. For the last six months, he was under homeopathic medication in addition to allopathic medicines for nocturnal epilepsy. The instructions from the homeopathic doctor were to not give him any drug without his consultation, as it may interfere with his treatment. The same doctor was consulted for his fever. For the next 2 days, there was no improvement, high fever continued. As advised, we got the pathological tests for typhoid, malaria, and dengue done. Reports were negative, only his platelets count was drastically low. The reason quoted by the doctor was high fever, and nothing to worry about. Two more days passed with the same condition, even though homeopathic remedies had been changed.

On 31st December evening, my son vomited. The vomit had some traces of blood. Immediately, the allopathic doctor was called. He visited, examined him and advised urgent hospitalization. Treatment started, blood sample was sent and urgent report was requested. It revealed the active dengue virus that had caused the drastic reduction of platelets for which platelets were given. Not only this, but the other 359 bottles, which were given in the due course of time, were managed with the mercy of God and help from friends, students, well-wishers and known and unknown people.

On the night of 1st January, in spite of continuous supply of platelets, my son started bleeding internally. There was blood in his lungs, liver, kidneys and every other organ. Doctors were trying hard. On 3rd morning, he started having difficulty in breathing, he was put on oxygen. As I went to him in the ICU, he was frightened, and

I had to console him that he would be ok. At this point, he asked me not leave him alone, I should be with him 24 hrs. I promised him, and then I was asked to leave the ICU.

Within 2-3 hours all specialist doctors were called to the hospital. My husband and I were called to the doctor's cabin. We were told one-by-one, by each specialist, that my son's liver had collapsed, kidneys had failed, there was bleeding in his stomach etc. Essentially, he had a multi-organ failure, his survival was difficult, and he was on 100% ventilator support.

The doctors said that the only thing that could be done, was to give him a minimum of 3 injections of vitamin K (these are very expensive, almost Rs. 1,00,000 each). But they said that there was no guarantee of his survival. We asked them to immediately do whatever was medically needed. I told them that I had complete assurance, and that my son would come home on his feet. I left the cabin shivering in fear. I prayed to my Guru, Bhagavan from the bottom of my heart for his help.

News of his condition spread to friends, family members and devotees of my Guru. Everyone prayed for his life. By evening, his bleeding was reduced but his life was still in danger. He was being given platelets. The platelet count was fluctuating in a number before and after every bottle as the dengue virus was very active and was creating havoc within his body.

A few days passed with the active virus in the body and a continuous supply of platelets. Most of our relatives from different cities visited Nagpur to see him. One of them was my youngest brother-in-law from Bangalore. After 3-4 days of his returning, he called my husband. He asked whether we would like to take the help of a spiritual healer. We didn't want to leave any stone unturned and readily accepted. Till that time, my husband had visited every temple, every mosque, did all sorts of offerings, poojas. Around 30-40 devotees, came to the hospital daily and did mass prayers. The result of all this was that my son was that my son was alive but in a bad condition.

A day before we got in touch with Naveen, my son had to go through a surgical procedure. Doctors were going to cut a hole in his throat to insert the ventilator tube. This was a life threatening procedure, as he was already bleeding. If there was excessive bleeding during the operation, then survival was impossible. We were all in intense prayer mode with full faith on the Guru and the Almighty. It worked. Operation was successful. Before the operation, his doctor asked me to pray for a successful surgery.

My son's other parameters for kidney, liver etc., were far from the normal range. Platelets were fluctuating. When I called Naveen and informed him the details of my son's health, he explained to me how to meditate when he would be healing. The process of healing started on the same day.

After a few days, probably on the evening of 22nd January, when I was meditating as per the plan, Naveen was healing my son from Delhi.

The next morning, we experienced a miracle, my son's blood test showed the absence of the dengue virus.

On 26th January, he couldn't breathe again. There was a blood clot in his respiratory tract due to earlier bleeding in the body. He needed urgent bronchoscopy otherwise his life was in danger.

The decision to go for the procedure was to be taken. I wanted to believe that all would go smoothly, and I consented to the procedure. The procedure started and Naveen and I started our healing routine (it had become a routine by now). The procedure was successful, and he got one more life.

Again on the 28th and 30th January, the same problem of blood clots in the respiratory tract occurred. This time, Naveen began and finished healing before the procedure started. When the specialist doctor came with a bigger bronchoscope and examined my son, he found that the clot disappeared from that place. The same thing happened for the third time on 2nd February. We were happy that his bronchoscopy got cancelled 3 times.

On 3rd February, he was coughing a lot and was very uneasy. As it turned out, he had a chest infection, due to the long-term use of the ventilator. Again, new drugs were introduced, and healing was on. He was cured from the infection. His blood count for the liver and the kidney's functioning started improving. He was fully conscious now.

On 6th February, my son became irritable and quick-tempered, not cooperating with doctors. I was called into the ICU by doctors. He was insisting that we take him to home, not wanting to stay there anymore. He is a spiritually aware child, as he had attended many discourses of our Guru. I reminded him of the teaching that when you cannot change the situation, accept it, your *sufferings* will vanish. I told him that the ventilator cannot be removed, and he needs to be under a doctor's supervision and treatment. If he accepts this and cooperates, he can go home early. Otherwise our stay here will be longer. I told him to decide what he wants to do. He understood and started cooperating. The next day, he was complaining of nightmares and crying. As per Naveen's advice, his elder sister spoke to him. She told him about the things he had gone through during his hospitalization – all surgical procedures, daily blood tests etc. After listening to it, he never had nightmares.

On 8th February, he had another bacterial infection in the chest. This time, those bacteria were resistant to all drugs available in the world. Naveen was apprised of the situation. Every time some problem occurred, everyone around us, including doctors were negative. I was now at my breaking point, but Naveen assured me that nothing would go wrong. My hope and positivity was supported and backed strongly, only by Naveen. I believed a person, who I had never met or seen and whose name I'd never even heard of before. I only knew that he was sent by the Almighty to help us come out of our situation. I never felt that I needed to know him more.

The next day, my son was taken to a diagnostic center for spiral X-ray to know the exact condition of his chest. He had to be put on oxygen instead of the ventilator for this. It was a huge risk to remove him from the ventilator. Again, with the help of Naveen, that hurdle was overcome. The same evening, a medical representative visited the hospital and introduced a new drug produced by his company. The doctor decided to try it on my son and it worked.

It was now 10th February, my son was better, the treatment was on, but only his heart rate was very high. Doctors were seeking expert opinion to remove the ventilator, but no doctor was ready to boldly suggest taking him off the ventilator. I explained the situation to Naveen. He told me that this was enough, he was coming to Nagpur to see that he gets well and gets discharged from hospital. He arrived in Nagpur the same evening. Naveen was working on healing him the whole night. The next day, my son's ventilator was removed, and he was put on oxygen. During the day, his recovery was very fast. By the next morning, his oxygen supply was stopped and that evening, he was discharged from the hospital.

This is not the end of the story. My son was *suffering* from nocturnal epilepsy for 12 years. After he came back home from the hospital, Naveen started to carry out healing for this issue too for 15 days. His epileptic fits have never returned.

My 12 years of continuous prayers were answered through Naveen. No doctor in the world is capable of doing what Naveen did. We take this opportunity to express our deep gratitude and heartfelt thanks to Naveen for standing firmly with us and helping us in this tough situation in our lives. Thanks to the Almighty too, for sending Naveen into our live

17. HER TRANSFORMATION CALMS HER HYPERACTIVE SON TOO.

I was referred to NV Life through a friend for my son who was mildly hyperactive. My friend's husband, who himself was under treatment with Naveen, the founder of NV Life, spoke to me in detail about it and had immense faith in what Naveen offered. I contacted Naveen via email mentioning my son's condition, and I heard back from him, where he mentioned that he would need to work on me and not my son. I did not understand his reply but then I thought, let us see what it is all about in the workshop. I then did some research on NV Life on YouTube, and watched his videos.

In Jan 2016, I attended the workshop, the place was beautiful and there were around 30 people who were attending the workshop. People were of different age groups and from different backgrounds, we all had different issues but Naveen addressed all of us with equal attention and explained the techniques. Correct breathing for meditation was taught to us as it was the foundation for all the techniques of NV Life. This workshop made me understand the basics of NV Life and I was determined to follow the techniques. I practically could do two techniques very well and after the workshop there was a support group created to help novices like me.

This part was going on well, I was doing my practice sincerely and I could see changes in me and in the whole environment of my home.

When I was told earlier that my energies were affecting my child, I did not understand it well then but as I was consistent with my practice of the techniques taught to us, this became quite obvious. My son was calmer but more than him, it was me who needed to be at peace and more calm in my handling things on all fronts. I was happy and things were good, for the first time I was my priority in my life after a long, long time.

As the months passed, I unknowingly started settling into my old routine and that's where things again started getting disturbing. My tensions and worries started surfacing again and everything became so difficult that I contacted Naveen for help again. He told me that there would be a treatment week in June, which I could join.

I reached the centre in Bangalore, with two other ladies and my son. We had a strict routine and proper schedule of meditation, the environment inside the centre was so serene and calm, and that in itself was healing. We were taught few more techniques or I can say that all the techniques of NV Life were practiced and practiced to get the essence of it, no short cuts. Naveen gave enough attention to all of us for our learning and healing. I must say, he is a hard task master who never gives up on anyone.

Everyday was a new discovery about myself and was I again started moving towards wellness. My joining NV Life has certainly made positive changes in my life. I was looking for meditation path for years, and I had tried different techniques with various groups of people, but never found anything suiting my needs. NV Life gave me methods, that work well for me, and that it is only me who has to work regularly to be at higher energy vibration and impact all around me.

Now I am more in control, and am able to handle my issues with a calm and peaceful mind. Practicing NV Life techniques has to be part of life to lead a healthy and fulfilling life. My son who was the reason I joined NV Life, has had so many positive developments.

I can say NV Life shows us how to live our life well.

Thank you.

18. AWAKENING THE POWER WITHIN, WITH NV LIFE.

There is a power that exists inside you, and me. This power – you can call it God, Source, Divine, the Ultimate Power that makes the flowers bloom, the earth spins around the sun, and the acorn into an oak tree.

The power, where there is no ego, but true wisdom that when channeled in a way aligned to the highest good for all, can help bring about so much good, not only for yourself, but as a result of it, it can allow you to transform you from the acorn to the oak tree – To shine your Truth. That has been my journey and continues to be, with NV Life and the unraveling of my truth and power.

I was introduced to Naveen a few years ago and was intrigued with his work. I had heard about his ability to help so many people with what is considered allopathically impossible, chronic conditions, mental conditions, and so much more. I wanted to know more and learn more from him. That was my angle then. Nothing happened after that, as it was just not possible to go and attend one of his workshops to learn more about his ways of working.

In my own work, having a science background, and now combining science with spirit, I help people get in touch with this power that resides within them. I personally had worked with many healing modalities to work on myself to do the same. But you know, how horses have blinders so that they don't see more then they need to? That was my state. I had blinders on to what else was possible. My heart and soul knew there was more, and I was always on the search for more ways to unravel this truth within me, but it never was able to see fully because of these blinders.

Life had an interesting way to bring me back around to meet with Naveen and to take off my blinders. Certain life events happened that were very traumatic in my family, and I was feeling helpless and just not knowing how to help the people in my family. First, my partner went through an extremely difficult situation at work, leaving the whole family traumatized, and following that my father had a heart attack. These situations were not easy to deal with for our whole family. I had called Naveen to ask him for his help for them, as everything in my life felt chaotic, and I was being pulled in all directions. He began to work on them one after another remotely.

Little did I realize that it wasn't the people in my family that needed the help, but me. About a month into this work, Naveen said to me, "This isn't about anyone else around you, this is about you. You are creating this chaos, and creating these situations around you." Up until now, I had always told people, "they create their reality, and that they need to work on themselves to shift this outside reality." But my blinders had prevented me from seeing the destruction I was creating. That is when the gears shifted in this work, and he began to work on me remotely.

I had no idea what was going to begin unraveling, because from that day the blinders were removed, and I felt unsure and uncertain as you would when you are in a different land, where nothing is familiar any more.

A few months into this work, I attended his workshop. It was destiny. You know when you look back and see all the events that have happened till now, to get you somewhere. It is only when you look back that you see the dots connecting each event. It was divine perfection, each and every step, all to help me open up to my power. The workshop was phenomenal in every way, and helped continue to allow me to blossom into my Being and Truth. This has continued on after the workshop, as I am practicing the techniques he taught us. The depth and wisdom of these techniques, albeit simple, are profound, and have the ability to open anyone up to their power if done with sincerity and authenticity.

What struck me most about Naveen from the beginning, which I can see in his eyes, is his compassion and kindness – a gift to humanity. This essence of his is like a sweet fragrance that reminds you of the sweet fragrance you are. His every word and action comes from this place. It is connected to this power in him, and he lights this power in others to be able to do the same.

During the workshop, he said these words that still ring in my ears, "You are the Cure." – Words so profound. You see, if we can connect with this power within, we *do* become the Cure. You open up to the Truth of your Being, and Cure is one part of that.

For me, every relationship, situation, circumstance, event that had been showing up right up to this moment in my life was coming from me. It was a result of the conditioned mind and separate mind, due to an accumulation of karma or past conditioning. This was creating the weakness in my intention of what was showing up in my life i.e., the chaos of events in my family. But now having worked with Naveen, what is happening is that I am moving beyond that conditioning, step-by-step, and toward the whole mind or free mind, where power resides.

This work, his techniques are helping me refine myself in a way that I never knew was possible. To open to the power, which is not here to control others, or influence others, but a power that is here to help make a difference on the planet. It is the power that is helping me transform from the acorn to the oak tree.

It hasn't been an easy journey over the last few months because I have had to face my biggest fears, come face-to-face with my own demons. I have never looked back, as it is has been the biggest gift in my life, to remove these blinders, as I can begin to see so much more of what resides inside me. The chaos in my life has calmed down considerably since beginning this work with Naveen and is a reflection of the truth in the words he had shared when we changed gears from working with my family members to me.

My partner's attitude has shifted around the work events, allowing him to have more peace within himself. My father, recovered well, but what was amazing in this case was that the heart attack was as a result of his old vein graft closing, and the artery that had been 100% closed, now opened! The vein graft was from a heart bypass he had 12 years ago. Instead the doctors were baffled as to how an artery that had been 100% was now open. Not only that, but the collateral arteries which support the heart health were also open, leaving his heart with very little damage from this event.

With quantum physics, we know there is no time and space. Einstein said *"Time is an illusion"*. I know that the healing was done after he had the heart attack, but there is no doubt in my mind that Naveen's intervention had a part to play in this, because the outcome could have been far worse, and this work does go beyond time and space.

This has all been possible because of his guidance for me to step back into myself. As I continue to spread my wings to learn to fly and soar, he continues to guide me. He has awakened within me the knowledge that I am whole, I am love, and this is just the beginning of my journey to take flight and chart my way into freedom within myself. From here to be able to create a life that is aligned to this Freedom and Power within. I am forever grateful to him for this.

This book that you are holding in your hands has the ability to do this for you too. See it as that gift that can help you fly into the freedom within and touch the sacred power, where your health and well-being resides on all levels. It really is and can be that life-changing, and it is all within You.

Thank you Naveen, for all that you are and will be, because it is changing the hearts of everyone you touch with your sweet fragrance. Personally, I can say, my seeking outside myself has stopped, and instead I am learning to navigate my way to discovering the treasure that exists within. Ultimately, isn't that where everything we desire reside, what everyone is seeking in their lives, peace, joy, harmony, and health? I can never look back now, as this journey, albeit easy, is rich and so very rewarding.

BOOKS THAT INFLUENCED AND INSPIRED MY JOURNEY

*B*ooks have been my great teachers. Here are some of the books which have helped along my journey. I am listing them down in various categories with my recommendations. Please do not feel you have to read them because they are not a prerequisite for you to realize you are The Cure. If you can afford to read them (always buy them), this may enhance your understanding of The Cure.

1. List of books which will directly enhance your understanding of The Cure:

    *   Living with Himalayan Masters - Swami Rama

    *   Celestine prophecy - James Redfield

    *   Seat of the Soul - Gary Zukav

    *   Eastern Body, Western Mind - Dr Anodea Judith

    *   Quantum Healing and Ageless body -Timeless Mind by Dr Deepak Chopra

If you have read them before, then read them again after reading The Cure. Your consciousness will receive them differently.

2. The books which have been a reference to my understanding and have led to my curiosity are:

    *   Secret - OSHO

    *   Integral Healing - Sri Aurobindo

- Breath, Mind and Consciousness - Harish Johari

- Time is illusion & Ecstasy - Chris Griscom

- The tantric path to higher consciousness - Sunyata Saraswati, Bodhi Avinasha

3. Books which have stimulated my curiosity:

- The power of Myth - Joseph Campbell

- Riding with the Lion - Kyriacos c Markides

- Trick to money is having some - Stuart Wilde

4. Books which are closest to my heart and I personally relate with:

- Intimate history of humanity - Theodore Zeldin

- The Spirit in Man, art and literature - Carl Jung

- Letters to a young Poet - Rainer Maria Rilke

- All the books of Nirmal Verma, who shaped my inner core in my younger days

NV FISHING

og Nidra leads to insight and a deeper state of *Yog Nidra* leads to revelation. This technique and healing prayers (used for energizing the cotton) are a revelation I received in my meditation and have proven to be miraculous in contributing to healing and transformation.

NV fishing is the most powerful, yet simplest technique when it comes to purifying the mind. I use this as a tool to diagnose my students to check their mental health conditions. In case of patients with mental disorders, I see this report as validation of the cure and in every other case, it is a great diagnostics tool. This report tells me within seconds if the person is free from any risk of relapse or if his mind is still complex.

Let me try to explain. So here is the woman who comes to me in distress because her husband is having an affair and is threatening to leave her. She is a healer in her own practice and likes to believe she is a spiritual being (whatever that means to her). So if you scan her mind and emotions, what would you expect to see? Pain, rejection, insecurity and feeling unloved, unworthy, especially when you know for 20 years that the relationship is the only thing she did. When she does NV FISH, we discover in the first round itself that her mind shows her mystical symbols. In the second round, she goes into past lives, and in the third round, she sees some images and colors. In reality, in a healthy mind, we shall see insecurity (immediate concern) and then shall see anger/pain/fear etc. This shows that she has already accepted that she has lost a relationship and the conscious mind is numb and right away goes into the subconscious and creates an illusion that she is a spiritual being and God is giving her some messages. She creates an illusion that she is in a trance. This is a huge distortion and in this state, there is no way she can attract any solution to her problem.

Printed in Great Britain
by Amazon